Zoopolis

D0843501

Zoopolis

A Political Theory of Animal Rights

Sue Donaldson and Will Kymlicka

OXFORD

UNIVERSITY PRESS

Great Clarendon Street, Oxford OX2 6DP
United Kingdom

Oxford University Press is a department of the University of Oxford.
It furthers the University's objective of excellence in research, scholarship,
and education by publishing worldwide. Oxford is a registered trade mark of
Oxford University Press in the UK and in certain other countries

© Sue Donaldson and Will Kymlicka 2011

The moral rights of the author have been asserted

First published 2011
First published in paperback 2013
Reprinted 2014

All rights reserved. No part of this publication may be reproduced, stored in
a retrieval system, or transmitted, in any form or by any means, without the
prior permission in writing of Oxford University Press, or as expressly permitted
by law, by licence or under terms agreed with the appropriate reprographics
rights organization. Enquiries concerning reproduction outside the scope of the
above should be sent to the Rights Department, Oxford University Press, at the
address above

You must not circulate this work in any other form
and you must impose this same condition on any acquirer

Published in the United States of America by Oxford University Press
198 Madison Avenue, New York, NY 10016, United States of America

British Library Cataloguing in Publication Data
Data available

Library of Congress Cataloging in Publication Data
Data available

ISBN 978-0-19-967301-8

Links to third party websites are provided by Oxford in good faith and
for information only. Oxford disclaims any responsibility for the materials
contained in any third party website referenced in this work.

Acknowledgements

We have received much encouragement and assistance in writing this book, for which we are extremely grateful. For research assistance, we'd like to thank Chris Lowry, Mike Kocsis, and Jenny Szende. For encouragement to take on this project, and for their inspiration and advice, we are indebted to Paola Cavalieri and Franco Salanga. For helpful written comments, we'd like to thank Alasdair Cochrane, Steve Cooke, Christine Overall, and Byoung-Shup Park. We were fortunate to receive timely and helpful advice at two different points from the referees for Oxford University Press: Clare Palmer and Bob Goodin, who reviewed the book proposal, and Frank Lovett and Jonathan Quong, who commented on the penultimate draft.

Versions of the arguments in this book were presented at the Uehiro Centre for Practical Ethics at Oxford, the Political Theory programme at Luiss University in Rome and at the Humanities Center at the University of Pittsburgh. We're grateful to the audiences for their challenging questions, to Roger Crisp, Sebastiano Maffetone, and Jonathan Arac respectively for the invitations, and to Michael Goodhart for his commentary at the Pittsburgh talk.

Special thanks to the students in Will's seminar in the autumn 2010 term on 'Animal Rights and the Frontiers of Citizenship', where the first draft of this manuscript was discussed. Their healthy scepticism pushed us to make a number of improvements.

Many of the most helpful ideas and reading suggestions arose in the course of informal conversations with friends, family, and colleagues. Everyone, it seems, has some interesting story about a human–animal interaction that confounds our familiar ways of thinking, and that requires new ways of theorizing animal rights. We have shamelessly borrowed those stories as raw materials for our research, some of which appear in this book. There are too many such conversations to list here, but we'd particularly like to thank our parents and our friends Joyce Davidson, Colin Macleod, Jon Miller, Christine Overall, Mick Smith, and Christine Straehle for extended and lively discussions. Sue's mom, Anne Donaldson, died before we completed this project. We know how much she would have liked to have seen the resulting book, and we hope it embodies her deep affection and respect for animals.

Acknowledgements

For insight and inspiration of a different order we are deeply indebted to our dog companion, Codie (and his best buddies: Tika, Ani, Greta, Julius, Rolly, and Watson). Codie died in 2005, but his spirit has guided us throughout the writing of this book, and we hope he would approve the outcome—even if books were never really his thing.

Jennifer Wolch coined the term 'Zoopolis' (1998) to describe an urban environmental ethics that embraces an integrated vision of human and animal community. We have been inspired by her project, and gratefully borrow her term, although our focus is on a broader understanding of the 'polis' as political community, and a broader set of ways in which animals relate to that community.

Finally, we'd like to thank our editor at Oxford University Press, Dominic Byatt, for his unwavering enthusiasm for this project, and Carla Hodge for her help with the production process.

SD and WK

Kingston, February 2011

Contents

1

Introduction

The animal advocacy movement is at an impasse. The familiar strategies and arguments for articulating issues and mobilizing public opinion around animal welfare, developed over the past 180 years, have had some success, on some issues. But the built-in limits of these strategies have increasingly become clear, leaving us unable to address, or even to identify, some of the most serious ethical challenges in our relations with animals. Our aim in this book is to offer a new framework, one that takes 'the animal question' as a central issue for how we theorize the nature of our political community, and its ideas of citizenship, justice, and human rights. This new framework, we believe, opens up new possibilities, conceptually and politically, for overcoming current roadblocks to progressive change.

Animal advocacy has a long and distinguished history. In the modern era, the first Society for the Prevention of Cruelty to Animals was established in Britain in 1824, primarily to prevent the abuse of carriage horses.[1] From those modest beginnings, the movement has grown into a vibrant social force, with countless advocacy organizations around the world, and a rich tradition of public debate and academic theorizing about the ethical treatment of animals. The movement has also scored some political victories, from the banning of blood sports to anti-cruelty legislation in the areas of research, agriculture, hunting, zoos, and circuses. The 2008 California Proposition 2 referendum—in which 63 per cent of voters supported a ban on the use of gestation crates for pigs, veal crates, and battery cages—is just one of many recent examples where activists have managed to focus public attention on the issue of animal welfare, and to develop a broad political consensus in favour of limiting practices of extreme cruelty. Indeed, across the United States, 28 of 41 referenda for improved animal welfare measures in the past 20 years have passed—a dramatic improvement compared with the almost total failure of such initiatives between 1940 and 1990.[2] This suggests that the concerns of the animal advocacy movement have increasingly taken root in public consciousness, and not just in the United States, but also in Europe, where animal welfare legislation is more advanced (Singer 2003; Garner 1998).[3]

Viewed this way, the movement can be seen as a success, cumulatively building on its victories, gradually pushing the goalposts further. But there is another, darker, side of the story. In a more global perspective, we would argue that the movement has largely failed. The numbers tell the story. The relentless expansion in human population and development continues to take away habitat for wild animals. Our population has doubled since the 1960s while wild animal populations have dropped by a third.[4] And the factory farm system keeps growing to meet (and fuel) the demand for meat. World meat production has tripled since 1980, to the point that humans today kill 56 billion animals per year for food (not including aquatic animals). Meat production is expected to double again by 2050, according to the UN report *Livestock's Long Shadow* (UN 2006). And corporations—always looking to cut costs or to find new products—constantly search for new ways to exploit animals more efficiently in manufacturing, agriculture, research, and entertainment.

These global trends are truly catastrophic, dwarfing the modest victories achieved through animal welfare reforms, and there is no sign that these trends will change. For the foreseeable future, we can expect more and more animals every year to be bred, confined, tortured, exploited, and killed to satisfy human desires. In Charles Patterson's provocative words, the general state of human–animal relations is best characterized as an 'Eternal Treblinka',[5] and there is no sign that this basic relationship is changing. The reality is that animal exploitation underpins the way we feed and clothe ourselves, our forms of entertainment and leisure, and our structures of industrial production and scientific research. The animal advocacy movement has nibbled at the edges of this system of animal exploitation, but the system itself endures, and indeed expands and deepens all the time, with remarkably little public discussion. Some critics argue that the so-called victories of the animal advocacy movement—such as California's Proposition 2—are in fact strategic failures. At best, they distract attention from the underlying system of animal exploitation, and at worst, they provide citizens with a way to soothe their moral anxieties, providing false reassurance that things are getting better, when in fact they are getting worse. Indeed, Gary Francione suggests that these ameliorist reforms serve to legitimate, rather than contest, the system of animal enslavement, blunting what might otherwise be a more radical movement for real reform (Francione 2000, 2008).

Francione's claim that ameliorist reforms are counterproductive is enormously controversial in the field. Even amongst animal advocates who share the goal of eventual abolition of all animal exploitation, there is disagreement on strategic questions around incremental change, just as there is disagreement about the relative merits of educational reform, direct action, pacifism, and more militant protest on behalf of animals.[6] But what surely is clear, after 180 years of organized animal advocacy, is that we have made no demonstrable progress towards dismantling the system of animal exploitation. Campaigns ranging from the very first nineteenth-century anti-cruelty laws to the 2008 Proposition 2 may help or hinder at the margins, but they do not challenge—indeed, do not even address—the social, legal, and political underpinnings of Eternal Treblinka.

In our view, this failure is a predictable result of the flawed terms in which animal issues are publicly debated. To oversimplify, much of the debate operates within one of three basic moral frameworks: a 'welfarist' approach, an 'ecological' approach, and a 'basic rights' approach. As currently elaborated, none has proven capable of generating fundamental change in the system of animal exploitation. We believe that such change will only be possible if we can develop a new moral framework, one that connects the treatment of animals more directly to fundamental principles of liberal–democratic justice and human rights. That, indeed, is the goal of this book.

We will discuss the limits of existing welfarist, ecological, and rights approaches throughout the book, but it might be useful to give a brief overview of how we see the field. By 'welfarist', we mean a view that accepts that animal welfare matters, morally speaking, but which subordinates animal welfare to the interests of human beings. In this view, human beings stand above animals in a clear moral hierarchy. Animals are not machines—they are living beings who suffer, and so their suffering has moral significance. Indeed, a 2003 Gallup poll found that 96 per cent of Americans favour some limits on animal exploitation.[7] Yet this concern for animal welfare operates within a framework that takes for granted—in a largely unquestioned way—that animals can be used within limits for the benefit of humans. In this sense, welfarism could also be described as the principle of the 'humane use' of animals by humans.[8]

By 'ecological', we refer to an approach that focuses on the health of ecosystems, of which animals are a vital component, rather than on the fate of individual animals themselves. Ecological holism provides a critique of many human practices that are devastating to animals—from habitat destruction to the polluting and carbon-generating excesses of factory farming. However, when the killing of animals can be claimed to have a neutral or indeed positive impact on ecological systems (e.g., sustainable hunting or livestock farming, or culling of invasive or overpopulated species), the ecological view comes down on the side of favouring the protection, conservation, and/or restoration of ecosystems over saving the lives of individual animals of non-endangered species.[9]

The shortcomings of both the welfarist and ecological approaches have been extensively discussed in the animal rights literature, and we have little to add to those debates. Welfarism may prevent some truly gratuitous forms of cruelty—literally senseless acts of violence or abuse—but it becomes largely ineffective when confronted with cases of animal exploitation for which there is some recognizable human interest at stake, even the most trivial (such as testing cosmetics), or the most venal (such as saving a few pennies in factory farming). As long as the basic premise of moral hierarchy goes unchallenged, reasonable people will disagree about what constitutes an 'acceptable level' of animal exploitation, and our widespread but vague impulse to limit 'unnecessary' animal cruelty will continue to be overwhelmed by the self-interested and consumerist pressures heading in the opposite direction. Ecological approaches suffer from the same basic problem of elevating human interests over those of animals. In this case, the interests may be less trivial, venal, or self-interested. Nevertheless, ecologists elevate a particular view of what constitutes a healthy, natural, authentic, or sustainable ecosystem, and are willing to sacrifice individual animal lives in order to achieve this holistic vision.

In response to these limitations, many advocates and activists in the field have adopted an 'animal rights' framework. In strong versions of this view, animals, like humans, should be seen as possessing certain *inviolable rights*: there are some things that should not be done to animals even in pursuit of human interests or ecosystem vitality. Animals do not exist to serve human ends: animals are not servants or slaves of human beings, but have their own moral significance, their own subjective existence, which must be respected. Animals, as much as humans, are individual beings with the right not to be tortured, imprisoned, subjected to medical experimentation, forcibly separated from their families, or culled because they are eating too many rare orchids or altering their local habitat. With respect to these basic moral rights to life and liberty, animals and humans are equals, not master and slave, manager and resource, steward and ward, or creator and artefact.

We fully accept this core premise of the animal rights approach, and will defend it in Chapter 2. The only truly effective protection against animal exploitation requires shifting from welfarism and ecological holism to a moral framework that acknowledges animals as the bearers of certain inviolable rights. As many defenders of animal rights theory argue, and as we will discuss, this rights-based approach is a natural extension of the conception of moral equality underpinning the doctrine of human rights.

However, we must also acknowledge that, to date at least, this approach remains politically marginalized. Animal rights theory (hereafter ART) has taken a foothold in academic circles, where it has been developed in sophisticated ways for over forty years. And its ideas circulate amongst a narrow circle of activists engaged in vegan outreach and direct action for animals. But it has virtually no resonance amongst the general public. Indeed, even those who believe in ART sometimes downplay it when engaged in public advocacy, since it is so far removed from the contours of existing public opinion (Garner 2005a: 41).[10] Campaigns by organizations such as PETA (People for the Ethical Treatment of Animals), whose long-term goal is to dismantle the animal exploitation system, often advocate welfarist goals of reducing suffering in the meat, egg, and dairy industries; or curbing the excesses of the pet industry. In other words, they often promote a goal of reducing 'unnecessary suffering' that leaves unchallenged the assumption that animals can be bred, caged, killed, or owned for human benefit. PETA may simultaneously espouse a more radical message (e.g., 'meat is murder'), but they do so in a selective way, to avoid alienating the large numbers of their supporters who don't share the strong rights view. The animal rights framework remains, for all intents and purposes, a political non-starter. And, as a result, animal advocacy campaigns have largely failed in the fight against systemic animal exploitation.

A central task for the movement is to figure out why ART remains so politically marginal. Why is the general public increasingly open to welfarist and ecological reforms, such as Proposition 2 or endangered species legislation, while remaining implacably resistant to animal rights? Having acknowledged that animals are living beings whose suffering matters morally, why is it so hard to take the next step and acknowledge that animals have moral rights not be used as means to human ends?

Many reasons for this resistance come to mind, not least the depth of our cultural inheritance. Western (and most non-Western) cultures have for centuries operated on the premise that animals are lower than humans on some cosmic moral hierarchy, and that humans therefore have the right to use animals for their purposes. This idea is found in most of the world's religions, and is embedded in many of our day-to-day rituals and practices.[11] Overcoming the weight of this cultural inheritance is an uphill battle.

And there are innumerable self-interested reasons to resist animal rights (AR). While citizens may be willing to pay a few cents extra for more 'humane' foods or products, they are not yet willing to give up entirely on animal-based foods, clothes, or medicines. Moreover, there are powerful vested interests in the system of animal exploitation. Whenever the animal advocacy movement starts to threaten those economic interests, animal-use industries mobilize to discredit AR advocates as radicals, extremists, or even terrorists.[12]

Given these cultural and economic obstacles to animal rights, it is perhaps not surprising that the movement to abolish animal exploitation has remained politically ineffective. But we believe that part of the problem lies in the way that ART itself has been articulated. To oversimplify, ART to date has been formulated in a very narrow way: it has typically taken the form of specifying a limited list of *negative* rights—particularly, the right not to be owned, killed, confined, tortured, or separated from one's family. And these negative rights are seen as applying *generically* to all animals possessing a subjective existence—that is, to all animals that have some threshold level of consciousness or sentience.

By contrast, ART has said little about what *positive* obligations we may owe to animals—such as an obligation to respect animals' habitat, or obligations to design our buildings, roads, and neighbourhoods in a way that takes into account animals' needs, or obligations to rescue animals who are unintentionally harmed by human activities, or obligations to care for those animals who have become dependent upon us.[13] Relatedly, ART has had little to say about our *relational* duties—that is, duties arising not just from the intrinsic characteristics of animals (such as their consciousness), but from the more geographically and historically specific relationships that have developed between particular groups of humans and particular groups of animals. For example, the fact that humans have deliberately bred domesticated animals to become dependent on us generates different moral obligations to cows or dogs than we have to the ducks or squirrels who migrate to areas of human settlement. And both of these cases differ yet again from our obligations to animals in isolated wilderness who have little or no contact with humans. These facts of history and geography seem to matter morally in ways that are not captured by classical ART.

In short, ART focuses on the universal negative rights of animals, and says little about positive relational duties. It's worth noting how this differs from the way we think about the human context. To be sure, all humans have certain basic inviolable negative rights (e.g., the right not to be tortured, or be killed, or to be imprisoned without due process). But the vast bulk of moral reasoning and moral theorizing concerns not these universal negative rights, but rather the positive and relational obligations we have to other groups of humans. What do we owe to our neighbours and family? What do we owe to our co-citizens? What are our obligations to remedy historic injustice at home or abroad? Different relationships generate different duties—duties of care, hospitality, accommodation, reciprocity, or remedial justice—and much of our moral life is an attempt to sort out this complex moral landscape, trying to determine which sorts of obligations flow from which types of social, political, and historical relationships. Our relations with animals are likely to have a similar sort of moral complexity, given the enormous variation in our historic relationships with different categories of animals.

By contrast, ART presents a remarkably flat moral landscape, devoid of particularized relationships or obligations. At one level, ART's single-minded focus on negative rights to non-interference is understandable. The inviolability of basic rights is the crucial premise needed to condemn the daily (and ever-growing) violence of animal exploitation. Compared with the urgent task of securing negative rights not to be enslaved, vivisected, or skinned alive, the question of, say, redesigning buildings and roads to accommodate animals, or developing effective guardianship models for animal companions, may seem like challenges that can be left for another day.[14] And in any event, if AR theorists are having trouble persuading the general public to accept that animals have negative rights, then it may simply make the struggle more difficult if we insist that animals may also have positive rights (Dunayer 2004: 119).

But this tendency within ART to focus exclusively on universal negative rights is not merely a matter of priority or strategy. Rather, it reflects a deep-seated scepticism about whether humans should be involved in the sorts of relationships with animals that might generate relational duties of care, accommodation, or reciprocity. For many AR theorists, the historical process by which humans entered into relationships with animals was an inherently exploitative one. The process of domesticating animals was a process of capturing, enslaving, and breeding animals for our human purposes. The very idea of domestication is inherently a violation of animals' negative rights. And if so, many AR theorists argue, the conclusion is not that we have special duties towards domesticated animals, but rather that the very category of domesticated animals should cease to exist. As Francione puts it:

> we ought not to bring any more domesticated nonhumans into existence. I apply this not only to animals we use for food, experiments, clothing, etc. but also to our nonhuman companions... We should certainly care for those nonhumans whom we have already brought into existence but we should stop causing any more to come into existence... it makes no sense to say that we have acted immorally in domesticating nonhuman animals but we are now committed to allowing them to continue to breed. (Francione 2007)

The general picture, then, is that insofar as humans historically have entered into relations with animals, these are exploitative relations that should cease to exist,[15] leaving only wild animals with whom we have no economic, social, or political relations (or at least none that generate positive duties). The goal, in short, is to make animals independent of human society in a way that precludes the very idea of positive relational duties. We can see this, for example, in Joan Dunayer's formulation:

> Animal rights advocates want laws that will prohibit humans from exploiting and otherwise harming nonhumans. They don't seek to protect nonhumans within human society. They seek to protect nonhumans *from* human society. The goal is an end to nonhumans' 'domestication' and other forced 'participation' in human society. Nonhumans should be allowed to live free in natural environments, forming their own societies... We want them to be free and independent of humans. In some ways, that's less threatening than giving rights to a new group

of humans, who then share economic, social, and political power. Nonhumans wouldn't share power. They would be shielded from *ours*. (Dunayer 2004: 117, 119)

In other words, the development of a theory of positive relational rights is unnecessary since, once the abolition of animal exploitation is achieved, domesticated animals will cease to exist, and wild animals will be left alone to lead their separate lives.

Our goal is to challenge this picture, and to offer an alternative framework that is more sensitive to the empirical and moral complexities of human–animal relations. We believe it is a mistake, intellectually and politically, to equate ART with universal negative rights while setting aside positive relational duties. For one thing, the traditional ART view ignores the dense patterns of interaction that inevitably link humans and animals. It rests implicitly on a picture in which humans live in urban or other human-altered environments, assumed to be largely devoid of animals (except for unjustly domesticated and captured ones), while animals live out in the wild, in spaces that humans can and should vacate or leave alone. This picture ignores the realities of human–animal coexistence. In fact, wild animals live all around us, in our homes and cities, airways, and watersheds. Human cities teem with non-domesticated animals—feral pets, escaped exotics, wild animals whose habitat has been enveloped by human development, migrating birds—not to mention the literally billions of opportunistic animals who gravitate to, and thrive in, symbiosis with human development, such as starlings, foxes, coyotes, sparrows, mallard ducks, squirrels, racoons, badgers, skunks, groundhogs, deer, rabbits, bats, rats, mice, and countless others. These animals are affected every time we chop down a tree, divert a waterway, build a road or housing development, or erect a tower.

We are part of a shared society with innumerable animals, one which would continue to exist even if we eliminated cases of 'forced participation'. It is simply not tenable for ART to assume that humans can inhabit a separate realm from other animals in which interaction, and therefore potential conflict, could largely be eliminated. Ongoing interaction is inevitable, and this reality must lie at the centre of a theory of animal rights, not be swept to the periphery.

Once we recognize these brute ecological facts about the inevitability of human–animal interaction, a host of difficult normative questions arise about the nature of these relations, and the positive duties they give rise to. In the human case, we have well-established categories for thinking about these relational duties. For example, certain social relationships (e.g., parent–child, teacher–student, employer–employee) generate stronger duties of care because of the dependencies and power asymmetries involved. Political relationships—such as membership within self-governing political communities—also generate positive duties, because of the distinctive rights and responsibilities of citizenship involved in governing bounded communities and territories. A central task of any plausible theory of animal rights, we believe, is to identify analogous categories for the animal context, sorting out the various patterns of human–animal relationships and their associated positive duties.

In the classical model of ART, there is only one acceptable relationship to animals: treating animals ethically means leaving them alone, not interfering with their negative rights to life and liberty. In our view, non-intervention is indeed appropriate in some cases—particularly in relation to certain wild animals who live far from human settlement and activity. But it is hopelessly inadequate in many other cases, where animals and humans are connected through dense bonds of interdependence and shared habitat. This interdependence is clear in the case of companion animals and domesticated farm animals who have been bred for millennia to be dependent on humans. Through this process of intervention we have acquired positive duties towards them (and advocating the extinction of these animals is a strange way of fulfilling our positive obligations!). But the same is true, in a more complicated way, of the many animals that gravitate uninvited towards human settlement. We may not want the geese and groundhogs who seek out our towns and cities, but over time they become co-inhabitants of our shared space, and we may have positive duties to design that space with their interests in mind. We discuss many such cases in the course of this book where any plausible conception of animal ethics will involve a mix of positive and negative duties, adapted in light of histories of interaction and interdependence, and aspirations to just coexistence.

In our view, limiting ART to a set of negative rights is not only unsustainable intellectually, it is also damaging politically, since it deprives ART of a positive conception of human–animal interaction. Recognizing relation-specific positive duties may make ART more demanding,[16] but in another sense, it also makes it a much more appealing approach. After all, humans do not exist outside of nature, cut off from contact with the animal world. On the contrary, throughout history, and in all cultures, there is a clear tendency—perhaps even a human need—to develop relationships and bonds with animals (and vice versa)—quite apart from the history of exploitation. Humans have always had animal companions, for example.[17] And from the first paintings at Chauvet and Lascaux, animals have preoccupied human artists, scientists, and myth-makers. Animals have 'made us human', in Paul Shepard's phrase (Shepard 1997).

To be sure, this human impulse for contact with the animal world—our 'special relationships' with animals as companions, icons, and myths—has usually taken a destructive form, forcing animals to participate in human society on our terms, for our benefit. But it is also true that this impulse for contact motivates much of the animal advocacy movement. People who love animals are key allies in this movement, and most of these people seek not to sever all relationships between humans and animals (if that were even possible), but to reconstruct those relationships in ways that are respectful, compassionate, and non-exploitative. If ART insists that all such relationships must be abolished, it risks alienating many of its potential allies in the campaign for animal justice. It also risks giving ammunition to anti-ART organizations, which delight in citing 'anti-pet' statements by AR advocates, and using these statements to argue that the true agenda of the animal rights movement is to sever all human–animal relationships.[18] These critiques are invariably distorted, but they contain a grain of truth about how ART has boxed itself into a position in which the human–animal relationship is inherently suspect.

Thus ART flattens our moral landscape in a way that is not only intellectually implausible but unattractive: it ignores the inevitability of, and desire for, ongoing and morally significant relationships with animals. If ART is to gain political traction, we need to show that prohibiting exploitative relationships with animals does not entail cutting ourselves off from meaningful forms of animal–human interaction. The task, rather, is to show how ART, when specified to include both positive and negative duties, sets the conditions under which these interactions can be respectful, mutually enriching, and non-exploitative.

The narrow version of ART is politically unsustainable in yet another way. It needlessly exaggerates the gulf between AR activists and ecologists, making enemies of potential allies. To be sure, some conflicts between ART and ecological views reflect fundamental moral differences. For example, in genuine conflicts between ecosystem health and the lives of individual animals, most ecologists will deny that animals have a right not to be killed by humans in an effort to manage an ecosystem, whereas AR advocates view so-called therapeutic culling as a clear violation of basic rights (as it would be in the human case). This is a real and indeed foundational moral disagreement about our moral duties to animals, to which we return in Chapter 2.

However, there are many other alleged conflicts between ART and ecologists which could be resolved by a broadened AR theory that included positive and relational rights. Ecologists worry that a theory of animal rights that is limited to a set of basic individual rights will be either indifferent to issues of environmental degradation, and/or too willing to intervene in the environment. On the one hand, if we focus only on the rights of individual animals, then we may be unable to criticize even large-scale devastation of habitat and ecosystems. Human pollution of an ecosystem may undermine a species' ability to survive, yet not involve the direct killing or capturing of any individual animal. Defenders of ART could respond by saying that 'the right to life' of individual animals includes the right to the means of life, including a safe and healthy environment. But if the right to life is interpreted in this expansive way, it seems to license large-scale human interventions in the wilderness in order to protect animals from predators, food shortages, and natural disasters. Defending the right to life of individual animals could lead to humans taking over the management of nature to ensure that every individual animal has a safe and secure food source and shelter. In short, if ART's conception of basic individual rights is interpreted narrowly, it provides no protection against degradation of the environment; but if its conception of basic rights is interpreted expansively, it seems to license massive human intervention in nature.

As we will see in Chapter 6, AR theorists have responded in various ways to this 'too little– too much' dilemma. But we believe that the dilemma cannot in fact be resolved within a theory that focuses only on a narrow set of universal individual rights. We need a richer and more relational set of moral concepts to guide us in determining our obligations to wild animals and their habitats. In addition to asking what we owe to individual animals as such, we need to ask about the appropriate relations between human and wild animal communities, where each is understood to have legitimate claims to autonomy and to territory. These fair terms of interaction between communities, we argue, can provide ecologically informed guidance on issues of both habitat and intervention that avoids the too little–too much dilemma.

More generally, ecologists worry that ART is simply naive about the complexity of human–animal interactions and interdependence. This could be addressed by an expanded ART which acknowledges that human–animal interactions are pervasive and inevitable, and that we cannot run away from these complexities with the seductive simplicities of a 'hands-off' approach. In all of these ways, a more relational theory of ART would close the gap with ecological thinking.

In sum, we believe that a more expansive account of ART—one that integrates universal negative rights owed to all animals with differentiated positive rights depending on the nature of the human–animal relationship—provides the most promising avenue for progress in the field. We argue that it is more intellectually credible than the existing welfarist, ecological, or classic AR approaches to human–animal justice, and that it is more politically viable, offering the resources needed to generate greater public support.

The idea that we need a more differentiated and relational approach to animal rights is not new. Many critics have questioned ART's exclusive focus on universal negative rights. For example, Keith Burgess-Jackson notes that animals are not an 'undifferentiated mass', and hence it is not true 'that whatever responsibilities one has to *any* animal one has to *all* animals' (Burgess-Jackson 1998: 159). Similarly, Clare Palmer asks: 'Does it make sense to make "across the board" rules concerning our moral obligations to animals, given the different kinds of relationships we have with them?' (Palmer 1995: 7). She calls for a situated animal ethics focused on context and relationships. We can find similar ideas in a range of authors working in the feminist and environmental ethics traditions.[19]

In our view, however, existing relational accounts suffer from a number of flaws. For one thing, while several authors have *called* for a more relational theory of animal rights, few have actually attempted to develop such a theory. Most focus on one particular type of relationship—Burgess-Jackson, for example, focuses on the special duties owed to companion animals—rather than on developing a more systematic account of the different types of relations and contexts relevant to animal rights. As a result, existing discussions sometimes look ad hoc, or even as special pleading, disconnected from more general principles about the basis of obligations.

Second, many of these authors suggest that a relational approach is an *alternative* to ART, as if we have to choose between recognizing either universal negative rights *or* positive relational rights.[20] Palmer, for example, says that her relational approach 'differs from the thrust of utilitarianism or rights theories, since they tend to the view that ethical prescriptions are invariant among urban, rural, oceanic, and wilderness environments' (Palmer 2003a: 64). But in our view, there is no need or justification for viewing these as competing rather than complementary approaches. There are certain 'invariant' ethical prescriptions—certain universal negative rights owed to all beings with a subjective experience of the world—and there are also variable ethical prescriptions based on the nature of our relationships.[21]

Third, we believe that these alternative accounts tend to invoke an incorrect, or overly narrow, basis for categorizing human–animal relationships. They typically distinguish between different categories of animals on the basis of subjective feelings of affective attachment (e.g., the 'biosocial' theory developed in Callicott 1992), natural facts of ecological interdependence (Plumwood 2004), or causal relations generating harm or dependency (Palmer 2010). In our view—and this is the crux of our project—we need to understand these relationships in more explicitly *political* terms. Animals have variable relationships to political institutions and practices of state sovereignty, territory, colonization, migration, and membership, and determining our positive and relational obligations to animals is in large part a matter of thinking through the nature of these relationships. In this way, we hope to shift the debate about animals from an issue in applied ethics to a question of political theory.[22]

We hope to offer an account of animal rights that seeks to combine universal negative rights and positive relational rights, and that does so by locating animals within a more explicitly political framework. This is a tall order. As we will see, there are many difficult puzzles in building such an expansive account of ART, and integrating universal negative rights with more differentiated and relational positive duties. We do not claim to have resolved all of these, by any means.

But while the task is difficult, we can learn from recent developments in cognate fields of political philosophy, which have long grappled with the challenges of combining universal individual rights with sensitivity to variations in context and relationships. We will focus in particular on the idea of *citizenship*, which has proven to be a crucial concept in this regard.[23] According to contemporary theories of citizenship, human beings are not just persons who are owed universal human rights in virtue of their personhood; they are also citizens of distinct and self-governing societies located on particular territories. That is to say, human beings have organized themselves into nation states, each of which forms an 'ethical community' in which co-citizens have special responsibilities towards each other in virtue of their co-responsibility for governing each other and their shared territory. Citizenship, in short, generates distinctive rights and responsibilities, beyond the universal human rights owed to all persons, including foreigners.

If we accept this premise, we are quickly led to a complex and highly group-differentiated account of our obligations. There will obviously be a distinction between co-citizens and foreigners. But there will also be groups that fall in-between the two basic categories: migrant workers or refugees, for example, often have the status of 'denizens' rather than 'citizens'. They reside on the territory of the state, and are subject to its governance, but are not citizens. The facts of human mobility will inevitably lead to situations where people are neither fully insiders nor fully outsiders of a self-governing community. There will also be cases where the territorial boundaries of these self-governing communities are contested: indigenous peoples, for example, may assert that they retain rights to collective self-government on their traditional territory, and hence to their own citizenship, even as they are nested within larger political communities. Or there may be cases of disputed territories that are subject to various forms of shared sovereignty, and hence overlapping citizenship regimes (as in Northern Ireland, or perhaps a future settlement regarding Jerusalem). The facts of human history will inevitably create disputes about the boundaries and territories of self-governing communities.

Thus, we have multiple, overlapping, qualified, and mediated forms of citizenship, all of which flow from the more basic fact that human society is organized into distinct, territorially bounded, self-governing communities. This fact requires us to take seriously the moral significance of our membership of specific political communities, and to address a broad range of issues about membership, mobility, sovereignty, and territory. And so, today, liberalism contains not just a theory of universal human rights, but also a theory of bounded citizenship, which in turn rests upon conceptions of nationhood and patriotism, of sovereignty and self-determination, of solidarity and civic virtue, of linguistic and cultural rights, as well as the rights of aliens, immigrants, refugees, indigenous peoples, women, people with disabilities, and children. Many of these theories generate group-differentiated positive duties, depending on people's membership status, individual capacities, and the nature of the relationships involved. What makes all of these theories liberal, however, is that they seek to show how these more 'collective' or 'communitarian' measures are consistent with, and indeed often enhance, the exercise of basic universal individual rights. Liberalism, today, involves a complex integration of universal human rights and more relational, bounded, and group-differentiated rights of political and cultural membership.

In our view, the evolution of citizenship theory provides a helpful model for thinking about how to combine traditional ART with a positive and relational account of obligations. At a minimum, it shows the intellectual possibility of reconciling invariant ethical prescriptions with relational duties. But we want to go further and argue that citizenship theory provides a helpful framework for this reconciliation in the animal case as well. Many of the same political processes that generate the need for a group-differentiated theory of human citizenship also apply to animals, and as a result some of the same categories apply as well. Some animals should be seen as forming separate sovereign communities on their own territories (animals in the wild vulnerable to human invasion and colonization); some animals are akin to migrants or denizens who choose to move into areas of human habitation (liminal opportunistic animals); and some animals should be seen as full citizens of the polity because of the way they've been bred over generations for interdependence with humans (domesticated animals). All of these relationships (and others we will discuss) have their own moral complexities that can be illuminated by using ideas of sovereignty, denizenship, migration, territory, membership, and citizenship.

We explore how these categories and concepts can be adapted from the human to the animal context. The sovereignty of animal communities is not the same as the sovereignty of human political communities, nor is their colonization the same as the colonization of indigenous peoples; the denizenship of migrant or opportunistic animals living in urban contexts is not the same as the denizenship of migrant workers or illegal immigrants; and domesticated animal citizens are different in key respects from other citizens who may be unable to exercise their citizenship rights without assistance, such as children, and people with intellectual disabilities. But we argue that these ideas are genuinely illuminating, identifying morally salient factors that are often ignored in the existing literature. (Indeed, we think that applying these ideas to the animal case helps to sharpen our thinking about citizenship in the human case as well.)

In short, we argue that an expanded citizenship-based ART helps to integrate universal negative rights with positive, relational duties, and does so in a way that speaks to the powerful intuitions that underpin ecological concerns, while still preserving the core commitments to inviolable rights needed to address the entrenched apparatus of animal exploitation. We believe this approach is not only intellectually compelling, but also helps to overcome the political impasse that has stalled the animal advocacy movement.

We begin in Chapter 2 with our defence of the idea that animals possess inviolable rights in virtue of being sentient individuals with a subjective experience of their world. As just noted, our aim is to supplement the traditional ART commitment to universal basic rights, not to replace it, and so we begin by clarifying and defending this commitment.

In Chapter 3, we distinguish the logic of universal basic rights from the logic of citizenship rights, explore the distinctive functions that citizenship serves within political theory, and show why this citizenship logic is compelling and applicable in the case of both humans and animals. Many people have argued that some of the core values of citizenship—such as reciprocity or political participation—cannot in principle be applied in relation to animals. We show that such objections rest both on too narrow a conception of the practice of citizenship, even in relation to humans, and on too narrow a conception of the capacities of animals. Once we think about how citizenship is enacted across the full range of human diversity, we can start to make sense of how animals too can be brought into practices of citizenship.

In Chapters 4–7, we apply this citizenship logic to a range of human–animal relationships, beginning with the case of domesticated animals. In Chapter 4, we explore the limitations of existing ART approaches to domesticated animals, and how they fail to recognize the moral obligations that arise from the domestication of animals and their incorporation into our societies. In Chapter 5, we defend the claim that the appropriate way to recognize this incorporation is through citizenship, showing how the facts of domestication make co-citizenship both morally necessary and practically feasible. In Chapter 6, we explore the case of animals in the wild. We argue that they should be seen as citizens of their own sovereign communities, and that our obligations to them are those of international justice, including respect for their territory and autonomy. In Chapter 7, we turn to the non-domesticated liminal animals who live amongst us, and argue that a form of denizenship is the appropriate status for them, a status which recognizes that they are co-residents of our urban spaces, but that they are neither capable of, nor interested in, being recruited into our cooperative scheme of citizenship.

We conclude in Chapter 8 by returning to some of the more strategic and motivational issues laid out in this chapter. Our main focus in Chapters 2–7 is on the normative arguments for a citizenship approach, but, as we have suggested already, we believe this approach has potential for expanding public support and political alliances for the animal advocacy movement. In Chapter 8, we attempt to redeem that promise by exploring how a citizenship approach makes sense of the most promising developments in human–animal relations. Individuals and societies are already experimenting on a small scale with new forms of relationship with domesticated, wild, and liminal animals in ways that we believe instantiate the impulses of a citizenship approach. Far from being utopian, we believe that the citizenship approach can be seen as a case of theory catching up with the practice of thoughtful ecologists, animal advocates, and animal lovers of various stripes.

Part I
An Expanded Theory of Animal Rights

2

Universal Basic Rights for Animals

An important strand of animal rights theory (ART) starts from the premise that all animals with a subjective existence—that is, all animals who are conscious or sentient beings—should be viewed as the subjects of justice, and as the bearers of inviolable rights. The idea that animals possess inviolable rights is a very distinctive view which goes beyond what is normally understood by the term 'animal rights'. So it is important for us to clarify what we mean by inviolable rights, and why we think animals possess them.

In everyday parlance, anyone who argues for greater limits on the use of animals is said to be a defender of animal rights (AR). Thus, someone who advocates that pigs being raised for slaughter should have larger stalls, so as to improve the quality of their short lives, is described as a believer in animal right. And indeed we can say that such a person believes that animals have a 'right to humane treatment'. Someone defending a more robust rights view might argue that humans should not eat animals since we have lots of nutritious alternatives, but that medical experiments on animals are permissible if this is the only way to advance crucial medical knowledge, or that culling wild animals is permissible if this is the only way to save key habitats. We can say that such a person believes animals have a 'right not to be sacrificed by humans unless an important human or ecological interest is at stake'.

These views, whether they endorse a weaker or more robust conception of, are crucially different from the idea that animals have inviolable rights. The idea of inviolable rights implies that an individual's most basic interests cannot be sacrificed for the greater good of others. In Ronald Dworkin's famous phrase, inviolable rights in this sense are 'trumps' which cannot be violated no matter how much others would benefit from their violation (Dworkin 1984). For example, a person cannot be killed in order to harvest her body parts, even if dozens of other humans might benefit from her organs, bone marrow, or stem cells. Nor can she be made a subject of non-consensual medical experimentation, no matter how much the knowledge gained from experimenting on her would help others. Inviolable rights in this sense are a protective circle drawn around an individual, ensuring that she is not sacrificed for the good of others. This protective circle is usually understood in terms of a set of basic negative rights against fundamental harms such as killing, slavery, torture, or confinement.

The idea that human beings have such inviolable rights is controversial. Utilitarians, for example, believe that morality requires us to bring about the greatest good of the greatest number, even if this means sacrificing one person to do so. If we can save five people by killing one, we should do so, all else being equal. As the great utilitarian Jeremy Bentham famously put it, the idea of inviolable rights is 'nonsense upon stilts' (Bentham 2002). Since utilitarians do not believe that humans are owed inviolable rights, they obviously do not accord such rights to animals either.[1]

Today, however, the idea that humans possess inviolable rights is widely accepted, despite ongoing philosophical debate regarding the grounding for human rights. Inviolability is the basis of our medical ethics, of domestic bills of rights, and of international human rights law. The idea that all human beings are entitled to the protection of certain inviolable rights is part of the 'human rights revolution' in law, and of the shift to 'rights-based' theories in political philosophy. One of the central motivations for Rawls's *A Theory of Justice*, widely seen as heralding the rebirth of political philosophy, was precisely his belief that utilitarianism was unable to account for the wrongness of sacrificing individuals for the good of others, whether that is experimenting on individuals to gain useful medical knowledge, or discriminating against racial or sexual minorities to satisfy the preferences of majorities (Rawls 1971). An adequate defence of liberal democracy, he believed, required a more 'Kantian' conception of respect for individuals, which emphasizes that we should never be treated simply as a means for the good of society.[2]

While the idea of inviolability is now widely accepted in relation to human beings, very few people have been prepared to accept that animals too might possess inviolable rights. Even those who accept that animals matter morally, and that they deserve to be treated more humanely, often think that when push comes to shove, they can be violated—endlessly sacrificed—for the greater good of others. Whereas killing one human to harvest organs to save five other humans is unacceptable, to kill one baboon to save five humans (or five baboons) is permissible, and perhaps even morally required. As Jeff McMahan puts it, animals are 'freely violable in the service of the greater good', whereas human persons are 'fully inviolable' (McMahan 2002: 265). Robert Nozick famously summarized this view under the label 'utilitarianism for animals, Kantianism for people' (Nozick 1974: 39).

The approach we develop in this book rejects this claim that only humans possess inviolable rights. The human rights revolution has been a profound moral achievement, but it is incomplete. As we will see, the arguments for inviolability do not stop at the boundaries of the human species. As Paola Cavalieri puts it, it's time to take the human out of human rights (Cavalieri 2001). If it is wrong to kill a human for her organs, even if we can save five people by doing so, so too is it wrong to kill a baboon for his organs. Killing a chipmunk or a shark is a violation of their basic inviolable right to life, just as killing a human being is.[3]

The claim to inviolable rights for animals has already been ably defended by several AR theorists, and we have little new to add to their arguments.[4] Those who are already persuaded of this view can skip this chapter, and move directly to the more original part of our argument, regarding the group-differentiated and relational rights we owe to different groups of animals.

Most readers, however, are unlikely to be persuaded of this view, and may indeed find it wildly implausible. If so, we hope that the arguments we develop in the rest of this book will still be of interest. Even if you endorse 'utilitarianism for animals, Kantianism for people'—or indeed, even if you endorse utilitarianism for both animals and people (or some other theory altogether)—we believe there is still a compelling case for adopting a more political and relational account of animal rights. Many of the arguments we give for according citizenship to domesticated animals, sovereignty to wild animals, and denizenship to liminal animals do not depend on endorsing the idea of inviolable rights for animals.

However, our own elaboration of these arguments will be developed within a strong AR framework that includes a commitment to inviolability. This affects how we elaborate these arguments, and the conclusions we draw from them. So in this chapter we attempt to defend that starting point, and to address some of the objections and anxieties that this view is likely to provoke.

Why do so many people find the idea of inviolable rights for animals implausible? Some people think it is simply self-evident that the death of a human being is more tragic, and more of a loss to the world, than the death of a baboon, and that killing a human being must therefore be a greater wrong than killing a baboon. We hope that our discussion in this chapter will give readers a livelier sense of the loss when animals die, and of the complexity of making such judgements of comparative loss. But in any event, this entire line of argument is misplaced. After all, we can and do make similar judgements about the relative loss when different human beings die. We may think that it is more of a tragedy when a young person dies in an accident than when a very old person dies, and more of a tragedy when someone who loves life dies than when a misanthrope dies. Yet these judgements about comparative loss have no implications whatsoever for the inviolable right to life. The fact that it may be more tragic when a young person dies does not mean that we can kill the old person to provide organs for the young person. We cannot kill misanthropes to harvest organs to use for people who love life.

Indeed, this is the essential point of inviolable rights, and how they differ from utilitarianism. From a strict utilitarian perspective, the strength of people's right to life depends on how much they contribute to the greater good. We are all 'freely violable in the service of the greater good', and so you have to earn your right to life by showing that your continued existence serves the overall good. Those who are young, talented, and gregarious are therefore bound to have a stronger right to life than those who are elderly, infirm, or miserable. The strength of one's right to life varies with the comparative loss from one's death.

The human rights revolution is precisely a repudiation of this way of thinking. The principle of inviolability says that people's right to life is independent of their relative contribution to the overall good, and is not violable in the service of the greater good. This is now firmly established in the human case, and we argue that it must extend to animals as well. The death of some individuals may be more of a tragedy or loss than the death of other individuals, within and across species, but they all possess inviolable rights: they all have an equal right not to be sacrificed for the greater good of others.

To say that animals have an equal right not to be sacrificed for the greater good of others raises another set of worries and objections. Does this entail that animals have 'equal rights' with humans, including, say, the right to vote, or to religious freedom, or to post-secondary education? This is often invoked as a *reductio* of the idea of animal rights, but here again, it misunderstands the logic of the rights revolution. Even within the category of human beings, many rights are differentially allocated on the basis of capacities and relationships. Citizens have rights that visitors do not have (e.g., to vote, or to social services); adults have rights that children do not have (e.g., to drive); people with certain rational capacities have rights that those with severe intellectual disabilities do not have (e.g., to decide how to manage their finances). But again, none of these variations has implications for claims to fundamental inviolability. Citizens have rights that foreign tourists do not have, but citizens cannot enslave tourists, or kill them to harvest their organs. Adults have rights that children do not have, and competent adults have rights that people with severe intellectual disabilities do not have, but children and the intellectually disabled cannot be sacrificed for the greater good of competent adults. Equal inviolability is compatible with variations in a wide range of other civil, political, and social rights, which track variations in underlying capacities, interests, and relationships. Again, all of this is clear enough in the human case, and we argue that it is equally true in the case of animals.

In short, the issue of inviolable rights needs to be kept clearly in mind, and not conflated with a range of other issues regarding our obligations to humans and animals. The issue of inviolability is, to repeat, the question of whether one's basic interests can or cannot be sacrificed for the greater good of others. The human rights revolution says that human beings possess such inviolability. The strong AR position says that sentient animals also possess such inviolability. Some readers may worry that extending inviolability to animals 'cheapens' the hard-won achievements of the rights revolution. We argue, on the contrary, that any attempt to restrict inviolability to human beings can only be done by radically weakening and destabilizing the scheme of human rights protection, leaving many humans as well as animals outside the scope of effective protection.

Our focus in this chapter on the issue of inviolable rights should not be taken as minimizing the importance of other civil, political, and social rights, such as issues regarding the duties of medical care we have to domesticated animals, or the duties we have to protect the habitat of wild or liminal animals. On the contrary, our entire project is intended precisely to show that we can only address these broader issues by situating them within an explicitly political theory of animal right. Our concern is that while animal rights theory has provided strong arguments for the principle of inviolable rights, it has lacked the conceptual resources to address these broader issues, which require a more relational theory of justice. But before we develop our account of relational justice, we need first to explain why we believe that animals do indeed fall within the scope of a strong rights-based theory, as opposed to being freely violable for the benefit of others.

As noted earlier, the arguments we go on to discuss in this chapter are not new. We believe that the case for a (strong) AR position has already been made, and our primary aim in this book is to take the next step, and to connect ART to broader political theories of justice and citizenship, so that we can identify more clearly potential models of animal–human relationships.

However, to lay the groundwork for our more original arguments in Part II, we provide a brief overview of the moral status/animal personhood debate, in order to explain why we view the strong AR position as the most compelling account. We begin, in section 1, with an argument about animal selfhood, and why this requires the recognition of universal basic rights.[5] In sections 2 and 3, we examine why plants and inanimate nature do not possess selfhood, although this does not mean that we have no duties towards them, nor that they lack intrinsic value. In sections 4 and 5, we address some possible ambiguities or objections regarding the idea of the 'universality' and 'inviolability' of basic rights.

We hope that readers will find these arguments compelling. However, we do not underestimate the difficulty of 'arguing' others into recognizing animals as vulnerable selves, each in possession of a life as precious as our own. For some people the route to this recognition is an intellectual process, but for many others, it comes (if at all) through relationships with individual animals. And this is one of the reasons we are anxious to extend the debate beyond the question of basic rights and moral standing to considerations of our actual relationships with animals in their full complexity and richness. We ask readers, even if they reject our starting premise of animal selfhood and the extension of human rights, to hang in for the journey in Part II of this book. It is an exercise in expanding the moral imagination to see animals not solely as vulnerable and suffering individuals but also as neighbours, friends, co-citizens, and members of communities ours and theirs. It imagines a world of human–animal relationships that takes seriously the idea that animals and humans can co-exist, interact, and even cooperate on the basis of justice and equality. We hope that sketching out this more positive vision of human–animal relationships, albeit in broad strokes, can prove compelling even to those readers who have not been persuaded to date by standard AR arguments regarding animal capacities, animal suffering, or the philosophical bases of moral standing.

1. Animal Selves

The assumption of most mainstream contemporary Western political theory is that the community of justice is coextensive with the community of human beings. Basic justice and inviolable rights are owed to all humans by virtue of their humanity, and should be blind to intra-human differences such as race, gender, creed, ability, or sexual orientation. Against this mainstream background, ART poses the question: why just humans? The universalizing impulse of human rights is to extend basic protections across boundaries of physical, mental, and cultural difference, so why should this impulse stop at the boundary of the human species?

The premise of ART—reflected in the writings of Sapontzis (1987), Francione (2000), Cavalieri (2001), Regan (2003), Dunayer (2004), Steiner (2008), and others—is that these protective rights are owed to all conscious or sentient beings, human or animal.[6] Conscious/sentient beings are selves—that is, they have a distinctive subjective experience of their own lives and of the world, which demands a specific kind of protection in the form of inviolable rights. To limit these rights to humans is morally arbitrary or 'speciesist'. Such rights can, and ought to, play a crucial role in protecting all vulnerable beings.

Sentience/consciousness has a distinct moral significance because it enables a subjective experience of the world. According to Francione, 'the observation that animals are sentient is different from saying that they are merely alive. To be sentient means to be the sort of being who is conscious of pain and pleasure; there is an "I" who has subjective experiences' (Francione 2000: 6).

Steiner's formulation is that 'sentience is a capacity shared by all beings for whom the struggle for life and flourishing *matters*, whether or not the being in question has a reflective sense of which things matter or how they matter' (Steiner 2008: xi–xii). Beings who experience their lives from the inside, and for whom life can go better or worse are selves, not things, whom we recognize as experiencing vulnerability—to pleasure and pain, to frustration and satisfaction, to joy and suffering, or to fear and death.

Recognizing others as sentient in this way changes our attitude towards them. Cora Diamond speaks of recognizing the other as a 'fellow creature' (Diamond 2004). Steiner says that recognizing other beings as sentient creates 'a kinship relation to one another that binds them together in a moral community' (Steiner 2008: xii). Barbara Smuts says 'the "presence" we recognize in another when we meet in mutuality is something we feel more than something we know . . . In mutuality, we sense that inside this other body, there is "someone home"' (Smuts 2001: 308).[7]

The basic premise of ART is that whenever we encounter such vulnerable selves—whenever we encounter 'someone home'—they need protection through the principle of inviolability, which provides a protective shield of basic rights around every individual. One natural way to express this claim is to say that animals should be recognized as persons, and this is indeed how many AR theorists summarize their position. Francione, for example, entitles his recent book *Animals as Persons* (Francione 2008). Since existing human rights norms are often phrased as 'all persons have the right to X', we can restate the ART position as saying that because animals have selfhood, they too should be included in the category of persons.

Many critics of this ART position reassert the traditional view that only human beings are entitled to the protection of inviolable rights. Some critics appeal to religion. The sacred texts of many faiths, including Judaism, Christianity, and Islam, state that God gave humans dominion over animals, including the right to use them for our benefit, and for some devout religious believers this biblical sanction is sufficient grounds to reject ART.[8] We will set this aside, since we are interested in arguments that draw upon public reasons, not private faith or sacred revelation.

Other critics attempt to deny that animals really do have a subjective experience of the world or that they experience pain, suffering, fear, or pleasure. But the scientific evidence on this point is overwhelming and growing daily. As Palmer notes, it is now accepted by the 'overwhelming majority of biologists and philosophers' (Palmer 2010: 15), so we will set that criticism aside too.[9]

A more serious critique of ART accepts that animals are sentient, but denies that sentience is sufficient for being entitled to the protection of inviolable rights. According to this line of argument, inviolable rights are only owed to persons, and personhood is something more than mere selfhood; it requires more than the fact of there being 'someone home'.[10] As we noted earlier, many AR theorists effectively equate selfhood and personhood; since animals are sentient selves, they should be treated as persons. But critics have argued that personhood requires some further capacity found only amongst humans. People disagree about what this further capacity is. Some appeal to language, others to the capacity for abstract reasoning or long-term planning, yet others appeal to the capacity for culture or to enter into moral agreements. According to these views, the fact that there is someone home is not sufficient to trigger inviolable rights: the 'someone' at home must also be capable of complex cognitive functioning. Since allegedly only humans possess these cognitive capacities, only humans deserve inviolable rights. And since animals lack these inviolable rights, they can legitimately be used for the benefit of humans.

The multiple flaws in this attempt to reject ART by appeal to personhood have been extensively discussed in the literature. First, even if we could draw a coherent distinction between 'selves' and 'persons', it would not in fact justify ascribing rights on the basis of species membership. Any attempt to draw a line between selves and persons will cut across the species line, treating some humans and some animals as persons, while relegating other humans and other animals to the status of 'mere' selves. Moreover, the very attempt to make a sharp distinction between personhood and selfhood is not conceptually sustainable. It attempts to draw a single clear line in what is really a continuum, or indeed a series of continua along which individuals move at different stages of life. And this in turn reveals the flimsy moral foundations of the appeal to personhood. There is simply no plausible moral justification for ascribing inviolable rights based on personhood rather than selfhood.

We do not want to rehearse all of these arguments, but it is important to clarify not just the futility, but also the grave risks, of trying to invoke personhood as the basis for privileging humans over animals. We cannot assume a priori that only humans will pass a test of personhood. It is not true that only humans use language, for example, or that only humans engage in planning. Every day we learn more about animal minds and capacities, and every day the line in the sand allegedly establishing a unique human personhood is obliterated. It is on this basis that recent authors have argued, for example, that the great apes (Cavalieri and Singer 1993), dolphins (White 2007), elephants (Poole 1998), and whales (Cavalieri 2006) possess the cognitive and moral capacities that establish personhood.

One could try to overcome this by raising the bar of personhood so that it requires not only language or planning but, say, the capacity to engage in reasoned moral argumentation and to make commitments to comply with principles reached through such argumentation.[11] In this view, personhood requires the ability to articulate one's beliefs verbally in a form that meets certain standards of public accessibility and universalizability, to be able to understand other people's moral arguments, to engage in some process of rational reflection about the relative merits of these different views, and then consciously and deliberatively to conform one's behaviour to the principles that result from such a process of moral reasoning.

It is clear that apes and dolphins are not persons in this Kantian sense. But it is equally clear that many humans are not persons in this sense either. Many humans (e.g., infants, the senile, the mentally disabled, those temporarily incapacitated due to illness, or others with severe cognitive impairments) don't possess the alleged prerequisites of personhood, and in some cases their capacities are clearly exceeded by apes and dolphins and other non-humans. And yet are children and the cognitively impaired not persons? Are they not precisely the most vulnerable kinds of human beings whom the concept of inviolable human rights ought to protect?

In the philosophical literature, this is often described as the 'argument from marginal cases',[12] but this way of stating the objection misses the point. The problem is not that we have a clear majority of 'normal' humans who pass the test of personhood and then a few 'marginal cases' of humans who possess selfhood but not personhood. The problem, rather, is that the capacity for Kantian moral agency is, at best, a fragile achievement that humans have to varying degrees at varying points in their lives. None of us possesses it when we are very young, and we all face periods of shorter or longer duration when it is temporarily or permanently threatened by illness, disability, and aging, or by lack of adequate socialization and education and other forms of social support and nurturance. If personhood is defined as the capacity to engage in rational argumentation and to conform to consciously understood principles, then it is a fluctuating characteristic that varies not only across human beings, but also across time within a life.[13] To ground human rights in the possession of personhood in this sense would be to render human rights insecure for everyone. And this would defeat the purpose of human rights, which is precisely to provide security for vulnerable selves, including (and indeed especially) in those conditions or periods of life when capacities are limited.

AR theorists sometimes make the point about insecurity in another way. If the protected status of personhood is based on humans possessing superior cognitive capacities to animals, then what happens if an even more evolutionarily advanced species from another planet comes to Earth? Imagine that we encounter a species—let's call them Telepaths—who can engage in telepathy, or who can engage in complex reasoning that exceeds even our most advanced computers, or who can engage in forms of moral self-control that exceed the notoriously weak-willed and impulsive human species. And imagine that Telepaths start to enslave humans, and use us for food, or sport, or as beasts of burden, or as subjects of medical experimentation for their health research. And imagine that they justify our enslavement and exploitation on the grounds that our primitive forms of communication, reasoning, and impulse control do not meet their tests of personhood. They recognize us as having selfhood, but deny that we have the complex capacities needed for the inviolable rights of personhood.

How would we respond to such enslavement? Presumably we would respond that our alleged inferiority in these respects is irrelevant to our possession of inviolable rights.[14] We might indeed have primitive forms of communication or moral self-discipline in the estimation of Telepaths, but that does not make us mere instruments for the use and benefit of more advanced beings. We have our own lives to lead, our own experience of the world, our own sense of how our lives go better or worse. We are, in short, selves, and it is in virtue of our selfhood that we are owed basic rights, and the presence of allegedly more advanced beings does nothing to reduce our selfhood. Inviolable rights are not a prize awarded to whichever individual or species scores highest on some scale of cognitive capacities, but rather a recognition of the fact that we are subjective beings, and as such should be recognized as having our own lives to lead. But of course we can only respond in this way to the Telepaths if we abandon our quest to deny inviolable rights to animals. The very arguments of cognitive superiority invoked to justify excluding animals are precisely the basis on which Telepaths would justify our enslavement.[15]

In these and other ways, basing human rights on a demanding conception of personhood rather than selfhood would render human rights insecure. Indeed, the evolution of the theory and practice of human rights in the last sixty years has been in the opposite direction, repudiating any limitation based on the rationality or autonomy of the beings involved. We can see this internationally with the adoption of the UN Convention on the Rights of the Child (1990) or the UN Convention on the Rights of Persons with Disabilities (2006), as well as in domestic laws and court cases. For example, in an important case dealing with a profoundly intellectually disabled man who could not understand language or conceptualize death, the Massachusetts Supreme Court in 1977 emphasized that 'the principles of equality under the law' have 'no relation to intelligence' or to an individual's ability to 'appreciate' life in a conceptual sense.[16] None of these developments make sense if we tie human rights to a cognitively demanding conception of personhood. In short, invoking personhood to deny inviolable rights to animals only succeeds in eviscerating the theory and practice of human rights for human beings.

Confronted with these objections, critics of ART have responded in various ways. Some bite the bullet and accept that some human beings will not qualify as persons who are entitled to the protection of inviolability, even as some animals might qualify (Frey 1983). We can identify a range of such imagined geographies of personhood, with various mixes and matches of 'normal' humans and 'higher' animals inside the protected tent, while 'marginal' humans and 'lower' animals are outside.[17] Any intellectually honest attempt to apply a cognitively complex definition of personhood will almost certainly lead to this sort of patchwork quilt of variable and insecure moral status. Some people might think that this is a philosophically respectable position that needs to be taken seriously, but in our view, it is deeply unappealing (not to mention unworkable), and in any event it runs directly counter to the real-world development of human rights theory. The evolving trajectory of human rights has been precisely to erect the strongest of safeguards for the most vulnerable, protecting subordinated groups from dominant groups who question their cognitive capacities, protecting children from adults who can rationalize their abuse, protecting people with disabilities from eugenicists who would deny that their lives have dignity. Anyone who endorses these developments, as we hope our readers do, cannot endorse a theory of moral status that demands cognitively complex personhood.

A surprising number of theorists, however, cling to the hope that personhood can be invoked to reject inviolable rights for (all) animals while preserving the claim to inviolable rights for (all) humans. To preserve this illusory hope, theorists engage in increasingly contorted intellectual gymnastics to defend the privileging of human beings. Some appeal to the idea that all humans, whatever their actual capacities, have the 'species potential' for personhood, or that all humans belong to the 'kind' of being that has the potential for personhood (e.g., Cohen and Regan 2001)—forms of argumentation that are widely discredited in all other areas of moral and political philosophy, but which get revived in a desperate attempt to preserve the right of humans to exploit animals. When the multiple fallacies of such arguments are pointed out (e.g., Nobis 2004, Cavalieri 2001), the last line of defence is to stipulate that all human beings should be seen as inviolable persons simply because of their species membership, regardless of their actual or potential capacities. In rejecting the idea of animal personhood, Margaret Somerville, for example, says that 'universal human personhood means that every human being has an "intrinsic dignity" that comes simply with being human; having that dignity does not depend on having any other attribute or functional capacity' (Somerville 2010). Here we reach the nadir of appeals to personhood, which become nothing more than the bald assertion of speciesism. For Somerville, we should treat every human as an inviolable person because they are one of us (whatever their needs, capacities, or interests), and we should deny inviolable personhood to every animal because they are not one of us (whatever their needs, capacities, or interests).[18]

Much of the literature on animal rights has been consumed with these arguments and counter-arguments around personhood. In our view, however, this way of framing the debate leads us astray. What morally justifies the attribution of inviolable rights is selfhood, not a more cognitively demanding conception of personhood. Indeed, talk of personhood starts us down the wrong path. It suggests we must first develop some canonical list of attributes or capacities that ground inviolable rights, and then look around to see which beings possess these attributes. Rather, we believe that respecting inviolability is, first and foremost, a process of intersubjective recognition—that is, the first question is simply whether there is a 'subject' there, whether there is 'someone home'. This process of intersubjective recognition precedes any attempt to enumerate his or her capacities or interests. Once we know there is someone home, we know we are dealing with a vulnerable self, a being with subjective experience whose life can go better or worse as experienced from the inside. And so we know we should respect their inviolable rights, even before we know their variable capacities such as intelligence or moral agency.[19]

All of this is clear enough in the human case. When dealing with sentient humans, we do not assign degrees of basic human rights or inviolability according to differences in mental complexity, intelligence, or emotional or moral range. Simple or brilliant, selfish or saint, torpid or vivacious—we are all entitled to basic human rights because we are all vulnerable selves. Indeed, it is often humans with the most limited capacities who are most vulnerable, and most in need of the protections of inviolability. Moral status does not rest on judgements of mental complexity, but simply on the recognition of selfhood. Talk of personhood obscures this, and creates false barriers to the recognition of animal rights.

The idea that inviolable rights are grounded in the capacity for language, moral reflection, or abstract cognitive ability strains common sense, and seems disconnected from any plausible account of how we actually reason morally.[20] Focusing on these capacities may be tempting to anyone whose driving motivation is to exclude animals from the protection of inviolable rights. But that end can only be achieved by hollowing out the theory, making a mockery of the idea of protecting the vulnerable and the innocent.[21]

Given the way talk of personhood obscures our moral reasoning, and the way it has been used for exclusionary purposes, it might be better to avoid the language of personhood entirely, and simply to talk, in both the human and animal cases, of selfhood, and of the inviolable rights that protect selfhood. But the language of personhood is too deeply woven into our everyday discourses and legal systems to simply be expunged. For many legal and political purposes, advancing an animal rights agenda will require using the pre-existing language of persons and extending it to animals. And so we too, like Francione, will sometimes speak about 'animals as persons'. But it is important to emphasize that, for the rest of this book, we are treating personhood as a synonym for selfhood, and that we reject any attempt to distinguish personhood from selfhood as the basis for inviolable rights. Such efforts are conceptually unsustainable, morally unmotivated, and radically destabilizing of the very idea of universal human rights.[22]

Our fundamental position, then, is that animals have inviolable rights in virtue of their sentience or selfhood, the fact that they have a subjective experience of the world. This naturally raises the question of which beings are indeed conscious or sentient in this sense. Which animals are selves? The truth is, we may never be able to fully answer this question. There is something fundamentally unknowable about other minds, and this chasm increases the further we move from forms of consciousness and experience that most resemble our own. Are molluscs conscious? Insects? The evidence to date suggests they are not, but this may just reflect the fact that we are looking for a distinctly human form of subjective experience, and not considering other possible forms.[23] Scientists are still learning how to study animal minds, and there will undoubtedly be hard cases and grey areas for a long time to come when trying to identify consciousness. However, this doesn't change the fact that we can readily identify it in many instances. Indeed, the types of animals that are most cruelly abused are precisely those whose consciousness is least in doubt. We domesticate species like dogs and horses precisely because of their ability to interact with us. We experiment on species like monkeys and rats precisely because they share similar responses to deprivation, fear, or rewards. To invoke the difficulty of determining a threshold of basic consciousness as a justification for continuing animal exploitation is dishonest. As Francione argues, even if we don't know enough about animal minds to be sure about whether all animals are sentient/conscious, we know that many of them are, and that the ones we routinely exploit most certainly are (Francione 2000: 6; cf. Regan 2003).

Moreover, it is important to emphasize that recognizing selfhood does not require that we be able to unravel the mystery of an animal's mind. The point of the Smuts quote about 'someone home' is that we can recognize consciousness without being able to understand what it is like to be a bat, say, or a deer. (Just as we can recognize the selfhood of other humans whose subjective experience is profoundly different from our own.) This doesn't mean that we shouldn't seek greater understanding of animal minds. Science has made remarkable strides in recent years in demonstrating the range and complexity of animal intelligence and emotion.[24] This understanding has been vital in changing human attitudes towards animals, especially in overturning the old scientific consensus that animals were insentient—a prejudice with remarkable staying power, given the overwhelming evidence (and common sense) to the contrary. Scientific understanding is also vital in helping us understand the specific interests of individual animals and species, and in interpreting what they are able to communicate to us about those interests. The better we understand animals, the greater the opportunities for rich and rewarding (and just) intersubjective relationship. There will always be some animals whose world and experience are so removed from ours—like the eelpout fish living deep in the Pacific Ocean thermal vents—that the best we can do is recognize that there is a self there, respect their basic rights, and leave them to get on with life.[25] But there will be countless others with whom greater understanding and relationship is possible. This is where the science of other minds becomes crucial—not in determining *who* has basic rights, but in helping us to understand *how* best to interact with them.

Thus we eagerly await new developments from the ethical exploration of animal minds. However, the moral claim to basic rights does not hinge on these findings. We already know that in the case of most animals, there is 'someone home'. This, in our view, is sufficient to ground respect for basic inviolable rights. Admittedly, ours is a minority view, and we have no doubt that debates will continue to rage concerning moral status, selfhood, personhood, and universal basic rights. Defenders of human superiority will continue to engage in increasingly contorted intellectual gymnastics to defend the privileging of human beings, and animal advocates will continue to strip the last vestiges of human chauvinism from our moral theories. As we said earlier, our aim in this book is not to reproduce all these arguments and counter-arguments—readers who are interested in them can consult a number of good collections of key texts (Sapontzis 2004; Sunstein and Nussbaum 2004; Cohen and Regan 2001; Donovan and Adams 2007; Palmer 2008; Armstrong and Botzler 2008). And no doubt there will continue to be new and more ingenious efforts to defend speciesism in all its dimensions. But as Peter Singer notes, we have now had thirty years of such attempts, and 'the continuing failure of philosophy to produce a plausible theory of the moral importance of species membership indicates, with increasing probability, that there can be no such thing' (Singer 2003).

2. Justice for Persons and the Value of Nature

This then is our basic starting point: like many other AR theorists, we defend inviolable rights for animals as a response to the vulnerability of selfhood or individual consciousness. So far, we have primarily been concerned with defending this position against critics who seek to restrict moral personhood to human beings (or to a few 'higher' animal species). But it's worth noting that there is another, very different, line of critique of ART found amongst ecological theorists. As we noted earlier, they often criticize ART for not extending moral standing far enough. ART extends moral standing to sentient beings, but not to forests, rivers, or nature more generally. Indeed, some ecologists argue that ART remains fundamentally an anthropocentric theory: it takes human beings as the measure of moral status, and simply argues that some other species share enough human-like characteristics to qualify for human rights.

Let us start with the anthropocentric objection, and then turn to the issue of the value of nature. Anthropocentrism, as we understand the term, is an approach to moral theory that takes humanity as its standard: it starts by asking what the essence is of 'being human' or of 'humanity', and assumes that human beings are entitled to rights and justice in virtue of this essential humanity. Animals, in this anthropocentric view, achieve moral standing only if they can be seen as possessing or approximating some aspect of this essence of humanity.

That is not our approach. Our theory is not one based on any account of the essence of being human, any more than it is based on the essence of, say, being a dog. Our theory is instead based on an account of one of the key purposes of justice, which is the protection of vulnerable individuals.[26] Being an 'I'—a being who experiences—represents a particular kind of vulnerability, calling for a particular form of protection from the actions of others, in the form of inviolable rights. This is not imposing a human-centric moral criterion on animals—on the contrary, what happens to sentient beings matters because it matters *to them*. It is the fact that sentient beings care about how their lives go that generates a distinctive kind of moral claim on us.

It's true that when we ask questions about what we mean by justice, it is often helpful to start from the familiar human case, and to examine our intuitions about what constitutes human justice, and why it is important. As we noted above, we believe that if one attends carefully to those intuitions, we will see that what matters is the presence of subjective experience (which all humans share), and not higher cognitive functions (which only some humans possess, at particular points in life). But the fact that we start from the human case in this sense doesn't mean that we are privileging some theory of humanity, nor that we are privileging a distinctly *human* state of subjectivity. We could equally have started from our intuitions about dogs, and whether they seem to be the kinds of beings who are vulnerable in ways that could be protected by inviolable rights, and if they are, what it is about dogs that makes them vulnerable in the relevant kind of way. And we would arrive at an answer concerning dog sentience, consciousness, or subjectivity, regardless of how close or distant dog subjectivity is to human subjectivity.

Let us turn now to the deeper question about the value of nature. As noted, ecological theorists have argued that it's not just individual animals who are vulnerable to harm from humans. Entire species are obliterated. Watersheds are polluted, mountain ranges pulverized, and once-flourishing ecosystems degraded. These processes harm both humans and animals, but for ecological theorists, their harmfulness is not reducible to their impact on sentient beings. Many ecological theorists have argued that non-animal nature has an interest in flourishing which must be taken into account, and that plants, ecosystems, etc. must be given moral standing, along with humans and animals, to protect their interests (Baxter 2005; Schlossberg 2007). According to this view, insofar as ART ascribes rights on the basis of selfhood, it lacks the conceptual resources to recognize the moral significance of nature more broadly.

Part of the difficulty here lies in the language of moral standing, invoked by both defenders of ART and their ecological critics. We need different, and more precise, terms to capture the way in which different types of considerations enter into our moral reasoning. To say that humans, animals, and nature all have moral standing, or that they can all be harmed, is unhelpful. A watershed can be harmed, and an otter can be harmed, but only the otter has the subjective experience of being harmed. This does not mean that subjectively experienced harm is necessarily more serious than other types of harm, but it does mean that it is different, and calls for different remedies or protections. Consider a standard example advanced by ecological theorists, in which a flourishing ecosystem has been overrun by deer. Natural predators are absent, so the deer population runs out of control and decimates the local flora endangering the ecosystem, including the last specimens of a rare orchid. Imagine the situation has been allowed to fester, and the habitat is on the verge of collapse. Non-lethal solutions such as propagating the orchid elsewhere, or controlling the deer population through fertility drugs or the creation of habitat corridors, won't work quickly enough, and the only apparent solutions are for humans either to kill the deer or allow them to destroy the ecosystem and its orchid.

In this sort of case, ecological theorists criticize ART for granting moral standing only to individual deer, while withholding moral standing to the ecosystem as a whole, or to a particular species of flower. But does granting moral standing to the ecosystem really help us identify the moral considerations at stake? If we grant moral standing to both the deer and the ecosystem, the implication is that these are moral considerations of the same type, to be weighed against each other, such that it might be acceptable to kill the deer to protect the ecosystem from degradation, or to protect the orchid from extinction. The interests of nature might outweigh those of the deer, who are a dime a dozen over in the next county.

Yet surely this way of framing the issue obscures rather than clarifies the moral factors at work. Consider what happens when we substitute human persons for deer in this example. In that case, we would not favour killing humans to save the orchid. We would try to dissuade humans from their destructive behaviour, we would try to protect the ecosystem and its orchids, but if worst comes to worst we're not going to be culling any people. The orchid will be lost, and we'll try to do better next time. Why is this? Because the nature of the moral standing at play is qualitatively different. The orchid, or the local habitat, does not have the kind of interest that can override the inviolability of persons and their right not to be killed.

Indeed, ecological theorists typically accept this. When ecological theorists first proposed that plants or ecosystems should have moral standing in theories of justice, critics raised the objection that the protection of an ecosystem or species could be used to justify the killing of humans. Ecological theorists were quick to respond to these 'ecofascism' charges by insisting that granting moral standing in a holistic way to species and ecosystems could not be used to justify the trampling of basic human rights. While holistic entities (e.g., species or ecosystems) have moral standing, it is not equivalent to human moral standing. As Callicott puts it, recognizing the moral status of the ecosystem supplements pre-existing moral systems of inviolable human rights, and cannot be invoked to limit or reject those pre-existing human rights (Callicott 1999).[27] Moral standing is a hierarchy, in other words. Natural systems have a moral standing such that ecological values must be taken into account, but these values do not trump basic human rights.[28]

This move, however, shows that the ecological discourse of moral standing is systematically misleading, obscuring fundamental differences in what we mean by moral standing. As much as ART, ecological theory implicitly operates with the assumption that certain beings are bearers of inviolable rights. But it simply assumes, without argument, that only humans qualify as persons with inviolable rights, while putting both sentient animals and non-animal nature into a residual category of moral standing whose basic interests are subject to trade-offs.

This may be a defensible position, but it's not illuminated or defended by asking whether non-animal nature has moral standing. Rather, the fundamental issue is about how we identify the set of beings whose selfhood generates inviolable rights. The question of selfhood is separate from, and constrains, the ways we respond to the value of nature. Ecological theorists implicitly presuppose that the selfhood of animals, unlike the selfhood of humans, does not generate the protection of inviolable rights. But they give no argument for this position, which therefore amounts to the naked assertion of speciesism, just like Somerville.

In our view, it is misleading to suggest that humans, animals, non-sentient life forms, and inanimate nature all have interests in the same sense, and hence that all have moral standing. On the surface, it appears to challenge the anthropocentric privileging of human beings, but in fact it presupposes a hierarchical concept of moral standing in which only one group of vulnerable individuals, namely humans, are inviolable, while all other animals are subject to trade-offs. And as we've seen in Chapter 1, the inevitable result of this hierarchical concept is the perpetuation and expansion of the (ecologically disastrous) system of animal exploitation.

A more plausible approach, we have argued, is to start with the question of selfhood. What sorts of beings have a subjective experience of the world, and hence have interests in that specific sense? This question of selfhood or personhood identifies the set of beings to whom justice and inviolable rights are owed. There are many good reasons to respect and protect nature, including instrumental as well as non-instrumental ones. But it is wrong to characterize these reasons as protecting the *interests* of orchids or other non-sentient entities. Only a being with subjective experience can have interests, or be owed the direct duties of justice that protect those interests. A rock is not a person. Neither is an ecosystem, an orchid, or a strain of bacteria. They are things. They can be damaged, but not subject to injustice. Justice is owed to subjects who experience the world, not to things. Non-sentient entities can rightfully be the objects of respect, awe, love, and care. But, lacking subjectivity, they are not rightfully the objects of fairness, nor are they agents of inter-subjectivity, the motivating spirit of justice.

Ecological theorists will counter that we're not eliminating the hierarchy, just changing its membership. But this is to misunderstand the claim. We do not deny that humans have moral duties to plants and inanimate nature. Nor do we claim that humans and animals are higher in some cosmic hierarchy than trees or mountains. Rather, we claim that they are different—sentience generates distinctive vulnerabilities, and hence distinctive needs for the protection of inviolable rights. If non-sentient entities shared this interest, and we denied the protections of inviolability to them, then we would be guilty of subordinating them. But they do not have this interest, and therefore there is no disrespect in declining to treat orchids and rock faces as persons.[29]

3. Nature's Otherness

As we have seen, the ART position on basic rights has been criticized from both directions—that is, by those who think only humans have moral status, and by those who think all of nature possesses moral status. Both critiques perform the same sleight of hand by ignoring animal subjectivity. Both tend to collapse the question of animals into the question of nature writ large, denying that animals, as subjects, need to be protected the way human subjects are, and not simply as components of nature.

What explains the puzzling resistance of so many people—both humanists and ecologists—to acknowledging the selfhood of animals? There are no doubt many reasons, including the long history of the denigration of animals as mere brutes or things. But it is worth noting that another factor, paradoxically, may be the ways in which we often admire, respect, and value animal life—and nature more generally.

People often view animals as simply part of nature, and hence as something fundamentally 'other'—indifferent to human projects and unknowable to human minds. And while this otherness can sometimes be threatening or alienating, it can also generate powerful aesthetic and moral responses of respect and awe. These are the moments when great natural beauty takes us out of ourselves, briefly silencing the ego and allowing us to lose ourselves in something larger, and something which is essentially indifferent to the self. This 'unselfing' is famously described in Iris Murdoch's account of the kestrel:

> I am looking out of my window in an anxious and resentful state of mind, oblivious of my surroundings, brooding perhaps on some damage done to my prestige. Then suddenly I observe a hovering kestrel. In a moment everything is altered. The brooding self with its hurt vanity has disappeared. There is nothing now but kestrel. And when I return to thinking of the other matter it seems less important. (Murdoch 1970: 84)

This is sometimes cited as an example of how nature can and should be valued by human beings, in ways that go beyond its instrumental value as a resource or commodity. The presence of a larger natural order, wholly indifferent to our daily projects and preoccupations, provides a necessary context to, and perspective on, our lives.

Consider a related description by mountain climber Karen Warren:

> One recognizes the rock as something very different, something perhaps totally indifferent to one's own presence, and finds in that difference joyous occasion for celebration. One knows 'the boundary of the self,' where the self—the 'I,' the climber—leaves off and the rock begins. There is no fusion of two into one, but a complement of two entities *acknowledged* as separate, different, independent, yet *in relationship*; they are in relationship *if only* because the loving eye is perceiving it, responding to it, noticing it, attending to it. (cited in Slicer 1991: 111)

Deborah Slicer quotes this passage, describing the relationship between climber and rock face as an exemplar of a kind of 'loving attention' which should be the basis for our ethical relations with 'the other', including animals, plants, and non-living nature.

Loving attention and respect for nature's otherness (including its beauty, self-containment, and self-sufficiency) represent a critical moral ability and opportunity for many humans (and perhaps for some animals). And the experience of such moments of selfless attention or connection may be vital in motivating humans to care for nature, including animals. But it is a mistake to see this kind of 'loving attention' as exhausting our moral response and duty towards animals. Warren speaks of being 'in relationship' with the rock, but it is a one-sided relationship in which it is the human self who does all of the perceiving, responding, noticing, and attending. In the case of the kestrel, on the other hand, there are two selves. The kestrel may be indifferent to Murdoch at the moment she is looking out her window (just as another human self would be, were she unaware of being observed). But there is a potential for intersubjective relationship, and with it, different kinds of moral duties.

Imagine that the kestrel suddenly hits the window and slides to the ground, or that a fragment of rock which Warren has just climbed has been jarred loose and falls to a ledge below. In the first instance, moral action to attend to the kestrel is called for. Murdoch has an obligation to go to the bird and help her if she can. The latter instance demands no comparable moral action. Warren may chide herself for sloppy climbing, and regret marring the rock face, but there is no other self who is suffering, and demanding moral action. The incident may prompt Warren to reconsider whether rock climbing really is consistent with loving attention for rock faces, but there is no call upon her to climb down to the ledge to assist the rock fragment she has dislodged.

If we overemphasize animals' separateness from us—their independence, distance, inscrutability, or indifference—we are at just as much risk of moral error as if we overemphasize our similarity by projecting onto them needs, desires, or interests that are distinctly our own. (And the same might be said of our relationships with other humans.) The fact is that many animals are far from indifferent to us, and quite capable of communicating a great deal about their needs, desires, and interests as individual selves.

Barbara Smuts, in her work with baboons and domestic dogs, is an expert witness of the process of interspecies communication and connection— 'the capacity to feel our way into the being of another' (Smuts 2001: 295). In her field research observing baboons, she describes a critical moment in the baboons' response to her presence amongst them. Initially, they simply retreat from her, in a unilateral and instinctive response to a potential threat. Over time, Smuts learns to 'talk baboon', changing everything from 'the way I walked and sat, the way I held my body, and the way I used my eyes and voice'. As she gradually communicates to the baboons that she can respond to their cues indicating emotions, motivations, and intentions, they come to recognize her as a subject:

> This may sound like a small shift, but in fact it signalled a profound change from being treated as an *object* that elicited a unilateral response (avoidance), to being recognized as a *subject* with whom they could communicate. Over time they treated me more and more as a social being like themselves, subject to the demands and rewards of relationship. This meant that I sometimes had to be

willing to give more weight to their demands (e.g., a signal to 'get lost!') than to my desire to collect data. But it also meant that I was increasingly often welcomed into their midst, not as a barely-tolerated intruder but as a casual acquaintance or even, on occasion, a familiar friend. (Smuts 2001: 295)[30]

Smuts came away from her time with the baboons with a profoundly different awareness of the individuality of animals, and the possibilities for intersubjective encounters:

Before Africa, if I were walking in the woods and came across a squirrel, I would enjoy its presence, but I would experience it as a member of a class, 'squirrel'. Now, I experience every squirrel I encounter as a small, fuzzy-tailed, person-like creature. Even though I usually don't know this squirrel from another, I know that if I tried, I would, and that once I did, this squirrel would reveal itself as an utterly unique being, different in temperament and behaviour from every other squirrel in the world. In addition, I am aware that if this squirrel had a chance to get to know me, he or she might relate to me differently than to any other person in the world. My awareness of the individuality of all beings, and of the capacity of at least some beings to respond to the individuality in me, transforms the world into a universe replete with opportunities to develop personal relationships of all kinds. Such relationships can be ephemeral, like those developed with the birds in whose territories we might picnic, or life-long, like those established with cats, dogs, and human friends. (Smuts 2001: 301)

This attention to the possibilities of intersubjective relationship is very different from Murdoch's moment of 'unselfing'. The latter encounter is possible with many kinds of other—sentient and otherwise. The former is only possible with other 'selves', creating the basis for intersubjectivity, and the special protections entailed by its unique form of vulnerability. Generalized discussion of 'the other' (meaning animals and nature) obscures the fact that animals are not just 'other', they are other *selves*. And it is selfhood that motivates the specific moral attitudes of fairness and compassion which underlie our duties of justice.[31]

4. The Great Debate: Summing Up

The foregoing, in essence, describes the 'great debate' initiated by ART for the last forty-five years. The debate is by no means over, but we believe that the arguments to date clearly support the strong AR position: namely, that animals should be recognized as vulnerable selves with inviolable rights (against those who would restrict basic rights to humans), and that these protections of selfhood should be extended to animals without being watered down, or displaced by other moral priorities (against those who would place animals and nature lower than humans in a hierarchy of moral standing, or advocate a moral standing for animals that disregards the importance of selfhood).

As we have noted, ART remains intensely controversial. And yet, for all their efforts, critics of animal rights have been unable to make a convincing case for the unique moral selfhood of human beings. As Martha Nussbaum rather reluctantly concedes, 'It seems that there is no respectable way to deny the equal dignity of creatures across species' (Nussbaum 2006: 383).

We do not expect our brief discussion in this chapter to persuade anyone who has not already been persuaded on its merits. How, in the end, can you persuade anyone to look in the eyes of another and recognize a person? And so, in the rest of the book, rather than trying to advance new arguments for why animals are selves/persons, we want to explore the implications of recognizing animals as persons, and also as friends, as co-citizens, and as members of communities—ours and theirs. We hope that fleshing out a conception of possible human–animal relationships in these ways will make it easier for readers, the next time they look into the eyes of an animal, to recognize the person there—familiar, yet mysterious, an independent locus of meaning and agency.

5. The Inviolability and Universality of Basic Rights for Animals

While our main goal is to develop an expanded and group-differentiated conception of human–animal justice that goes beyond ART's current preoccupation with basic rights, this is not to diminish the significance of these universal rights. Quite the contrary. They are vital to ending the ongoing tragedy of animal exploitation, and the most egregious forms of violence. So we will conclude this chapter with a brief overview of how we understand these rights, and how they set the foundations for the more expanded conception we develop in later chapters.

What are the implications of recognizing animals as persons or selves with inviolable rights? In the simplest terms, it means recognizing that they are not means to our ends. They were not put on earth to serve us, or feed us, or comfort us. Rather, they have their own subjective existence, and hence their own equal and inviolable rights to life and liberty, which prohibits harming them, killing them, confining them, owning them, and enslaving them. Respect for these rights rules out virtually all existing practices of the animal-use industries, where animals are owned and exploited for human profit, pleasure, education, convenience, or comfort.

We have described these basic rights as both 'inviolable' and 'universal', just as human rights are typically understood as both inviolable and universal. However, inviolability and universality are concepts that require some further clarification. Let us start with inviolability. As we have already noted, this term does not mean that basic rights are absolute and exceptionless. This is not true in either the human or animal case, as in cases of self-defence. Human beings have an inviolable right to life, but killing another human being is permissible if it is done out of self-defence or necessity.[32] So, too, with animals. There is also a historical dimension to the issue of inviolability. At different stages of human history, or in particular contexts, humans have had to harm and/or kill animals in order to survive. In that sense, too, basic inviolable rights are not absolute or unconditional.

This raises a more general point about the nature of justice: namely, that it only applies in certain circumstances—what Rawls (following Hume) calls the 'circumstances of justice'. Ought implies can: humans only owe justice to each other when they are in fact able to respect each other's rights without jeopardizing their own existence. Rawls calls this the requirement of 'moderate scarcity': justice is *necessary* because there isn't an unlimited pool of resources such that everyone can have everything that they want; but for justice to be *possible*, the competition for resources must be moderate rather than severe, in the sense that I can afford to recognize your legitimate claims without undermining my own existence.

We can contrast this with what are sometimes called 'lifeboat cases', when there is too little food or shelter for all to survive. In these lifeboat conditions, the most extreme actions may need to be contemplated. In order to avoid everyone on the boat dying, one person may be sacrificed, or sacrifice themselves, and various proposals have been made about how to decide who should live and who should die. But the existence of such extreme lifeboat cases tells us nothing about the basic rights we owe each other in the normal case where the circumstances of justice do apply. In conditions of moderate scarcity, rather than lifeboat cases, murdering other humans for food or shelter is wrong.[33]

Similarly, there are lifeboat cases in the relations between humans and animals. Indeed, in the past the circumstances of justice may not have applied to many human–animal interactions, and the killing of animals may unavoidably have been a central and enduring part of a group's survival strategies. And there may still be some isolated communities of humans dependent on limited local options for survival, who arguably are not in the circumstances of justice with animals.

But circumstances change. Ought implies can, but what we can do changes over time, and so, therefore, does the 'ought'. Today, most of us are no longer in the circumstances that would justify imprisoning and killing animals for food, labour, or clothing. We have no need to engage in the tragic necessity of harming animals in order to meet our needs.[34]

This does not mean that we never need to kill animals. Animals sometimes attack humans, or pose a lethal risk to humans by their presence (e.g., venomous snakes who take up residence in human houses). And the nature of these risks can change over time: a particular species of animal with whom we used to have benign relations may develop a virus that is lethal to us, and we may need to take protective action that had not been required beforehand. On the other hand, we may develop technologies (e.g., inoculations, barriers) that allow us to manage long-standing risks from animals, rendering unnecessary harmful self-defence measures that had previously been required.

Assessing and sustaining the circumstances of justice is therefore an ongoing task. Whether one is in the circumstances of justice towards animals is not a simple or one-shot 'yes/no' judgement. While human societies no longer need to routinely kill or enslave animals in order to survive, there will be ongoing cases of potentially lethal conflict, and these cases may evolve and change over time. What does not change, however, is our obligation to try to sustain the circumstances of justice where they exist, and to move towards the circumstances of justice where they do not yet exist. We should not recklessly put ourselves in situations where we are likely to face lethal conflicts with animals, and we should make reasonable efforts to identify practices that would allow us to reduce existing conflicts, in order that, to the extent possible, we can respect the inviolable rights of animals.[35]

What precisely this will require of us will vary considerably. For those of us who live in wealthy urban environments, the vast bulk of our daily interactions with animals clearly falls within the circumstances of justice. For those living in more remote areas alongside potentially aggressive wildlife, or in poorer societies without adequate infrastructure (e.g., waste disposal, impermeable housing barriers), the necessities of daily life may create more regular risks of lethal conflict, and greater measures would be needed to extend the circumstances of justice. In each case, there is a duty to sustain and extend the circumstances of justice, so as to respect as far as possible the inviolable rights of animals, but obviously more can be expected and demanded of those of us living in more propitious circumstances.

The idea of inviolable rights for animals, therefore, is more complex than it initially appears, and not as absolute or unconditional as it may sound. But all of this is equally true in the case of human rights. We may need to sacrifice humans who pose a lethal risk, or in lifeboat cases. The existence of such tragic cases does not put into question the basic inviolable rights of animals or humans—on the contrary, these cases are tragic precisely because we cannot respect the inviolability that people are owed. And so, in both cases, we have a duty progressively to extend the circumstances of justice so that, wherever possible, we can respect these inviolable rights.

Moreover, while inviolable rights are not exceptionless, we should not overstate these exceptions. For most societies, it is very rare indeed that self-defence or necessity requires violating the basic rights of animals. Some people try to extend the logic of self-defence to the case of medical experimentation on animals, on the grounds that it might lead to cures for lethal human diseases, and so qualifies as a case of 'kill or be killed'. According to this view, either animals or humans will die, and so it's okay for humans to choose their own survival.

But this is a gross distortion of the idea of self-defence or necessity. Consider a comparable human case. Human subjects make much more reliable models for human medical research than animals do, but we do not condone conscripting humans for dangerous, invasive, and non-consensual research purposes. We are rightly appalled by the idea of sacrificing human individuals in order to expand medical knowledge or to develop medical technologies in order to help other humans. This is one of the kinds of exploitation that the inviolability of the individual is intended to protect. Basic rights are needed precisely to prevent one individual's most basic interests being sacrificed for the greater good of others. It doesn't matter if sacrificing one human would generate knowledge that would potentially save a thousand others; we simply don't accept 'benefit to others' as sufficient cause for violating the basic rights of the person. And in the human case, we do not confuse 'benefit to others' with 'self-defence'. If a woman is holding hostages and threatening to shoot them, it may be necessary to kill her to save them. But picking a woman off the street and infecting her with the HIV virus in order to work for a cure is an act of unconscionable violence.

Medical experimentation on animals is often viewed as a hard case for animal rights. Even those who abhor factory farming, cosmetic testing, or recreational hunting will often condone medical research, as though giving up our access to unlimited, if imperfect, research subjects is too great a sacrifice to contemplate (e.g., Nussbaum 2006; Zamir 2007; Slicer 1991; McMahan 2002). But to view this as a sacrifice is already to misunderstand the moral situation. After all, there are countless medical technologies and medical advances that don't exist today because we refuse to use human subjects for invasive experiments. It is hard to overestimate the advances that medical science could have made by now if researchers had been able to use human subjects, rather than imperfect animal stand-ins. Yet we do not view this as a sacrifice. We do not wake up every day lamenting all that untapped knowledge; we are not bitter about the restriction on human subjects that has so hampered medical advance; we do not worry that an overly squeamish attitude about respecting the rights of a few humans is standing in the way of longer and healthier lives for the rest of us. Indeed, anyone who viewed prohibitions on using humans as research subjects as a sacrifice would be seen as morally perverse. We fully understand, in the human context, that medical knowledge must advance within ethical boundaries, or it simply isn't knowledge that we have a right to. This may force us to be more creative about how we learn, or to be more patient in waiting for results. Either way, it's not something we view as a sacrifice. It's a recognition that a world in which better or longer lives for the many are purchased by sacrificing the few is not a world worth living in.

It will require a huge adjustment for societies to accept that medical knowledge gained by harming and killing animals is not knowledge to which we are entitled. But the costs of the adjustment would be temporary. After a few decades in which new practices became customary, and a new generation of researchers trained, animal experimentation would be perceived much as human experimentation is viewed today. Its prohibition would not be viewed as a cost, just as the absence of human experimentation is not viewed as a cost. Nobody would think that giving up animal experimentation constitutes a sacrifice on the part of humans. Rather, they would wonder how we ever rationalized such a practice in the first place.

This then is how we understand inviolability, in both the human and animal cases: it is conditional on the circumstances of justice, but where those circumstances exist, it provides firm protection for basic rights, even when (and indeed especially when) sacrificing the interests of the few could benefit the interests of the many.

Let us now turn to the issue of 'universality'. Following Cavalieri (2001) and others, we have presented our account of animal rights as a logical extension of the doctrine of human rights, and as sharing in its aspirations to universality. To say it aspires to universality is to say, amongst other things, that it is not offered simply as the interpretation of a particular cultural tradition or religious worldview, but as a global ethic, based on values or principles that are accessible to and shared by the world as a whole.

All such claims to universality immediately raise issues of cultural pluralism. Given that the world's cultures and religions have very different views of the moral standing of animals, how can any one view claim to be universally valid? Is it not a form of Eurocentrism and moral imperialism to impose 'our' views of the rights of animals on other societies? This objection has been particularly salient and controversial in relation to indigenous peoples, some of whom engage in forms of hunting and trapping that animal rights activists have sought to ban (e.g., whale hunting, seal hunting). Viewed against the long history of Western imperialism against indigenous peoples, it is difficult not to see this as yet another example in which Western societies claim the right to exercise power over indigenous societies on the grounds that the latter are backward, primitive, or even barbaric. And so even ardent animal rights activists sometimes seek ways to exempt indigenous peoples from laws or conventions that would prohibit their traditional hunting practices.

Yet few people in the animal advocacy movement would wish to endorse a generalized 'cultural exemption' that could be invoked whenever traditional cultural practices violate the rights of animals. For example, when Spain joined the European Union, it negotiated an exemption from European animal welfare laws to allow bullfighting on the grounds of 'respecting cultural traditions' (Casal 2003: 1). Most animal rights activists view this as scandalous: what is the point of endorsing animal rights principles if not to stop these sorts of traditions?

In-between Spanish bullfighting and traditional indigenous hunting, there are a wide range of controversial cases, many tied up with religion. Should Jews and Muslims be exempted from animal slaughter laws that are intended to minimize suffering? Should adherents of the Santeria religion be allowed to use animals in ritual sacrifices as part of their religious services? More generally, is there a conflict between respect for cultural diversity and respect for animal rights? And if so, does that mean, in Paula Casal's words, that 'multiculturalism is bad for animals' (Casal 2003)?

This is an important issue, or, more accurately, a nest of different issues that needs to be carefully unpacked. We cannot hope to fully address them here, but it's important to note that the same debate arises in relation to human rights. From the origins of the Universal Declaration of Human Rights in 1948, there have been ongoing contestations over whether the idea of human rights is truly universal, or whether it reflects the imposition of Eurocentric ideas on other cultures, particularly in relation to the rights of women and children, or family life more generally. And so, as with animal rights, we see a number of calls for cultural or religious exemptions from human rights standards. Many countries have entered 'reservations' when signing international human rights norms, particularly in relation to the rights of children and women, which are seen as central to a society's way of life or its religious self-identity. And this in turn has led to questions about whether there is a conflict between respect for cultural diversity and respect for women's rights, and hence whether 'multiculturalism is bad for women' (Okin 1999).

If we compare these debates, the similarities are striking. In relation to their claims for universality, and the contestability of these claims, human rights and animal rights are on a par, and we see no reason to think that animal rights are any more or less capable of universality than human rights. Indeed, if our arguments in this chapter are correct that animal rights flow from the logic of human rights, then their universality stands or falls together. Defending the universality of animal rights despite the persistence of deeply rooted cultural disagreement is a difficult challenge, but it is a challenge we already face in defending the universality of human rights in the face of equally persistent cultural disagreement, and our answer to the latter challenge is likely to apply to the former.

Much has been written about how best to defend the universality of basic rights in light of these facts and claims of cultural diversity, and we cannot hope to reproduce those debates here, let alone to resolve them. But we can perhaps at least set aside some misunderstandings. Much of the opposition to the universality of human or animal rights rests on a particular view about how cultural values emerge or evolve. As Bielefeldt (2000) notes, when people discuss whether human rights are Western, they often operate implicitly with the model of cultures as acorns that turn into oak trees. To say that human rights are Western is to say that human rights were somehow present in the very acorn of Western civilization, present in its cultural DNA as it were, and hence destined to blossom as the tree grew. By contrast, human rights are said to be missing from the acorn of Islamic or Eastern societies, not part of their cultural DNA, and hence not part of their natural evolution, but can only be at best a foreign graft that does not truly fit into their tree. Similarly, someone who denies the universality of animal rights might argue that animal rights are part of the cultural DNA of the West, but not of the East.

This model of acorns and oak trees is hopelessly misleading, in relation to both human rights and animal rights. To state the obvious, the same Western civilization that nurtured ideas of human rights also nurtured Nazism and Stalinism, not to mention centuries of patriarchy and racial supremacy, all of which drew upon deeply rooted ideas in Western culture about order, nature, evolution, and hierarchy. If most people in the West today embrace ideas of human rights, it is not because these ideas were the only ones that matched our cultural DNA. Rather, people have judged that amongst the many diverse and contradictory moral sources that are found in our history and culture, ideas of human rights are worthy of being endorsed and defended, while other moral sources are judged unworthy of our continued allegiance.

This process is one that takes place within every culture, not just the West. Within every culture and religion, there is a diversity of moral sources (or a diversity of interpretations of moral sources), some of which fit comfortably with ideas of universal human rights, others of which do not. Whether members of a society endorse human rights is not predetermined by their primordial cultural DNA, but rather is determined by their ongoing judgement about which of their diverse moral sources are worthy of allegiance. Human rights achieve universality, therefore, not through a series of alien grafts into societies that lack the appropriate cultural DNA, but through processes of reflecting on diverse moral sources, leading ideally to an 'unforced consensus' on a set of shared values or principles (Taylor 1999).

This is the model that most theorists invoke today to explain the universality of human rights,[36] and we believe that the same model applies to animal rights. No society is predetermined to embrace ART, but nor is any society predetermined to reject it. Every society contains a diversity of moral sources on the status of animals, some of which lead comfortably in the direction of ART, others of which do not, and it is up to all of us to judge which of these moral sources we find compelling.[37] This, we believe, is as true of indigenous societies as of European societies. Indeed, the conception of inviolability we have just defended—that is, one which condones the killing of animals only if and when it is a tragic necessity—is arguably closer to traditional indigenous attitudes than to the mainstream attitudes of Western societies for the past few centuries.

The available evidence suggests that many human cultures have viewed the killing of animals as a tragic necessity. For millennia, the fact that humans had to exploit animals in order to survive was a source of psychic stress. It's easy to forget this now, when most people go through their daily lives with barely a thought for the billions of animals who suffer and die to serve human wishes. But in ancient times, to the credit of our ancestors, the exploitation of animals was recognized as tragic and morally problematic. In many Mediterranean cultures, for example, it was considered taboo to consume unsacrificed meat. When animals were sacrificed a token amount was offered to the gods, and the remainder distributed for human consumption. James Serpell describes sacrifice culture as a form of blame-shifting, in which the gods are ultimately held responsible for the killing of animals by demanding that humans offer sacrifice. Animals were delivered to the temple or priest, who performed the ritual slaughter after eliciting (alleged) consent from the animal, thus further mitigating blame. And priests had to cleanse themselves after performing the dreadful deed (Serpell 1996: 207). In modern times, most humans live at a remove from direct animal exploitation, and seem to have successfully repressed any need for redress, although blame-shift and mitigation practices continue amongst traditional hunting societies and religious groups.[38]

In some respects, endorsing ART may well involve a greater cultural shift for the mainstream of Western societies than for societies that maintain this older view of killing animals as a tragic necessity to be atoned for. And not surprisingly, there is indeed debate within indigenous societies about the wisdom and necessity of various hunting and trapping practices, and some indigenous leaders resent the way the fur industry, for example, uses indigenous peoples in their marketing and publicity to whitewash their industrial-scale exploitative and abusive practices.[39]

In any event, there is no basis for saying that ART is somehow in the West's cultural DNA but can only be a foreign graft for other societies. The universality of animal rights, as of human rights, is something to be debated openly through a process of reflecting on our moral sources, not prejudged by simplistic assumptions about the primordial essence of cultures.

Obviously, we believe that the claim to universality for both human and animal rights can be vindicated, and that this process of moral reflection can lead to an overlapping consensus on basic rights for all vulnerable selves. But we would emphasize that claiming universality for ART is not the same thing as endorsing its *imposition* on other societies. As with the case of human rights, there are powerful moral and practical reasons for limiting coercive intervention to the most grievous violations, and for focusing our efforts instead on supporting societies to move towards the fulfilment of human and animal rights. This is particularly true when dealing with historically subordinated groups that have good reason to distrust the motives of their erstwhile oppressors.[40]

We should also note that claiming universality for human or animal rights does not justify the *instrumentalizing* of such rights. As noted earlier, there is a long history in which dominant groups have justified their exercise of power over minorities or indigenous peoples by appealing to the 'backward' or 'barbaric' way that they treat women, children, or animals. In this context, human and animal rights are used, not out of a good-faith concern for the rights-holders, but rather to justify the reproduction of existing power relations (Elder, Wolch, and Emel 1998). In the case of animals, dominant groups typically ignore the ways in which they are directly complicit in the abuse of millions of captive and enslaved domesticated animals, while hypocritically complaining about the hunting practices of rural communities and indigenous peoples, or the ritual use of animals by religious minorities, even though these latter practices represent only a tiny fraction of abused animals overall. Dominant groups also complain about the way developing countries fail to protect their charismatic or endangered wildlife, while engaging in rampant extermination campaigns at home against non-endangered animals that often pose much less of a threat. In these ways, dominant groups invoke animal welfare instrumentally, to reaffirm their sense of superiority over other peoples and cultures.[41]

In all of these cases, concern for animals is being manipulated and invoked selectively to legitimate injustice between humans, in ways that discredit the underlying norms. We must guard against these forms of moral imperialism. But the solution to this instrumentalization, we believe, is not to disown the universality of human or animal rights, but on the contrary to make that universality more explicit, to ensure consistency and transparency in the way we interpret these principles, and to create forums in which all societies can participate equitably in debating and shaping these principles. Activists in the human rights field have adopted the same approach in response to worries about the instrumentalization of human rights.

This, then, is how we understand universality: we believe that the view of animals as vulnerable selves who need the protection of inviolable rights is one that is accessible to all societies from within their diverse moral sources, and cannot be treated as the unique property of any one culture or religion. If the arguments for AR are indeed found persuasive, then we all have a duty to respect the inviolable rights of animals once we are in the circumstances of justice, and we all have a duty to try to bring those circumstances into being. What this will require will vary from society to society, but it is a task we all face.

6. Conclusion

Accepting that animals are selves or persons will have many implications, the clearest of which is to recognize a range of universal negative rights—the right not to be tortured, experimented on, owned, enslaved, imprisoned, or killed. This would entail the prohibition of current practices of farming, hunting, the commercial pet industry, zoo-keeping, animal experimentation, and many others.

This is the core agenda of ART, and for many of its defenders it is the totality of that agenda. Animal rights is about abolishing exploitation and liberating animals from enslavement. As we have seen, an influential strand within ART—sometimes called animal abolitionists or liberationists—assumes that these prohibitions against exploitation rule out virtually all forms of interaction.

But we do not believe that ART can stop here. Respecting the basic rights of animals need not, and indeed cannot, stop all forms of human–animal interaction. Once we recognize the basic rights of animals, we need to ask about the appropriate forms of animal–human interaction that respect those rights. Ending the human exploitation of animals is a necessary start, but we need to know what non-exploitative relations might look like. What is the potential for mutually beneficial relations between humans and animals? And what kinds of positive obligations do we owe to animals—whether those in our direct care, those in symbiotic relationship with us, or those who live more distantly and independently of us? These are the questions to which we now turn.

3

Extending Animal Rights via Citizenship Theory

In our introduction, we defended the necessity of supplementing and extending animal rights theory (ART) through the inclusion of various relational and differentiated animal rights, in addition to the more familiar universal rights typically defended by animal rights (AR) theorists. The first step in such a process is to develop some account of the sorts of relationships between humans and animals that can give rise to morally significant obligations and responsibilities. As we have noted, this is a complicated task, given the enormous variability in these relations. Human relations with animals differ in their beneficial and harmful impacts, levels of coercion and choice, interdependencies and vulnerabilities, emotional attachments, and physical proximity. All of these (and other) factors seem potentially morally relevant.

We need to bring some conceptual order to this confusing profusion of relations. In this chapter, we argue that citizenship theory can help in this task. Thinking about human–animal relations in light of the familiar categories of citizenship theory—such as citizens, denizens, aliens, sovereigns—can help us identify both the distinctive claims that certain animals have upon us, and also the distinctive sorts of injustices we visit upon them. We begin by explaining what we mean by citizenship theory, and the conceptual resources it provides for thinking through issues of relational rights. We then consider and reject two immediate objections to applying this framework to animals.

1. Universal Rights and Citizenship Rights

Let's begin with citizenship in the human case. Imagine that we come across a crowd of human beings getting off a plane at an airport somewhere in our country. Without knowing anything about our more specific relationships with particular individuals in the crowd, we already know that we have certain universal obligations to all of them, simply because they are sentient beings with a subjective good. These are the universal rights we owe to all persons as such (for example, we cannot torture, kill, or enslave them).

But as the crowd proceeds to passport control, it quickly becomes apparent that these individuals have quite different relational rights. Some of them are our co-citizens and, as such, they have the unqualified right to enter and reside in the country, and, once inside, they have the right to be considered full and equal members of the political community. That is to say, they are co-guardians of the country, with the right that their interests and concerns count equally with those of others in determining the direction of the country. As citizens, they are members of 'the people' in whose name the government acts, they have the right to share in the exercise of popular sovereignty, and society has a duty to create mechanisms of representation or consultation by which their interests will be counted equally in determining the public good or the national interest.

By contrast, other passengers on the plane are tourists, foreign students, business visitors, or temporary workers, who are not citizens. As such, they do not have an unqualified right to enter the country, and may need to have secured permission beforehand (by obtaining a visa, for example). Even if they have permission to enter, they may not have the right to settle permanently, or to work, in the country. Perhaps their visa only allows them to stay for a short period of time before having to leave. As such, they are not included in the people in whose name the government acts, they do not participate in the exercise of popular sovereignty, and there is no duty to create mechanisms of representation to ensure that their interests are counted in determining the public good.

Of course, to repeat, these non-citizens are still human beings and therefore have certain universal human rights. It would be impermissible to kill or enslave them, or to engage in other acts that deny their essential personhood and dignity. But there is no obligation to restructure our public spaces to make them more enjoyable for, or accommodating of, such non-citizens, or to restructure our political institutions to make them more accessible to such non-citizens. It may be that the hundreds of thousands of Chinese tourists who now vacation around the world would enjoy visiting New York or Buenos Aires more if there were more Chinese-language street signs. And if a city wishes to attract tourists, it may well choose to make such changes. But there is no obligation on citizens to make their cities more welcoming to visitors, and it is the citizens, not the visitors, who make this collective decision about the shape of their society and its public space. The visitors do not get to vote in elections or referenda determining policies about street signs.

In short, we typically distinguish between *universal human rights*, which are not dependent on one's relationship to a particular political community, and *citizenship rights*, which are dependent on membership in a particular political community. As they embark from the plane, all passengers possess the former, but only some possess the latter in relation to the country of disembarkation. And this means that their interests count in different ways. To oversimplify, we could say that the interests of citizens determine the public good of the political community, whereas the interests of non-citizens set *side-constraints* on how political communities pursue that public good. For example, in deciding whether to build more public housing, nursing homes, or subways, it is the interests of citizens, not those of tourists, that are determinative. However, we cannot enslave tourists to help us build those houses or subways; the universal human rights of non-citizens set constraints on how citizens of a political community pursue their public good.

This is an oversimplification because, as we will see, there are various 'in-between' categories of people who are more than mere visitors but not (or not yet) citizens, and whose interests need to be considered in a way that is more complicated than this simple dichotomy allows. For example, immigrants who gain long-term residency acquire a certain legal and political standing that differs from that of temporary visitors, even if they do not yet have citizenship. There may also be groups who are affiliated to the state through some form of historic political association other than standard citizenship—for example, the status of American Indian tribes as 'domestic dependent nations'—in recognition of the fact that they form a distinct sovereign people within the boundaries of a larger sovereign people. But the existence of such in-between groups with partial or overlapping citizenship status simply confirms the underlying point: namely, that the fact of being a 'person' with universal human rights under-determines one's legal rights and political status. (And we must also remember all of the potential visitors who were never allowed to get on the plane in the first place, and who therefore remain resident in some other sovereign political community.)

At first glance, this multiplicity of legal status may seem puzzling. After all, the passengers are all human beings with the same inherent moral dignity and the same vulnerable selfhood. How, then, is it possible that they end up having such different legal rights? Indeed, some cosmopolitans deny that such distinctions are legitimate. They argue that everyone everywhere should automatically have their interests counted equally in political decision-making, either by creating a world of open borders in which all persons have the right to move freely across the face of the earth and take their full citizenship rights with them, and/or by eliminating the very category of citizenship, and simply attributing rights solely on the basis of personhood. Whether we universalize the category of citizenship or abolish it, the result would be the same—everyone would have an equal right to get on the plane, and everyone would have the same social and political rights (to settle, work, and vote) as they exit the plane.

But that is not the world we live in, and arguably it is not a desirable world. There are good reasons why human beings have organized themselves into distinct political communities that regulate their membership. This is partly for pragmatic reasons. Practices of democratic self-rule are easier to sustain in contexts where people see themselves as co-nationals, with a common national language and sense of attachment to a shared national territory, rather than simply as globetrotters who happen to be momentarily residing here rather than there. Democracy and the welfare state require levels of trust, solidarity, and mutual understanding that may be difficult to sustain in a borderless world that forgoes a sense of bounded and rooted political citizenship.

The commitment to bounded citizenship is not just pragmatic. There are powerful moral values tied up with citizenship, including values of national identity and culture, and of self-determination. Many people see themselves as members of collectivities that have the *right* to govern themselves and their bounded territory, and to govern themselves in ways that reflect their national identities, languages, and histories. These aspirations to national self-government reflect deep attachments to a particular community and a particular territory, and these attachments are legitimate and worthy of respect. Indeed, part of what it means to respect people is to respect their capacity to develop such morally significant attachments and relationships, including attachments to particular individuals and communities, to territory, to ways of life, and to schemes of cooperation and self-government. Bounded citizenship expresses and enables such attachments. Any form of cosmopolitanism that denies the legitimacy of such attachments in the name of universal personhood is missing a key aspect of what it means to respect personhood—namely, our capacity to develop morally significant attachments to bounded communities and territories.[1]

For these and other reasons, virtually all major traditions of political theory—whether liberal, conservative, or socialist—have operated on the assumption that human beings organize themselves into distinct bounded political communities. In any event, for the purposes of this book, we will assume that liberal political theory operates in a world of bounded political communities, and hence operates through a theory of citizenship as well as a theory of universal human rights. Whereas a liberal theory of universal human rights tells us what all human beings are owed in virtue of their personhood, a liberal theory of citizenship needs to tell us how we determine membership rights in distinct political communities. And this in turn requires answering a host of difficult questions: Which people should have which *membership* rights in which political communities? How do we determine the *boundaries* of the various distinct and bounded political communities? How should we regulate *mobility* between such communities, and how should we determine the rules of *interaction* between various self-governing communities?

Some of the most interesting work in liberal political theory over the past thirty years has been concerned with precisely these questions in 'citizenship theory'. (We are using 'citizenship theory' here in a broad sense to encompass all these questions about the definition of boundaries and membership in distinct political communities, and hence to subsume questions about rights to sovereignty and territory, regulation of international mobility, and access of newcomers to citizenship.) Our central claim is that a similar sort of citizenship theory is appropriate, indeed essential, in the case of animals. We argue that, as in the human case, some animals are best viewed as co-citizens in our political community whose interests count in determining our collective good; others are best viewed as temporary visitors, or non-citizen denizens, whose interests set side-constraints on how we pursue our collective good; and yet others are best viewed as residents of their own political communities, whose sovereignty and territory we should respect.

This idea of extending citizenship theory to animals will seem counter-intuitive to many readers. It will undoubtedly be contested by those who deny that animals have the sort of selfhood or personhood that warrants inviolable rights. But even those AR theorists who advocate recognition of the moral personhood of animals have rarely suggested that they could or should be seen as citizens. For a number of reasons, people have trouble connecting the concepts of 'animals' and 'citizenship': they belong to different intellectual registers.[2]

Our full response to this worry unfolds over the course of the next four chapters. The proof is in the pudding, and we hope to show that applying a framework of citizenship theory is not only coherent, but helps to clarify a number of inconsistencies and dead ends that have afflicted animal rights to date. However, to begin with, it may help to address two major roadblocks to thinking about animals and citizenship. In our view, much of the reluctance to link animals and citizenship theory rests on either (a) a misunderstanding about the nature and function of citizenship, even in the human case; and/or (b) a misunderstanding about the nature of animal–human relationships, both as they exist today and as they might exist in the future. We briefly address these two misunderstandings in the rest of this chapter, in order to prepare the ground for the more detailed discussions to follow.

2. The Functions of Citizenship

One reason why many people have trouble thinking of animals as citizens is that our everyday ideas of citizenship often carry with them connotations of active political participation—citizens are people who vote, engage in public debate, and mobilize politically around contested public policies. At first glance, it might seem that animals are simply incapable of being citizens in this sense. Whatever status animals have, surely it cannot be that of citizens.

However, this is too quick. We need to disentangle the idea of citizenship. Ideas of active political participation are just one aspect of citizenship, and we need a fuller sense of the function of citizenship in our normative political theories before we can judge how it might apply to animals. We can think of citizenship as serving at least three different functions in political theory, which we label rights to nationality, popular sovereignty, and democratic political agency.

1. Nationality: The first function of citizenship—and still the predominant one in international law—is to allocate individuals to territorial states. To be a citizen of country X is to have the right to reside in the territory of X, and the right to return to X if you travel abroad. Everyone should have the right to live somewhere on the globe, and so international law seeks to ensure that no one is stateless. Everyone should be a citizen of some country, with a secure right of residence in it, and a right to return to its territory. Note that citizenship in this passport sense does not yet tell us anything about the nature of the country that people are citizens of. People can be citizens of undemocratic theocracies, monarchies, military juntas, or fascist or communist dictatorships, and hence entirely lacking in rights of political participation. This is citizenship in a very thin sense.

2. Popular sovereignty: Starting with the French Revolution, the idea of citizenship began to take on a new meaning, associated with a particular theory about the basis of political legitimacy. In this new view, the state belongs to 'the people', rather than to God or some particular dynasty or caste, and citizenship is about being a member of the sovereign people. As Allen Buchanan puts it, it is part of the 'gospel' of liberal theory that the state is not the property of dynastic or aristocratic divisions in society, but rather belongs to the people.[3] The legitimacy of the state derives from its role as the embodiment of the inherent sovereignty of the people—in short, 'popular sovereignty'. This was initially a revolutionary idea that had to struggle, often violently, against older theories of political legitimacy. However, today it is virtually universal, and provides the essential presupposition for international law, and for the United Nations. To gain recognition and legitimacy, states must define themselves as the embodiment of the sovereignty of the people.

As a result, even illiberal and undemocratic regimes today insist that they embody popular sovereignty. Twentieth-century communist and fascist dictatorships, for example, described themselves as 'people's republics' to emphasize that they too endorsed the idea that state legitimacy flows from the will and interests of 'the people'. Indeed, they often justified their suppression of multiparty electoral democracy on the grounds that such factionalism impedes the proper recognition and expression of the popular will, which is better left to a strong leader or vanguardist party. Citizenship in this sense means belonging to the people in whose name the state governs. Not everyone who is a 'national' in the first sense is necessarily included in the 'people' in this second sense. Slaves in the USA, for example, were considered American 'nationals', at least for some purposes—they were not viewed as nationals of some other country, or as stateless refugees. But they were not American 'citizens', in the sense of being included in the sovereign people in whose name the state governs. Many racial and religious minorities have suffered this fate of being nationals of a state, but not considered citizens in the sense of being members of the sovereign people (think about Jews in medieval and early modern Europe). To be a citizen in this second sense reflects a more robust idea of citizenship than mere nationality, connected to a distinctly modern conception of state legitimacy. But it is not yet a fully democratic conception, since it does not entail that citizens are able to exercise their popular sovereignty through democratic means.

3. Democratic political agency: With the defeat of fascism and communism, we take for granted today that the only legitimate way to exercise popular sovereignty is through open multiparty electoral democracy, in which individuals have rights of political dissent, political mobilization, and free political debate. Indeed, we often say that people living in non-democratic regimes are really 'subjects' rather than 'citizens', even if those regimes claim to be grounded on ideas of popular sovereignty. To be a citizen, in this new understanding, is not just to be a national of a state (as in the first meaning), or to be a member of the sovereign people in whose name the state governs (as in the second meaning), but also to be an active participant in the democratic process (or at least to have the right to engage in such active participation). Citizenship, in this view, involves being the co-author of the laws, and not just a passive recipient of the laws. It therefore rests on assumptions about the illegitimacy of paternalistic rule, and about the capacity of individuals to represent themselves in the democratic process. The subjects of a non-democratic regime may have the benefit of the rule of law, but citizenship involves taking on the right and responsibility to shape the law. And this in turn entails assumptions about the skills, dispositions, and practices involved in political participation, including ideas of deliberation, reciprocity, and public reason.

In our view, all three of these dimensions play a vital and irreducible role when thinking about citizenship, and we need to consider all three when considering whether and how to extend citizenship theory to animals.

Unfortunately, in everyday parlance, and in much of the contemporary political theory literature, the focus is entirely on the third dimension. A theory of citizenship, it is widely assumed, is first and foremost a theory of democratic political agency. And it is this third sense of citizenship that seems, at first glance, to rule out citizenship for animals. After all, animals are not capable of engaging in the processes of 'public reason' or deliberative rationality that theorists like John Rawls and Jurgen Habermas say are essential to democratic agency.[4]

We contest the assumption that ideas of political agency are irrelevant to animals, but before we get to that, it is important to emphasize that citizenship cannot be reduced to democratic political agency, even in the human case. If we define citizenship narrowly as the exercise of democratic political agency, we immediately exclude large numbers of humans from citizenship rights. Consider children, or people with severe mental disabilities, or people with dementia. None of them are capable of engaging in Rawlsian public reason or Habermasian deliberation. Yet they are certainly citizens of the political community, in the first two senses of the term. That is, they have the right to reside in, and return to, the territory of the state. And they have the right to have their interests counted in determining the public good or in the delivery of public services (e.g., health and education).

In both of these senses, children and the mentally disabled are very different from, say, tourists or business visitors. The latter lack citizenship, and so lack rights to nationality and to be included in the sovereign people, even though they may have highly developed capacities for political agency. A tourist may have a profound ability and desire to engage in democratic agency, but that skill and desire by itself does not give them a right to reside in the country, or a right to have their interests counted in the public good. The former, by contrast, are citizens, and so have rights to nationality and to membership in the sovereign people, despite the limitations on their capacities for political agency. We cannot understand the rights of children or the mentally disabled if we ignore their status as citizens. They do not simply have universal human rights, on a par with tourists or business visitors. They also have certain fundamental *citizenship rights*—rights that are independent of capacities for political agency. The capacity for political agency is neither necessary nor sufficient for citizenship in these first two senses.

So it is important not to ignore the first two dimensions of citizenship. A central task of any citizenship theory is to explain who has rights to reside in and return to a particular territory, and to explain who is included in the sovereign people in whose name the state governs. We argue that any plausible answer to these questions must attend to animals as well as humans. Particular groups of animals should be seen as citizens of our political community in these first two senses. They have the right to reside in and return to the territory of our shared political community, and the right to have their interests included in determining the public good of the community. This is particularly true, we argue, of domesticated animals.

Not all animals will be citizens of our political community, just as not all humans are citizens of our community. Some will be citizens of their own separate communities on their own bounded territories, and then our main obligation is to comply with fair terms of intercommunity interaction. Others will be residents in our community, but not full citizens, and then our main obligation is to respect their rights as side-constraints on how we pursue our public good. In both the human and animal cases, a key task of citizenship theory is to explain how we determine membership in political communities, and on that basis to determine which citizenship rights apply to which individuals. Indeed, we argue that categorizing animals within this sort of citizenship framework clarifies a number of puzzles that historically have afflicted AR theory.

So even if we accepted that animals are incapable of democratic political agency, it would not follow that citizenship theory is irrelevant to thinking about their rights. However, we do not in fact accept the premise that animals are incapable of political agency. This third dimension of citizenship is an essential feature of modern understandings of citizenship, and in many ways can be seen as a culmination or fulfilment of the first two senses. Any conception of citizenship that stopped with rights to nationality and popular sovereignty, without addressing rights of political agency, would be an impoverished idea of citizenship. As we noted earlier, ideas of agency are now so central to our understanding of citizenship that we are inclined to say that where people are denied agency, they are really subjects rather than citizens. The ideal of citizenship involves a deep commitment to political agency.

We share this commitment, but it is important to clarify the nature of it. It is a serious mistake to treat political agency as a threshold or criterion that determines *who is a citizen*, such that those who are incapable of this or that form of agency are relegated to a status of non-citizenship. As we have seen, this would have the perverse effect of excluding children and the mentally disabled from citizenship. Rather, we should think of this third dimension as a value—or rather a cluster of related values—that informs how we treat those who (on prior and independent grounds) we recognize as citizens. Citizenship theory, in this third dimension, affirms values such as autonomy, agency, consent, trust, reciprocity, participation, authenticity, and self-determination, and says that part of what it is to treat people *as citizens* is to treat them in ways that affirm and respect these values.

We agree that to treat someone as a citizen involves facilitating and enabling their political agency. This commitment rests on a recognition of the dangers of paternalism, the harms of coercion, and the value to individuals of being able to act upon their own desires and attachments. But it is essential to note that *how* we affirm and respect these values varies enormously, even in the human case, as well as in the animal case.

Consider, for example, the contemporary disability movement. As many commentators have noted, this movement has 'adopted citizenship as the central organizing principle and benchmark' (Prince 2009: 16), demanding to be treated 'as citizens' rather than as 'clients' or 'patients' in the care of 'guardians' (Arneil 2009: 235). As such, it is widely counted as one of the paradigmatic instances of contemporary 'citizenship movements' (Beckett 2006; Isin and Turner 2003: 1). Obviously citizenship in this context refers to the third dimension of agency, since people with disabilities typically have already been counted as citizens in the first two senses—they have had rights to reside and return to a country, and have been considered as members of 'the people' in whose name the state governs. However, until recently, people with disabilities have been treated as passive recipients of paternalistic policies decided by their guardians, with little or no input into this process. Against this older model, the disability movement has insisted on rights to agency, participation, and consent, captured in the well-known movement slogan 'nothing about us without us'. This is the core of the claim of people with disabilities to be treated 'as citizens'.

Yet what it means for people with disabilities to be treated as citizens is complex, particularly in the case of those with intellectual disabilities. It is not just a matter of inviting them to engage in Rawlsian public reason or Habermasian deliberation, since they may be unable to communicate linguistically (Wong 2009). Nor is it a matter of giving them the right to vote for a particular political party, or for a particular legislative proposal, since they may be unable to comprehend political platforms or legal proposals, or to formulate judgements about how these platforms would impinge on their own interests (Vorhaus 2005). If they are to participate, it will require new models of 'dependent agency' (Silvers and Francis 2005) or 'supported decision-making' (Prince 2009) for 'non-communicating citizens' (Wong 2009). Older models of paternalistic guardianship are being challenged by newer models in which the goal is to find ways of eliciting a person's sense of their subjective good, often through 'embodied' rather than verbal communication. In these new models, people with mental disabilities can enact their citizenship, but it requires other people—whom Francis and Silvers call 'collaborators'—to help construct a 'script' of their conception of the good life, drawing on both verbal and nonverbal expressions of preference.[5] As they put it, 'The collaborator's role is to attend to these expressions, to fit them together into an account of ongoing preferences that constitutes a personalized idea of the good, and to work out how to realize this good under existing circumstances' (Francis and Silvers 2007: 325), and to bring this information into the political process, so that their views can shape ongoing debates about social justice.

Some of the most interesting work in citizenship theory in the past few years has focused on this idea of enabling and exercising citizenship through 'dependent', 'assisted', or 'interdependent' agency. This may sound like an exceptional case, but in fact we all go through stages of our lives when we are in need of such assisted agency, whether as infants and children, or when temporarily incompetent due to illness, or in old age. Immigrants may need translation help to understand political debates; people with speech or hearing impediments may need accommodations or assistance if they are to participate. Any plausible conception of citizenship must acknowledge the value of agency, but it must also acknowledge that capacities for agency expand and contract over time, and vary across persons, and that a central task of a theory of citizenship is to support and enable what is often a partial and fragile achievement. This needs to be central to, and not incidental to, a theory of citizenship. As Francis and Silvers put it, 'The difference between the majority of people and the minority of dependent agents is the extent of dependency, not the fact of it' (Francis and Silvers 2007: 331; cf. Arneil 2009: 234).[6]

Stated another way, political agency, as a third dimension of citizenship, should be seen as something that inheres in a relationship amongst citizens, not as an attribute of individuals that exists prior to their interaction. It is not that people are first agents, and therefore are accorded citizenship. Nor do we strip citizenship from our co-nationals who are temporarily or permanently limited in their cognitive abilities or rational agency. Rather, entering into relations of citizenship is, at least in part, entering into relationships that involve facilitating the agency of our co-citizens, at all stages of their life course and at all levels of mental competence.

This new field is opening up important possibilities for citizenship amongst people with disabilities, but we believe it equally opens up the possibility of citizenship for animals, at least for those (domesticated) animals with whom we live in close proximity, and whom we have rendered dependent on us through domestication.[7] Here, too, we can elicit a range of expressions of preference to construct scripts of domesticated animals' interests, and can bring those into the political process to help determine ongoing fair terms of interaction. Domesticated animals, we argue, should be seen as co-citizens in this sense, with the right to be represented through forms of dependent agency in our political decision-making. As we show in Chapter 4, insofar as proposals regarding the ethical treatment of domesticated animals do not enable citizenship in this sense—and this is true of some proposals from AR theorists (amongst those who do not advocate extinction for domesticated animals)—they are prone to perpetuating relations of exploitation, oppression, or unwarranted paternalism.

As with the first two senses of citizenship, not all animals will be our co-citizens in the sense of active political participants. Constructing relations of dependent agency involves a degree of intimacy and proximity that is neither feasible nor desirable for animals in the wild. But recall that this is true in the human case as well. Citizenship is a relationship that holds amongst those who cohabit a common territory and who are governed by common institutions. That is true for both humans and animals. We argue that citizenship is both possible and morally required for those (domesticated) animals whom we have brought into our society, and is neither necessary nor desirable for those (wild) animals who should be seen as belonging instead to their own sovereign communities. And, as in the human case, there are yet other groups of animals who fall into in-between categories, neither fully inside nor fully outside our political communities, and hence with their own distinctive status. In all of these cases, the citizenship status of animals—just as in the human case—is determined not by their cognitive capacities, but by the nature of their relationship to a particular bounded political community.[8]

In short, the common view that animals cannot be citizens rests on a misunderstanding about the nature of citizenship, even in the human case. Many people assume that animals cannot be citizens because (a) citizenship is about the exercise of political agency; and (b) political agency requires cognitively sophisticated capacities for public reason and deliberation. Neither claim is correct, even for human beings. Citizenship is about more than political agency, and political agency takes forms other than public reason. Citizenship has multiple functions, and all of them are, in principle, applicable to animals. Citizenship operates to allocate individuals to territories; to allocate membership in sovereign peoples; and to enable diverse forms of political agency (including assisted and dependent agency). Not only is it conceptually coherent to apply all three citizenship functions to animals, but we argue in the remaining chapters that it is the only coherent way to make sense of our moral obligations. Versions of ART that are unable or unwilling to categorize animals through these citizenship frames, we show, are incapable of recognizing morally salient differences in our relationship with different animals, and, as a result, are incapable of recognizing specific forms of oppression against certain animals.

3. The Diversity of Animal–Human Relationships

Reluctance to apply citizenship theory to animals does not just stem from an unduly narrow understanding of citizenship in the human case. It also, and perhaps more importantly, stems from an unduly narrow understanding of how animals relate to human communities. Adopting a citizenship framework presupposes that animals and humans will inevitably be linked through diverse relations of interaction and interdependency, and the task of citizenship theory is to evaluate the justice of these relations, and to reconstruct them on fairer terms. As we discuss below, there are literally dozens of such patterns of interaction and interdependency, for which citizenship theory is potentially relevant.

However, in everyday understanding, and in much of the academic literature on animal rights, animals are seen as falling into just two possible categories: wild and domesticated. The former are free and independent, inhabiting the wilderness 'out there' (unless they have been captured for zoos, exotic pet-keeping, or research purposes). The latter are captive and dependent, living under our management at home (as domesticated pets), in the laboratory (as experimental subjects), or on farms (as livestock) (Philo and Wilbert 2000: 11). If one starts from this dichotomy, as many AR theorists do, then it may seem that the idea of citizenship for animals is at best irrelevant and at worst a pretext for continued oppression.

According to classic ART, animals who are wild (human-independent), or capable of living so, should be protected from human intervention. We should 'let them be' to get on with their lives. Wild animals do not need to be included within human citizenship regimes: rather, what they need is precisely to be protected from interaction with, or interdependency on, human beings. The idea of citizenship might seem more relevant to domesticated animals, who have been rendered dependent on human beings, and who have lost their ability to live independently in the wild. Extending citizenship status to domesticated animals might ensure that they are treated justly in a mixed human–animal society. However, many AR theorists deny that justice is possible for animals that have been bred to be dependent on, and forced to participate in, human society. The status of dependency is said to be inherently exploitative and oppressive. Thus some AR theorists call for a complete end to domestication and the extinction of domesticated species. Reform is not possible. According citizenship to domesticated animals, in this view, would simply serve to give a veneer of morality to an inherently oppressive relationship of paternalistic dependency and forced participation in a human world.

So for many AR theorists, the idea of extending citizenship to animals is irrelevant, and potentially pernicious. Citizenship would be an appropriate framework if the goal were to develop better or fairer patterns of interaction and interdependency amongst humans and animals. But for many AR theorists, it is the very fact of interaction and interdependency that is the problem. And the solution is to end these patterns, first by leaving wild animals alone, and second by abolishing relations with domesticated animals. In an ideal world, all animals will be 'wild' or 'liberated', living freely and separately from humans, with no animals having citizenship claims on humans (or vice versa).

We believe that this picture of a world without sustained human–animal interaction and interdependency is fatally flawed, descriptively and normatively. The most obvious problem is that it ignores the many types of animal–human relations that do not fit either the wild or domesticated categories. Consider squirrels, sparrows, coyotes, rats, or Canada geese. These 'liminal' animals are not domesticated, but nor are they living independently of humans in the wilderness. They are living here amongst us in our garages, backyards, and local parks, and indeed have often sought us out because of the benefits of living close to humans. They exhibit their own distinctive patterns of interaction and interdependence that differ from those of both wilderness and domesticated animals. These liminal animals cannot be dismissed as anomalies. There are millions of them, and many of our most difficult ethical dilemmas arise in relation to them. Yet ART provides virtually no guidance regarding these cases.

But even if we focus solely on wilderness and domesticated animals, there will be ongoing relations of interaction and interdependency linking such animals with humans that need to be regulated by norms of justice. In relation to domesticated animals, it is true that domesticated animals should cease to be enslaved, and as we see in Chapter 4, many current proposals for reforming the status of domesticated animals are just a veneer for continued exploitation. However, it is premature to claim that the best or only way to redress the injustices suffered by domesticated animals is to seek their extinction. Historic processes of domestication were unjust, as is the existing treatment of domesticated animals, but histories of injustice (in both the human and animal cases) often generate ongoing responsibilities to try to create new relationships that comply with norms of justice. We argue in Chapter 5 that such relationships are possible, and that pursuing the extinction of domesticated animals is an abdication of our historic and ongoing responsibilities to them.

In terms of wild animals, it is true that animals in the wilderness often need to be left alone, but even wild animals exist in complex relations of interdependency with humans that need to be regulated by norms of justice. Consider animals that feed off a single plant species that is disappearing due to acid rain or climate change. These animals are, in one sense, being 'left alone'—no one may be hunting or capturing them, or even entering into their habitat—yet they are extremely vulnerable to human activity.

More generally, it is a fatal mistake to think that our duties to wild animals can be met by designating no-go zones (e.g., protected wilderness areas). For one thing, it is simply impossible to turn the full extent of wild animals' habitats into a no-go zone. When scientists in 1991 put a radio collar on a wolf and tracked its movements, it covered 40,000 square miles in two years, starting in Alberta (Canada), moving south to Montana, west to Idaho and Washington, and then north to British Columbia, before returning to Alberta (Fraser 2009: 17). Wolves are wild animals who avoid humans, and some of the movement of this wolf was through protected wilderness (e.g., National Parks), but we can hardly turn all 40,000 square miles into a no-go zone for humans. Most of this territory is criss-crossed by roads, railways, farms, power lines, fences, and indeed international borders, creating multiple forms of human impact on wolves and other wild animals. The vast majority of wild animals live in, or move across, areas that are directly influenced by humans. According to the Wildlife Conservation Society and the Center for International Earth Science Information Network at Columbia University, 83 per cent of the earth's land surface is influenced directly by human beings, whether through human land uses, human access from roads, railways, or major rivers, electrical infrastructure (indicated by lights detected at night), or direct occupancy by human beings at densities above one person per square kilometre.[9] Wild animals live 'in the wild', but they rarely live in pristine wilderness untouched by humans, and we need a theory of animal rights that addresses these inevitable entanglements between humans and wild animals.

This is not to say that we should stop trying to establish or expand protected wilderness zones. Indeed, our citizenship-based sovereignty model developed in Chapter 6 is intended to support that project, by providing a clearer rationale for the territorial rights of wild animals than is currently available within ART. However, we need to recognize that we cannot solve the problem of wild animals simply through designating no-go zones where we let them be. Given the relentless human expansion and habitat destruction that has already taken place, such protected zones will almost certainly be too small to cover the full range of habitat that many wild animals need. And so, predictably, wild animals have adapted to the human influences in their environment, such that certain forms or degrees of coexistence are now natural for them. As Gary Calore argues, human domination of the planet has in effect turned human-independence into a losing evolutionary strategy, leading to an 'age of interdependent forms' (Calore 1999: 257). Of course, this sort of interdependency is different from that characterizing either domesticated or liminal animals. But as we will see, it is a relationship that raises its own distinctive issues of justice, and we need some way of conceptualizing this field of coexistence and interdependency between humans and wild animals.

In short, animal–human relationships come in a remarkable array of forms, with varying levels of interaction, mutual vulnerability, and interdependency. And in all of these cases, we argue, citizenship theory, with its differentiated and relational model of rights, is needed to supplement the universal rights that ART has focused on to date.

The failure of ART to consider a citizenship model, we believe, is largely due to its failure to recognize the inevitability of such diverse forms of human–animal relations. But this just pushes back the problem a level: what explains this failure to recognize the enduring nature of human–animal relationships? After all, the idea that animals and humans belong in hermetically separated compartments—with humans here in humanized environments and animals out there in untouched wilderness—cannot survive even cursory inspection. It is contradicted by our everyday experience of constant human–animal interaction, and at odds with all the scientific studies of such interactions. How then did this idea take hold in ART?

An uncharitable explanation is that it took hold because it allows AR theorists to sidestep a number of thorny dilemmas that arise once we acknowledge the enduring nature of human–animal interdependence. A more charitable answer is that AR theorists have focused on the most egregious violations of animal rights, leaving positive and relational duties for another day. But the full answer, we believe, lies in some deeper misunderstandings about the underlying factors that generate these enduring patterns of human–animal interdependence and interaction. The simplistic division of animals into 'free and independent' animals inhabiting the wilderness and 'captive and dependent' domesticated animals living with humans rests on a series of widespread myths that need to be continually guarded against. We mention three such myths, relating to agency, dependency, and geography. In perpetuating these myths, ART reflects a more general cultural blindness regarding human–animal relations.

Agency

The traditional ART view assumes that humans are the primary agents or initiators of human–animal relationships. Humans either choose to leave animals alone to get on with their lives, or choose to hunt, capture, or breed them in order to serve human wants and desires. If we stopped interfering with animals, relationships between humans and animals would largely cease.

In reality, however, animals also exhibit various forms of agency. Animals can choose to avoid human settlement, but they can also choose to seek it out for the opportunities it offers. There are literally millions of liminal animals who seek out areas of human settlement. And they can also choose whether to avoid individual humans, or seek them out for food, assistance, shelter, companionship, and other needs. Given a range of non-coercive alternatives, animals can express preferences (i.e., 'vote with their feet') about how to live their lives, and under what circumstances, if any, to engage with humans. A crucial task of any theory of animal rights is to consider what justice requires in terms of these animal-initiated relations with humans, as well as what justice requires in terms of human-initiated interactions with animals.[10]

To be sure, the capacity for agency seems to vary widely amongst animals. An adaptive and social animal like a dog, rat, or crow is capable of great behavioural flexibility, of choosing between options depending on context and needs. Other animals are more tightly 'scripted'; they are 'niche specialists' who cannot readily adapt to changes in their environment, either because their needs are inflexible, or because they lack the cognitive flexibility to explore alternatives. But any plausible theory of animal rights must be attentive to the potential for animal-initiated forms of interaction, and for animal agency in response to human-initiated interaction.

Dependence/Independence

The traditional ART view tends to misinterpret the nature of animals' dependence on, or independence of, human beings. As we have seen, the traditional ART view is that wild animals live 'independently' of humans (and therefore need simply to be left alone), whereas domesticated animals are 'dependent' on humans (and therefore are condemned to relations of oppressive subservience). In reality, dependency is a multidimensional continuum which varies for every individual according to activity and context, and over time. There are important respects in which animals living in the most remote wilderness are nonetheless dependent on human beings, and there are important respects in which domesticated animals can exercise independence.

In thinking about dependency it is useful to distinguish two dimensions: inflexibility and specificity. A mouse living in a cage in Johnny's bedroom is dependent in both inflexible and specific ways. Her dependence is inflexible because she is without alternative options if Johnny fails to feed her. She can't transport herself to another location, or start deriving nutrition from fun wheels and cardboard tunnels. Her dependence is also highly specific: she is dependent on one particular human (or one particular human family) to feed her. Contrast this with a rat living at the city dump. The rat is dependent on humans for its food source, but not on any specific humans. It doesn't matter to the rat whether Johnny and his family drop off garbage in any given week, as long as humans collectively don't close up the landfill and withdraw all their garbage at the same time. And even if the dump were to close entirely, the rat's dependency isn't entirely inflexible. He might be able to relocate and find alternative food sources.

Viewed this way, domesticated animals often exhibit dependence along the specificity dimension: that is, they are typically dependent on specific humans to feed and shelter them. By contrast, wild and liminal animals—virtually by definition—are not dependent on specific human beings for food, shelter, or other basic needs. But notice that wild animals are often more dependent on the inflexibility dimension. Many animals in the wilderness are niche specialists who are intensely vulnerable to even the indirect side effects of human activity. Consider a bird species which migrates along a specific route where humans have erected a significant barrier. If the birds can't figure out how to get around the barrier and continue on their way, they are in trouble. Or consider polar bears whose ice-floe habitat is being lost due to global warming, or monarch butterflies who are dependent on one food source, the milkweed. These animals may live in the wilderness, but even if they are 'left alone' in the sense that no one attempts to hunt, capture, or domesticate them, they are nonetheless highly vulnerable to any human activity that alters their environment. By contrast, many liminal and domesticated animals, though living amongst human beings, may actually be less inflexibly dependent on them. Domestic and liminal animals are often adaptive generalists (rather than niche specialists) who can readily respond to changes in the natural or built environment. Consider racoons and squirrels, and their amazing ability to adapt to (and defeat) every new generation of 'squirrel-proof' feeder or garbage bin enclosure. Consider the feral dogs of Moscow, Palermo, and countless other cities who demonstrate remarkable skills in adapting to a constantly changing urban environment.

In this respect, as Calore notes, certain wild animals are much more 'dependent' on humans than many liminal or domesticated animals. Some of the animals we think of as 'majestic, fierce, and free', such as the tigers of Nepal, are in fact dependent on highly elaborate and costly human schemes of 'rewilding' intervention, whereas many liminal animals can survive, even flourish, in the face of almost total human indifference to them (Calore 1999: 257).[11] We need a much more sophisticated understanding of these diverse forms of (inter)dependence.

Spatial Dimensions of Human–Animal Relations

Cultural sociologists and cultural geographers have long emphasized that modern societies operate with a very specific conception of space. Certain spaces—cities, suburbs, industrial and agricultural zones—are defined as 'human' rather than 'animal', as 'cultural' rather than 'natural', or as 'developed' rather than 'wilderness'. These dichotomies underpin our 'culturally derived modernist conceptions of proper, morally appropriate, spatial relations between animals and society' (Jerolmack 2008: 73). In this cultural imaginary, companion animals stay safely on the leash (rather than becoming feral), wild animals stay in zoos or in pristine wilderness far removed from humans, and livestock stay on the farm. Whenever any animal is found outside its 'proper, morally appropriate' space, it is seen as 'matter out of place', and hence as morally problematic.[12] 'Urban living has resulted in the incorporation of animals into the private sphere (as pets) or urban culture has removed them to a real or imaginary "wild" or some rural past' (Griffiths, Poulter, and Sibley 2000: 59), and if any animals cross the boundary they are 'doomed to be considered morally transgressive as they transgress the spaces that we have defined as "for humans only"' (Jerolmack 2008: 88).

This high modernist conception of space systematically distorts our understanding of human–animal relations. It recognizes the existence of pets in cities (if safely leashed), but ignores the non-domesticated animals around us. And so, liminal animals come into view only when their numbers or behaviour turn them into 'pests'. In other words, they are visible when they become a problem, but invisible as ubiquitous members of the community. We have paid remarkably little attention to the diversity of these animals, the kinds of spaces they inhabit, and the ways we interact with them—from the mice who inhabit our houses, to the sparrows and feral pigeons who scavenge in city cores, to the deer and coyotes who thrive in the suburbs, to the countless species who have evolved in symbiosis with traditional agricultural practices (e.g., the birds, rodents, and small mammals who feed on agricultural crops, and the larger mammals and raptors who prey on them in turn).

There are similar spatial complexities to our relations with wild and domesticated animals. Some wild animals live truly remote from human settlement—like the eelpout fish living deep in the thermal vents of the Pacific Ocean. Others, however, live in little pockets of wilderness completely surrounded by human development, and many wild animals spend at least some of their time negotiating human environments because of the ways our roads, shipping lanes, flight paths, fences, bridges, and tall buildings interrupt their travel and migration routes. In the case of domesticated animals, some, like pet mice or goldfish, spend their entire lives in microworlds inside our houses. Some, like dogs, accompany us out onto the streets and into public spaces. Others, like horses, tend to live in rural areas because their housing and exercise needs are so much more expansive.

These spatial dimensions of human–animal relations interact with the agency and interdependency dimensions identified above in ways that create a dizzying array of relationships, with diverse causal origins, differing types of interaction, and varying levels of vulnerability—and all of these variations are important for identifying the relevant issues of justice, and for assessing our moral responsibilities. The simplistic dichotomy of wild and domestic animals—and the accompanying call to simply 'let animals be'—needs to be replaced with a more complex matrix of relationships, and a more complex set of moral prescriptions. Indeed, a chief goal of this book is to dismantle the simple wild/domestic dichotomy, and to replace it with what Jennifer Wolch describes as 'a *matrix* of animals who vary with respect to the extent of physical or behavioural modification due to human intervention, and types of interaction with people' (Wolch 1998: 123). In the next four chapters, we highlight several distinctive patterns of human–animal relationships, and show how each of them can be illuminated by drawing upon citizenship theory.

Part II
Applications

4

Domesticated Animals within
Animal Rights Theory

In applying citizenship theory to animals, we begin with the case of domesticated animals. Humans have domesticated a variety of animals to serve a remarkably diverse array of uses, from providing food, clothing, and replacement body parts (e.g., heart valves); serving as military and medical research subjects; to performing hard labour (e.g., ploughing, hauling) or skilled labour (e.g., patrol, search and rescue, hunting, guarding, entertainment, therapy, assistance to people with disabilities); and providing companionship.

This is a heterogeneous category, and in much of the animal literature the different types of domesticated animals are discussed separately: the ethics of farm animals is discussed separately from the ethics of keeping pets or the ethics of animal experimentation. In our view, however, a crucial factor in thinking about the political status of these animals is precisely the fact of domestication itself. Domestication creates a particular sort of relationship between humans and animals, and a central task of any political theory of animal rights is to explore the terms under which that relationship can be rendered just.

Throughout much of human history, this relationship has been deeply unjust—domestication has been characterized by the coercive confinement, manipulation, and exploitation of animals for the benefit of humans. Indeed, this injustice is so deep that, for many animal advocates, it is irredeemably unjust; a world in which humans continue to maintain domesticated animals cannot be a just world. In this view, the 'original sin' of exploitative domestication is beyond reform. We argue, however, that this is too quick. Relations between humans and domesticated animals can be reordered in a just way if they are reconceived along the lines of membership and citizenship. Where domesticated animals are accorded the status of co-citizens in a political community that governs in the name of both its human and animal members, justice is possible.

Needless to say, when humans first embarked on the process of domesticating animals, they did not intend to include them as 'members' or 'citizens' of their society. In this respect, the domestication of animals is like the importation of slaves from Africa, or of indentured labourers from India or China, who were brought into countries solely to provide labour, without the expectation of membership and without the right to become citizens. Indeed, it's quite possible that the people who purchased slaves and indentured labourers would not have done so had they realized it would eventually lead to co-citizenship for people they viewed as inferior or unworthy. But whatever the original intent, the only legitimate response today—the only possible basis for reorganizing relationships on a just foundation—is to replace older relations of hierarchy with new relations of co-citizenship and co-membership in a shared community.

So too, we argue, with domesticated animals. In virtue of the causal role that humans have played in bringing these animals into human society, in breeding them to be adapted to human society, and in closing off alternatives, we must accept that domesticated animals are now members of our society. They belong here, and must be seen as co-members of a shared human–animal political community.

As we will see, reconceptualizing domesticated animals as citizens is not a magic formula for resolving all the ethical dilemmas raised by their presence in a shared political community. It does, however, offer a fresh perspective for thinking about the rights of animals, and we argue that it is more compelling, and more fruitful, than existing alternatives promoted by animal rights theory (ART) to date.

1. Defining Domestication

To begin with, we need to clarify the term 'domestication'. According to the *Encyclopaedia Britannica*, domesticated animals are 'created by human labour to meet specific requirements or whims and are adapted to the conditions of continuous care and solicitude people maintain for them'.[1] There are several logically separable components at work in this definition, and it will be helpful to distinguish these for our discussion:

a. The *purpose* of domestication—that is, the breeding and use of animal bodies to 'meet specific requirements or whims' of humans.

b. The *process* of domestication—that is, the 'human labour' of selective breeding and genetic manipulation to adapt the animal's nature for specific ends.

c. The *treatment* of domesticated animals—that is, the 'continuous care and solicitude people maintain for them'.

d. The *state of dependency* of domesticated animals on humans for ongoing care—that is, the fact that animals are 'adapted' to the conditions of continuous care.

The components are separable in the sense that it is possible to imagine one or more of them existing independently, or in various combinations. If humans stopped breeding animals, and stopped exploiting them for human use, we would still have a class of animals in existence who are dependent on humans for ongoing care. Or, we could imagine humans continuing to breed animals, but doing so with the intent of serving the animals' interests, rather than human interests. For example, a breeding programme could be designed to eliminate a congenital defect that plagues a particular species or breed of animal, solely with the intent of benefiting the offspring of the animals bred. (There could also be instances when animals' interests coincide with human interest, as in the case of eradicating a disease that affects both species.) Or one could imagine a breeding programme undertaken to protect an animal species from overpopulation and hardship from the resulting scarcity of resources. One could also imagine a breeding programme that doesn't result in dependency of the species in question, or even one which results in greater independence from the need for human management or care (like some existing breeding programmes designed to re-establish wild populations of endangered species). Or one could imagine individual animals being treated justly even when their species generally has been, and continues to be, subject to unjust breeding and treatment (as in the case of a particularly fortunate animal companion).

In thinking about the ethics of human–animal relations we need to distinguish these aspects of domestication. The overwhelming direction of domestication has been to breed specific traits in animals which increase both their dependency on humans and their utility for humans, with no attention to the animals' own interests. But in examining the potential for an ethical relationship between humans and domesticated animals, it is important to distinguish issues of purpose, process, and treatment. Not all forms of controlled reproduction involve instrumentalization or a violation of basic rights, and not all forms of dependency involve abuse or domination. Too much of the existing ART literature fails to make these distinctions, and so prematurely closes off possible models of just relations with domesticated animals.

2. Myths of Humane Treatment and Reciprocity

To date, the ART literature has been more effective in detailing what is wrong with the existing treatment of domesticated animals than in exploring possible remedies to those wrongs. This is understandable, since one of the major obstacles to effective action on the rights of domesticated animals is the persistence of romanticized myths of their humane treatment.

For anyone who takes animal rights seriously, the history of human domestication of animals is a story of ever-intensifying degrees of enslavement, abuse, exploitation, and murder. Intensive farming has reduced animals to widgets, their brief and brutal lives utterly mechanized, standardized, and commodified.[2] Biotechnology goes a step further and alters the very genetic nature of animals in order to make them better widgets. The animal rights AR movement has worked tirelessly to expose this treatment, and the ways in which it is tied to underlying beliefs about the moral insignificance of animals, and human entitlement to use them as we see fit.

And the rot doesn't stop at the doors of research labs and factory farms. While recognizing the extreme violations of modern farming, most AR theorists have been adamant that there is no such thing as 'humane meat', even under less industrialized conditions. Animals may have enjoyed a more natural existence under traditional farming techniques than they do in industrialized farms, but they were exploited and killed nonetheless, and frequently neglected and abused. The scope and intensity of exploitation have increased, but the underlying relationship of domination is the same. There never was a 'good old days' as far as domesticated animals are concerned.[3] And the idea that 'modern', 'clean', and 'efficient' methods can contribute to a system of 'humane slaughter' is simply to replace the old myth of happy plantation slaves with the new myth of a brave new world.

When these myths of humane treatment are exposed, defenders of animal exploitation often retreat to a different myth: namely, that domestication is actually in animals' interests, and expresses a form of moral reciprocity. In the case of domesticated animals, we give them life, shelter, food, and care, and in turn they supply us with their meat, skins, and labour. Domesticated animals would not exist if they were not useful to us, and measured against non-existence, a brief life under suitable care ending in a quick death is a reasonable reciprocal arrangement.[4]

We would never accept this sort of argument in the human case. Imagine that someone proposed bringing a group of humans into existence in order to exploit and kill them at age twelve, or to harvest their organs. This is the realm of horror movies and genocidal crime, not moral theorizing. Children would not exist if their parents did not bring them into existence, and yet this gives parents no right to exploit or otherwise violate the rights of their children. The very fact that such rationalizations are contemplated for farm animals shows how little we value animals, and the extent to which much domestication is premised on the denial of their moral dignity.

Similar myths distort the discussion of pets. Many people love their animal companions and care for them reasonably well, and yet the story does not have a happy ending for countless animals. Millions of cats and dogs are killed each year in animal shelters. These include strays, feral animals, animals abandoned by their families (according to a widely cited statistic families keep their pets on average for only two years),[5] and animals considered unadoptable due to age, health, or temperament.[6] Companion animals are often bred at puppy mills by unscrupulous profit-seekers. They are sometimes bred to achieve aesthetic ideals which compromise their basic health and mobility. They can be subject to painful and unnecessary procedures (tail-docking, de-barking, de-clawing) to make them more attractive or suitable for human companionship, and to training methods using violence and coercion. Their basic needs for food and shelter are often unmet. Even when they live amongst humans who love their companions and have good intentions, sheer ignorance often results in animals' needs for exercise and companionship going unmet.[7] And when disaster strikes, such as war, famine, or floods, companion animals, along with other domesticated animals, are usually abandoned to a terrible fate as humans scramble to save themselves.[8]

3. The Abolitionist/Extinctionist Approach to Domesticated Animals

AR advocates have worked relentlessly to expose the extent of our mistreatment of domesticated animals across a spectrum of traditional and modern practices, practices which put the lie to myths of benign human dominion over domesticated species. However, the question remains: what should we do about these injustices?

To oversimplify, the ART literature offers two approaches, which we will call the 'abolitionist/extinctionist' and 'threshold' views. The former seeks the abolition of relations between humans and domesticated animals, and since domesticated animals can rarely survive on their own, this in effect means the extinction of domesticated species. In this view, we should care for existing domesticated animals but should employ systematic sterilization to ensure that no more are created. The latter envisages ongoing relations between humans and domesticated animals, subject to various reforms and safeguards designed to ensure mutual benefit and the protection of basic interests. We discuss each view in turn, and explain why we think neither is sufficient, before going on to elaborate our own citizenship-based alternative in Chapter 5.

According to the abolitionist/extinctionist view, the horrendous history of injustice leads to an inescapable conclusion: we must remove ourselves from the equation—whether as owners, overlords, stewards, or ostensible co-contractors. Our power and control inevitably lead to domination and abuse of domesticated animals. We cannot have domestication without mistreatment, because mistreatment is intrinsic to the very concept of domestication. Gary Francione says:

> we ought not to bring any more domesticated nonhumans into existence. I apply this not only to animals we use for food, experiments, clothing, etc. but also to our nonhuman companions... We should certainly care for those nonhumans whom we have already brought into existence but we should stop causing any more to come into existence... it makes no sense to say that we have acted immorally in domesticating nonhuman animals but we are now committed to allowing them to continue to breed. (Francione 2007: 1–5)

The view that respecting animal rights requires the end of domestication, and the eradication of currently existing domesticated species, is a hallmark of the abolitionist/extinctionist position (Francione 2000, 2008; Dunayer 2004).[9] The bottom line is that we must end all human use of, and interaction with, domesticated animals. To speculate about possible relations of justice between humans and domesticated animals is to fall into the error of welfarist reformism.

Defenders of this position invoke a mixture of arguments, including the wrongness of the original act of domestication, the viciousness of current treatment, and a condemnation of the very state of domestic animal dependency. We can see all of these at work in Francione's claim that:

> Domestic animals are dependent on us for when and whether they eat, whether they have water, where and when they relieve themselves, when they sleep, whether they get any exercise, etc. Unlike human children, who, except in unusual cases, will become independent and functioning members of human society, domestic animals are neither part of the nonhuman world nor fully part of our world. They remain forever in a netherworld of vulnerability, dependent on us for everything that is of relevance to them. We have bred them to be compliant and servile, or to have characteristics that are actually harmful to them but are pleasing to us. We may make them happy in one sense, but the relationship can never be 'natural' or 'normal'. They do not belong stuck in our world irrespective of how well we treat them. (Francione 2007: 4)

Note how this position bundles together the different aspects of domestication identified earlier—the intent of domestication, the process of domestication, the fact of dependency, and the actual treatment of domesticated animals. Whether we treat existing animals well ('make them happy in one sense') or badly (i.e., exploit and kill them) does not change the intrinsic wrongness and 'unnaturalness' of their situation. This intrinsic wrongness contaminates any possibility of us having an ethical relationship with the class of domesticated animals. Francione's position here echoes that of environmentalists such as Callicott, who famously described domesticated animals as debased and unnatural, as 'living artifacts' whom humans have bred to 'docility, tractability, stupidity and dependency' (Callicott 1980).[10] Similarly, Paul Shepard refers to pets as human creations, as 'civilized paraphernalia', 'vestiges and fragments', and 'monsters of the order invented by Frankenstein' (Shepard 1997: 150–1).

In our view, the abolitionist/extinctionist call to end all relations with domesticated animals has been a strategic disaster for the AR movement. After all, many people have come to their concern for animal rights precisely through their relationship with a companion animal, which has opened their eyes to the rich individuality of animals' lives, and to the possibility of a relationship with animals that is not based on exploitation. To insist that support for AR requires condemning all such relationships is to alienate many potential supporters. It has also provided an easy political target for those hostile to ART, including hunter and breeder organizations, which invoke these extinctionist quotes as a *reductio* of the very idea of animal rights.[11]

Strategy aside, however, we believe that the abolitionist position is simply not intellectually sustainable. It rests on a series of fallacies and misunderstandings about human–animal relationships. Some versions of the abolitionist position rest on a rather crude claim that because it was historically unjust to bring domesticated species into existence, therefore we should seek to take these species out of existence. Consider Francione's claim that 'it makes no sense to say that we have acted immorally in domesticating nonhuman animals but we are now committed to allowing them to continue to breed' (Francione 2007: 5). But this is an obvious fallacy. Consider the case of slaves brought from Africa to the Americas. Justice certainly requires abolishing slavery, but that does *not* mean abolishing the existence of the former slaves and their offspring. Shipping slaves to America was certainly an injustice, but the remedy is not to seek the extinction of African Americans, or to repatriate them to Africa. The original process by which Africans entered America was unjust, but the remedy to that historic injustice is not to turn back the clock to a time when there were no Africans in America. Indeed, far from remedying the original injustice, seeking the extinction or expulsion of African Americans compounds the original injustice, by denying their right to membership in the American community, and by denying their right to found families and reproduce themselves.[12]

Similarly, there is no reason to assume that the remedy to the original injustice of domestication is to extinguish domesticated species. Indeed, we might well think that this abolitionist proposal compounds the original injustice, since it can only be achieved by coercively restricting domesticated animals further (e.g., by preventing them from reproducing). The remedy, rather, is to include them as members and citizens of the community.

Some abolitionists might respond that the analogy fails, on two grounds: (a) a good life was possible for former slaves and their descendants, whereas there is no possibility of a good life for domesticated animals, due to their unnatural or degraded condition; and (b) preventing the reproduction of former slaves would involve unjust coercion, but there is no comparable injustice in controlling the reproduction of domesticated animals.

Both of these claims are suggested in the quotes we listed earlier, but they are rarely defended in depth and, in our view, they cannot be sustained. Take first the issue of controlling reproduction. In much of the abolitionist literature, talk about phasing out domesticated animals is remarkably vague, even euphemistic. Consider Francione's view that we 'should certainly care for those nonhumans whom we have already brought into existence but we should stop causing any more to come into existence' (Francione 2007: 2). Compare this with Lee Hall's statement that 'declining to create more dependent animals is the best decision an animal-rights activist can apply' (Hall 2006: 108), and John Bryant's view that pets 'should be completely phased out of existence' (Bryant 1990: 9–10). The language here is very interesting: 'stop causing any more to come into existence', 'decline to create', 'phase out'. The descriptions conjure up images of labs in which humans 'create' domesticated animals, as if these animals left to their own devices would not want to reproduce, or would have no interest in doing so.

Now it's true that most domesticated animal reproduction is under human control, and that it can be a highly invasive and mechanized process. Assisted insemination is widely practised (some breeds of domesticated turkey are unable to reproduce without assistance), as is the use of rape racks (also called, more euphemistically, 'mating cradles'). In other cases, reproduction is strictly monitored by humans, but not mechanically assisted (as, for example, when breeders bring animals together and 'allow' them to mate if/when/how they choose).

The abolitionist position implies that if humans stopped 'creating' domesticated animals, they would cease to exist. But this isn't the case. For domesticated animals to be 'phased out of existence' would not just require a cessation of human creation of animals, but a massively increased (and probably impossible) human effort to forcibly sterilize and/or confine all domesticated animals. It would mean not just limiting the procreation of domesticated animals, but preventing it entirely—denying them the opportunity ever to mate and raise a family. It would, in short, involve precisely the sort of coercion and confinement that AR theorists say makes domestication unjust, and in that sense compounds rather than remedies the original injustice.

In our view, there is a serious question here concerning the infringement of individual liberties which is glossed over by language such as 'decline to create' or 'phase out of existence'. By masking the process as one of human, rather than animal, agency, the abolitionist position evades important questions about infringements of animals' basic liberties.

This isn't to say that it is always wrong to control or limit domesticated animals' fertility. For example, there may be valid paternalistic justifications that appeal to the interests of the animal whose reproduction is being curtailed. It is justifiable to prevent conception in an elderly ewe who will not survive another pregnancy, or to delay opportunities of conception for a young animal who is fertile but too young to bear offspring without compromising her health. As in the case of paternalistic actions undertaken for children or people with intellectual disabilities, such restrictions must meet tests of proportionality, and use the least invasive or restrictive means available to meet a justifiable objective serving the individual's interests. In Chapter 5 we defend a more complex basis for paternalistic restrictions on domesticated animal fertility as part of a reciprocal citizenship model. So, we do not deny the possibility of justifiable restrictions on domesticated animal reproduction. Our concern is that the abolitionist/extinctionist position supports a massive intervention and makes no attempt to justify it in relation to the individuals whose liberty is being restricted.[13]

But even if we set aside for now the concern about the level of coercion needed to 'phase out' species, a deeper objection to the abolitionist position is its inability to conceive good lives for domesticated animals. It presupposes that domesticated animals will continue to be exploited, and that it is impossible for them, or their descendants, to lead good lives. In our view, this claim is deeply implausible. We all know of companion animals who seem to be leading good lives. And in the case of farm animals, anyone who has visited a farm sanctuary knows that even those animals rescued from factory farms can live out full and happy lives under human care, in the company of their own and many other species. Many seem to thrive in the interspecies community of farm life, forming cross-species friendships—creating a kind of farm culture in which the whole is greater than the parts, offering a rich form of existence to a wide variety of individuals, including humans. If it were possible to have this kind of world, without the exploitation, wouldn't this be preferable to the extinction of domesticated animals?[14]

On what basis then can abolitionists claim that domesticated animals cannot have good lives? As we said earlier, this claim is rarely defended in depth, but insofar as it is defended, it seems to rest on deeply problematic assumptions about the relationship between freedom/dignity and dependency, and about the alleged unnaturalness of human–animal interaction.

Dependency and Dignity

While we agree with abolitionists that human domestication of animals is wrong, it is important to be clear about why this is so. Earlier, we disaggregated the different aspects of domestication—its intent, the actual process, and the resultant state of dependency. We agree with abolitionists that the original *intent* of animal domestication—to alter animals to serve human ends—is wrong, just as it would be to engage in the selective breeding of a human subclass in order to serve other humans. Moreover, we agree that the *process* of domestication—confinement and forced breeding—involves a violation of basic rights of liberty and bodily integrity. Any attempt to re-establish relations with domesticated animals on the basis of justice will need to change both the characteristic ends and means of human control over domesticated animals. Our citizenship model, described in Chapter 5, aims to address just these sorts of changes.

However, abolitionists go further and argue that the resultant state of dependency is also inherently wrong in a way that cannot be reformed or redeemed. It is now part of the very nature of these animals to be dependent—as a result of decades, centuries, or millennia of breeding—and for many abolitionists, this inbred dependency condemns domesticated animals to lives without integrity and dignity. Let's return to the quote from Francione, cited earlier:

> Domestic animals are dependent on us for when and whether they eat, whether they have water, where and when they relieve themselves, when they sleep, whether they get any exercise, etc. Unlike human children, who, except in unusual cases, will become independent and functioning members of human society, domestic animals are neither part of the nonhuman world nor fully part of our world. They remain forever in a netherworld of vulnerability, dependent on us for everything that is of relevance to them. We have bred them to be compliant and servile, or to have characteristics that are actually harmful to them but are pleasing to us. We may make them happy in one sense, but the relationship can never be 'natural' or 'normal'. They do not belong stuck in our world irrespective of how well we treat them. (Francione 2007: 4)

We see here a condemnation of the very nature of domesticated animals. They are 'unnatural', 'dependent on us for everything', 'compliant and servile', comparable to children who never grow up and become fully functioning, and so on. Similarly, Hall justifies extinction of domesticated animals because 'it's disrespectful to afford them an autonomy that's incomplete and not in their best interest' (Hall 2006: 108).

The alleged unnaturalness of domesticated animals has two dimensions. In terms of their physical and mental characteristics, selective breeding has resulted in *neotonization* (retention of juvenile characteristics in the adult of the species, such as cute features, low aggression, playfulness, and other characteristics). Dogs more closely resemble juvenile wolves than adult wolves (in size, head shape, eagerness to learn and play, retention of begging and barking behaviours). Concerning their ability to function in the world, domesticated animals have been bred for *dependency*. They are 'dependent on us for everything that is of relevance to them'—much like human children, only in the case of domesticated animals they are forever stuck in this 'netherworld of vulnerability'. These two characteristics—neotonization and dependency—are seen by abolitionists as locking domesticated animals into an undignified state of perpetual immaturity.

In our view, this entire way of understanding domesticated animals is misguided, and indeed morally perverse. There is nothing inherently undignified or unnatural about either neotony or dependency, and to condemn domesticated animals on these bases is not only unjustified, but would have pernicious consequences for humans as well.

Consider first the issue of dependency. It is puzzling that AR theorists continue to use unproblematized notions of independence (or autonomy) and dependence at precisely the same time when philosophy and political theory more generally are increasingly attentive to the many fallacies and distortions involved in this sort of binary opposition. Traditionally, human political theory, like abolitionist ART, took the state of independence to be the natural and highest goal of human life. Decades of feminist critique have demonstrated how this view is the product of male bias and the socially constructed division of public and private spheres (Okin 1979; Kittay 1998; Mackenzie and Stoljar 2000). It is increasingly recognized that humans, at all stages of life, are vulnerable and dependent beings. Our sense of independence and self-sufficiency rests on a fragile foundation. This fragility becomes all too apparent when we are confronted by natural or human-caused disaster; when we lose loved ones, our livelihoods, or our homes; when we experience serious injury or illness, or when we become responsible for dependants. There are important questions of degree, and some humans (for example people with physical or mental disabilities) experience significant levels of dependency throughout their lives. But even in the case of humans who are acutely vulnerable and dependent, such as those with severe mental disabilities, we have come to recognize the indignity involved in perceiving them strictly in terms of their dependency or alleged lack of functioning. Disability advocates have continuously demonstrated how this perspective blinds us to the ways in which different enabling conditions allow individuals with disabilities to exercise significant kinds of agency and independence. Similar arguments have been made in the feminist literature, and on writings about the rights of children (e.g., Kittay 1998). Dependence, in this richer view, is not the binary opposite of independence; rather, recognizing our inevitable (inter) dependence is a precondition to supporting people's ability to express preferences, develop capacities, and make choices.

Dependency doesn't intrinsically involve a loss of dignity, but the way in which we *respond* to dependency certainly does.[15] If we despise dependency as a kind of weakness, then when a dog paws his dinner bowl, or nudges us winningly to remind us it is walk time, we will see ingratiation or servility.[16] However, if we don't view dependency as intrinsically undignified, we will see the dog as a capable individual who knows what he wants and how to communicate in order to get it—as someone who has the potential for agency, preferences, and choice. When we view others as servile dependants, we don't have to consider them as particular individuals, with unique perspectives, needs, desires, and abilities that can be nurtured. If we look beyond their dependency, however, we can learn how to understand and respond to their wishes, demands, and contributions. We can ask how best to restructure society to enable their potential functioning.

The idea that 'natural and normal' relations do not contain dependency is a strange one. Domesticated animals are made very vulnerable by their dependency on humans for food, shelter, and companionship. But non-domesticated animals are also acutely vulnerable—to weather conditions, food sources, and predators. Some wild animals are relatively mobile, adaptable, and social, with a wide scope of independent agency for meeting their food, shelter, and companionship needs, for avoiding hazards, or generally enjoying life. Others are acutely vulnerable due to limited mobility or ecological niche specialization, rendering them utterly dependent on a single food source or climate phenomenon. We humans become acutely aware of our own dependency when the internet crashes, the power grid fails, or the 'just in time' food delivery system is disrupted. Dependency, though highly variable, is an inescapable fact of life for us all. Indignity does not arise from this fact. Indignity arises when our needs are belittled, exploited, and/or unmet by those who should know better. And indignity arises when the fact of dependency is used to occlude or stifle opportunities for agency. There is no question that domesticated animals are subject to appalling indignities (in addition to the direct violation of their basic rights). However, it is a mistake to equate this indignity with their state of dependency on humans per se. The indignity arises in our response to that dependency—both in the way we fail to meet needs when others are truly dependent on us, and also in the way we fail to recognize the many ways in which domesticated animals are individuals capable of developing considerable scope for independent agency.[17]

Is Neotony Unnatural?

Domestication and neotonization go hand in hand. When you select for a single juvenile trait, such as low aggression or 'tameability', other juvenile traits follow—such as floppy ears, flatter snouts, playfulness, and so on.[18] Over time, adults of the domesticated species come to exhibit traits that formerly were limited to juveniles amongst their ancestors. Abolitionists seem to view this process as unnatural, and as demeaning. But is it really?

On the contrary, neotonization is a perfectly natural form of evolution. If juvenile traits are the most adaptive in a particular environment, then they will be selected for. Juvenile traits include willingness to explore, ability to learn, and a weakened sense of species boundaries in social interaction. One can see that under a variety of environmental situations these would be extremely adaptive traits to maintain into adulthood. For example, Stephen Budiansky argues that the climate fluctuations of the last ice age favoured adaptive animals over niche specialists, and selection for juvenile traits (e.g., willingness to explore new territories in search of food, ability to learn to adapt to changing circumstances, willingness to cooperate across species boundaries) allowed some species to survive while others perished (Budiansky 1999). Many animals underwent a process of 'self-domestication' during this period of climate and environmental upheaval.

Indeed, Budiansky and others have argued that dogs and other domesticated species underwent prolonged periods of self-domestication long before humans began actively breeding for selected traits. Another example of a 'self-domesticating' species is bonobos. If you compare bonobos to chimps, you see a very similar relationship as between dogs and wolves. Bonobos are neotonized chimps, displaying physical traits such as reduced head size (and smaller teeth, jaw, and brain), and social traits such as reduced aggression, increased desire to play and learn, increased sociality and cooperation, and increased sexual interest and availability. A very similar relationship obtains between domesticated dogs and wolves.

And here's the kicker. Stephen Jay Gould, Richard Wrangham, and others have argued that humans have also self-domesticated. Substitute humans for bonobos in the above example, and you can see that humans also display traits of neotonized chimps. (And that includes brain size, which has decreased by about 10 per cent in humans over the last 30,000 years, during the same period that body, head, jaw, and tooth size have declined.)[19] This process of self-domestication has been critical to human development, and our ability to live and cooperate as part of ever larger societies.

When we look at human development, we see the evolution of a more gracile form; reduced aggression; increased ability to play, learn, and adapt; and increased social bonding and cooperative behaviour as positive developments. These attributes are positively valued in humans, yet these same attributes in domesticated animals lead to accusations that they have been bred to be stupid (smaller brain size), infantile, compliant, and servile.[20] Apparently neotonization is compatible with dignity in the human case, but renders domesticated animals undignified. As in the case of dependency, we would argue that this alleged indignity is in the eye of the beholder, not the intrinsic nature of the domesticated animal. As Burgess-Jackson says: 'If dogs and cats are to be viewed as unauthentic or infantile versions of their wild cousins, then, for the sake of consistency, human beings should be viewed as unauthentic or infantile versions of the primates from which they descended and to whom they are presently related' (Burgess-Jackson 1998: 178 n61).

Abolitionists are right to condemn the confinement and forced/selective breeding of domesticated animals, especially the purposive selection of traits that harm animals while making them more useful to humans. Where we part company with the abolitionist position is in its condemnation of dependency and neotonization per se. Domesticated animals are not intrinsically degraded by these aspects of their evolution, such that they have no opportunity for a good life, or no interest in reproduction. And so the remedy for the historic and ongoing injustice to domesticated animals is not to seek their extinction, but to reconstruct our relationships on grounds of justice.

The Inevitability of Relationship and Symbiosis

The abolitionist assumption that animal dependency on humans is unnatural is related to another core abolitionist assumption—namely, that it is unnatural for animals to be interacting with humans in the first place. In the passage cited earlier, Francione implies that it is unnatural for domesticated animals to be 'stuck in our world'. Similarly, Dunayer equates domestication with 'forced participation' of animals in human society (Dunayer 2004: 17). The implication is that animals, left to their own devices and free of human interference, would live in their own world separate from humans. Living in human society is an unnatural state of affairs for them, one resulting from misguided human interventions, and leading to unnatural dependency.

Here again, this is a misunderstanding of the relationships at work. As we discuss in more detail in Chapter 7, it is quite natural for many animals to seek out human society and the opportunities it offers. Adaptive opportunists like raccoons, mallard ducks, rats, squirrels, and countless others thrive in human settlements, and persist in urban living even in the face of aggressive human efforts to discourage them.[21] Humans are not hermetically sealed from the surrounding environment, but are part of it. A human-altered landscape is just as much an ecosystem as an undisturbed wild one. Nature abhors a vacuum, and as our patterns of settlement and activity alter the environment, other species will inevitably adapt to fill available ecological niches. So there always have been, and always will be, animals who adapt to live in symbiosis with human activity, drawn to the opportunities offered by our forms of shelter, waste disposal, agricultural, and resource practices.[22]

Histories of domestication suggest that the ancestors of today's dogs, cats, and domesticated herbivores were the adaptive opportunists of their day. Dogs' wolf-like ancestors were drawn to human settlement for food scraps, warmth, and shelter. The advent of agriculture and large-scale grain storage attracted rodents to human settlement, which in turn attracted cats and other predators of rodents. Herbivores (like deer today) were attracted to human settlement by feeding opportunities, and the protection afforded from some of their human-wary predators. Prior to active domestication by humans, symbiotic relationships developed between humans and many species of animal. These relationships initially resulted just as much, if not more, from animal agency and adaptation as they did from human agency or intervention. Then, over time, humans learned how to manipulate the breeding of opportunistic animals in order to select for attributes useful to humans, thereby altering the animals' evolutionary trajectory. However, if humans had never clued in to selective breeding, we would not currently be living in a world with a neat separation of human and other animals—humans in cities, wild animals out in the wilds. Rather, we would be sharing our communities, as we do now, with countless adaptive species. This suggests that we cannot escape the ethical complexities of human–animal relationships simply by bringing an end to domestication. Animals are part of our daily lives whether or not we 'invite' (or force) them into 'our world'. There is no such thing as an 'our world' that doesn't include animals, and our task is to identify appropriate forms of human–animal relations.

An interesting example here concerns the Sami relationship with reindeer in northern Scandinavia. Reindeer are considered only semi-domesticated. They exist in free roaming herds, and their breeding is not manipulated. However, over time they have adapted to the presence of humans, and some forms of husbandry. Humans manage the herds, and they kill reindeer for meat, skins, and antlers, and sometimes they milk the animals. The animals are not confined. They could run away from humans if they wanted.

This sort of case raises important issues that cannot be addressed, or even identified, within an abolitionist framework. Our point is not (as some non-AR theorists claim) that the human use of animals should be seen as non-exploitative whenever animals have 'chosen' domestication (or semi-domestication, in this instance).[23] We've already rejected that view.[24] The fact that opportunistic animals gravitate to human community does not give us a licence to exploit them (just as, in the human case, the fact that desperate refugees would sell themselves into slavery does not make slavery legitimate).[25]

Indeed, our point is just the opposite. Even when relations between humans and animals arise through symbiosis rather than 'forced participation', there are still important moral questions to be asked about the fair terms of interaction. We need to determine which ways of interacting with adaptive animals or semi-domesticated animals are permissible, since they will interact with us whether we like it or not. Such relationships are inevitable, and because of superior human power, they carry the endemic risk of turning into relations of exploitation. A central task of any theory of animal rights is to identify the terms under which these relations are non-exploitative. We need a basis for distinguishing parasitic and exploitative relationships from mutually beneficial ones. We need to know the boundaries of acceptable uses of animals by humans, and our duties to animals who adapt to our presence, whether invited or not. And once we have identified the principles of non-exploitative relations, there is no reason for ruling out of court the possibility that relations with domesticated animals can also be reconstructed along just terms. The abolitionist framework ignores these issues, and pre-empts important moral possibilities, by assuming that it is only forced participation that brings humans and animals together.

In short, we believe that the abolitionist approach is multiply flawed; it wrongly treats states of dependency as inherently undignified, and wrongly treats human–animal interaction as somehow unnatural. Once we set aside these misconceptions, there is no reason to assume that domesticated animals are stuck in a condition of intrinsic and unalterable injustice that can only be remedied through their extinction (a goal which itself could only be achieved through further unjust exercises of coercion and confinement).

We hasten to add that we are not, in any way, trying to deny or diminish the gravity of the original injustice done in domesticating animals. Domestication involves wrongs on several levels—infringing basic liberties through forced confinement and breeding; breeding animals in ways that compromise their health and lifespan, and that thwart their potential to return to the wild; and more generally turning them into a means to human ends, rather than respecting them as ends in themselves. We fully share the abolitionist view that these harms to domesticated animals are at the heart of the human oppression of animals—it is domesticated animals that suffer the full horrors of human oppression—even if public opinion seems to care more about, say, seal hunting or endangered species.

Confronted with this historic record of unending misery, it is understandable that abolitionists want to bring the entire existence of domesticated animals to an end. For abolitionists, the remedy is to turn back the clock to a time before domesticated animals existed in order to undo the historic wrongs. In Francione's words, 'it makes no sense to say that we have acted immorally in domesticating nonhuman animals but we are now committed to allowing them to continue to breed'. But this is the wrong remedy—indeed, it is a perverse remedy, compounding the original injustice. Here again, it's instructive to think about debates on ending slavery in the USA in the early nineteenth century. When abolitionism was first seriously debated, many whites held the view that justice required turning back the clock, as it were. Blacks were wronged when Europeans captured them, transported them to the Americas, and enslaved them. To right this wrong, the only solution was to transport them back to Africa and restart the clock of history. But of course this was neither the only nor the just solution—it was an attempt to evade the forward-looking demands of justice. African Americans were forcibly incorporated into white society as slaves, and then as second-class citizens. Over time, the experience of slavery changed them. It changed their cultures, their physical being, their sense of identity, their aspirations and options. With the end of slavery, the path of justice was not to transport African Americans back to a historical trajectory that no longer existed for them; it was to move forward in recognizing them as full and equal citizens. We face a similar moral challenge with domesticated animals.

To be sure, this will require radical changes in the way we treat domesticated animals, including the underlying purposes (serving human interests), the means (forced confinement and breeding), and the standard forms of treatment (exploiting and killing for food, experimentation, and labour). But as we will see, such changes are possible.

4. Threshold Approaches

Not all AR theorists endorse the abolitionist/extinctionist position. Some defend what we are calling a 'threshold' approach, which allows for the possibility that human relations with domesticated animals could be drastically altered in order to meet the demands of justice. The threshold approach does not seek the phasing out of the existence of domesticated animals, but rather seeks a mutually beneficial symbiosis between humans and domesticated animals. In this view, the goal is to define certain thresholds for allowable 'uses' of domesticated animals, while prohibiting their 'exploitation' or 'sacrifice'. Steve Sapontzis, for example, argues that liberating domesticated animals does not rule out all human uses of them:

Rather, [the] goal is to provide for animals the same sort of protection against the routine sacrifice of their interests currently enjoyed only by humans. Just as it is ordinarily in our best interest not to be hermits but to be of benefit to others in certain ways, so it may well be in the best interest of animals to be of benefit to us in certain ways... Just which uses of animals are really mutually beneficial is, of course, the controversial issue. (Sapontzis 1987: 102)

Sapontzis himself does not develop a theory of mutually beneficial relations between humans and domesticated animals—he defers this question 'for a much better world than ours' after gross forms of exploitation have been ended (Sapontzis 1987: 86). This, indeed, is rather typical of the non-abolitionist ART literature: theorists acknowledge the need for some theory of mutually beneficial relations, but then leave it for some future occasion.[26]

However, a couple of important attempts have been made to specify principles for regulating our relations with domesticated animals. In this section we discuss the ideas of David DeGrazia, Tzachi Zamir, and Martha Nussbaum. Each account offers valuable insights, but also suffers from serious limitations. In particular, we argue that they mischaracterize the nature of the community of justice. In our view, the result of domestication is that animals are now appropriately seen as members of our society, where membership entails rights of residency (this is their home, they belong here), the right to have their interests counted when determining the collective or public good of the community, and the right to shape evolving rules of interaction. In the human case, this fact of social membership is captured in the idea of citizenship, and we argue that this is the appropriate framework for thinking about domesticated animals as well. As we will see, existing ART accounts of the appropriate threshold of animal use do not acknowledge the significance of these facts of membership, and so end up legitimating forms of injustice.

DeGrazia and Zamir on Use and Exploitation

The threshold view presupposes that we can distinguish (permissible) 'use' of domesticated animals from (impermissible) 'exploitation' or oppression. The idea of using animals may seem inherently committed to viewing animals in unacceptably instrumental terms, simply as a means to our own ends. But this is a mistake. We regularly and permissibly use other people—our family, friends, acquaintances, and strangers—in order to achieve our own ends. Most relationships have instrumental aspects which are unproblematic as long as we don't view others' very existence in a totalizing instrumental fashion. This use is part of the give and take of society, and only tips over into exploitation under certain conditions. Indeed, in the human context, we don't simply use people who happen to be available, we actually bring new people into the community, at least in part, in order to make use of them. For example, parents often have multiple motives in deciding to have children. They may simply wish to bequeath the gift of life onto another. But having children also serves their own ends—a desire to be a parent, a desire for companionship, the hope of an heir to carry on a family tradition or business, and so on. Consider also the case of immigration policy. Countries routinely favour immigration applicants of a particular age, or possessing particular skills, depending on the labour needs of the host country. We bring individuals into the community on the expectation of using them to benefit particular industries, or society more generally. Precisely because others have an interest in using them, both children and immigrants are vulnerable to exploitation. But the solution is not to eliminate reproduction or immigration, or to eliminate the ways in which children and immigrants help us to achieve our aims. Rather, justice requires defining a set of criteria and safeguards to ensure that use is mutually beneficial—that it is indeed part of a give and take of social life amongst members of a shared community—rather than the one-sided exploitation of the weaker by the stronger.

There is no reason in principle why a comparable distinction cannot be made in the case of domesticated animals, allowing us to distinguish permissible uses of animals from impermissible exploitation. Perhaps domesticated animals can permissibly be used for companionship, or for certain forms of labour (e.g., protecting sheep), or for certain products (e.g., manure), while ruling out exploitation that is substantially detrimental to the freedom and well-being of animals (e.g., long work hours, unsafe conditions, lack of options).

But how should we draw this distinction in the case of domesticated animals? In the human case, as we have indicated, we answer this question in light of an ideal of membership: use involves the give and take of social life amongst members of a shared community; exploitation involves treating people in ways that presuppose (or result in) their relegation to the status of second-class citizens—as slaves or lower-caste members. Preventing exploitation, therefore, involves a set of criteria and safeguards intended to affirm ideas of membership and citizenship, and to ensure that use remains confined within the mutual give and take of social life amongst members.

This is not, however, the framework used by existing threshold accounts of the rights of domesticated animals. Instead, theorists like DeGrazia (1996) and Zamir (2007) offer a much weaker set of criteria and safeguards—criteria that, we believe, reproduce relations of subordination and exploitation.

Both DeGrazia and Zamir accept that humans have acquired special duties towards animals as a result of domestication—duties that prohibit exploitation of animals. However, in each case, they define exploitation not by reference to some ideal of the give and take of membership in a shared community, but rather by reference to two criteria: (a) some 'floor of well-being' that ensures that animals' lives are worth living and their most basic needs are met; and (b) some counterfactual of what would have happened in the absence of human action—that is, that animals are not worse off than they would have been in the absence of human care and control.

It is this second criterion that interests and worries us.[27] The two theorists define this counterfactual in different ways. For DeGrazia, the criterion involves comparison with life in the wild. If an animal would be better off living in the wild, then we harm it by keeping it as a pet or in a farm or zoo. But so long as our treatment of animals does not leave them worse off than they would be in the wild, then our use is permissible.[28] As DeGrazia acknowledges, this is a very weak requirement, at least in relation to domesticated animals. It may set a very strong presumption against capturing wild animals for display in zoos: such animals are almost always better off left alone in the wild. In the case of domesticated animals, however, many animals would not survive, let alone thrive, in the wild—after all, they have been bred for centuries to be dependent on humans. Even if one treated a dog simply as a beast of burden, to be used (and used up) in difficult labour without the opportunity for play or companionship, it might still live longer than if simply turned out onto the street and left to fend for itself.[29]

For Zamir, the relevant contrast is with non-existence. In the case of domesticated animals, their very existence depends on whether humans bring them into being, and so the question for Zamir is whether animals have an interest in being brought into existence for use by humans. He argues that in general, animals do benefit from having a chance to live, provided that the forms of human use do not subject animals to levels of suffering or harm that make their lives not worth living.[30] In Zamir's view, many uses of domesticated animals will pass this threshold, for example no-kill milk and egg farming, pet ownership, and animal-assisted therapy using dogs and horses. He acknowledges that these activities involve harms to animals, but not enough to make their lives qualitatively bad. Harms can be justified if they are 'reasonable' prerequisites for humans to be willing to bring these animals into being. For example, humans won't have domestic chickens unless they can raise them in large enough flocks to have an economically viable egg operation. This might mean that painful debeaking is necessary, but it is worth it for the chickens in exchange for existence. Unless calves are removed from cows, they will drink the lion's share of the cow's milk, which might make a dairy operation unviable. Zamir says that if we believe that removing calves from cows is more of a temporary distress than a long-term harm, then separation may be acceptable, being worth it for the cows in exchange for existence. In other words, he allows for various violations of rights (separation of families, non-consensual surgical procedures, coercive training) in exchange for the opportunity to live.

Zamir rules out extreme violations (e.g., killing animals, or subjecting them to ongoing suffering), but allows for less serious violations because they are (allegedly) in the animals' interest overall, as compared with the counterfactual of non-existence.

There are important differences between DeGrazia's and Zamir's versions of the counterfactual, but it should immediately be clear how weak both are, and how far they depart from the way we think about use and exploitation in the human case. Consider some analogies. As noted above, we often bring new members into our society for instrumental reasons: we bring children or immigrants into society in part because of expectations of their use to us. However, once a child is born, or an immigrant settles permanently, they become co-members of the society, whose use must be regulated by norms of citizenship. We don't allow parents to violate the rights of their children on the grounds that they wouldn't have given them life otherwise. Imagine someone who justifies removing a child's vocal chords on the grounds that she would never have become a parent in the first place if she had known she would have to listen to a child's crying or screaming, and that even without vocal chords the child's life is still worth living. In the human case, we don't accept that the value of existence to the child justifies such harms.

Or imagine that a couple with two biological children decides to adopt a third child from a foster home in which the child is neglected. The couple meets the basic needs of the adopted child such that his life is worth living, and he is better off than he would have been in the foster home. However, when it comes to funding music lessons, sports activities, or university education, the parents only support their biological children, while using their adopted child as a household servant. Or consider a rich country with an active immigration programme that brings in workers from poor countries, primarily to perform jobs that the rich country's native-born population avoids, and allows them to settle permanently. The rich country ensures that immigrants are paid enough to meet their basic needs, but it denies them access to legal protections regarding overtime and vacation policies, employment insurance, workplace training opportunities, pensions, etc. The workers are better off than they would be back in their poor country, and can meet their basic needs. However, they are second-class citizens, not entitled to share in the host society's wealth and opportunities, no matter how long they live there or how much they contribute. In both of these cases, we should surely condemn the treatment of the adopted child or the immigrants as unjust.

As these examples suggest, our sense of justice within the family and the larger community is governed by something more than the fulfilment of DeGrazia's and Zamir's thresholds. It is governed by a conception of membership. Justice is not measured against the counterfactual of non-existence, or

93

the counterfactual of banishment or exile or return to some prior state outside the community. It is measured in terms of an egalitarian vision of the social community, and when we bring new people into the community (via birth or immigration) we must allow them to become full members, and not condemn them to permanent second-class status. Why should the standard be different for animals whom we bring into our community? What justifies treating humans as members first class (encompassed within an egalitarian conception), and animals as members second class (entitled to the lesser threshold of basic needs and the two counterfactual requirements)? Far from contesting the exploitation of animals, these approaches legitimize and institutionalize their subordinate status.

In our view, what both versions of the counterfactual ignore is that humans have already brought domesticated animals into a mixed society. This has to be the starting point of any credible account of the rights of domesticated animals: they are already here, living amongst us, the product of a long history of interaction and interdependence. Both DeGrazia and Zamir write as if humans could simply walk away from domesticated animals, and that if we do decide to continue interacting with them, our only obligation is to not make them worse off than they would be if we did walk away. This is a bizarre view to take, ignoring the fact that human societies, collectively speaking, have acquired special duties to domesticated animals, stemming from centuries of captivity and breeding. Our actions, over generations, have foreclosed for many domesticated animals the possibility of a life in the wild. We can't evade this responsibility by choosing as individuals not to adopt an animal companion, or not to keep chickens in our yard. It is a collective responsibility stemming from the cumulative impact of our treatment of domesticated animals.[31]

A comparison with human immigration is again instructive. When newcomers enter a community, there are often specific individuals with special responsibilities to help them (e.g., sponsoring family members or church groups). However, the members of society have a collective responsibility towards newcomers—a duty to help them integrate and become successful members of society. This collective responsibility is usually discharged via government programmes of language training, citizenship education, settlement supports, job training, and so on. Similarly, duties towards children are conceived in both private terms (the duties of parents to their children) and public terms (the duties of society to nurture development and socialization through provision of education, health care, etc.). DeGrazia and Zamir miss this socio-political dimension. Domesticated animals are part of a shared community with us, a mixed community which has existed over time, generating collective and intergenerational obligations. As a result, we not only have an obligation as individuals not to make others worse off through our personal actions, but also a collective responsibility arising from domestication to create fair terms of membership.

These problems with existing threshold models may help to explain why so many AR theorists endorse the abolitionist/extinctionist approach. Given that domestication is driven by human purposes, and given the enormous incentives to exploit animals, there is an omnipresent danger that threshold models will simply become a pretext for ongoing exploitation, and that assessments of harm will be biased by human self-interest. (Consider Zamir's speculation that the separation of calves is only a temporary distress to them and their mothers; or that 'breaking' horses is not a serious harm.) The various thresholds that have been proposed may simply become another version of the sort of welfarist reforms that we've already seen are inadequate in addressing animal exploitation. Neither welfarist reforms aimed at the reduction of 'unnecessary suffering' nor threshold accounts aimed at reducing 'exploitation' can effectively block the human domination of domesticated animals. Only the complete abolition/extinction of domesticated animals can end the injustice.

We take this objection seriously. However, as we have seen, the abolitionist approach is, in its own way, an abdication of our responsibility to domesticated animals, and perhaps even a compounding of that original injustice. In our view, neither threshold nor abolitionist views take sufficiently seriously our ongoing obligations to domesticated animals. Both, in their own ways, provide a licence for humans to evade these responsibilities. The citizenship model we develop in Chapter 5 offers a fundamentally different approach.

5. Nussbaum and the Species Norm Principle

Before elaborating our own citizenship model, we'd like to briefly consider one other approach, developed by Martha Nussbaum in her *Frontiers of Justice* (Nussbaum 2006). Unlike Zamir and DeGrazia, Nussbaum seeks to apply the same general framework of justice to animals as to humans: our obligation, in both cases, is to enable individuals to achieve as far as possible their 'capabilities'. Our obligations to animals are not constrained by some artificial counterfactual of non-existence or life in the wild; rather, as with humans, we have an open-ended obligation to promote flourishing through the enabling of capabilities.

Pitched at this very abstract level, we are sympathetic to Nussbaum's 'capability approach'.[32] However, we believe that, like DeGrazia and Zamir, she elaborates her approach in ways that ignore the fact that humans and domesticated animals already form mixed societies, and as a result she misses the implications of this shared sociopolitical context for animal justice. The problem, in brief, lies with the way Nussbaum ties her capability theory of justice to what she calls 'the species norm'. According to Nussbaum, individuals thrive in ways typical for members of their species. Therefore justice requires that we enable individuals to achieve (insofar as possible) the capabilities as defined for typical members of their species. The question on her approach is not, what does this individual require in order to flourish, but what do individuals of this type (i.e., species) typically require in order to flourish?

Nussbaum uses the idea of species norm to ensure that even for those individuals who don't possess the 'normal' capacities for their species (severely disabled humans, for example), the target of social policy should be to ensure that they achieve the species-defined capabilities as far as possible. In order to flourish, humans need to learn a human language and be socialized to human society so that they can enjoy contact and relationships with other humans. It is a matter of justice that human individuals be able to achieve these capabilities. In the case of humans with severe mental disabilities, it might not be possible to achieve the full capability, but it is a duty of justice that we devote the necessary time and resources to help them achieve this capability insofar as they are able, providing them with a life as 'normal' as can be achieved. 'We should bear in mind that any child born into a species has the dignity relevant to that species, whether or not it seems to have the "basic capabilities" relevant to that species. For that reason, it should also have all the capabilities relevant to the species, either individually or through guardianship' (Nussbaum 2006: 347).

Applied to animals, this means that justice for animals requires access to the capabilities that are typical for members of their particular species:

> In short, the species norm (duly evaluated) tells us what the appropriate benchmark is for judging whether a given creature has decent opportunities for flourishing. The same thing goes for nonhuman animals: in each case, what is wanted is a species-specific account of central capabilities ... and then a commitment to bring members of that species up to that norm, even if special obstacles lie in the way of that. (Nussbaum 2006: 365)

For Nussbaum, species membership sets not only a baseline for justice, but also an outer limit. She says, for example: 'For chimpanzees, language use is a frill, constructed by human scientists; their own characteristic mode of flourishing in their own community does not rely on it' (Nussbaum 2006: 364). Sign language (or computer-assisted language) for chimpanzees is a frill, because normal chimpanzees don't sign, or share a language with humans. By contrast, normal dogs are mobile, so if your dog companion is injured Nussbaum argues that it is appropriate to provide a prosthetic device if that will allow the dog to regain normal mobility. In the case of injury or disability, as in more general circumstances, the species norm is the appropriate guide for whether or not a particular intervention is appropriate.

In our view, this preoccupation with species norm might make sense in a world where humans and animals lived separately: chimpanzees would flourish according to their species norm 'in their own community' in the wild; while humans would flourish according to their species norm in their own community. But the challenge of domesticated animals is precisely that we already live in a society that contains both animals and humans who must find a way to live together on terms of justice. And this means that we need a theory of capabilities that is premised on enabling humans and domesticated animals to flourish in mixed communities, rather than enabling each species to flourish separately 'in their own community'.

For chimpanzees living in the wild, a concept of flourishing tied to a species norm is probably a reasonable standard. Species membership is a useful short-hand classification for making a rough and ready assessment of the likely needs and capabilities of any particular individual. But in the case of domesticated animals, our positive duties towards them cannot be fully captured by a conception of the species norm. They are members of a species, but they are also members of an interspecies community. The relevant capabilities for any particular animal will be greatly affected by this context. Wolves or feral dogs may need to communicate primarily with other wolves or feral dogs, but companion dogs need to communicate with humans and other species with whom they live, and to function in a mixed human–animal society. For a dog or donkey at a rural farm sanctuary, relevant capabilities might relate to getting along with a variety of other animals (of varied species), education about the hazards of farm machinery, or the learning of useful skills like protecting sheep or shooing crows from the corn crib. For a city dog, learning to take the subway, or to activate accessible door devices, or learning the niceties of where to defecate, may all be relevant capabilities. In other words, these capabilities relevant to flourishing are defined by social context as much as species membership. We have made domesticated animals part of human society, and we have a duty to ensure that they can flourish in that interspecies context, which will involve capabilities not relevant to their feral or wild cousins.[33]

Moreover, this need for an interspecies account of capabilities goes in both directions. Our conception of *human* flourishing must also take into account the fact that humans live in mixed communities, and that interacting justly with other species is both a responsibility and an opportunity. Our conception of human flourishing shouldn't assume that our most significant relationships must be with other humans, as opposed to individuals of other species. For many humans this is simply not the case, and it's not clear why this should be conceptualized as a failure to achieve a species norm, rather than simply an individual proclivity or choice.

Consider Nussbaum's discussion of Arthur, her nephew, who is diagnosed as having forms of Asperger's and Tourette's syndromes. His intellectual capacities are formidable, but he is enormously challenged in terms of social relations with humans. Nussbaum says:

> Arthur will flourish, if he does, as a human being; and that fact means that special efforts must be made to develop his social capacities. It is clear that without such efforts he will not form friendships, wider social relationships, or useful political relationships. Such a lack matters for Arthur, because the human community is his community. He has no option to go off and search somewhere in the universe for a community of intelligent aliens with minimal social capacity (such as Mr. Spock). Humans expect certain things of him, and so education must nourish those capacities, even if it is very expensive to devise such forms of education. The relevance of the species norm is that it defines the context, the political and social community, in which people either flourish or do not. (Nussbaum 2006: 364–5)

While this position helps to underpin a powerful set of entitlements for people with disabilities, it is too rigid and potentially cruel in its blindness to individual capacities and interests. Rather than spending countless hours trying to learn the niceties of human social interaction with very limited success, someone with severe autism spectrum disorder, for example, might derive greater happiness and satisfaction from interacting with dogs, or horses, or flocks of chickens with whom he or she is able to communicate more intuitively and rewardingly. Setting benchmarks for individuals based on a species norm, rather than on their actual capacities and preferences, may simply set them up for frustration and failure. Their unique individuality might include capacities and inclinations that are better realized in the company of animals, and if so, their flourishing might be stunted by rigid adherence to a species norm rather than a more species-ecumenical conception of community.

We cannot speak to Arthur's situation, but it seems possible that individuals with severe (human) social inhibitions or incapacities might flourish with alternatives to so-called normal levels of human contact. Someone like Arthur might find intellectual challenge and satisfaction through interaction with computers, with highly intelligent humans who understand and make allowances for his conditions, or with others who share his lack of human social functioning. Some of his emotional needs might be satisfied through friendships with dogs or pigs or other animals who have limited social expectations, but abundant capacity for love and attachment. Why isn't this a valid conception of individual human flourishing? Why should concepts such as community, sociality, friendship, and love be hedged by species?[34] Throughout history countless humans have chosen animals over human company, just as today many humans prefer to live with animal companions instead of human partners, children, or housemates. To pathologize these preferences as deviating from an alleged human norm is to close ourselves off from the potential richness of interspecies sociality. Indeed, research on (human) children highlights how they naturally see themselves as part of a shared society with animals. They have to be socialized into making a sharp separation between humans and other animals, and marking the boundaries of a strictly human society (Pallotta 2008). There is no reason why we must mark the boundaries of society in this way.[35]

Nussbaum's focus on a species norm eclipses both ties across species and diversity within species. Consider the case of an infant chimpanzee, orphaned and injured in the wild, who is adopted by humans and who is unlikely, due to injuries and socialization, to be able to return to life as a wild chimpanzee. The appropriate conception of flourishing for this animal is not a capability list for chimpanzees qua species. It's a capability list for this particular individual chimpanzee, who will be making his life primarily in human society. For him, learning rudimentary human language (and various other aspects of human culture), far from being a 'frill', might be essential to flourishing—to being able to function and thrive in his environment. We are not just members of species. We are members of societies, and the two don't necessarily overlap. A theory of justice needs to take account of our social context, not just our species membership.

Similarly, differences from the norm are not necessarily 'disabilities' in which the appropriate remedy is to try to replicate the norm. Individual variation can also lead to simply different or even superior abilities. Why shouldn't justice attend to these unique capacities rather than straitjacketing individuals according to a species norm? This indeed has been a familiar critique of Nussbaum's approach within the field of disability studies. As Silvers and Francis put it, 'on her capabilities approach, just treatment of the disabled seems to mean permitting, encouraging, or obliging the nondisabled to relate to the disabled primarily by improving them, whether or not they can be improved and whether or not they prefer to be improved' (Silvers and Francis 2005: 55; cf. Arneil 2009).

For both humans and animals, justice requires a conception of flourishing that is more sensitive to both interspecies community membership and intraspecies individual variation. It should also be open to evolution, as new forms of interspecies community emerge, opening up new possibilities for forms of animal and human flourishing. As we argue in Chapter 5, this is precisely what is offered by a citizenship model.

6. Conclusion: The Limitations of Current ART Approaches

The abolitionist, threshold, and species-norm approaches we have canvassed differ in many respects. Whereas abolitionists seek the extinction of domesticated animals, threshold and species-norm approaches accept that human–animal contact is inevitable and sometimes desirable. However, at another level, they share some important assumptions. For all, domesticated animals' status is conceived as a kind of deviation from their true or natural community in the wild, which remains the default position for thinking about our moral obligations. And this in turn is related to the assumption, shared by both abolitionists and threshold approaches, that domesticated animals are the objects of human action and decision-making, never agents. Both assume that in human–animal communities humans will inevitably 'call all the shots' (Zamir 2007: 100), and typically go on to provide a list of practices that are deemed acceptable (rather than exploitative) without seeking to solicit the preferences of individual animals themselves.

In our view, we need an entirely new starting point. We need to start from the premise that humans and domesticated animals already form a shared community—we have brought domesticated animals into our society, and we owe them membership in it. This is now their home, where they belong, and their interests must be included in our conception of the common good of the community. And this in turn requires enabling animals to shape the evolution of our shared society, contributing to decisions about how their (and our) lives should go. We need to attend to what sorts of relationships animals themselves want to have with us (and with each other), which are likely to develop over time, and to vary from individual to individual. The results are difficult to predict, but they are almost certainly going to be different from the sort of life animals would have led in the wild, or from what is entailed by a static notion of species norm. In short, we need to recognize that domesticated animals are co-citizens of the community.

5

Domesticated Animal Citizens

In this chapter, our aim is to spell out in more detail our citizenship model for domesticated animals. As suggested earlier, our approach rests on two main ideas:

(1) domesticated animals must be seen as members of our community. Having brought such animals into our society, and deprived them of other possible forms of existence (at least for the foreseeable future), we have a duty to include them in our social and political arrangements on fair terms. As such, they have rights of *membership*—rights that go beyond the universal rights owed to all animals, and which are hence relational and differentiated;

(2) the appropriate conceptual framework for thinking about these relational membership rights is that of *citizenship*. Citizenship, in turn, has at least three core elements: residency (this is their home, they belong here), inclusion in the sovereign people (their interests count in determining the public good), and agency (they should be able to shape the rules of cooperation).

In both respects, we've likened domestic animals to the case of former slaves, indentured labourers, or foreign migrants who were initially brought into a community as a subordinated caste, but who rightly demanded inclusion in the 'we' of the political community. When we bring newcomers into our society on a permanent basis, we owe them and their descendants membership, in the form of citizenship, above and beyond universal human rights. Our aim is to extend this principle to domesticated animals.

To some extent, these two ideas are separable, and someone could accept the idea of membership rights for domesticated animals without accepting that citizenship provides an appropriate framework for conceptualizing these membership rights. One might think that while domesticated animals stand in morally significant relations with humans that generate relational membership rights, these cannot be relations of co-citizenship. Indeed, as we have seen, animal rights (AR) theorists to date have been surprisingly reluctant to invoke the idea of citizenship in relation to domesticated animals, perhaps because citizenship seems to presuppose a set of capacities that many animals lack. Citizenship is often said to require a reflectively held sense of one's own good, and the ability to articulate that good within a democratic process, as well as a sense of justice, and the ability to comply with fair terms of cooperation that are themselves rationally negotiated and consensually endorsed. In this view, since animals lack such competences, their membership could not take the form of citizenship, but could perhaps be conceptualized as wardship. The difference is that whereas citizens are active co-authors of the community's laws and institutions, wards are the passive recipients of our duty to protect the vulnerable.[1]

In this chapter, we argue for the appropriateness of a citizenship model. But it is worth noting that both wardship and citizenship entail the idea of relational rights, and hence go beyond many existing AR theories. At the start of this book, we stated that our aim was to show the necessity of supplementing the universal rights defended by traditional animal rights theory (ART) with a differentiated theory of animal rights that tracks morally significant differences in the relations between animals and humans. Wardship is one possible framework for articulating a distinctive type of morally significant relationship, with its own rights and duties, beyond the respect for universal rights owed to all sentient animals.

Indeed, wardship and citizenship are likely to generate similar conclusions on at least some issues. For example, both wardship and citizenship are likely to say that we have duties to provide forms of care (such as medical interventions) to domesticated animals which we do not have to wild or liminal animals. However, we want to argue strongly for the preferability of a citizenship model. We believe that the reluctance to conceive of domesticated animals as co-citizens is rooted, fundamentally, in two pernicious misunderstandings. First, there is an unwillingness to recognize the competences of domesticated animals for agency, cooperation, and participation in mixed human–animal settings. As biologists have long recognized, animal species were selected for domestication precisely because of these competences. The wardship model ignores these capacities, and treats domesticated animals as wholly passive and dependent on humans. Second, and relatedly, there is an unwillingness to accept that humans and domesticated animals already form a mixed community that belongs to all its members. The wardship model, implicitly or explicitly, treats domesticated animals as a leftover or remainder, located on the (literal and figural) margins of human society, having no claims regarding how the broader community governs itself and its public spaces. It treats domesticated animals as something like protected aliens or guests, who don't really belong here, but whom we have a duty to treat humanely.[2]

Our aim in this chapter is to show that a citizenship model better captures both the empirical realities and the moral imperatives of our relations with domesticated animals. To that end, we begin by exploring the sort of competences that are required for citizenship. Drawing on recent work in disability theory, we show that there are many ways for individuals with varying levels of cognitive ability to be treated as citizens and to exercise their citizenship, and that there is no reason why domesticated animals cannot be included within these more expansive ideas of citizenship (sections 1–3). We then explore what this citizenship model would mean for a range of specific issues, including the socialization and training of domesticated animals, their rights to mobility, their medical care and protection from harm, and their reproduction (section 4). In all of these cases, we argue, the citizenship model provides more plausible answers than either the abolitionist/extinctionist or threshold views we discussed in Chapter 4.

1. Rethinking Citizenship

Can animals be citizens? As we discussed in Chapter 3, citizenship involves not just a list of rights or entitlements, but also an ongoing role as a co-creator of the community, participating collectively in the shaping of one's society, and its culture and institutions. Citizenship is thus an active role, in which individuals are contributing agents and not simply passive recipients of benefits. Such an active role clearly requires certain capacities, which we need to spell out explicitly. If we look at familiar accounts of citizenship in the human case, citizenship is often said to require at least three basic capacities, or what Rawls calls 'moral powers':[3]

- (i) the capacity to have a subjective good, and to communicate it;
- (ii) the capacity to comply with social norms/cooperation;
- (iii) the capacity to participate in the co-authoring of laws.

We do not dispute this basic list. We do, however, dispute the way in which these three capacities are typically interpreted.

In most political philosophy, these capacities are interpreted in highly intellectualist or rationalist ways. For example, the capacity for a subjective good is seen as requiring that individuals reflectively endorse a conception of the good. It is not enough to have a good, you need to have a reflective good. Similarly, the capacity to comply with social norms is understood to require that individuals rationally understand the reasons for those norms, and comply with them for those reasons. And the capacity to participate in the co-authoring of the law is understood as requiring that individuals be able to engage in 'public reason' or other forms of 'communicative rationality' that involve being able to articulate one's own reasons for defending certain laws, and to understand and evaluate other people's reasons. It is not enough to cooperate in social life, you need to be able to reflect on and deliberate about the terms of cooperation.

If interpreted in these highly cognitivist ways, then animals do indeed seem incapable of being citizens. However, large numbers of human beings would also be excluded: children, the mentally disabled, people with dementia, and those who are temporarily incompetent due to illness or injury.[4] As a result, cognitivist restrictions on citizenship have progressively been challenged and abandoned, in large part due to the legal and political struggles of the disability movement, which has campaigned explicitly for citizenship, rather than merely humanitarian protection.[5] In the words of Michael Prince, 'struggling for "full citizenship" is the paradigmatic form of political action' within the disability movement, whose activists 'have adopted citizenship as the central organizing principle and benchmark' (Prince 2009: 3, 7).

For people with mental disabilities, this challenge to the cognitivist conception of citizenship operates on two levels, both of which are highly relevant for the animal case. First, the disability movement insists on the capacities the mentally disabled actually have (e.g., capacities to have a subjective good, to communicate that good, to participate and co-create public life, and to form relations of trust and cooperation), and on the continuities between these abilities and those of the 'abled'. Second, the movement has reconceived how these capacities can sustain the recognition and exercise of citizenship (e.g., how those with mental disabilities can enact their citizenship, at least under appropriate conditions).

At the heart of these new accounts of the capacities for citizenship is the idea of trust-based 'dependent agency'. In this view, even the severely cognitively disabled have the capacity for agency, but it is agency that is exercised in and through relations with particular others in whom they trust, and who have the skills and knowledge needed to recognize and assist the expression of agency. Where such supportive and trusting relations exist, those with mental disabilities have the requisite capacities for citizenship, including (i) the capacity to express their subjective good, as revealed through various forms of behaviour and communication; (ii) the capacity to comply with social norms through the evolution of trusting relationships; and (iii) the capacity to participate in shaping terms of interaction.

We spell out some of these ideas in more detail below, since in our view they are applicable to domesticated animals. Indeed, one of the important facts about the process of domestication is that it presupposes and reinforces precisely these sorts of capacities for dependent agency. Domestication only works for animals that are sociable, able to communicate, and to adapt to and trust humans, and domestication over time has worked to strengthen these capacities (Clutton-Brock 1987: 15).[6] As a result, domesticated animals are capable of forming relations with humans that allow them to manifest a subjective good, to cooperate, and to participate—in short, to be citizens.

Not all animals have the sorts of relations with human beings that enable this sort of dependent agency, and hence citizenship. Indeed, in the following two chapters, we argue that such relations do not exist, and should not exist, for a wide range of non-domesticated animals, whether living in the wild or amongst us in the liminal zone. For such animals, we need to find alternative ways of recognizing their rights and interests other than by according them citizenship in our shared political community. But for domesticated animals, citizenship is both possible, we argue, and morally required.

2. Recent Disability Theories of Citizenship

Before examining the case of domesticated animals in more detail, we'd like to briefly explore the important new literature on disability theory with regard to citizenship for people with severe intellectual disabilities (hereafter SID), since our own ideas have been strongly shaped by it. As we noted, this literature raises two profound challenges to traditional citizenship theory. It calls upon us to recognize the capacities that already exist amongst people with SID, and calls upon us to recognize ways in which those capacities can sustain practices of citizenship.

The first is the capacity to have a subjective good, and the ability to communicate it. Theorists emphasize that people with SID have projects and preferences, even if they lack 'the more specific abilities required to form judgements about their own interests' (Vorhaus 2005), and even if they are unable to articulate their subjective good without the assistance of others (Francis and Silvers 2007). In order to communicate this good, various models of 'dependent agency' have been developed. For example, Eva Feder Kittay emphasizes the role of caregivers in achieving a kind of transparency for communicating the preferences of people with SID, through intimate acquaintance and careful and loving attention (Kittay 2005b). This may involve the interpretation of body language, and subtleties of expression, gesture, and sound. As Francis and Silvers put it, 'the collaborator's role is to attend to these expressions, to fit them together into an account of ongoing preferences that constitutes a personalized idea of the good, and to work out how to realize this good under existing circumstances' (Francis and Silvers 2007: 325).

John Vorhaus (2007) provides the example of Kaylie, a child with SID. She cannot answer a question about how she wants to spend her day. However, shown pictures representing different options, she is able to gesture to indicate a preference.[7] Whereas traditional theories assume that a subjective good for people with SID either does not exist or is inaccessible and therefore cannot be a basis for citizenship, disability theory argues that this dismissal is an artefact of undue reliance on linguistic models of articulation (Clifford 2009), and an overly individualistic (and internal) conception of how we arrive at our understanding of the subjective good (Francis and Silvers 2007). With the right enabling conditions in place, the subjective good for people with SID can be articulated and can help to shape our conceptions of justice.[8]

Citizenship is not just about articulating or advancing one's own good. It is also about the ability to consent to, and comply with, fair terms of cooperation. Traditional theories of justice frequently invoke the idea of negotiating a social contract as a way of envisioning how we come to agreement about principles of justice. We first engage in a rational debate about the appropriate terms of cooperation, and then, having collectively endorsed the preferred principles of justice, we comply with those principles (and do so for the right reasons). This model obviously won't work for people with SID. But as Silvers and Francis note, there are alternatives to this 'negotiation' model of how social cooperation develops. They propose instead a 'trust' model, in which parties first develop trusting relations with particular others, and through the evolution of these trusting relations, come to participate in the shaping and sustaining of larger cooperative schemes. In the traditional negotiation model, the parties 'are portrayed as articulating, examining and then selecting basic principles', which are then 'put immediately in place'. The trust model, by contrast, 'emphasizes that cooperation-facilitating conditions develop over time, as social activity evolves to exemplify principles of cooperation that strengthen and systematize people's natural proclivities to depend on each other. People need not be able to articulate these principles, or to ponder them, to be committed to them' (Silvers and Francis 2005: 67). This trust model begins with 'the discretionary commitment to trusting each other by parties whose capabilities differ', but these particular interactions 'enrich another kind of entity, the cooperative scheme (or the social climate, the community culture, or society itself)' (Silvers and Francis 2005: 45).

In this trust model, people with SID can both assent to, and comply with, schemes of social cooperation, envisioned as a process of enacting and revising social norms in the context of ongoing cooperating relationships, rather than a one-time negotiation. People with SID participate in and enrich the cooperative scheme through their relationships of love, trust, and mutual dependency, capacities which are overlooked by traditional models of citizenship participation.[9]

This is just a brief sketch of recent theorizing on citizenship for people with intellectual disabilities. But we can already see the seeds of a new and more inclusive conception of citizenship. In the traditional account, people with SID are either entirely ignored or treated as 'outliers' or 'marginal cases' to be incorporated as 'moral patients', subject to permanent wardship in accordance with social norms that they have no role in shaping. With this new approach, citizenship is reconceived to enable individuals with a much broader range of capabilities to act as, and to be treated as, full citizens. And this in turn requires treating citizens as distinct and unique individuals, rather than just as instances of some generic category. Respecting people as citizens means attending to their subjective good (rather than treating them according to some list of objective goods or capacities decided without reference to the person's own expressed wishes), and attending to their individualized capacities (rather than making global judgements of competence or incompetence based on a generic diagnosis of disability, without reference to a specific person's actual abilities to negotiate this or that particular challenge in life). To treat someone as a citizen is to look for evidence of their subjective individualized good, and to look for and support areas of individual agency.[10]

The main virtue of this new approach is its capacity to extend justice and membership to a historically subordinated group. But it's worth noting that this approach arguably offers a more accurate account of what citizenship means for all of us. All of us need the help of others to articulate our subjective good; all of us need the help of supportive social structures to participate in schemes of social cooperation. We are all interdependent, relying on others to enable and sustain our (variable and contextual) capacities for agency.

This indeed is a central point emphasized within the disability movement: we can learn something important about the human condition generally by exploring how identity and agency can be supported for those with mental disabilities. Acknowledging the facts of dependency should not be seen as an embarrassment to theories that stress the moral importance of autonomy and subjective identity, but as an opportunity to enrich such theories, by highlighting the many ways in which social relationships and social structures either enable or inhibit these values. As Francis and Silvers put it, the facts of interdependency 'do not bring with them a loss of individuality or difference. To the contrary, understanding that subjective accounts can be achieved rather than precluded or marred through dependent agency enriches the way we think about the good' (Francis and Silvers 2007: 334). Similarly, Barbara Arneil notes that since we are all highly dependent on structures that enable us to function independently, dependency should be seen 'not as an antonym of autonomy but as in some sense, its precursor' (Arneil 2009: 236). An adequate theory of citizenship needs to explain how we enable agency in light of our varying forms and degrees of dependency, rather than simply wishing the facts of dependency away.

In other words, the significance of this new model of interdependent citizenship isn't simply to expand the circle of individuals encompassed by citizenship theory, but to change our conception of citizenship for everyone, regardless of dependency status and innate capacities. Rather than dividing the polity between those who are independent and those who are dependent — or into those who are agents and those who are patients—this new conception of citizenship recognizes that we are all interdependent, and experience varying forms and degrees of agency according to context, and over the life-course. Bringing people with SID into the realm of citizenship not only alters our conception of their capacities (because it forces us to establish enabling conditions in which their capacities can be recognized and fostered), it also highlights the ways in which capacities of the rest of the population are not simply innate, but socially enabled.[11]

3. Can Domesticated Animals be Citizens?

These new conceptions of citizenship arising from disability theory have important implications for how we think about domesticated animals, since they offer a model of how the core capabilities of citizenship can be enacted without rational reflection. Individuals with SID can be citizens—they can have and communicate a subjective good; they can comply with schemes of social cooperation; and they can participate as agents in social life—without being capable of rational reflection. If so, can domesticated animals also exercise these capacities, and thereby be citizens?

Our answer is yes. In a way, this should now be obvious. As we noted earlier, the animal species that were historically selected for domestication were picked precisely because they possessed these competences. But given the novelty of thinking of animals as citizens, it may be worth reviewing the evidence.

Having and Expressing a Subjective Good

Anyone who has lived with a domesticated animal knows that they have preferences, interests, and desires, and that they communicate these in a variety of intentional ways. They walk to the gate to indicate that they want to go outside. They meow in front of the fridge to ask for food. They nuzzle your arm to ask for affection. They charge at you flapping their wings and squawking to tell you to back off. They drag a leash from the cupboard to signal walk time. They bow to invite you to play. They point towards the couch or bed to ask if it's okay to jump up. They come to a halt if you've inadvertently taken a wrong turn while walking with them through the park. They walk across the field and nuzzle your pocket to ask for an apple treat. They mass at the barn door to indicate that they want to get out of the rain. Through a vast repertoire of vocalizations, gestures, movements, and signals, domesticated animals tell us what they want and need from us.

This communicating of their subjective good requires that we attend to them, and learn to understand their ways of communicating. First we must recognize that animals are trying to communicate, then we need to observe carefully to interpret individual repertoires, and finally we need to respond appropriately—confirming for the animal that attempts to communicate with us are not a wasted effort. Over time—through a collaborative process of recognition and response—knowledge, trust, and expectation increase and repertoires expand. This is a classic instance of dependent agency. If we start from the premise that animals lack agency, and so do not attend to their signals, this belief becomes self-fulfilling as animals give up their attempts. However, the more that agency is expected and enabled, the greater the resulting capacity to express their subjective good.

Consider some examples. Many humans think that their dog companions aren't fussy about what they eat, or that even if they are, it is up to humans to assert control over their diet. A paternalistic frame reigns. But while some paternalism is inevitable, we exercise far more control over animals' lives than is necessary for their safety. It's true that humans need to ensure that dogs meet their nutritional needs, and that they don't overeat, or eat foods that will poison them. But this still leaves a large area in which dogs can express their food preferences and make their own choices. Through trial and error (and choice amongst options), it became perfectly clear to us that our dog Codie's favourite foods included fennel, kale stems, and carrots. And peas were so prized he simply helped himself from the veggie garden. Fruit really wasn't of interest. On the other hand, his buddy Rolly was mad for bananas. Dogs have individual preferences, and (to varying degrees) the competence to make choices based on their preferences.

Our friend Christine is a great walker, and she and her (late) dog companion Julius spent hours on their daily outings. Christine was always of the view that these walks were for Julius, that they constituted his special time of the day, and that as much as possible she should defer to his wishes about what route to walk, how long to walk, whether to play along the way, whether to swim in the river, and so on. Julius usually walked off leash, and simply led the way. If he fell behind to stop and sniff, and meanwhile Christine came to a decision point in the route and chose the wrong way, then he would stop at the decision point and sit and wait until she looked back, recognized her mistake, and turned back to join him on his chosen route for the day. In other words, not only did he exercise route choice, he understood that this was his prerogative.

Food choices and walk routes may seem like trivial matters in the context of thinking about citizenship, but are they really? In the life of a dog companion, wouldn't questions about what you eat, and how you spend the most active part of your day, in fact be of enormous importance?

What are the outer limits of this potential scope for agency? That's not a question that can be answered in the abstract. It can only be answered by engaging in the process—expecting agency, looking for agency, and enabling agency. And indeed there have been some remarkable examples of people who have gone much further in exploring the possible scope for dogs (and other domesticated animals) to exercise agency. Barbara Smuts describes her relationship with Safi, the dog she adopted from an animal shelter. Smuts didn't 'train' Safi, but very patiently communicated with her, repeated signs, and attended to Safi's signals in return:

> [Safi] understands (in the sense of responding appropriately to) many English phrases, and she, in turn, has patiently taught me to understand her language of gestures and postures (she rarely uses vocal communication). Some dogs bark when they want to go out, but Safi instead gazes at the door, even if she's standing far away, and then looks at me (it took me a while to catch on). If we're out walking, and I become too absorbed in my own thoughts or in talking with other people, she regains my attention by gently touching her nose to the back of my leg in that sensitive spot behind the knee. As I write this paragraph, she leaves the spot where she's been resting for the last hour and gently prods my elbow with her nose, signaling a desire to connect. When I approach her with a similar desire, she's nearly always willing to pause in her activities to attend to me, and I do the same for her. I stop typing, meet her gaze, say her name, and brush the top of her head with my lips. Apparently fulfilled by this brief contact, she leaves me uninterrupted for another hour or two, a restraint specific to those times when I am writing (Smuts 1999: 116).

Elizabeth Marshall Thomas has also engaged in a lengthy project of figuring out how to respect the agency of her dog companions. In *The Hidden Life of Dogs* she provides detailed observations of their individual capacities and choices when given scope for agency, rather than being trained to conform to her expectations:

> To the dogs who stayed with me I gave food, water, and shelter, but after my project began I made no effort to train them, even for housebreaking or coming when called. I didn't need to. The young dogs copied the old dogs, which in their case resulted in perfect housebreaking, and all the dogs naturally came when called most of the time, declining to do so only if our demands conflicted with something that was genuinely important to them. A dog who feels free to make such a distinction shows more of his thoughts and feelings in a single day than a

rigidly trained, hyperdisciplined dog can show in a lifetime. (Thomas 1993: xx–xxi)

Thomas found significant individual variation amongst her dogs in terms of capabilities, and preferences about how, and with whom, to spend their time. The dogs were often allowed to roam and explore freely around the city of Cambridge (Mass.). Mischa was a master navigator, going on long journeys without ever getting lost or running into difficulty coping with cars and other dangers of city life. Maria also loved to roam, but, a hopeless navigator, she inevitably got lost when she wasn't with Mischa. Her solution was to wait on the porch of a house until someone noticed her, checked her tags, and called Thomas to come and collect her. This proved a reliable mechanism which Maria depended on often. It's a classic instance of dependent agency. Maria loves to roam, but can't navigate, so the solution is to find humans to play key enabling roles as a kind of scaffold to support her autonomy.

The capacity for agency is not restricted to companion animals. Farm animals are also capable of expressing their subjective good. Rosamund Young has spent decades observing the cows and other animals on her family's farm in Worcestershire—their friendships and enmities, their individual preferences across a range of activities, their distinctive personalities and intelligences. Kite's Nest Farm offers 'an environment which allows all of the animals the freedom to communicate with or disassociate themselves from us as they choose' (Young 2003: 22). In the space created by this freedom, individual personality and agency emerge.

> For many years we have noticed that if you give cows the opportunity and the time to choose between several alternatives—for instance between staying outside or coming in for shelter, or walking on grass or on straw or concrete, or a choice of diet—then they will choose what is best for them and they will not all choose the same thing... The decision-making process animals are constantly involved in includes choosing exactly what to eat. Nibbling and browsing all sorts of different grasses, herbs, flowers, hedges and tree leaves gives them vital trace elements in their daily diet in the amounts they feel are appropriate: such decisions could not be made so effectively by us. The animals are all individuals. Mass 'legislation' for the entire herd in terms of feed might suit the majority but we have always been concerned with minorities. We have watched cows and sheep eat extraordinary plants in prodigious quantities. Cows will eat dark green, vicious-looking stinging nettles by the cubic yard and sheep often choose pointed, spiky thistle tops or tall, tough dock leaves, particularly after parturition when their energy reserves are depleted... One particularly satisfying fact we have discovered is that if the animals have sustained an injury they like to eat quite large quantities of willow. We hope that this is connected to the origins of aspirin. (Young 2003: 10, 52)

All of these writers provide compelling accounts of dependent agency—agency which arises out of respectful relationship. Smuts describes this respect in terms of a relationship between equals, between persons:

> relating to other beings as persons has nothing to do with whether or not we attribute human characteristics to them. It has to do, instead, with recognizing that they are social subjects, like us, whose idiosyncratic, subjective experience of us plays the same role in their relations with us that our subjective experience of them plays in our relations with them. If they relate to us as individuals, and we relate to them as individuals, it is possible for us to have a *personal* relationship. If either party fails to take into account the other's social subjectivity, such a relationship is precluded. Thus while we normally think of personhood as an essential quality that we can 'discover' or 'fail to find' in another, in the view espoused here personhood connotes a way of being *in relation to others*, and thus no one other than the subject can give it or take it away. In other words, when a human being relates to an individual nonhuman being as an anonymous object, rather than as a being with its own subjectivity, it is the human, and not the other animal, who relinquishes personhood. (Smuts 1999: 118)[12]

Domesticated animals may not *reflect* on the good, but they *have* a good—interests, preferences, desires—and an ability to act, or communicate, in order to achieve their good. Recall Arneil's claim that dependency is a precursor to autonomy, not its antonym. Domesticated animals are dependent on humans to establish a basic framework of security and comfort for them. With this framework in place, they are capable of exercising agency in many areas of their lives, either directly (as when the cows choose which plants they need to eat), or through supported agency (as when Maria uses her 'sit on a stranger's porch' routine to muster up her drive home).

Political Participation

So animals have, and can express, a subjective good. But can this be translated into political participation? Participation is linked to the idea that citizens consent to being democratically governed. In traditional views, this is conceived primarily in terms of the responsibility to be informed, to participate in elections on the basis of this information, and thereby help to shape the shared political community. Once again, we see the strong rationalist inflection at work in this concept of citizenship—participation as an intellectual process of rational reflection, negotiation, and consent.

Earlier, we noted that disability advocates have offered a different conception of political participation—one that reconceives participation and assent in more 'embodied' terms. Clifford (2009) notes how the sheer presence of people with SID alters the political process and debate. Silvers and Francis (2005) propose a trust model in place of the negotiation model of social contract, in which citizens participate in and shape the political community by engaging in social relationships. In other words, assent is reconceived in terms of the continuation of an ongoing relationship of trust, rather than a fixed-in-time agreement.

Can we see domesticated animals in this picture? Much has been written about the invisibility of domesticated animals in modern society. A casual glance at a nineteenth-century newspaper underscores the change—the papers are filled with accounts of 'unruly' cows and pigs running amok in towns and cities. The history of industrialized agriculture is a history of the gradual separation of domesticated animals from human spaces—increasing restriction and confinement, and gradual removal of animals from the centre to the periphery of urban areas. Cities and towns have passed ever more restrictive by-laws to regulate domesticated animal bodies, including animal companions. The latter are more visible than farm animals, but their mobility and access, too, have been significantly curtailed. In recent years there has been a growing challenge to this trend towards confinement and invisibility. People are starting to keep backyard chickens, for example, and challenging by-laws that prevent them from having pigs as companions. The trend is most apparent in the case of dog companions and the burgeoning movement demanding access for them to off-leash parks, public transportation, and holiday destinations.

The invisibility and exclusion of domesticated animals has parallels in the history of people with disabilities—the move towards separation, confinement, and invisibility in the nineteenth century, countered by the late twentieth-century demands for reintegration, mobility, and access. When people with disabilities were rendered invisible from the public sphere, the shape of the political community was altered. Absent bodies could no longer act as a corrective presence, or a shaping force in political life. It is no coincidence that the escalation of separation and invisibility coincided with the height of the eugenics movement, and the most egregious assaults on the rights of people with disabilities. The modern disability movement is focused on issues of reintegration and access, not just because of the difference this makes to the lives of particular individuals, but because of the way that the presence of people with disabilities alters our conception of the political community, and the institutions and structures of communal life. Sheer presence, in other words, constitutes a form of participation.

When we think about the growing movement challenging leash laws and a variety of other restrictions controlling access and movement of dogs in public spaces, we might be inclined to conceptualize this advocacy in terms of human citizenship. It is humans who are doing the advocacy on behalf of themselves and their dogs. Humans are the agents here, doing the articulating and advocating. Dogs are the objects of agency, not the agents themselves. But this is to miss the way in which dogs, by their sheer presence, are advocates and agents of change. Consider some examples. North Americans who travel in Europe, especially France, are often struck by the presence of dogs in public spaces. Dogs travel on the buses and trains. They accompany their humans to movie theatres, shops, and restaurants. In North America, this sort of integration of animals in public spaces is strictly limited by a range of by-laws justified primarily on grounds of public health and safety. Now, if you've never travelled to France, you might unthinkingly accept the standard justifications for this exclusion of animals. You might believe that if dogs were integrated into public spaces there would be epidemics of disease and injury. But then you travel to France and see the dogs everywhere, and you see that civilization hasn't collapsed, and you are forced to reconsider the highly restrictive treatment of animals back home. Notice, in this scenario, that the change in attitude is not the result of human advocacy. It is not necessary for the North American to have a conversation with a French citizen about the integration of dogs in their society. The dogs themselves, by their presence, are agents of change. They are not deliberate agents. But they are agents—leading their lives, doing the things they do—and because this agency is exercised in the public realm it serves as a catalyst for political deliberation.

A similar process is happening within North America through the agency of service dogs. Formerly strict prohibitions on dogs are being relaxed to allow service dogs who assist people with disabilities or who perform other services for humans. The justification for integration of these dogs is to benefit humans, but the impact of their presence is often to raise doubts about more general restrictions on dogs.[13] It becomes much harder to cling to ideas about the dangers of dogs in public spaces when you regularly witness the opposite. In this way, service dogs are acting as agents in the public sphere, altering attitudes, and changing the terms of public debate. In fact, the category of 'service dog' is becoming a site of civil disobedience in the struggle for social reintegration. In a town in eastern Ontario, the owners of a local cheese shop have a companion dog, Justine, who likes to hang out at the shop. This would normally contravene local health by-laws, but Justine has false service dog credentials indicating that she warns her human of impending epileptic seizures, and on these grounds Justine is allowed to accompany her human into otherwise restricted areas.[14] In this way Justine, by her embodied presence, educates the cheese shop customers that she is not a menace to their health, but a welcome addition to society.

A fascinating account of dogs as political participants and agents of change is described by Jennifer Wolch in her discussion of urban dog park activism (Wolch 2002). A public park had become a hang-out for drug-users and prostitutes, abandoned by families and others intimidated by the presence of illegal activity. Then it was 'taken back' by an informal group of dog-owners who invested in improvements and security, and used the presence of large off-leash dogs—illegally—to discourage less desirable uses. Paradoxically, just as the park became more attractive, other local residents signaled their desire to use the park but objected to off-leash dogs, framing the issue as 'dogs versus kids'. Dog-owners prevailed in part by normalizing dogs as legitimate members of the American family and urban community. Like other urban dog parks, this park is now a distinctive place for both people and animals, and remains a locus for grassroots participation in the governance of urban park and recreation facilities. (Wolch 2002: 730–1)

Humans are essential 'enablers' in this story, but it couldn't have happened without the participation of the dogs. Their physical presence and actions played a key role in the political process, resulting not only in their reintegration into public life and space, but in a more general change to grassroots activism in the city. The fact that the dogs cannot reflect about the goals of activism, or their role in it, doesn't change the fact that they are participants in the process. And they are not coerced or captive participants. They are agents, doing what they want to do—exploring, playing, hanging out with their human and dog friends—and by virtue of being present, and carrying on their lives, helping to shape their shared community with humans.

This theme is explored in a recent study on the ripple effect of companion animals on community ethos and interactions (Wood et al. 2007). The presence of companion animals increases social interactions in communities, for example when dogs act as an ice-breaker to conversation. Their presence prompts reciprocal relations between neighbours, such as helping out by feeding the goldfish when the family goes on vacation. Because humans and their dog companions have a presence on the streets and in parks, they increase community members' sense that they live in a vibrant, cohesive, and safe neighbourhood. And finally, companion animals serve as a spur for their humans to participate in community activities. In these myriad ways, companion animals actively foster contact, trust, and reciprocity within communities—the essential glue of citizenship relations.

Political participation also includes protest and dissent. Jason Hribal has explored this dimension of working animals' political agency, including actions such as work stoppages and slow downs, destruction of equipment, escape attempts, and violence (Hribal 2007, 2010). Indeed, Hribal argues that part of the explanation for the rapid transition from horse power to the internal combustion engine in the early twentieth century lies in industrial management's desire to be rid of a disruptive workforce who regularly challenged their working conditions (Hribal 2007). Hribal also examines resistance amongst zoo and circus animals. He argues that zoo/circus authorities have deliberately mislabelled resistance actions by elephants, dolphins, and primates as unintentional accidents or random and instinctive behaviours, ignoring the obvious intent and planning involved. Authorities are well aware that public support for their institutions would be undermined by revelations that animals are desperate to escape their situation, and engaged in active resistance (Hribal 2010).

Cooperation, Self-Regulation, and Reciprocity

Citizens are engaged in the cooperative project of social life. This means that they must engage in various forms of self-restraint—in terms of their actions, and their demands and expectations—in order to foster mutual cooperation and trust. Put colloquially, citizenship is about responsibilities as well as rights, including the responsibility to comply with fair terms of cooperation. As noted, traditional citizenship theory puts a rationalist inflection on the idea of reciprocity. It is not enough to regulate your behaviour in ways that foster social cooperation, you are supposed to do this for the right reasons—that is, out of concern for justice, and respect for your fellow citizens.

However, self-control, compliance with social norms, and cooperative behaviour are all possible without rational reflection. Rational reflection is only sometimes part of the mix, and is always a matter of degree—varying enormously between individuals, and for the same individual in different contexts. Political philosophy typically idealizes reciprocal behaviour motivated by rational reflection, but in terms of the ongoing functioning of society, it is the behaviour, not the motivation, that matters most.

Most of us go through our daily lives respecting social norms forbidding violence, theft, or harassment of others. Social life is only possible because we all know and respect these norms, by and large. Much of the time, our conformity to these norms is completely unreflective. We do it unconsciously, automatically, habitually. If we're given to philosophizing we may occasionally sit back and examine these practices, and changing circumstances might prompt us to pause and reflect. However, it would be paralysing if we stopped to reflect all the time about the ethics of our actions. Most ethical behaviour is habitual. This is particularly striking in the case of heroic moral action. People who have risked their lives to save others—running into a burning house, jumping into a freezing river, breaking cover to help a fallen comrade—often say that they did not stop to reflect. They responded directly to a situation of need in which they perceived they could act. We consider these people moral heroes. Moral action is not just about doing things out of commitment to abstract justifications; it is about moral character and action, and motivations such as love and compassion and fear and loyalty. We all know people who think very carefully about the nature of morality, and yet are quite selfish in their relationships or social actions. And we all know people who engage in unstinting and altruistic social action, and yet are not all that interested in reflecting on the ethics of their conduct.

In the human case, we recognize that morality is deeply complex in this way, involving questions of motive (both rational and emotive), character, action, and consequence. When it comes to animals, however, we focus on just one aspect—rational reflection—and conclude that because animals seem incapable of reflecting on the nature of the good, they are not moral agents. Even in much of the animal advocacy literature, it is assumed that animals are moral patients (the objects of moral action by humans), and never moral agents themselves.

This view is strongly challenged by recent findings in the science of animal behaviour, which shows that animals experience a wide range of emotions, and exhibit a range of moral behaviours such as empathy, trust, altruism, reciprocity, and a sense of fair play.[15] The existence of cooperative and altruistic behaviour amongst animals is not particularly controversial. We all know that wolves and killer whales and countless other animals engage in cooperative hunting and other activities. We are also all familiar with stories of animals helping each other, and helping humans, even in circumstances of great cost to themselves.[16] Less familiar is the research on reciprocity and fairness. Bekoff and Pierce summarize some of the primate research conducted by Sarah Brosnan and Frans de Waal:

> Capuchin monkeys are a highly social and cooperative species in which food sharing is common; the monkeys carefully monitor equity and fair treatment among peers...Brosnan first trained a group of capuchins to use small pieces of rock as tokens of exchange for food. Pairs of females were then asked to barter for treats. One monkey was asked to swap a piece of granite for a grape. A second monkey, who had just witnessed the rock-for-grape trade, was asked to swap a rock for a piece of cucumber, a much less desirable treat. The short-changed monkey would refuse to cooperate with the researchers and wouldn't eat the cucumber and often threw it back at the human. In a nutshell, the capuchins expected to be treated fairly. They seemed to measure and compare rewards in relation to those around them. A single monkey who traded a rock for a cucumber would be delighted with the outcome. It was only when others seemed to get something better that the cucumber suddenly became undesirable. (Bekoff and Pierce 2009: 127–8)

Reciprocal altruism and aversion to inequity (the capuchins' reaction to perceived unfair treatment) indicate that social animals play close attention to the fair sharing of social goods. But it is not just food sharing that is governed by norms of reciprocity. Social animals adhere to norms governing many aspects of their lives, such as mating, playing, and grooming. We tend to dismiss a lot of this behaviour as blind instinct (a drive to dominate, or to reproduce), when in fact it reflects a process of conscious learning, negotiating, and developing social norms.

This is well illustrated by Bekoff's fascinating observations of play behaviour amongst wolves, coyotes, and dogs. Play is related to morality because both involve systems of rules and expectations, and sanctions for violations. Through play, community members are introduced to social norms of reciprocity and fairness.[17] Social play

> rests on foundations of fairness, cooperation, and trust, and it can break down when individuals cheat. During social play, individuals can learn a sense of what's right or wrong—what's acceptable to others—the result of which is the development and maintenance of a social group (a game) that operates efficiently. Thus, fairness and other forms of cooperation provide a foundation for social play. Animals have to continually negotiate agreements about their intentions to play so that cooperation and trust prevail, and they learn to take turns and set up 'handicaps' that make play fair. They also learn to forgive. (Bekoff and Pierce 2009: 116)

Canids invite one another to play by bowing, indicating that play is under way, with its special set of rules. For example, you have to control your power and the strength of your bite so that others aren't hurt. You have to recognize that during play it is okay to transgress rules that apply outside of the play context (e.g. a subordinate animal challenging a dominant one, or a dominant animal submitting to a subordinate). In other words, play levels the playing field, as it were. Self-handicapping of power and status ensures that behaviours that would be threatening in other contexts (biting, mounting, or tackling) are understood to be play. Violations of play are not tolerated—as when a dog becomes too aggressive, or attempts to translate play mounting into an actual sexual act. When a violation occurs play is potentially disrupted, so animals constantly negotiate and reassure each other that they are still playing. Bekoff has observed that the bow is used widely in canid play, not just to initiate play, but to negotiate it on an ongoing basis. If a dog hits or bites a little too hard, and his partner reacts with confusion, the violator will bow by way of apology and reassurance—'Sorry, my bad. Let's keep playing'. If he's about to make an apparently aggressive move he will bow first to indicate 'don't worry, this is just play'. Canids who violate the rules of fair play are excluded from play, and sometimes expelled from the social group altogether (Bekoff and Pierce 2009, Horowitz 2009).[18]

This digression into the fascinating world of canid play shows that dogs have the capacity for understanding and negotiating social rules, and for observing and responding to the expectations of others in the social group. But what does this tell us about the potential for domesticated animal citizenship in mixed human–animal communities? Dogs may understand the rules of good citizenship amongst their own kind, but how does this translate to mixed society? The fact is that dogs display a very similar capacity for negotiating the social rules of human–dog society. Indeed, one of the most striking differences between dogs and wild canids is that dogs are highly attuned to humans, and look to them for social clues and guidance. Tamed wolves and coyotes don't do this. In other words, dogs' repertoire of skills for social cooperation (learning and negotiating norms of acceptable and fair behaviour, attending to the expectations of others) has evolved in a dog–human community. Dogs are remarkably adept at reading human behaviour, and negotiating terms of cooperation.[19]

A wonderful study by Alger and Alger explores friendships between dogs and cats living in the same households. Dog and cat friends often sit or sleep curled up together, and greet and touch each other regularly. They like going for walks together, and will protect one another from outside threats. Most of all, they enjoy playing together. Dogs and cats have specific forms of play which they engage in with their conspecifics. To cross the species divide they must correctly communicate and interpret play overtures and behaviours. For example, cats quickly learn to understand a dog's bow as an invitation to play, even though cats don't themselves bow. Similarly, dogs correctly interpret that cats are inviting play when they do a quick run past, or lie on the ground with all four legs extended. Cohabiting cats and dogs don't understand all of each other's behaviour, but they negotiate a repertoire for communicating with one another. Moreover, this repertoire is not restricted to tight scripts used in their own species play. For example, Alger and Alger found that cats successfully adapted cat greeting and affection behaviours (such as headbutting or tail curling) as invitations to play with dogs, even though they would not use the same behaviours to engage other cats in play (Alger and Alger 2005; see also Feuerstein and Terkel 2008).

It is not just dogs and cats who recognize that they are part of a cooperative community with humans (and each other). Most domesticated animals know to seek out humans for help, either for themselves or for others. Young describes several instances in which cows, anticipating a difficult birth, or concerned for the welfare of another cow, sought human assistance (Young 2003). Masson describes the case of Lulu the pig who saved her human companion Joanne Altsmann. Altsmann was in the kitchen one day and feeling very unwell. Lulu sensed that something was seriously wrong. She forced her body through a dog door, scraping herself and drawing blood in the process. She ran out to the road and lay across it until a car stopped, then led the driver back to the kitchen where Altsmann had suffered a heart attack (Masson 2003). Most animals recognize when vets are trying to help them, even if the process (setting a limb, receiving an injection, undergoing porcupine quill extraction) is uncomfortable. In other words, they understand that they form part of a cooperative society with humans.

We can see this in some of the dog stories we related earlier. It is evident that under conditions of mutual respect, animals can recognize that cooperative society is negotiated on an ongoing basis. Julius knew that his walks with Christine were his special time of the day, and that it was his prerogative to negotiate how this time was spent. Elizabeth Marshall Thomas describes how her dogs respond most of the time when she calls them because she doesn't make unreasonable demands. They ignore her requests only when they have reasonable grounds for doing so. Barbara Smuts gives a wonderful account of this kind of negotiation with her dog Safi over contentious areas such as how to interact with squirrels, cats, and other animals sharing their environment. And the negotiation of social life goes in both directions. Safi has also trained Smuts in a variety of ways—to not step over her when she is asleep, to not clean mud off her stomach except with a very soft cloth. As for the much-hated bath:

> I bring her into the bathroom and suggest that she climb into the tub. Usually, with great reluctance, she does so. But sometimes she chooses not to, in which case she voluntarily travels to the kitchen where she remains until the mud has dried enough for me to brush it off. Similarly, when playing fetch with a toy, Safi drops it when I ask her to only about half the time. If she refuses to drop it, it means either that she's inviting a game of keep-away, or that she wants to rest with her toy for a while before chasing it some more. Since the toys belong to her, and since she never substitutes objects like my new shoes, it seems fair that she decides when to keep the toy and when to share it with me. (Smuts 1999: 117)

All of these cases challenge our conventional notions about humans issuing directives, and dogs obeying them. These dogs are clearly inclined to cooperate and please their human companions, but they are also quite prepared to assert their own preferences, and to (re)negotiate terms of cooperation—in short, to exercise a form of citizenship involving both rights and responsibilities.

We can look at these stories and say, oh well, those are obviously very special and unique animals. Maybe so. But a more appropriate response might be to say, oh well, those are obviously very special and unique humans, that is, humans who recognized dogs as beings who have individual preferences, who are capable of communicating these, and of negotiating the terms of coexistence with their human companions. It's not simply that these animals have special innate capacities (though that is no doubt part of the equation), but that their human companions are prepared to enable the development of these capacities.[20]

How many animals are capable of this kind of self-regulation and negotiation of cooperative life? We can't answer that question, since we've only just begun to ask it. There is enormous uncharted territory here once we recognize domesticated animals as our fellow citizens, rather than chattels, slaves, or alien intruders.

One of the most important unknowns is whether domesticated animals will continue to choose to be part of a mixed society with humans, once given greater freedom and assisted agency. When Elizabeth Marshall Thomas moved to the country and created a very large enclosed territory in which her dogs were free to establish lives of their own choosing, the result was that while they certainly never cut off contact with her, and continued to rely on her for food and emergency assistance, they did withdraw somewhat, gradually reorienting their lives around each other rather than human companions (Thomas 1993). In *The Dogs Who Came to Stay*, George Pitcher describes a story with an opposite trajectory—of Luna the stray dog who gradually came to trust and adopt Pitcher and his partner (Pitcher 1996). Rita Mae Brown describes how her eleven-year-old dog, Godzilla, adopted the next-door neighbour as her primary human, though she returned almost daily to visit Brown on her farm (Brown 2009). And Thomas describes a similar experience with her free-roaming cat, Pula, who opted to live with a family up the road, though she still greets Thomas eagerly when their paths cross (Thomas 2009). In both of these latter instances Godzilla and Pula left multi-animal houses for homes where they were the only animal companion and the sole focus of human attention.

Animal sanctuaries provide some insight into a possible future with domesticated animals. The donkeys at Dancing Star sanctuary in California inhabit a world that lies somewhere between traditional farm life and life in the wild. The donkeys are free to interact with humans on their own terms, and often choose to do so (especially with people they like). They are dependent on humans for certain supports (supplementation of free-roaming diet, security, veterinary care). At the same time, they are integrated into a larger ecosystem. Deer, turkeys, bob cats, mountain lions, and countless smaller birds and creatures also inhabit the sanctuary (Tobias and Morrison 2006). Young's description of the cows at Kite's Nest Farm indicates that they, too, are not cut off from the surrounding ecosystem, but integrated into it. Young's free-roaming cows encounter deer, badgers, foxes, wild cats, and many other creatures in their rambles. They have a foot in both worlds—a shared society with humans, and a role in the larger ecological system extending beyond human settlement (Young 2003). It's possible that some domesticated animals, given greater control over their lives, would choose to completely opt out of shared human–animal society. Masson argues that this might be the case with horses who seem to have the physiological and psychological traits to readily withdraw from humans and successfully 'rewild', but is much less likely with dogs, who are strongly bonded with humans (Masson 2010).

In short, the scope of agency for domesticated animals is unknown. The more we learn about animal capacities, the more potential we see. Moreover, the nature of dependent agency is that it is created through relationship, not deducible from the innate capacities of individuals. As Smuts says, subjectivity/personhood is not a capacity we can either 'discover' or 'fail to find' in another, but rather, a way of 'being in relation' with others.[21] So we must keep an open mind about the potential scope of animal agency, recognizing that it will always be highly variable, and dependent on individual, contextual, and structural factors. Recognizing domesticated animals as citizens means we have a duty to foster their agency, always aware that these capacities vary across individuals and over time, and that they can be blunted or enhanced by our actions, often in unintended or unpredicted ways. All of this is true, we should remember, for human citizens as well as animal ones.

4. Towards a Theory of Domestic Animal Citizenship

To recap the discussion so far, we have argued (a) that justice for domesticated animals requires accepting that they are members of our society, to be included in our social and political arrangements on fair terms; and (b) that citizenship is the appropriate framework for conceptualizing membership, given that domesticated animals have the requisite capacities to be citizens: capacities to have and express a subjective good, to participate, and to cooperate.

But what would this look like in practice? What would it mean to conceive domesticated animals through the lens of membership and citizenship? What forms of use of, or interaction with, domesticated animal citizens would be permitted, under what conditions? There is a natural tendency to want to answer this question by formulating a fixed list of citizenship rights and responsibilities. In our view, this is premature, since such a list can only be the outcome of a process of enabling agency and participation amongst all co-citizens. If domesticated animals were merely passive wards, we could formulate our humanitarian duties to them in advance of their own input or participation. But if animals are co-citizens, with the right to shape collective social and political arrangements, then we need to know more about how they are likely to express their subjective good, and how they are likely to comply with or contest social norms. This will be an ongoing process with unpredictable outcomes.

However, we can at least think about what is entailed or presupposed by ideas of membership/citizenship (and conversely what is inconsistent with them). We will try to identify the presuppositions of citizenship in nine areas:

1) basic socialization
2) mobility and the sharing of public space
3) duties of protection
4) use of animal products
5) use of animal labour
6) medical care
7) sex and reproduction
8) predation/diet
9) political representation

This is not an exhaustive list, but it does cover many of the most pressing moral issues regarding the relations between humans and domesticated animals. In each case, our aim is not to provide a conclusive resolution of all the challenges involved, but rather to show how a citizenship framework provides a distinctive lens for thinking about our obligations; one that goes beyond traditional ART, and one that is more compelling than the various abolitionist, threshold, and 'species norm' views we discussed in Chapter 4.

Basic Socialization

Membership in any community involves a process of socialization, and so any theory of citizenship has to say something about how individuals are socialized into membership. Existing members must pass on the basic skills and knowledge that children or newcomers will need to fit in and flourish. In the human case, failure to socialize a child is a form of abuse, like failing to feed, protect, or nurture. This is true of domesticated animals as well. Animals, like human infants, arrive in the world ready to learn, ready to explore, ready to figure out the rules, ready to find their place. If we fail to channel this readiness appropriately, we harm them. Socialization in this sense is a right of membership. Failure to socialize domesticated animals blights their chances of flourishing in human–animal society.

We should note here that basic socialization is different from training for particular forms of labour (such as training dogs to be guide dogs for the blind). Socialization involves the basic and general skills/knowledge that individuals need to learn (insofar as possible) in order to be accepted into social community—like establishing control over bodily processes and impulses, learning basic communication, rules of social interaction, and respect for others. Training, on the other hand, is about developing a particular individual's capacities and interests. Socialization is a basic threshold precondition for social membership. (We return to the question of training for domesticated animals later in the chapter.)

We all have a basic right to be socialized into a community, but into which community? Here is where our citizenship model differs clearly from other accounts. How we define the boundaries and membership of the political community will shape our understanding of what constitutes appropriate socialization for any particular individual. For example, if we think of cat community as defined strictly by species, then we will think of cat socialization in terms of learning the basic norms and knowledge of cat society, a process guided by adult cats. But if we also think of cats as members of a mixed human–animal community, then the right of basic socialization encompasses the norms and knowledge needed for cats to flourish in that mixed society, not just in cat society. Moreover, the same goes for human members of mixed society. At the moment, learning how to live with the animals in our midst is part of socialization for some humans, within certain families or subcultures, but certainly not all. However, if we recognize domesticated animals as members of a joint political community, then a certain level of basic socialization in both directions becomes mandatory—part of recognizing and respecting each other as co-citizens. Just as socialization for citizenship involves learning how to respect, cooperate, and participate with people of different races and religions, so too it should involve learning about the sorts of cooperative relations with domesticated animals we discussed earlier.

However, the content of what constitutes appropriate socialization is an open question. It can vary widely according to the circumstances. A horse born into a free-roaming horse sanctuary who will have limited contact with humans doesn't need much socialization into mixed human society since his agency will be exercised primarily amongst other horses, and they will look after his basic socialization needs (including the basics of getting along with other animals, like rattlers or mountain lions, who might share the same geographic territory). A dog adopted into a human family, on the other hand, needs to learn quite a bit more about getting along in mixed human–animal society. The community in which she will flourish, and in which she must learn to respect some basic rights of others, is a community that includes not just other dogs and humans, but possibly cats, squirrels, birds, and others. She needs to be housebroken, to learn not to bite or to jump up on people, to be wary of cars, and not to chase the family cat (unless it's a play chase!), for example. She will learn not just from other dogs, but also from humans, and possibly the cat too. In other words, even if we conceive all domesticated animals as members of a mixed human–animal political community, requiring some degree of mutual socialization, the actual content of appropriate socialization will vary greatly according to circumstances.

Nevertheless, while the content of socialization is adaptable to individual and contextual factors, there are some general principles that should guide the process. The first, as noted, is that socialization should be conceived, not as the right of parents or states to mould individuals, but as the responsibility of parents or states to recognize individuals as members of the community, and to give them the skills and knowledge they need to thrive in that community, insofar as possible.

Second, socialization is not a lifelong process of control and intervention, but a temporary developmental process for bringing individuals into full membership of the community. It is justified, not as an end in itself, but because it facilitates the emergence of agency and the capacity to participate. By a certain point individuals have either internalized the basic norms, or they have not. Either way, the duty of others to mould them ends with childhood. At a certain point respect requires that we accept that people are who they are—full citizens, warts and all. After that, individuals who violate basic norms may be humorously tolerated, shunned, or, if they become a danger to others, locked up. But it would be disrespectful to continue to treat them like children. There are exceptions to this general picture, of course, as when childhood trauma, abuse, or neglect has severely delayed or limited socialization. But in general, we are 'moulded' when we are young, and then respected as autonomous agents as we achieve adulthood.

Recognizing domesticated animals as citizens implies that a similar approach is appropriate—that is, that we attend to basic socialization when they are young, but do not see them as subject to lifelong moulding. Acceptable paternalism allows for a limited period in which adults socialize the young, but it would be pernicious paternalism (indeed domination) to turn this into a lifelong relationship of moulder–moulded. And yet many people seem to view domesticated animals as permanent children in this sense, subjecting them to continuous efforts at moulding well past the age when they achieve adulthood. (People with SID are also frequently subject to this kind of pernicious paternalism.)[22]

In addition to limiting the duration of socialization, we also, in the human context, recognize strict limitations on *how* it is undertaken. There has been great variation in socialization methods over time and across cultures. In liberal democracies a clear trend has emerged away from coercive and authoritarian methods towards a positive reinforcement and gentle correction model of how the process should work. Harsh punishment and threats are generally viewed as unnecessary and unproductive (not to mention abusive). For the most part, wild animals also socialize their members without much violence or coercion. As is clear from Bekoff's discussion of wild canids, play is a key component in the socializing process, guiding the young towards knowledge of social norms in a non-threatening context. Many social animals, like humans, are generally amenable to socialization through methods of positive reinforcement and gentle correction.[23] We all come into the world eager and primed to learn how to fit in, a situation which calls for wise guidance, not threat and force. The fact that socialization of domesticated animals by humans is so often harsh and coercive is a comment, not on the capacities of animals, but on the ignorance, impatience, and disrespect of humans.[24]

Freedom of Movement and the Sharing of Public Space

To accept domesticated animals as members of our community means accepting that they belong here in the community, and have the prima facie right to share its public spaces. Acknowledging membership is inconsistent with confining individuals to private seclusion or to designated segregation zones. Yet that is precisely how contemporary societies typically treat domesticated animals. We greatly restrict the free movement of domesticated animals, both by the use of *physical restraint*—crates and cages, fenced runs, chains, leashes, etc.—and by the use of *mobility restrictions* on access to public spaces, businesses, beaches, parks, public transportation, or even city limits (in the case of agricultural animals). In fact, we devote a remarkable amount of time and energy to controlling domesticated animals—to keeping them in their place. This extreme containment helps maintain their invisibility, allowing us to delude ourselves about the ubiquity and significance of their presence in our lives.[25]

This enormous exercise of confinement constitutes a serious violation of domesticated animals' basic rights, and indeed violates even minimal standards of protection against cruelty. But what sorts of regulations on freedom of movement and access are permissible within a citizenship model? How do we distinguish acceptable from unacceptable restrictions? We consider first the case of the negative right against being restrained or confined. We then consider the more positive right to mobility.

In the human context, we consider the right against confinement/restraint as a fundamental right, to be suspended only under conditions that meet a very demanding test of need and proportionality. For example, we might restrain individuals who pose a serious threat to themselves or others, either intentionally (e.g., violent aggressors, suicidal individuals), or unintentionally (e.g., someone infected with a life-threatening contagion, or high on drugs/ alcohol and about to engage in high-risk behaviour). Most of these restraints are justified on a temporary basis only, until an immediate risk has been removed. But we also impose physical confinement in more enduring ways as a form of justified paternalism. We use forms of restraint and confinement with infants and children for several years until they can safely negotiate their environment. Such restrictions call for clear justification, however.

Historically, people with disabilities or mental illness have been confined in ways that far exceed an acceptable paternalism. This should make us wary of calls for confinement/restraint that are alleged to be in the interests of the person being subject to restriction.[26]

The positive right to mobility is viewed in less absolute terms than the negative right against restraint. Our right to mobility is circumscribed in a number of ways—most notably by international borders, and by private property laws. Both of these are modern developments, leading some commentators to equate modernity with growing restrictions on our mobility rights. However, mobility has always been circumscribed. In the modern world this takes the form of geographical/political boundaries, whereas historically it tended to take the form of social position (e.g., your movement was strictly controlled by your status as a serf, soldier, member of nobility, or cleric), but free movement has always been constrained by socio-political (not to mention practical) limitations.

While some cosmopolitan theorists call for an unqualified right to mobility, most theorists recognize that mobility matters because, and insofar as, it is necessary to provide us with access to a reasonable range of options for leading a flourishing life. We have a right to adequate or sufficient mobility, not unlimited mobility (Baubock 2009; Miller 2005, 2007). To be sure, restrictions on mobility can operate to perpetuate unjust inequalities within and between states. Under conditions of injustice, restrictions on mobility—such as the right of rich people to keep others off their property, or of rich countries to keep out people from poor countries—become a key mechanism for preserving privilege. However, the underlying problem here is inequality, not restrictions on mobility per se. If we imagine a world that has eliminated unfair inequalities between states, or between citizens within a given state, then restrictions on mobility are not inherently unjust. It's important to many people to be able to move and work freely within their country, and, for many, to travel and see other parts of the world. But it doesn't follow that we have a right to become citizens of any country of our choosing, or that all private property should be abolished, or that governments shouldn't be able to block off unsafe beaches and treacherous roads, or control access to fragile ecosystems and cultural sites. In other words, we need enough mobility to be able to lead our lives, make a living, socialize, learn, grow, and have fun—but, assuming this scope of mobility is in place, we do not have a right to go anywhere we want, or to move anywhere we want. Whereas physical restraint is always prima facie harmful, bounded mobility is not, so long as people have a sufficient range of good opportunities within those bounds.

Mobility is also a key relative marker of social standing and inclusion. Oppressed groups invariably find their mobility rights restricted—consider Nazi restrictions on Jews in the 1930s, the Bantustan system in South Africa, caste restrictions in India, Jim Crow in the USA, or travel restrictions imposed on women in Saudi Arabia. In other words, mobility is important not just because we need it to be able to carry out our lives as we see fit, but also because it functions as a way of distinguishing full citizens from subordinated groups, especially by restricting their access to public space. It is possible for a particular restriction to pass the 'sufficient options' test (i.e., it doesn't impose an unreasonable restriction on someone's ability to lead a flourishing life), while failing the social inclusion test. For example, even if the Jim Crow lunch counters for blacks were just as good as the ones for whites ('separate but equal'), they would have functioned as a mark of social exclusion and inequality. These forms of exclusion are designed to send the message that certain individuals or groups do not belong here with us, and that they need to be kept in their (subordinate) place.

In addition to blatant and intentionally discriminatory restrictions on mobility, there are unintentional forms of mobility discrimination. Consider the case of people with physical disabilities for whom the structure of modern cities, designed with the able-bodied in mind, acts as a barrier to mobility and access. These oversights may be unintentional, but they highlight unexamined assumptions about who is considered a full citizen. Full citizenship is measured not just by being included in a list of legal rights-holders, but by being considered when the institutions of a shared society are being conceived. Part of being recognized as a full citizen is that the very shape of public space and movement is designed with your input and your needs in mind.

So, differential restrictions of mobility can function as direct forms of social exclusion, or as indirect markers of inequality. But not all forms of differential restriction are an assault on dignity, or a marker of inequality. Often mobility rights are connected to occupational roles. For example, security or maintenance workers, theatrical performers, scholars, and countless other occupational groups have access to public spaces to which other citizens do not, and this is not problematic. Such restrictions do not compromise anyone's access to sufficient options. Nor do they function as a tool of social exclusion. Similarly, restricting children's access to strip clubs or adult cinemas is an acceptable form of paternalism which passes the sufficient options and social exclusion tests. And, as discussed in relation to confinement/restraint, there are times when mobility rights of adults are limited on paternalistic grounds, or by the need to protect others. We restrict people from driving if they cannot demonstrate competence; we restrict some people from air travel if they have a medical condition (or are in an advanced state of pregnancy) which might put them at risk; we issue injunctions to prevent individuals from approaching near to others whom they have threatened in the past. In yet other cases we allow people to move freely only on condition that they wear a monitoring device (e.g., certain parolees), or submit to chemical castration (e.g., as an alternative to incarceration for a repeat sex offender).

Our purpose here isn't to defend any particular catalogue of mobility rights and restrictions in a liberal society, but rather, to draw, in broad strokes, a general picture of how we think about the right of free movement. To summarize, in the human case, we can see three basic principles:

(1) a very strong presumption against any form of restraint or confinement, except in cases where individuals pose a demonstrable threat to themselves or to the basic liberties of others;

(2) a positive right to sufficient mobility providing access to an adequate range of options needed for a flourishing life;

(3) opposition to restrictions on mobility, even if they leave individuals with sufficient options, if (a) they are adopted in order to express second-class or subordinate citizenship (e.g., Jim Crow-style segregation); or (b) they have emerged inadvertently because certain groups were simply not considered when designing access to certain spaces and places (e.g., access for people with disabilities). Such restrictions are inconsistent with acknowledging the full membership of all individuals in the community.

In our view, the same basic principles can and should apply when thinking about the mobility rights of domesticated animals, although their detailed application will naturally differ. The first principle arguably does not depend on recognizing domesticated animals as co-citizens: it could be endorsed from within a wardship model, or indeed any approach that prohibits harm to sentient beings. But the second and third principles, we believe, are tied to recognition of domesticated animals as co-citizens. They reflect positive obligations we have in virtue of having brought domesticated animals into our community, thereby acquiring the responsibility to (re)shape our collective society to accommodate those animals fairly.

Our current treatment of domesticated animals violates all of these principles. It violates the strong prima facie presumption against confinement and restraint. Indeed, far from being presumptively illegitimate, there seems to be a general presumption that such restrictions are necessary and justifiable as a matter of human convenience. We restrain/confine domesticated animals with muzzles, leashes, chains, cages, and pens. We also violate the requirement to provide sufficient positive mobility, and we do so in ways that are both intentionally discriminatory (animals don't belong here, they need to be kept in their subordinate place), and unintentional (we just didn't consider their interests when designing access to public space).[27] All of this is done as a matter of course, with no sense that such extraordinary restrictions call for extraordinary justification. We have general proscriptions (e.g., 'all dogs must be leashed', 'no pets allowed', 'no chickens within city limits') restricting the free movement of animals, without any consideration of the capacity of individual animals to safely negotiate a range of human–animal environments without restraint, or the impact of these restrictions on either the flourishing of animals or their standing as members of a shared community.

This approach would no longer be acceptable if we recognized domesticated animals as co-citizens. This is not to say that restrictions cannot be justified. As in the case of humans, animals need sufficient mobility, not unlimited mobility. This need may be adequately met with large fenced ranges and pastures, and parks. And mobility restrictions are also justifiable on the grounds of protecting domesticated animals from predators, from highways, or from other dangers, and on the basis of protecting people from animals. Some forms of confinement and restraint can be justified as paternalistic developmental measures (e.g., to socialize a dog so that he will be able, in time, to exercise responsible adult agency). They can be justified for adult dogs who have not learned to be street smart, or to resist chasing squirrels, or jumping up on people. In other words, dogs vary greatly in terms of their ability to negotiate the reciprocal boundaries of social life. Some will need more restraint than others, either to protect them or to protect others. The point is that, as citizens, animals would be presumed to have the skills for negotiating social life, a right to be taught those skills, and an opportunity to appeal arbitrary restrictions on their freedom of movement. No doubt there would still be many justifiable restrictions on animals' movement, but these would always have a provisional status—open to appeal, negotiation, and ongoing evolution. We simply don't know what human–animal society might eventually look like under these conditions.

It may be difficult to fulfil this sufficient mobility principle for some domesticated animals. Consider goldfish or the recently domesticated budgerigars. On the one hand, domesticated budgies and goldfish have lost some of their fitness for survival in the wild, so we can't simply turn them loose. On the other hand, providing them with tanks or aviaries that meet the test of sufficient mobility is a large undertaking. In such cases, the commitments of a citizenship approach may not be achievable. Where there is no prospect for rewilding but nor can we provide the mobility conditions needed for a flourishing domesticated existence, a citizenship model may fail, and we may well be pushed towards the abolitionist/extinctionist position. But there is no reason to assume that this is true of all or most domesticated animals.[28]

A citizenship approach would not only challenge the acceptability of restrictions on the free movement of animals, it would also require us to learn how to enhance accessibility and reduce barriers to mobility. We need to ask how we can alter our infrastructure, habits, and expectations in order to help domesticated animals act as responsible co-citizens (i.e., citizens who can follow the basic rules of social community, and not endanger themselves or others), and to ensure that we aren't imposing arbitrary or unnecessary barriers to their mobility. Recall Catherine MacKinnon's famous dictum about the structure of American society being an affirmative action programme for men (MacKinnon 1987: 36). It's fascinating to start thinking about how human societies are an affirmative action programme for those who walk on two legs (instead of four, or use a wheelchair or a walker), whose sight lines are above five feet, who rely primarily on visual signs (instead of auditory or olfactory) or human language (rather than symbols or sign language), and so on. When you start thinking in this way, the issues don't always line up with humans on one side and animals on the other. Dogs, cats, and children, due to their height, are all vulnerable to being run over by cars backing up. People in wheelchairs find stairs a great impediment, as some animals do. Foreign visitors are often as mystified by linguistic information as most animals are. And, as is sometimes the case for people with disabilities, animals can have compensatory abilities. In the case of animals, these include a more acute sense of smell, attention to body language, physical speed and agility, and so on. Animals are better able to negotiate many contexts than humans (e.g., threading through crowds or streams of traffic, jumping obstacles, maintaining balance on precarious footing, locating food sources). In other words, integrating domesticated animals into the polis involves rethinking our shared spaces on multiple levels—not just removing barriers to mobility, but thinking about what special abilities animals bring to the mix.

Similarly, we need to think about whether, and how, restrictions on mobility and access can function as markers of inferiority. Consider North American bans on animal companions accompanying humans into restaurants. This is typically justified on grounds of food safety. However, as we discussed earlier, the absence of such bans in countries like France has not resulted in outbreaks of disease. In fact what seems to be at stake here are certain ideas about 'where animals belong', or disgust reactions to seeing animals in proximity to food. In other words, such blanket bans are more closely akin to 'Blacks to the back of the bus' or 'No Jews allowed' than they are to 'Employees must wash hands after using the restroom' or 'All passengers must wipe their feet on the antibacterial mat'. Such restrictions, in addition to violating the principles of demonstrated need and proportionality discussed earlier, function as social markers of hierarchy. They simultaneously bar certain groups from full citizenship and at the same time help to render invisible those who have been barred. In effect, we are back to the Victorian household in which the servants are restricted to the back stair—second class, and invisible.[29]

To summarize, recognizing animals as citizens has three key implications for mobility rights. First, it means extending to domesticated animals the same general presumption against restraint/confinement, and the positive right to sufficient mobility for leading a flourishing life. Second, citizenship theory encourages us to attend to questions of structural inequality—that is, is society constructed in ways that limit unnecessarily the mobility of certain individuals or groups? And finally, it asks us to attend to questions of recognition and respect—that is, are there ways in which society uses arbitrary restrictions on mobility as a way of marking inferior status?

Duties of Protection

Recognizing domesticated animals as co-citizens has implications for our duties to protect them from harm, including harm from human beings, harm from other animals, and more generally harm from accidents or natural disasters. We will say a few words about each of these cases. As with the issue of mobility, some of these duties do not depend on the status of domesticated animals as citizens, but simply on their status as beings with a subjective good whose basic rights should be respected. Others, however, are tied specifically to the fact of membership.

Citizens are entitled to the full benefit and protection of the law, and this means that the duty of humans not to harm animals is not simply a moral or ethical responsibility, but ought to be a legal one. Harms to animals, like harms to humans, should be criminalized. This would include both the criminalization of deliberate harm, and also of negligence leading to harm or death. But, as we all know, there is often a world of difference between the law on the books and what is actually enforced. Laws against wife assault were, for many years, simply ignored, and rarely investigated or prosecuted. The same is true today about many existing laws against animal cruelty. Indeed, one measure of the extent to which individuals are truly acknowledged as co-citizens is precisely whether they actually receive the effective protection of the law.

As a society, when it comes to serious crimes against human beings, we invest enormous resources to prevent these crimes in the first place, or, when they occur, to find the perpetrators, subject them to criminal proceedings, and pay for their incarceration and treatment if necessary. Our extensive criminal justice system serves several functions: protecting the vulnerable, deterring crime, enacting deserved retribution in proportion to the blameworthiness of the guilty party, and restoring communities to wholeness after a violation. But perhaps its greatest function is simply to show how seriously we, as a society, take the protection of basic rights by backing up our commitment with enforcement mechanisms. We all grow up under the umbrella of these mechanisms, learning from the earliest age that respect for the basic rights of others is a vital glue of social life. Most of us internalize these injunctions, and have no desire to contravene them. Recognizing that domesticated animals are co-citizens would entail viewing that they too are owed full protection under the law, and that the criminal law should be used to reflect and uphold their membership in the community.

Does this principle entail that people who intentionally kill a dog or cat should be subject to the same sorts of penalties as the murderers of humans? In a recent article about a chimpanzee who was shot after escaping confinement in the UK, Cavalieri asked why his killers were not tracked down and prosecuted, and looked forward to 'a time when this killing will be seen for what it is—murder' (Cavalieri 2007). We, too, look forward to such a time. But the relationship between criminalization and punishment is complex. Punishment serves a variety of functions: to deter future transgressions; to send a symbolic message of society's abhorrence of a particular action; to enact deserved retribution in proportion to the blameworthiness of the guilty party; and to enable the victim (or his/her family) to feel closure. These different functions often pull in different directions in the human case, and are likely to do so in the animal case as well. For example, the blameworthiness of an individual's transgression is often understood in terms of the extent to which she has deliberately and flagrantly violated well-established social norms that she was socialized to uphold. Where those social norms are not yet well established, or where individuals have not been socialized to uphold those norms, the guilty party is likely to be less deserving of punishment. However, it may be precisely in those circumstances that the deterrence function calls for stronger punishment, so as to establish more firmly these new social norms of respect for animal life. This suggests that sentencing guidelines are likely to change over time in light of evolving social norms and patterns of socialization.[30]

As we discuss in Chapters 6 and 7, the deliberate killing of non-citizen animals—whether animals in the wild or liminal animals in urban space—should also be criminalized (just as prohibitions on murder and harm apply equally to human visitors and aliens, not just to citizens).[31] But other duties of protection may apply only to co-citizen domesticated animals, rather than to all animals. For example, domesticated animal citizens need protection not only from humans, but also from other animals. We need to take steps to protect them from predators, disease, accidents, floods, or fires. In these cases, it is their status as members of our society, and not just their intrinsic moral status as sentient beings, that calls forth our duties of protection and rescue.

As we write this chapter, two interesting controversies have emerged that illustrate our theme. The first concerned news footage of the Los Angeles fire department rescuing a dog during a flood—one in a long series of similar controversies concerning the rescuing of domesticated animals in cases of disaster, such as the Katrina hurricane.[32] Some defenders of these efforts responded that rescuing animals provides good training for the rescue of humans. In our view, the moral injunction is much simpler: having brought such animals into our society, we take upon ourselves a duty to protect them. As we see in Chapter 6, we do not have a comparable duty to, say, protect squirrels in the wild from floods or forest fires, or to protect them from their natural predators. The second example concerned how to deal with a coyote that had moved into a neighbourhood of Toronto from the surrounding woods, and was believed to be killing local dogs and cats. Similar scenarios are occurring throughout coyotes' expanding North American range. In our view, there is a duty to protect domesticated animals from this sort of predation. (In Chapter 7 we discuss a variety of measures for doing so without violating the rights of urban coyotes.) Again, this is a duty owed to co-members. We have no comparable duty to protect, say, voles in the wild from the coyote, and no right to interfere with the predatory activities of coyotes living in the wild.

Use of Animal Products

As we discussed in Chapter 4, several ART authors have attempted to distinguish between the (legitimate) 'use' of animals and their (illegitimate) 'exploitation'. As these authors rightly note, in the human context, we often use others in a variety of ways to satisfy our needs and desires, and this is not necessarily morally problematic. Many economic and other forms of exchange in human society provide examples of benign use, including exchanges of human body products such as hair and blood. The question is, when do such uses tip into exploitation?

We argued that this distinction, while sound, can only be drawn in light of an underlying theory of membership. What counts as exploitation of immigrants, for example, cannot be answered simply by asking whether they are better off than they would have been in their country of origin. (For refugees fleeing famine or civil war, virtually any form of existence, even slavery, might be an improvement.) And what counts as exploitation of children cannot be answered simply by asking whether they are better off than they would have been if they had not been born at all. (Again, even the most slavish life for children might be better than not being born at all.) Rather, we need to ask what forms of use are consistent with full membership in society, and what forms of use condemn people to the status of a permanently subordinated caste or class.

In the human case, we have a number of guidelines and safeguards to mark this distinction. For example, children or immigrants may be temporarily denied the rights of full citizenship (while they mature, or integrate into a new society), but not permanently so. At a certain point, all citizens must have the freedom to make choices about their lives (where they live, work, socialize, etc.), determining for themselves how they will be 'used' by others. In other words, a chief protection against exploitation is that individuals have options, and the freedom to exit exploitative situations. We may bring children and immigrants into the community with the expectation of benefiting from them, but once they enter the community, they are full rights-bearing members. We can benefit from their work, but we cannot unilaterally impose a life plan on them, or restrict their access to the full benefits of citizenship.

So too, we believe, with domesticated animals. Using others is legitimate if the terms of the relationship reflect and uphold the membership status of both parties, rather than permanently subordinating one to the other, and this, in turn, requires (as far as possible) respecting their agency and choices. Because domesticated animals are significantly dependent on humans throughout their lives, they are particularly vulnerable to exploitation. It is very difficult for animals to exercise a right of exit, or to put up effective resistance to exploitative conditions. The tendency to ignore animal agency—for humans to 'call all the shots' in Zamir's words—is overwhelming. Given that humans have a great stake in using animals, there is an omnipresent danger that they will adopt a self-serving picture of animals' needs and preferences. This is why we have emphasized the need to recognize and enable animal agency. We have a responsibility to try to understand what animals are able to communicate to us about their needs and preferences, and to facilitate their realization of their own life projects.

This does not mean that we cannot use animals, or benefit from them, but it does mean that we can only do so under conditions that are consistent with their agency and their membership status. Let us first consider some uses that fall into the benign category. Many people derive enormous pleasure from watching dogs running freely and playing at the dog park. There is a sense in which we are using the dogs for our pleasure, but our use in no way impedes or harms them. Nor does it impose a totalizing instrumental conception on them—that is, the fact that we derive pleasure from them does not mean that 'dogs only exist to give humans pleasure'. Humans may bring dogs into their lives for pleasure (and company, love, and inspiration), but this is compatible with dogs existing in and for themselves (as it is in the case of humans).

Now let us consider a more obvious example of use. Imagine the town of Sheepville, in which a flock of sheep are full citizens of the community they share with humans. Their basic rights are protected. They enjoy the full benefits of citizenship. They roam freely in various large pastures with lots of shelter, and a variety of food sources, under the watchful eye of humans who protect them from predators, tend to their medical needs, and supplement their diet appropriately. Humans benefit from the company of the sheep, but they also benefit in other ways. At certain times of year the sheep roam public parks and keep the grass short. Or, as on the Danish island of Samso, they graze around the fields of solar panels, keeping the grass from growing up and obscuring the panels. Or, as in many parts of Europe, their grazing simply helps to maintain open pastoral areas which support a diversity of other flora and fauna (Fraser 2009; Lund and Olsson 2006). In addition to this grazing activity, humans benefit from collecting sheep droppings and using it to fertilize their flower and vegetable gardens. These uses seem to be utterly benign—the sheep are just doing what sheep do, and humans are benefiting from this uncoerced activity.

Now let us consider a trickier example. Should humans in Sheepville use wool from sheep? Commercial wool operations harm sheep in many ways, subjecting animals to painful and frightening procedures in order to make wool gathering a profitable business (quite apart from the fact that the sheep eventually go to slaughter). But one can imagine ethical conditions under which humans can benefit from the use of sheep wool. Whereas wild sheep naturally shed their coats, domesticated sheep have been selectively bred to increase wool production, and many breeds have lost the ability to shed their coats.[33] They need their wool to be shorn by humans once a year to protect them from disease and overheating. At Farm Sanctuary in upper New York State, the sheep are shorn annually because it is in their interest that shearing be performed. Indeed, it would be an abuse to fail to shear them. The sanctuary minimizes the discomfort and stress of shearing as much as possible. Their expert shearer is very careful to keep the animals calm, and to make sure they are not nicked by the shears. After shearing, the sheep are clearly relieved to be free of the weight of their coats. But what then to do with the wool? Since Farm Sanctuary is philosophically opposed to any human use of animals, the wool is not used by humans, but spread in the woods for use as bedding by birds and other animals.[34]

In a world that views domesticated animals in overwhelmingly instrumental terms, this may be an appropriate gesture for unsettling widespread human attitudes about our right to use animals. However, if we are attempting to imagine a just human–animal society in Sheepville, then a refusal to allow humans to use the sheep's wool, which must be shorn anyway for their own benefit, begins to look perverse. It rests on a presumption either that (a) any use is necessarily exploitative, or (b) use will inevitably lead down a slippery slope to exploitation. Regarding the first point—that use is necessarily exploitative—we have already challenged this conflation by reference to the human case. Use is not necessarily exploitative, and indeed a refusal to use others— effectively to prevent them from contributing to the general social good—can itself be a form of denying them full citizenship. (Consider, here, how denial of certain occupations to human groups—for example, excluding Jews from professions, or prohibiting Israeli Arabs from serving in the military—is a mark of second-class citizenship.) Citizenship is a cooperative social project, one in which all are recognized as equals, all benefit from the goods of social life, and all, according to their ability and inclination, contribute to the general good. Turning one group into a permanently subordinated caste that labours for others is a denial of citizenship, but refusing to consider that group as potential contributors to a common good is also a way of denying citizenship.

The mode of contribution will vary greatly. Some may contribute simply by participating in loving and trusting relationships, others might contribute in more material ways.[35] What is important is that all be enabled to contribute in a way suited to them. This is a vital component of dignity—not just the self-respect we derive from contributing (after all, not everyone has the mental capacities for feeling self-respect), but the respect in which we are held by others by virtue of our contributions. Farm Sanctuary separates domesticated animals out as a special class of protected beings, rather than conceiving of them as co-citizens of a mixed human–animal polity. But protection need not be antithetical to use. If Sheepville allowed the human use of wool, everyone's interests could still count equally, and everyone's rights could still be protected. Moreover, everyone would be viewed as contributing to the social good. Individuals would vary enormously in terms of their capacities, agency, and degrees of dependency and independence, but they would all be viewed as willing participants in the social project, not as a special class excluded from the give and take of communal life.

This still leaves the second worry: that there is a slippery slope from use to exploitation. But, as in all slippery slope concerns, we need to consider carefully the kinds of stoppers we have in place. The primary cause of slippery slope pressure is commercialization. When the profit motive is introduced, there is strong pressure towards exploitation. For example, steps to minimize the discomfort to sheep of the shearing process tend to cost more money. If you want to increase profit, you might be tempted to minimize these steps. Obviously, similar pressures exist in human economic activity—pressures to increase work hours, reduce pay, compromise workplace safety, and so on. In the human case, workers (in a just society) can resist the slippery slope through collective bargaining, political action, or the right of exit. Animals, too, can exercise forms of resistance (Hribal 2007, 2010). Moreover, it would be possible, in Sheepville, to ensure that similar protections are in place for sheep via trustees who bargain, agitate, or advocate on their behalf. If for some reason it were not possible to protect sheep from the exploitative pressures of the profit motive, then commercialization of wool and wool products could simply be banned. After the annual shearing, Sheepville could allow residents to use the wool as they see fit, but prohibit them from selling it, or products made from it. (Or, it could be a non-profit arrangement in which earnings are used entirely for the maintenance of the sheep.)

There is room here for reasonable disagreement about whether commercialization of wool products is antithetical to respecting the rights of sheep citizens—that is, whether in the context of a group of citizens who are distinctly vulnerable to exploitation, commercialization pressures are simply too dangerous to their interests. In the human context, we see similar concerns about vulnerable groups. Is it best to prohibit children from working for money, or to carefully regulate this work? Or, in the case of people with severe intellectual disabilities, should employment be prohibited, not for profit, or profit-oriented? Prohibition denies individuals an opportunity for reciprocal citizenship. The profit motive generates a responsibility for enormous caution and oversight to protect vulnerable workers from exploitation.

What about other animal products, such as eggs and milk? As in the case of sheep, the dangers here rapidly escalate with commercialization. If chickens or cows are brought into the world in order to derive profit from their eggs or milk, this will almost certainly entail sacrificing their basic rights. Currently, the egg system involves not only horrific confinement and abuse of hens, but the killing of male chicks, and the killing of hens when their egg production levels off, all of which is needed to sustain profitability.

But let us imagine citizen chickens whose rights are fully protected, and who enjoy the same rights as other citizens to be supported in leading a flourishing life. Domesticated hens produce many eggs. They could be allowed to incubate some fertilized eggs, and have the opportunity to raise young, and yet still have many surplus eggs. Indeed, it is possible to identify the sex of embryos in the egg, and to allow hens to incubate females only (or primarily). Is it wrong for humans to use these surplus eggs? (Or to feed them to their cats, as discussed below?) At Farm Sanctuary, consistent with their position on wool, human consumption of eggs is forbidden (instead they are fed back to the chickens). We would argue, analogously to the wool discussion, that human use of eggs is not inherently exploitative. Humans could have chicken companions on the farm or in large backyards—chickens with flourishing lives, allowed plenty of scope to do what chickens like to do, chickens who explore and play and form social bonds and raise young under the watchful eyes of humans who protect them, shelter them, and care for their food and medical needs. And meanwhile, humans could consume some of the chickens' eggs. It's true that this relationship would in part be based on use—that is, many humans who would choose to have chicken companions would do so at least in part because they want some eggs. But this fact of use need not compromise the full protection of chickens' rights and community membership. As in the sheep case, the primary concerns would be to ensure that mechanisms are in place to fully monitor and enforce these rights, and to regulate commercial pressures that might erode these rights.[36]

Using milk from cows is more problematic. Dairy cows have been bred to produce abundant milk, and this breeding has undermined their health and longevity. (For example, excess milk production reduces calcium stores, leading to weaker bones.)[37] In addition, to make dairy production a commercially viable process, male calves are killed to produce veal, cows are continuously impregnated to keep them producing milk (which wears them out, and contributes to many diseases), and calves are separated from cows in order to maximize the percentage of milk that goes to humans. Can we imagine a non-exploitative environment for cows, that is, one which recognizes them as full citizens and contributes to their flourishing in ways similar to those we have described for sheep and chickens? This would represent an enormous practical and financial undertaking on the part of humans (given the size and needs of cows), with limited return in terms of milk.[38] Assuming that cows would follow their own inclination in terms of mating, and would raise their calves, there might be some surplus milk, but probably not very much. Meanwhile, cows and calves (male and female, unless it would be possible to sex select in a non-invasive manner) require significant space and resources for their care. In other words, it's hard to imagine anyone having cow companions except for the pleasure of their company (or because they are prepared to go to great lengths for a bit of dairy).

This does not mean that there will be no cows, just not very many. There will always be people who want to have cow companions (or pig companions), but the reality is that since these animals are less 'useful' (under non-exploitative conditions), fewer of them would be brought into the human–animal community.[39] On the other hand, cautious commercialization of the use of cow's milk could lead to it becoming a luxury good, resulting in a limited but stable cow community.[40]

Use of Animal Labour

So far, we have focused on cases in which humans benefit from using animals engaged in doing what they do naturally—eating grass, growing wool, producing manure, eggs, and milk. A different form of use involves training animals to perform various kinds of work for humans, such as assistance and therapy training for dogs, or police training for horses. There are some jobs that dogs and other animals can perform without significant training. For example, if we return to Sheepville, we can imagine that the community also includes some dogs or donkeys who help to protect the sheep. This protective behaviour is a natural instinct (much nurtured by selective breeding of certain dog breeds) that does not require much training, and we can imagine a full and flourishing life for a dog or donkey which includes performing some guard duties. We would need safeguards in place to ensure dogs or donkeys were not exploited in Sheepville. For example, only dogs and donkeys who enjoy the work, and who enjoy the company of sheep (and of other working dogs and donkeys), would be considered. These animals would need to have the option of other activities (staying in bed, hanging out with humans, or sticking to a pasture with their own species, etc.) as a way of assessing their preference for guarding the sheep. And in any case, the hours of work would need to be strictly limited so the donkey or dog didn't feel that they were always on call. With all these provisos in place, we can imagine that a life involving a limited number of hours of guard duty could be a deeply satisfying life—offering variety, the satisfactions of directed activity, and plenty of social contacts.

There may be other kinds of dog work that fall into this category. For example, a gregarious dog might enjoy accompanying her human on social work visits to hospitals or homes for the aged. There may be kinds of work in which dogs (or rats) use their superior sniffing skills, without excessive training required, to assist humans in detecting tumors, or incipient seizures, or dangerous substances, or tracking lost individuals. We emphasize, however, that the possibilities for exploitation are very high, and the use of animals for these purposes would need to be carefully regulated. For such use to be non-exploitative, the animal must be in a position to give a clear indication that they enjoy the activity, that they thrive on the stimulation and contact, and that the work is not a price they need to pay to receive the love, approval, treats, and care that are their due (and need). Work must be balanced with lots of down time in which dogs engage in other activities and socialize with their human and dog friends. In other words, dogs (and other working animals) should have the same opportunity human citizens have to control the conditions under which they contribute to society, and to follow their own inclinations in terms of how they live their lives, and with whom they spend time.

One danger is that we will mould and manipulate these needs and preferences to our ends. This is the classic problem of 'adaptive preferences', long recognized within the field of human justice. One of the worst forms of injustice is manipulating or brainwashing the oppressed so that they come to accept their oppression as natural, normal, or deserved. This has been an issue in theorizing about justice for women, lower castes, and other groups that have been socialized to accept subordination.

It is clearly an issue for animals as well (Nussbaum 2006: 343–4). Earlier, we discussed the fact that all domesticated animals have a right to basic socialization so they can mature into competent citizens. Moreover, we discussed the right of individual animals to have their own special interests and abilities nurtured. But this is a delicate process. In the human case, we recognize the difference between nurturing individual potential and coercing, moulding, or brainwashing individuals to fill prescribed roles. There are some very bright animals who thrive on learning, testing, and developing their abilities, accomplishing tasks, and engaging in cooperative goal-oriented activity. One can imagine a very bright and energetic dog, for example, who couldn't be happier than when engaged in agility training with her human companion.[41] There may be a certain amount of restraint, correction, and manipulation necessary in this learning process, but dogs can benefit from a certain amount of 'stick to it' pressure from their humans, just as a child might benefit from parents who gently pressure her to give the piano lessons a few more tries before giving up. The parents may recognize musical talent, for example, and know that in the long term their child could derive enormous satisfaction from learning to play the piano, even if in the short term she might not see it that way. We trust parents to get this balance right because the overall context is one in which we know they have the child's interests at heart. We quickly lose trust in parents if we suspect that their intent is strictly to create a young performer to satisfy their own whims to hear live music, or to profit financially from the child's piano playing, or to enjoy bragging rights in conversation with other parents. These may all come to pass—that is, parents can benefit from their child's piano playing—but the primary motivation for education should be about the child's interests and development.

Viewed in this light, much training of domesticated animals is exploitative. Most therapy and assistance animals are not trained to develop their own potential and interests, but moulded to serve human ends (the same goes for horse riding, animals in the entertainment industry, and most other kinds of animal work). Animals with specific tractable temperaments are identified early, and pegged for future roles. Training, often very intensive over many months, involves significant restraint and confinement, and frequently, severe correction and deprivation. Even so-called positive reinforcement is usually thinly disguised coercion. If the only way a dog gets treats, play time, or affection from others is by performing tasks to please them, this is blackmail not education. Many working animals are denied any real down time in which they run free, or socialize with others, or simply explore and experience their world. Their work often puts them in stressful and even dangerous situations. They are often denied a stable environment and continuity in terms of their friendships and environment, and instead are shunted between trainers, workplaces, and human employers. Far from being nurtured to develop their potential, these animals are moulded into submission. Their agency isn't enabled, but suppressed in order to turn them into effective tools for crowd control, human entertainment, hippotherapy, or assistance to people with disabilities.

In between the donkeys whose presence in the sheep pasture keeps predators at bay, and the seeing-eye dog who undergoes months of intensive training in order to spend most of his life serving as a tool for others, we cross the line from use to exploitation. It is often difficult to know exactly when this line has been crossed, just as it is difficult to know the precise moment when someone crosses the line into baldness. But imprecision at the boundaries doesn't mean we cannot distinguish a full head of hair from a bald one. In general terms, that line is crossed when we bring domesticated animals into the community and then fail to treat them as full citizens. The problem is not that we benefit from animals, but that we almost always do so at their expense.

Medical Care/Intervention

Recognizing domesticated animals as members of the community includes accepting their equal right to communal resources and the social bases of well-being, such as medical care. Today, farm and companion animals are subject to a great number of veterinary procedures and medications, most of which are not in their interest, but rather in the interest of humans who wish to make animals into more productive, compliant, or attractive entities (e.g., growth hormones, castration, declawing, debeaking, debarking, tail- and ear-docking, and many others). Some interventions are rationalized as being for the good of the animal (e.g., antibiotics for mastitis and other infections, debeaking of chickens who would otherwise harm each other), but of course these problems are caused by human abuse of animals in the first place (e.g., overcrowding, stress, inadequate diet), and so are hardly indicative of a genuine concern for the well-being of community members.

However, animals also receive a great deal of veterinary care that is genuinely in their interest—from vaccines to emergency care. The amount of money spent on health care for pets is often criticized as an example of misguided moral priorities (e.g., Hadley and O'Sullivan 2009). And indeed there is something deeply perverse about the sacrifices many families make for their dogs' and cats' well-being, even as they happily participate in the abuse of farm animals. For some critics, spending on companion animal health care is simply a bad-faith gesture by people who want to think of themselves as animal lovers, even as they support the horrors of livestock farming or animal experimentation.

But even if the human motivation for providing health care to companion animals is hypocritical or inconsistent in this way, that in no way diminishes the claim of domesticated animals to health care. Health care is a right of membership in contemporary societies, and domesticated animals have the right to be treated as members. This indeed explains why we have duties to provide health care to domestic dogs and cats, and not (or not always) to wolves or leopards in the wild (we discuss our obligations to animals in the wild in Chapter 6). These duties would likely be fulfilled through some scheme of animal health insurance.[42]

However, there are difficult issues regarding the scope and nature of this obligation. For one thing, animals are not in a position to give informed consent to treatment, and so humans must make decisions on behalf of animals, much as parents do for children. While a paternalistic framework is unavoidable here, we should be open to the possibility that animals are able to communicate their wishes to us to some extent. For example, many animals are capable of understanding that a vet is trying to help them, even if in the short term a particular procedure is uncomfortable or painful, and so they willingly assent to the ministrations of the vet over the years. But imagine now that in her older years, a dog runs into chronic health problems and at a certain point begins to actively resist trips to the vet and treatment. This should be a red flag that perhaps imposing treatment, even if it still has a good chance of being effective and giving her a few more months or years of life, is not her choice.

Our best efforts at understanding what our animal companions would wish us to do will not significantly alter the basic paternalistic framework in which humans must decide what is right for their companions. Human adults, confronted with the prospect of invasive surgery followed by a lengthy period of discomfort and recovery, are able to understand what is happening to them, and to anticipate their lives post-recovery. Animals are not, and so we should assume that the process is more frightening and stressful for them. An invasive surgery, which might be the right choice for a young animal with psychological resilience and years of potential life ahead, might not be the right choice for a timid and elderly dog who will be subject to terrifying interventions in exchange for a few more months of life.

In the human case, there is much debate as to the ethics of euthanasia in the advanced stages of terminal illness. On the one hand, it seems right to want to spare people unnecessary pain in the final hours or days of life, even if they are not in a position to consent to, or request, intervention. On the other hand, there is a possibility that legalizing euthanasia will lead to abuses. In the case of domesticated animals, we see the term euthanasia used all the time for killings that have nothing to do with avoiding suffering in the last days of terminal illness. Animals are euthanized (so-called) simply because they are unwanted or abandoned, old, inconvenient, or expensive. However, the fact that most killing of domesticated animals is a terrible abuse does not mean that in a just society where domesticated animals are recognized as full citizens euthanasia would be completely prohibited. It means that, as in the human case, it would be morally fraught and contested, and, if legal, tightly regulated.

There are paradoxes here. Developments in veterinary care mean that many animals who once might have died of heart failure now have their heart conditions successfully controlled by medication, adding months or years to their lives. However, rather than dying from a quick heart attack, this can mean that they are more likely to die from painful and prolonged conditions, such as kidney failure or brain tumors. Our various interventions (whether good, like heart medications, or bad, like allowing animals to eat too much or exercise too little) have implications for what their dying hours and days will be like. It is a very difficult question what our role should be at that stage—to comfort and ease pain as much as possible, or to hasten death and end suffering. Either way, we can't avoid responsibility for the decision. And given how contested this question is in the human instance, it is unlikely to be any less contested in the case of domesticated animals.

Sex and Reproduction

One of the most difficult issues facing any theory of animal rights, including a citizenship approach, concerns rights to reproduction. Humans exert enormous control over domesticated animals' sex and reproductive lives—whether they *can* do it, whether they *may* do it, and *when*, *how*, and *with whom* they may do it. Many abolitionist/extinctionist AR theorists rightly condemn this sort of pervasive interference in breeding, and cite it as evidence of the ways that domestication inherently involves oppression. Yet, as we noted in Chapter 4, their own call for the extinction of domesticated species implicitly presupposes an equally systematic programme of coercion and confinement in order to *prevent* domesticated animals from reproducing. If current practices force animals to reproduce in ways that serve human purposes, the abolitionist/extinctionist approach involves forcing animals not to reproduce.[43]

Neither of these approaches takes seriously the legitimate interests of domesticated animals. If anyone proposed this level of intervention into the sexual and reproductive lives of humans it would be considered outrageous. But before confronting the question of what, if any, regulation by humans of the sex lives of domesticated animals is justified, it is helpful to consider briefly the human case, and the case of animals living in the wild.

In what ways are human sexuality and reproduction subject to regulation? On the one hand, it is very important for people to be able to have sex, if and when they want, with partners of their choosing, and to have a family if they wish. But it's not a free-for-all. We protect children from sexual exploitation and predation. We insist that sex be consensual: one's freedom to have sex isn't absolute, but dependent on finding a willing partner. We require that people take responsibility for the children they produce. We carefully regulate which aspects of sex and reproduction can be subject to market forces, especially where children are concerned (e.g., sale of sperm, eggs, reproductive services, or adoption services). And we regulate the extent to which reproduction can be manipulated to produce specific outcomes. (For example, we allow selective abortion to end pregnancies in the case of birth defects, but discourage it as a tool for sex selection. The use of foetal surgery to 'enhance' capacities rather than simply correct abnormalities is another area of ethical debate.) Many of these regulatory boundaries are highly contested.

In general, we expect individuals to be self-regulating and responsible when it comes to engaging in sex and accepting its consequences. When they are unable to do so, the state intervenes (e.g., to protect children, to protect unwitting partners from contracting HIV, or unwilling partners from sexual assault). There is no 'right to have (partnered) sex' as such, but, rather, a right to be free from sexual coercion, or unwarranted sexual regulation. And while most people would insist that we have a 'right to have a family' (a right which is enshrined in the UN's Universal Declaration of Human Rights), this right, too, depends on having a willing partner (or donor, or adoptee). And there is obviously great contention about the extent of any right to have a family. How far is such a right constrained by a corresponding responsibility to be able to care for your offspring, or a responsibility not to reproduce in the case of societal overpopulation (or a responsibility *to* reproduce in the case of population collapse)? Societies engage in extensive use of incentives (and sometimes more coercive measures) to encourage or discourage people from reproducing. Our sex and reproductive lives are in fact highly regulated, although the form that this regulation takes is largely internalized self-regulation and response to social pressures and incentives.[44]

Through self-regulation of reproduction, humans can (theoretically) ensure that their numbers don't exceed sustainable levels, or their (individual and collective) ability to care for the children they produce. Amongst animals in the wild, we see enormous diversity regarding the extent to which sex and reproduction are subject to social control and self-regulation. Amongst some species, almost all adult females mate and produce young. Often, huge numbers of young are produced, and adults invest almost no energy in caring for them. The population is kept in check by predation, exposure, disease, and starvation. This is the evolutionary strategy of many fish and reptile species. The picture is very different amongst social species. Wolves are a fascinating example of a species that strictly regulates sexual and reproductive activity. In wolf clans, it is common for only the alpha male and female to have sex and produce young. Few cubs are born, and they are a heavy investment. The entire clan cooperates to raise the young of the alpha pair. Many adult wolves go their entire lives without having sex. Wolves are highly self-regulating and socially regulating in this respect. Rather than population being controlled by external forces, it is strictly regulated by the social group in response to context and available resources.

When we turn to domesticated animals, it is important to remember that they belong to social species whose ancestors exerted some level of social control over reproduction and/or adult cooperation in the raising of young. However, human intervention has drastically disrupted these species' reproductive mechanisms—whether instinctual or learned. In other words, just as human intervention has made domesticated animals more dependent on humans to feed, shelter, and protect them from predators, it has also removed them from the mechanisms of population control that exist in the wild (a combination of self-regulation, social cooperation, and external controls).

In recognizing domesticated animals as citizens, to the extent that autonomous control over their sexual and reproductive lives is possible for such animals, then we should seek to restore it. However, we can only foster agency where individuals are capable of agency, and domesticated animals vary considerably in the extent to which they might be capable of self-regulating with respect to sex and reproduction. We have removed domesticated animals from conditions in the wild in which their numbers would be regulated either by their own self-regulation in response to external pressures (similar to wolves), or directly by those external pressures (in the form of predators, food shortages, etc.). Starving to death or being eaten by a predator are not exercises of agency, and it would not be in the interests of domesticated animals to return to such conditions. But if such mechanisms are removed, then what replaces them? Given the opportunity to live in social communities in which they mix with others of their choosing, mate by choice, and raise their young, we don't know how they would regulate these activities. So part of what it means to recognize them as citizens is to experiment and learn about what animals would do if given greater control over their lives. However, this is not an excuse for humans to simply step out of the picture. To the extent that domesticated animals are unable to exercise meaningful agency, humans have a responsibility to act in their interests. As members of the community, domesticated animals are entitled to protection, including, where necessary, paternalistic protection. Moreover, to the extent that they are not internally self-regulating, they are subject to the constraints of social life (e.g., to having regulation imposed on them in order to protect the basic rights of others and the sustainability of a scheme of cooperation).

Here, as elsewhere, citizenship is a package that involves a mix of rights and responsibilities. As citizens, domesticated animals have rights, including rights not to have their sexual and reproductive activities unnecessarily curtailed, and the right to have their offspring cared for and protected by the larger, mixed human–animal society. But, as citizens, domesticated animals also have the responsibility to exercise their rights in ways that do not impose unfair or unreasonable costs on others, and that do not create unsustainable burdens on the scheme of cooperation. Where animals do not or cannot self-regulate their reproduction, the costs to others of having to care for and maintain their offspring could become prohibitive. In these circumstances, imposing some limits on their reproduction is, we believe, a reasonable element in a larger scheme of cooperation. As in the case of mobility restrictions, reproduction restrictions would need to be carefully justified, and involve the least restrictive available methods. This justification is importantly different from the abolitionist call for universal birth control/sterilization leading to extinction. Abolitionists would restrict the liberties of individual animals without reference to the interests of those animals. With the citizenship model, restrictions can only be justified by reference to the interests of the individual, while recognizing that these interests include being part of a cooperative social project which involves both rights and duties.

It is worth distinguishing the question of how domesticated animals reproduce from the question of how many such animals should exist. Currently, domesticated animals are the most populous mammals and birds on earth by a long shot, so it would be hard to make a case that there should be more of them. Their numbers are unsustainable from an ecological point of view (as is likely the case for humans too). The only reason they exist in the numbers they do is because we intensively breed them to exploit them. So, no matter what, the liberation of animals will bring about a great reduction in the numbers of domesticated animals. Presumably we should head towards population sizes that are (a) ecologically sustainable, and (b) socially sustainable (i.e., reflect some sort of balance between the human duty to care for domesticated animals, and the ways in which animals contribute to joint human–animal society). It is in the interest of domesticated animals that humans regulate their numbers in a sustainable fashion, rather than allowing the ravages of ecological or social collapse to do so instead.

There are many relatively non-invasive ways in which we can control the reproductive rates of domesticated animals—birth control vaccines, temporary physical separation, non-fertilization of chicken eggs, etc. Moreover, insofar as possible, we can impose birth control measures after animals have had a chance to have a family, if they seem inclined to do so. In other words, rather than the current situation in which some domesticated animals are designated breeders, while the vast majority never reproduce, the opportunity for having (and raising) young could be dispersed amongst most animals, but limited in scope.

The fact that it is appropriate for us to control the overall numbers of domesticated animals (insofar as they are not socially self-regulating in this respect), does not mean that we need to control all aspects of this process, for example, choices about whether to have sex, with whom, and when. Again, we face tricky questions about the extent to which animals exercise agency in this regard. In *The Hidden Life of Dogs*, Elizabeth Marshall Thomas (1993) describes two strikingly different scenarios. In one, her dogs Maria and Misha, a strongly bonded and loving pair, clearly derive mutual pleasure and satisfaction from the sex act, and the resulting pregnancy and puppies. On the other hand, her dog Viva is clearly traumatized when an unknown male dog jumps the fence into the yard and rapes her, and she proves to be a frightened and uncertain mother. The first scenario might count as one in which dogs in a secure context have an opportunity to exercise responsible agency. Human involvement plays a key role in creating the conditions for this exercise of agency—that is, by providing a stable and secure environment in which dogs can choose a mate, while protecting them from unwanted sexual advances. In other words, human involvement doesn't necessarily restrict agency, it may be crucial for enabling it.

There are many unknowns here. For some species of domesticated animals, generations have been born through human-assisted insemination (to the extent that some animals cannot reproduce without assistance). We need to proceed cautiously when returning to them some control over the business of deciding if, when, and with whom to engage in the sex act. Our role should be guided by what is revealed about the extent to which (and conditions under which) they seem to exercise meaningful agency. In the meantime, we will undoubtedly continue to exercise a great deal of control over who breeds with whom. Even if we create circumstances in which animals can make many choices, we will still be controlling the pool of available partners, and the likelihood of any given partnership leading to pregnancy and birth. This control should be exercised in ways that respect the rights of current animals, and hopefully benefit future animals.

For example, human breeding of animals has resulted in a wide array of health problems—breathing problems, shortened lifespans, increased vulnerability to temperature extremes, flesh-to-bone ratios which mean that adult animals cannot support their own weight, and so on. Animals are incapable of making mating decisions to deliberately reverse these processes. We have removed them from natural conditions in which evolutionary pressures define and select for fitness. Fitness, for domesticated animals, is what enables them to thrive in mixed human–animal society. This means that humans, at least for the foreseeable future, need to exercise some control over breeding in the interests of domesticated animals. When providing an animal with a pool of possible partners, one of whom they might choose as a mate, humans should be selective about the pool in ways that benefit potential offspring in terms of their health, and their capacities for flourishing in mixed society, based on animal citizenship rather than animal exploitation.

This management of breeding can be justified if it is of benefit to future animals, and operates under conditions that respect the rights of the breeding pair (as to whether and when they mate).[45]

Domesticated Animal Diets

Amongst our many duties to domesticated animals, we are responsible for ensuring that they have adequate nutrition. And here we encounter another dilemma: do we have an obligation to feed meat to our domesticated animals, particularly if this is part of their (so-called) natural diet? Must we turn some animals into meat in order to fulfill our duties to our domesticated animal co-citizens?

It is worth stepping back and considering the issue of animal diets more generally. Some domesticated animals (especially chickens, cows, goats, sheep, and horses), given greater scope for exercising agency, will be able to take care of many of their own nutritional needs. Earlier we cited Rosamund Young's descriptions of how her free-roaming cows tailor their own feeding to eat a balanced diet, deal with ailments, prepare for childbirth, and so on (Young 2003). Other animals, however, will be dependent on us to provide for their nutritional needs for the foreseeable future. Dog and cat companions have been long removed from a wild context in which they could adequately feed themselves through hunting and scavenging. Feral dogs and cats can often survive on their own, but they rarely thrive unless their diets are supplemented by humans. Indeed, dogs and cats are long adapted to living with human families, and sharing their food. In recent decades we have gotten used to the idea of specially prepared cat and dog foods. (In part this reflects growing understanding that dogs and cats have different nutritional needs from humans. In part it reflects a desire to find markets for the by-products of an industrialized meat system.) But for most of human–pet history, dogs and cats have just eaten family leftovers and their own scroungings. Dogs especially have evolved to be highly flexible omnivores. There is ample evidence that dogs can thrive on a (suitably planned) vegan diet. There is growing evidence that cats, even though they are carnivores, can also thrive on high-protein vegan diets, suitably supplemented with taurine and other nutrients.[46] If this is the case, then transition to a just human–animal world will not pose insurmountable moral dilemmas when it comes to feeding our animal companions.

Critics will complain that a vegan diet is not natural for dogs and cats. But dogs and cats have been part of our world for centuries, adapting to a diversity of cultural diets (and there is nothing natural about commercial pet food). There is no natural diet for animal companions. What matters is for them to have a diet that meets all their nutritional needs, and which is palatable and pleasing to them. Cats and dogs have individual tastes, but there is plenty of evidence of their partiality to many vegan foods and palate enhancers (e.g., nutritional yeast, sea vegetables, and simulated meat, fish, and cheese flavours).

It is probable that even if a vegan diet can be nutritional and tasty, it wouldn't be the first choice of many cats and dogs. Given the option, they would probably go for the meat. We have made a point of enabling animal agency—allowing them to make choices about their own good when this is possible. So why, in the case of diet, are we advocating that meat should not be among the choices offered to them? Because the liberty of citizens is always constrained by respect for the liberties of others. Dog and cat members of mixed human–animal society do not have a right to food that involves the killing of other animals. As we discuss in Chapter 6, predator–prey relationships are a necessity for animals in the wild, but domesticated animals are citizens of a mixed human–animal society in which the circumstances of justice do exist. Justice requires acknowledging the rights of domesticated animals, as we have been emphasizing repeatedly, but it also requires that domesticated animals, like all citizens, respect the basic liberties of all. Many humans, too, would prefer to eat meat, but given the availability of nutritional alternatives it would be unethical to do so.

However, what if it turns out some cats simply cannot be adequately nourished without animal protein in their diet? How could we fulfill our duty to feed our cats without violating the rights of other animals not to be killed? Possible options include: (1) letting cats hunt; (2) scavenging corpses for them; (3) inventing 'frankenmeat' grown from stem cells; or (4) letting cats eat eggs supplied by domesticated chickens. The first option, that is, letting cat companions prey on mice and birds, is not much better than killing the birds and mice ourselves. Cat companions are part of our community, and this means that insofar as we are able, we need to limit their ability to inflict violence on other animals—just as we would inhibit our children from doing so. In other words, part of our responsibility as members of a mixed human–animal society is to impose regulation on members who are unable to self-regulate when it comes to respecting the basic liberties of others (e.g., by putting bells on cats to warn mice and birds that they are approaching, and by supervising them out of doors).

The option of scavenging corpses—for example, acquiring meat from animals who die of old age, or in accidents on roads—raises interesting questions. Showing dignity to corpses is one of the ways in which we mark respect. Some would argue that since animals are incapable of understanding the idea of disrespecting corpses, it is not possible to undermine their dignity by the way we treat their bodies after death. The idea that respectful relations can only exist between persons who understand the concept of respect has been challenged by disability theorists who argue that respect can inhere in the relationship between two people, even if it is not part of the self-understanding of one of them. Lack of respect, even if it is not understood that way by the person who is not respected, can have serious implications for how they are treated, and whether they are truly perceived as full members of the community. This conception of respect may have implications for the treatment of animal corpses. If we have a different standard in general for the treatment of animal corpses than for human corpses, this both marks a different level of respect and perpetuates an inability to see them as full members of the community. Therefore, we need to be careful about what it means to allow animal corpses to be treated differently from human corpses. On the other hand, our ideas of respecting human corpses are culturally variable and subject to change over time. Performing autopsies, using human bodies for scientific research, transplanting organs—all of these practices were once seen as examples of subjecting corpses to indignity. New technologies for composting human bodies are controversial for the same reason. Is it okay to recycle human bodies as fertilizer?

There is a further question here about whether the treatment of corpses belongs to the realm of basic rights concerning all individuals, or is it a right associated with citizenship that marks the boundaries of community and the duties of members towards each other. It seems to operate at both levels. On the one hand, there are some kinds of interference with human corpses—things we should refrain from doing—which are probably universally recognized as acts of contempt or disrespect. On the other hand, ideas about our positive obligations to corpses—what we *should do* to show respect—are culturally (and religiously) variable, marking the boundaries of community. This could mean that while there are some ways in which we should never treat bodies—human or animal, citizen or foreigner—there are special obligations we owe to members of the community. For example, if a human dies in a foreign land, it may be more appropriate to repatriate the body, or to treat it in accordance with the culture/religion/community to which the person belonged, rather than the culture in which he happened to be a visitor.

Perhaps, then, we ought to treat the bodies of domesticated animals the same way as human bodies in any given society or community, but the same obligation does not apply for corpses of those from outside the community. It may be appropriate to treat the corpse of my cat companion in a way that marks her citizenship in a shared human–animal society, while it may be inappropriate to do so with a wild animal. The wild animal belongs to a different society in which there is nothing undignified about dead bodies being scavenged and recycled in this way through the web of life. Does this mean that it would therefore be acceptable for us to scavenge those bodies to feed our cats? Or would this inevitably lead to a cheapening of wild animal life in our eyes?

Concerns about how we treat corpses, and how this may compromise our respect for the living, bring us to related concerns about the invention of frankenmeats—that is, meat grown in labs from stem cells. On the one hand, this kind of development seems to offer a potential end run around the problems of meat consumption. The idea is that no sentient being is created, just tissue. Thus nobody is directly harmed by the creation of this meat. One concern, however, is that such a development would have spillover effects in terms of respect for the living. If animal stem cells, but not human ones, are used to grow frankenmeat, does this not mark a crucial difference in terms of the dignity of persons? It seems unlikely we would grow meat for consumption from human stem cells. This would violate the taboo against cannibalism that says humans aren't for eating. But in that case, would it not be a similar violation to eat flesh grown from animal stem cells? For some vegans, even the idea of simulated meats (or fur, or leather) is disgusting. For others, these products are unproblematic. Issues of disgust are bound up with issues of respect, and reasonable people will no doubt continue to disagree about the appropriate boundaries.

The possibility of feeding cats non-meat animal protein, like eggs, obviously depends on whether there are any conditions under which it is ethical to use chickens to provide these foods within human–animal society. We discussed this issue earlier, and concluded that there are limited circumstances in which it is acceptable to do so. However, a commercial industry in egg (or milk) products is probably not viable (and would invite abuse), and so there can be no mass production to solve the problem of animal protein for cats. However, it could be that for people who want to live with cat companions, part of the deal, as it were, is that they might need to find an ethical source of eggs, perhaps by keeping their own chicken companions as well.[47]

Cats are the only true carnivores amongst domesticated animals, and thus pose a unique challenge in human–animal society. There may be no way for humans to have cat companions without dealing with a certain level of moral complexity regarding their diet and other restrictions necessary for them to be part of human–animal society. (Such restrictions are not just diet-related, but involve careful monitoring of cats outdoors to protect other animals from their predatory activities.) Does this level of restriction undermine the possibility of cats being flourishing members of mixed society? Does it mean that we would be justified in bringing about their extinction? At the very least, it means that any individual human contemplating having a companion cat is signing on for a great deal of responsibility in terms of doing the work to ensure their cat flourishes under the necessary restrictions (e.g., efforts to find palatable and nutritionally appropriate foods for them, and to create opportunities for them to enjoy the outdoors while not endangering others).

Political Representation

We have emphasized the way in which citizenship offers a perspective on individual freedom and flourishing which understands how these unfold within the cooperative and reciprocal project of social life. This requires that individuals internalize the basic rules of social life (e.g., not violating the rights of others, participating in social life) in order to enjoy its freedoms and opportunities. But the basic rules are always provisional, subject to ongoing negotiation through the democratic participation of all citizens. We have also emphasized that domesticated animals have the capacity to participate in this process, if assisted by those 'collaborators' who have learned how to interpret their expressions of preferences. But this sort of dependent agency is only going to be effective, politically, if there are institutional mechanisms that link domesticated animals and their collaborators to political decision-makers. We need, in short, some way to ensure the effective political representation of domesticated animals.

Obviously, this will not be through extending the vote to domesticated animals, since animals are not capable of understanding the political platforms of different candidates or political parties. This is also true of many people with severe intellectual disabilities, and, as Vorhaus notes, they, too, need a conception of representation that is not defined by, or exhausted by, the right to vote (Vorhaus 2005). How then should we think about political representation for animal co-citizens?

Little has been written on this within the ART literature—reflecting the priority on negative rights, and the assumption that the future of human–animal relations is one of minimal contact, not social and political integration. However, there is a related debate within the environmental literature on how to 'enfranchise nature'. Robyn Eckersley, for example, has recommended the constitutional entrenchment of an independent public authority such as an 'environmental defenders office' with responsibility for ensuring that the interests of future generations and non-human species are taken into account in decision-making (Eckersley 1999, 2004: 244). Similar proposals for creating political offices of environmental 'advocates', 'trustees', or 'ombudsmen' have been discussed by other authors (e.g., Norton 1991: 226–7; Dobson 1996; Goodin 1996; Smith 2003), although critics argue that in the end, the only reliable way of ensuring that the interests of either future generations or non-human species are taken into account is to change attitudes amongst the general human electorate (Barry 1999: 221; Smith 2003: 116).

As we noted, these proposals have not emerged from within the ART literature, but from within the Green/ecology literature. And as reflects the priorities of that literature, these proposals have rarely focused on the idea of defending even the basic rights of domesticated animals, let alone their citizenship status. The focus, rather, has been on preserving the sustainability of ecosystems, primarily in the wild—a commitment which, as we have seen in Chapter 2, has often gone hand in hand with endorsing the violation of the rights of individual animals (e.g., through support for sustainable hunting, or therapeutic culling of over-populated or invasive species).

From a more specifically animal rights perspective, there is the intriguing example of the office of 'animal advocate' within the Swiss canton of Zurich—a lawyer with the power to represent animals in court, and with the mandate to focus on animal well-being rather than environmental sustainability.[48] But this is more about ensuring the effective enforcement of existing legal protections against cruelty and harm than about political representation. The animal advocate is not authorized to renegotiate the terms of membership by representing animals as co-citizens in legislative processes.

As these examples make clear, what matters in the end is not the creation of this or that institutional mechanism—an 'ombudsmen' rather than a 'defender', for example—but rather the underlying picture of human–animal relations that drives the institutional reform. After all, there is already a well-established system of animal welfare officers in most jurisdictions, but their role is tightly circumscribed by the underlying welfarist philosophy that takes it for granted that animals exist to serve human ends, and that animal welfare therefore consists only in eliminating 'unnecessary' animal suffering.

To get out of this trap, we need first to clarify the goals of any new scheme of representation, which we have argued should be built around the idea of co-citizenship for domesticated animals. Effective representation within this scheme will require institutional reforms at any number of levels. It will involve representation in the legislative process, but it will also require representing animals in, for example, municipal land planning decisions, or on the governance boards of various professions and public services (police, emergency services, medicine, law, urban planning, social services, etc).[49] In all of these institutions, domesticated animals have been rendered invisible, and their interests ignored.

5. Conclusion

This is just a partial list of the sorts of changes that are entailed by thinking about domesticated animals as co-citizens. We hope that these examples give some indication of how the citizenship perspective works, and how it differs from both the abolitionist/extinctionist and threshold views that currently dominate ART. It's important to note that the core of the citizenship model in our view is not a static list of rights or responsibilities, but rather the commitment to constructing certain kinds of ongoing relationships that embody ideals of full membership and co-citizenship. We examine issues of animal training and socialization, animal products and labour, animal health care and reproduction, by asking what sorts of provisions and safeguards uphold the status of domesticated animals as full members of a mixed human–animal community, and which ones operate to erode that status, turning animals into a permanently subordinated caste.

On all of the issues, thinking about domestic animals as co-citizens does not provide a magic formula that resolves all of our moral dilemmas without remainder. As in the human case, what is required by respect for co-citizenship will be a matter of contestation and reasonable disagreement. But we have argued that thinking in these terms does clarify the goals and safeguards that should guide our judgements, and helps us avoid the dead ends and contradictions that afflict existing approaches within ART.

Moreover, this approach helps make sense of some of the seeming paradoxes of our current treatment of animals. One hears the criticism that human society goes overboard in its treatment of pampered domestic animals, such as companion cats and dogs, and that this treatment is sentimental, hypocritical, and self-indulgent. The criticism has two aspects. First, it notes the hypocrisy of paying for expensive cancer treatment for Rover, while sitting down to a dinner of pork chops or chicken wings. The second criticism is not comparative, but absolutist. It simply holds that animal companions are neither deserving, nor appropriate objects of, this level of care. They're just animals, after all.

We don't dispute the perversity of our current treatment of domesticated animals, but we think these two criticisms are miscast. On the first, a citizenship approach says that the appropriate response to hypocrisy is not to reduce the level of care we give to companion animals, but rather to treat all domesticated animals as citizens, with the full benefits and responsibilities of membership. On the second, a citizenship approach asserts the fundamental equality of all members of the community. Equal concern and respect for all citizens is not a sentimental indulgence, but a matter of justice. The love and care that many humans direct to their animal companions is not misdirected sentiment to be despised, but a powerful moral force to be harnessed and expanded.

6

Wild Animal Sovereignty

In the previous two chapters, we have focused on domesticated animals. Now we turn our attention to non-domesticated animals, those living relatively free of direct human management and meeting their own needs for food, shelter, and social structure. Within the broad category of non-domesticated animals we find many different kinds of human–animal relations. In Chapter 7 we consider liminal animals—wild animals living in close association with humans. In this chapter, we consider the case of 'truly wild' animals, that is, those animals who avoid humans and human settlement, maintaining a separate and independent existence (insofar as they are able to) in their own shrinking habitats or territories. For wild animals, the model of dependent agency and co-citizenship in a mixed human–animal community which we have just outlined for domesticated animals is neither feasible nor desirable.

Although wild animals avoid humans and are not dependent on us for their daily needs, they are nonetheless vulnerable to human activity. This vulnerability varies according to geographical proximity to human activity, adaptability of a particular species to ecosystem changes, and the pace of those changes. We can think of these vulnerabilities as resulting from three broad categories of impact:

1. Direct, intentional violence—hunting, fishing, and trapping; the kidnapping of animals from the wild in order to stock zoos and circuses, or to meet demand for exotic pet-keeping and trophy-collecting, or other wild animal body or body part uses; the killing of animals as part of wildlife management programmes; and harmful experimentation on wild animals in the name of scientific research.

2. Habitat loss—the continuous encroachment of humans (whether for habitation, resource extraction, or leisure and other pursuits) into animal-inhabited territory in ways which destroy habitat and deny animals the space, resources, and ecosystem viability they need for survival.

3. Spillover harms—the countless ways in which human infrastructure and activity impose risks on animals (from shipping lanes, skyscrapers, and roadways, to spillover effects like pollution and climate change).

While the vast bulk of human impacts on wild animals are negative in one of these three ways, we can also imagine a fourth category of potentially positive impacts:

4. Positive intervention—human efforts to assist wild animals, whether individual (e.g., rescuing a deer who has fallen through ice) or systemic (e.g., vaccinating a wild population against disease); whether in response to natural disasters and processes (such as volcanoes, food cycles, predators) or in an effort to reverse or prevent human-induced harms (e.g. rewilding and habitat restoration).

Any adequate theory of animal rights must provide guidelines for thinking about all four types of impacts.

In this chapter, we argue that traditional animal rights theory (ART) is inadequate in this regard, and suggest how it must be expanded and amended to meet the task. As we show, traditional ART has focused on the first category—the direct violation of basic rights—with much less attention to the other three issues. This is not just an accidental oversight, but rather reflects the limits of any theory that defines animals' rights solely on the basis of their intrinsic moral status. To address the other three issues adequately requires elaborating a more explicitly relational account of animal rights, one which articulates the sorts of relations between human communities and wild animal communities that are both feasible and morally defensible. As we will see, these are fundamentally political questions, and can only be addressed by identifying an appropriate structure of political relationships between human societies and wild animal communities. We argue that one helpful way to identify these relations is to think of wild animals as forming sovereign communities, whose relations to sovereign human communities should be regulated by norms of international justice. Just as Chapter 5 argued that citizenship theory helps us to identify our obligations to domesticated animals, so here we argue that ideas of sovereignty and international justice help us to identify our obligations to wild animals.

As will become clear, our aim is to expand ART, not to replace it. In this respect, our approach differs from much of the ecological literature, although we start from similar concerns. A number of ecological theorists have rightly criticized traditional ART for its inattention to issues of habitat destruction and other inadvertent harms, and for its inadequate understanding of the complex and devastating impact of human activity on wild animals (and ecosystems). We draw extensively on these insights. However, as we argued in Chapter 2, the general tendency in environmental theory is to subsume animals into the broader category of nature or ecosystem, thereby downplaying the distinctive moral significance of animal subjectivity, and denying the inviolability of individual (non-human) beings.[1] Indeed, many ecologists insist that a holistic concern with the health of ecosystems is incompatible with the idea of according rights to individual animals. Just as invasive plants may need to be removed to protect a vulnerable ecosystem, so too humans may need to engage in so-called therapeutic culling of animal species that are damaging the ecosystem.

From an ART perspective, however, it is essential to remember that amongst the many different types of entities within the ecosystem, some beings have a subjective existence that calls for distinctive moral responses, including respect for their inviolable rights. In fact, ecologists already accept this idea; after all, they would not recommend the therapeutic culling of human beings in order to protect a vulnerable ecosystem. Where humans are concerned, they accept that a commitment to protecting the ecosystem can and must operate within the constraints of the inviolable rights of individuals. We believe a similar principle can and should apply to animals. Our aim in this chapter, therefore, is to show how an expanded AR theory can address fundamental issues of habitat and ecosystem flourishing, while still maintaining ART's commitment to the inviolability of subjects.

We begin by outlining the limits of the traditional ART approach to wild animals, and then develop our alternative sovereignty-based model, explaining what we mean by sovereignty, clarifying the sense in which it can be attributed to wild animal communities, and identifying the ways in which this model can help to articulate compelling principles for addressing the full range of human impacts on, and interactions with, wild animals.

1. Traditional ART Approaches to Wild Animals

Of the four types of impacts that humans have on wild animals, ART has focused primarily on the first—the direct violation of rights to life and liberty. Enormous energy has been devoted to advocating for wild animals against the predations of hunters, trappers, exotic animal traders, zoos and circuses, and wildlife managers. And rightly so—the numbers of animals killed and harmed by these practices are horrendous.[2] This focus flows naturally from ART's theoretical emphasis on basic negative rights for all animals, and provides an appropriate starting point for wild animal advocates.[3]

But for traditional AR theorists, this emphasis on the direct violation of basic rights is not just the starting point, but also the end point, of animal advocacy. Their basic injunction is that humans should stop directly harming wild animals, and then leave them alone, even if this means leaving them vulnerable to indirect harms from human activity, or to being harmed by natural forces (such as floods or diseases) or by other animals (predation). Thus Tom Regan summed up our duty to wild animals in terms of 'letting animals be'.[4] Similarly, Peter Singer says that given the complexities of intervention in nature, we 'do enough if we eliminate our own unnecessary killing and cruelty towards other animals' (Singer 1990: 227), and that 'we should leave them alone as much as we possibly can' (Singer 1975: 251).[5] And Gary Francione argues that our duty to wild animals 'does not necessarily mean that we have moral or legal obligations to render them aid or to intervene to prevent harm from coming to them' (Francione 2000: 185), and indeed he too suggests that 'we should simply leave them alone' (Francione 2008: 13).

In short, traditional ART has endorsed a 'hands-off' approach to wild animals: strict prohibitions on direct harming, but no further positive obligations. Clare Palmer calls this the 'laissez-faire intuition', and notes that it runs very deep in the ART literature (Palmer 2010). However, this approach has been widely criticized as both too little and too much. It is too little because the injunction to 'let them be', at least as it has traditionally been understood within ART, doesn't address certain key ways that humans can harm wild animals, such as human expansion and habitat loss. As we have seen, the direct violation of basic rights is just one of three types of negative impacts humans have on wild animals, and even if we stopped hunting or capturing them, humans would still be imposing huge harms on wild animals by means of air and water pollution, transportation corridors, urban and industrial development, and agricultural processes. Of course, the idea of 'letting them be' could be interpreted in an expansive way that covers these indirect harms, but to date at least, ART has had little to say about how to determine when these indirect risks and harms constitute injustices, or how they should be remedied.

It has also been seen as potentially too much, because if we say that wild animals have a right to life, it is not clear why this only generates negative duties of non-intervention, and not positive duties as well. AR theorists may describe their theories in terms of letting wild animals be, but critics have pointed out that according a right to life seems to require not only stopping humans from killing animals, but also intervening whenever the lives of animals are threatened, including systematic intervention to end predation, and to protect animals from natural processes such as famine, floods, or exposure (Cohen and Regan 2001; Callicott 1980). If we should stop humans from hunting antelope in order to protect their inviolable rights to life and liberty, shouldn't we also try to stop lions from hunting antelope, perhaps by trying to fence all lions into their own separate space, or by putting them all into zoos? A *reductio ad absurdum* envisions the creation of soy protein worms for birds, or installation of central heating in wildlife dens in order to meet human duties of positive assistance to wild animals with a right to life (Sagoff 1984: 92–3; cf. Wenz 1988: 198–9). Invoking a right to life as grounds for prohibiting hunting of wild animals seems to open the floodgates to implausibly broad obligations to intervene in nature.[6]

AR theorists have responded to these two criticisms, and in the process refined their views, but as we will see, these modifications are both inadequate and ad hoc, although they do help point us towards a more adequate relational view. We will briefly review these refinements, and then show how they naturally lead towards something like our sovereignty model.

In response to the concern about loss of habitat, AR theorists have acknowledged that thriving ecosystems are a precondition for the thriving of individuals, and that ART must therefore find a way to accommodate these ecological concerns (e.g., Midgley 1983; Benton 1993; Jamieson 1998; Nussbaum 2006). Indeed, recent AR theorists have asserted that habitat protection is a key right for wild animals. Dunayer, for example, states that with 'the possible exception of the right not to be murdered by humans, the most important right for free nonhumans probably is the right to their habitats' (Dunayer 2004: 143). John Hadley argues that this right to habitat can be formulated in terms of property rights for wild animals, which would protect them from forced relocation due to human expansion and ecological destruction (Hadley 2005; see also Sapontzis 1987: 104).

In general, however, these recent ideas within ART of a property right to habitat are underdeveloped, and leave crucial questions unaddressed. It is one thing to say that a bird has a property right in its nest, or that a wolf has a property right in its den—specific bits of territory used exclusively by one animal family. But the habitat that animals need to survive extends far beyond such specific and exclusive bits of territory—animals often need to fly or roam over vast territories shared by many other animals. Protecting a bird's nest is of little help if the nearby watering holes are polluted, or if tall buildings block its flight path. It's not clear how ideas of property rights can help here. Which parcels of land should be seen as the property of which wild animals? How and to what extent should human activity be limited in these territories? How do we monitor the boundaries and regulate mobility across these boundaries (in either direction)? What additional duties, if any, do we owe to animals in their own habitats? (If property rights give animals the right not to be forcibly relocated due to human expansion, should we also protect animals from being forcibly dislocated due to the activities of other animals, or due to changes in climate?)

In our view, AR theorists have left these questions largely unaddressed because they cannot be answered within a framework that focuses solely on the intrinsic moral standing of animals. As we have seen, that question underdetermines our moral obligations to particular animals (or to particular humans), which vary with the nature of our relationship to them. Talk about a right to property or to habitat reflects an implicit recognition within ART that our relations with wild animals must be understood in more relational and political terms. However, as we will see, focusing exclusively on property rights is incomplete and indeed misleading as an account of these political relationships. We need first to ask what is the appropriate relationship between human and wild animal communities—a relationship we think is best framed in terms of sovereignty—and then address issues of habitat within that frame.

We see a similar impasse in relation to the worry that recognizing a right to life would entail a duty to intervene in predation. AR theorists typically endorse the 'laissez-faire intuition' that we should not intervene in nature, even to protect wild animals from starvation or predation. Yet this intuition seems to conflict with the insistence that the lives of animals matter morally, and that they have basic rights to life and liberty. In response to this worry, AR theorists have responded with a series of arguments as to why they are not committed to wholesale interventions in nature.

One set of arguments attempts to show why we have no *obligation* to interfere in cases of predation or starvation, even though giving aid to vulnerable animals might be laudable or praiseworthy. In the first edition of his classic book *The Case for Animal Rights*, Regan noted that our obligation to prevent injustice—the wrongful violation of rights—is typically stronger than our obligation to prevent mere misfortune. So we have a duty to protect wild animals from human hunting, since this is an unjust action undertaken by a responsible moral agent, but no comparable obligation to protect wild animals from predation and suffering due to natural causes, since these are not the result of moral agency, and hence are unfortunate but not unjust.[7]

Similarly, Francione notes that American law limits our 'duty to aid' even in the case of other humans:

> If I am walking down the street and see a person lying passed out, face down in a small puddle of water and drowning, the law imposes no obligation on me to assist that person even if all I need to do is roll her over, something I can do without risk or serious inconvenience to myself . . . The basic right of animals not to be treated as things means that we cannot treat animals as our resources. It does not necessarily mean that we have moral or legal obligations to render them aid or to intervene to prevent harm from coming to them. (Francione 2000: 185)

Other AR theorists likewise argue that while we have a 'perfect' duty not to violate the basic rights of others (human or animal), we only have 'imperfect' or discretionary duties to assist others in need. In general, our negative obligations to others (not to kill, confine, torture, enslave them, or rob them of the necessities of life) are 'compossible'—that is, these obligations do not conflict with one another. Fulfilling my duty not to kill one person does not make it impossible to fulfil the same duty with respect to another person. Many positive obligations, on the other hand, are not compossible. Assisting one animal in relation to one potential harm is likely to compete with other ways of helping other animals. With my limited time and funds I can support some assistance projects, but not all, and this constrains any prima facie duty to intervene, limiting them perhaps to cases where intervention is close by, low risk, and well known (Sapontzis 1987: 247).

This idea that positive duties to assist are only weak and imperfect is often accompanied by a 'concentric circles' model of positive duties. In this model, found in Callicott (1992), Wenz (1988), and Palmer (2010), our moral duties are determined by our (emotional, spatial, or causal) proximity to those in need. Those animals who are close to us, such as our companion animals, are owed positive duties, but those animals who are remote from us, such as wild animals, are owed only negative duties of non-harm.

These various responses suffer from two fatal problems. First, they save the laissez-faire intuition (LFI) towards wild animals only by dramatically weakening our moral obligation to aid humans in distress. It may be true that we have a greater obligation to prevent injustice than to prevent misfortune, but surely we do indeed have a strong obligation to rescue a drowning person at a beach, or to save someone from being hit by a falling rock, even though these are natural misfortunes, not acts of injustice. Francione may be right that American law does not currently impose such 'good Samaritan' obligations towards humans in distress, but other jurisdictions do, and these are widely seen as genuine moral obligations, not merely discretionary options. Similarly, it may be true that we have stronger obligations to help those close by, but surely we have positive obligations to people suffering in distant countries. I may have no personal connection to people starving in a remote country, and no causal responsibility for their plight, but their remoteness does not absolve me from positive duties to assist. It would be perverse to try to defend the LFI vis-à-vis wild animals by weakening our general moral obligation to aid those in distress from natural misfortune, or those whose suffering is remote from us (whether geographically or causally).

Second, these responses do not actually get to the heart of the issue, since the objection to ART is not that it would make intervening in nature to help wild animals *obligatory*, but that it would encourage and praise such intervention. Most of us would think it a good thing (even if not legally mandatory) to help a distressed human fellow citizen on the street. Yet most of us think it is a bad thing to systematically intervene in predator–prey relations. We simply should not be trying to physically separate lions from antelope to make sure the former can never prey on the latter. Treating aid to wild animals as merely discretionary rather than obligatory fails to capture this feeling. The ART response says that aid is permissible rather than obligatory, but the critics argue that intervention should, at least in some cases, be seen as impermissible—we ought not to intervene, even when it is in our discretionary power to do so.

Several AR theorists, therefore, have attempted to show why there are good reasons, from within an ART perspective, to limit our interventions in nature. Of course, to be consistent with ART, any such argument must start from the premise that there are prima facie moral reasons to reduce animal suffering. Since the moral basis of ART is the recognition that animals have a subjective experience of the world, it clearly matters morally what this experience is. Insofar as natural processes such as food cycles or predation cause suffering, these processes are not benign or sacred. However, there are a variety of both principled and pragmatic reasons why any duties to intervene are likely to be highly limited in the case of wild animals. We now briefly discuss two of these limitations.

The Fallibility Argument

Perhaps the most common argument invokes the enormous fallibility of human interventions in nature. When humans have attempted to intervene in nature, the results have often been not just unintended, but perverse. Consider all the cases of deliberate species introductions that have resulted in serious ecological impacts, or the many allegedly scientific management techniques that have led to disaster. For example, H. J. L. Orford describes 'Why the Cullers Got it Wrong' in the national parks of Namibia. Their culling interventions were based on an inaccurate model of static animal populations, whereas evolution is based on huge variations of population explosion and collapse, in which both extremes are critical for the creation of habitat and conditions favourable to other creatures in the ecosystem (Orford 1999).[8] Natural systems are enormously complex, and our understanding is limited. Under these conditions, it is likely that our interventions will cause as much harm as good, and quite possibly a great deal more.

This fallibility argument is a strong one. It is indeed difficult to predict the effects of our interventions. If you can save a deer by scaring off a pack of wolves, that seems like a clear benefit, but what if the wolves starve? Or, what if they kill a younger, healthier deer over the next hill? Or, what if the deer that you have just rescued from a terrifying but quick death, will now slowly starve through a long, food-scarce winter, or suffer the effects of a prolonged wasting disease? And here we're just talking about our ignorance concerning small-scale or isolated interventions. If we think about human intervention on a larger scale, then the risks of interference expand dramatically. Our past manipulations of ecosystems—introduction of invasive species, or destruction of keystone species, for example—should make us humble about the complexity of ecosystems, and cautious regarding our ability to understand the relevant variables for any particular act of intervention. Consider the example of crocodiles, an apex predator in many African rivers. Fraser (2009: 179–94) discusses how entire ecosystems, such as the Okavango Delta, are collapsing due to the destruction of crocodiles. On the one hand, their removal reduces the immediate threat to their prey, such as catfish. On the other hand, the catfish is itself a mid-chain predator, so its unchecked growth spells destruction for countless other species such as tigerfish and bream. Meanwhile, the fish and bird species (herons, storks, eagles) who normally feed on baby crocodiles are also devastated. The crocodile, with its large body, is vital to maintaining open water channels through the reeds of the Delta, vital to many other species. This activity, in addition to the crocodile's role in removing waste and recycling nutrients, is key to maintaining water quality upon which all of the animals in the Delta depend.[9] This kind of ecosystem complexity makes it very likely that interventions in predation will (at best) simply relocate suffering, rather than significantly reduce it, and may (at worst) create perverse effects.

Thus many AR theorists believe that ecological interdependencies and the precautionary principle argue against interventions in nature. Any duty we have to intervene to prevent suffering is limited by our obligation not to cause greater suffering (Sapontzis 1987: 234; Singer 1975; Nussbaum 2006: 373; Simmons 2009; McMahan 2010: 4).

However, as Palmer (2010) notes, this fallibility argument still seems to miss the target. It implies that if we just had more information, we should start re-engineering the natural world to prevent wild animals from competing for scarce food or territory, or to separate prey from predators—to give every wild animal its own safe and secure habitat, turning nature into a well-managed zoo in which each animal has its own safe enclosure and guaranteed food source. Perhaps we don't yet know how to do this, but if the only objection were fallibility, then we could at least be starting with small-scale pilot projects, in order to build up our knowledge about how to re-engineer nature so as to reduce suffering overall. Indeed, McMahan argues that since human impacts in the wild are already pervasive, we ought to direct our future interventions towards reducing suffering in the natural world (McMahan 2010: 3). In other words, we can't hide behind the fallibility argument for non-intervention insofar as our impact is already pervasive and unavoidable.

The Flourishing Argument

Neither the discretionary argument nor the fallibility argument gets to the heart of the issue. Most of us reject intervening in the suffering of wild animals, not just on grounds of fallibility or cost, but on a more principled basis—namely, that it undermines the flourishing of wild animals. This flourishing argument is perhaps the most important one, but also the least developed. How precisely does allowing suffering contribute to flourishing?

According to Jennifer Everett, the flourishing of wild animals depends on their being able to act in accordance with their characteristic traits and capacities, which have evolved precisely in relation to processes of predation. This applies at both the collective and individual levels. Wild animal communities flourish when they are able to self-regulate, and individual animals flourish when they act in accordance with the kind of being they are. Everett describes this in terms of attending to characteristic facts of a creature's nature, arguing that we have 'prima facie duties to assist them only insofar as such assistance is necessary as a matter of course for those creatures to flourish according to their nature'. We should not intervene to save a deer from a predator because deer 'do flourish qua deer without human protection from nonhuman predators. Indeed, if such assistance was consistently forthcoming, it is questionable whether they could flourish according to their natures' (Everett 2001: 54–5).

There is something important here, but it needs qualification and clarification. It is difficult to argue that preventing a deer's death is inimical to her flourishing. She can't flourish if she's not alive, and indeed various AR theorists have insisted that the flourishing argument cannot rule out all interventions at this level.[10] Everett seems to concede this with her reference to 'consistent' interference—perhaps it is only systematic intervention that undermines flourishing. Re-engineering nature to turn it into a zoo would make it impossible for deer to flourish according to their natures, but rescuing an individual deer trapped in the ice might not. To invoke the flourishing argument against all such interventions runs dangerously close to sanctifying natural processes as inherently morally good or benign. The fact that a deer's nature has been shaped by processes of predation does not mean that the deer finds fulfilment in being eaten alive.

So we need to think more carefully about which kinds of interventions, at which levels, inhibit flourishing. A similar need to distinguish individual interventions and state interventions arises in the human case. We may advocate a duty to assist in individual cases without thinking that the state should take on the role of protector or eliminator of risk. Regan notes that if one comes across a child being mauled by a tiger there is a duty to intervene to assist the child, but it doesn't follow that the state has the duty to eradicate all tigers to reduce the threat of mauling (Regan 2004: xxxviii). (Nor, we might add, does it support a public policy of tagging and tracking all tigers to warn people of their presence, or a policy of forbidding people from entering the forests.) People have to live with risk. Eliminating risk would involve a terrible curtailment of freedom, including the freedom to fully develop and explore one's capabilities. Individual action to protect a human child at the moment of harm contributes to her flourishing; collective action to prohibit the actions or processes that create the risk of harm is likely to undermine human flourishing. So, too, with animals.

Once we recognize this, however, we need to shift our level of analysis to a more relational and political plane. The question is no longer what sorts of obligations we owe wild animals in virtue of their intrinsic capacity for suffering. As we have seen, current ART answers to that question are ad hoc and selective. Rather, we need to ask: what are the appropriate sorts of relations between human and wild animal communities? In our view, current ART arguments reflect an implicit recognition of the need to understand this relationship in more political terms, as a relationship between distinct self-governing communities, but fall short of actually spelling out the terms of that relationship. Just as references to a right to property as a way of dealing with the habitat objection gesture at a more political understanding, so too these references to the dangers of excessive intervention indicate that we need to think about wild animal communities as organized and self-governing communities, whose relations to human societies must be regulated through norms of sovereignty and fair interaction.

Indeed, we can see glimpses of this idea within the ART literature.[11] Regan, for example, immediately after his famous comment about 'letting animals be, keeping human predators out of their affairs', goes on to add that we should 'allow these "other nations" to carve out their own destiny' (Regan 1983: 357). This suggests that in addition to our duty not to infringe the rights to life of individual animals, we also have a duty to respect their collective autonomy— their ability as 'other nations' to 'carve out their own destiny'. Similarly, Nussbaum says that 'the very idea of a benevolent despotism of humans over animals, supplying their needs, is morally repugnant: the sovereignty of species, like the sovereignty of nations, has moral weight. Part of what it is to flourish, for a creature, is to settle certain very important matters on its own, without human intervention, even of a benevolent sort' (Nussbaum 2006: 373). Here we can see ART reaching towards ideas of respect for collective autonomy and sovereignty, not just respect for the rights of individual conscious beings.[12] But neither Regan nor Nussbaum spells out what it would mean to treat wild animals as 'other nations' or as 'sovereign' species, and other passages in their works are hard to reconcile with this picture.[13]

In short, ART's approach to the issue of wild animals is, at best, underdeveloped. We began this chapter by describing four key ways in which wild animals are vulnerable to human activity: direct, intentional violence; habitat encroachment; other inadvertent harms; and positive interventions. ART's emphasis on basic rights for all animals provides a powerful check against direct violence. On the remaining issues, however, ART provides an inadequate framework. Many AR theorists state the importance of habitat protection for wild animals, but few have explored how this should be realized. The problem of other inadvertent harms to wild animals has received even less attention. On the question of positive obligations to assist wild animals (against predation, natural food cycles, and natural disasters), AR theorists have set forth various limits to positive intervention, which are sound as far as they go, but have a selective and piecemeal character. What is lacking is a more systematic theory of relations between humans and wild animal communities, one which ties together the various ad hoc arguments provided to date, and goes further in addressing a range of issues and conflicts which ART has so far ignored.

Our approach, outlined in the rest of the chapter, is a theory of sovereignty which recognizes that the flourishing of individual wild animals cannot be separated from the flourishing of communities, and which reframes the rights of wild animals in terms of fair interaction between communities. This has implications across the full range of human–animal interactions. The recognition of animal sovereignty limits our actions in terms of encroaching on wild animal territory, and imposes obligations on us to take reasonable precautions to limit our inadvertent harms to wild animals (e.g., by relocating shipping lanes, or building animal bypasses into road construction), but it also limits our obligations in terms of positive assistance to wild animals. It restricts the terms on which we can visit sovereign wild animal territory (or share overlapping territory), but at the same time it establishes terms for wild animals entering sovereign human societies. It obligates us to respect the basic rights of animals, but also protects us from violations in return. In other words, a theory of wild animal sovereignty provides an overarching framework for guiding our interactions with wild animals, for understanding the balance of our negative and positive obligations to them, and for doing so in a manner that is sensitive to the differences between the ethical duties of individual actors on the one hand, and state-level interventions on the other.

2. A Sovereignty Theory for Wild Animal Communities

As discussed in Chapter 3, ideas of citizenship and sovereignty are core organizing principles for how we understand the rights of individuals and self-determining communities, and our aim is to extend these principles to animals. In Chapters 4 and 5, we focused on the nature of citizenship *within*

self-governing communities, examining how domesticated animals have suffered injustices analogous to those of other historically marginalized or subordinated castes or classes, and how citizenship theory offers a framework for
addressing these injustices and for building more inclusive political communities embracing all of their members. In this chapter, we focus on the external
dimension of relations *between* self-governing communities. Here too, we
argue, wild animals have suffered injustices that are analogous to those suffered by various human communities whose self-government and sovereign
control of their territory have historically been denied.

There is no need to recount the sad history of colonization and conquest in
the human case, by which powerful nations have perpetrated injustices on
weaker nations. These acts of aggression, subjugating so-called primitive or
uncivilized peoples to colonial rule, were often justified by denying that the
victims were worthy of being self-governing. In the Nazi conquest of Eastern
Europe, for example, while some groups were targeted for wholesale extermination (Jews, gypsies), other peoples such as the Poles, Ukrainians, and other
Slavs were stripped of their national sovereignty, reducing them to something
like feudal serfs or slaves. In other cases of conquest, existing inhabitants such
as indigenous peoples were in an important sense simply rendered invisible.
Australia's colonizers famously conceived that continent as 'terra nullius'—a
territory empty of human (or other) citizens.

Confronted with such injustices, the international community has developed an evolving system of international law intended to safeguard weaker
nations from domination by stronger nations. This involves both recognizing
the sovereignty of nations (and hence criminalizing invasion or colonization),
and also articulating a series of principles to regulate the interaction between
nations, including fair terms of trade and cooperation, the creation of supra-
national institutions to address cross-border conflicts (arising from pollution
or migration, for example), and establishing rules for legitimate external
intervention in the case of failed states or gross human rights violations.
These form the heart of an evolving system of the 'law of peoples', or international justice.

All of these aspects of state-to-state relations are highly contested and
constantly evolving. They are a work in progress in response to centuries of
conquest and exploitation in which humans have simply employed raw
power to seize new territory, whether to settle or to extract resources, without
regard for the existing inhabitants who have been killed, displaced, enslaved,
or colonized.

In our view, wild animals have been subjected to similar sorts of injustices,
for which similar sorts of international norms are needed. As Jennifer Wolch
notes, the justifications given for colonizing animal habitat are strikingly

similar to the 'terra nullius' justifications for the colonizing of indigenous lands:

> In mainstream [urban] theory, urbanization transforms 'empty' land through a process called 'development' to produce 'improved land,' whose developers are exhorted (at least in neoclassical theory) to dedicate it to the 'highest and best use.' Such language is perverse: wildlands are not 'empty' but teeming with nonhuman life; 'development' involves a thorough denaturalization of the environment; 'improved land' is invariably impoverished in terms of soil quality, drainage, and vegetation; and judgements of 'highest and best use' reflect profit-centered values and the interest of humans alone. (Wolch 1998: 119)[14]

Even when it is acknowledged that wild lands have animal inhabitants, these inhabitants are not seen as having a right of sovereign control and occupation with respect to the territory they inhabit. For example, a common 'no-kill' solution to the conflict between development and animal-occupied habitat is to relocate animals to different habitat, as though forced relocation were not in itself a rights violation. As Hadley argues, a requirement not to harm animals in the process of development is a significantly weaker protection than respecting their right to property ownership (Hadley 2005). And as we discuss below, property ownership, in turn, is weaker than recognition of sovereign territorial rights.

In the human case, these injustices—terra nullius doctrines and relocation practices—are firmly prohibited by international law. Consider the involuntary relocation of peoples from their homelands. Let's say I want to develop land parcel A. It is currently occupied by an indigenous community, so I round up the inhabitants and relocate them to land parcel B, which is currently occupied by a different community. The inhabitants of neither location have been consulted about this reassignment of citizenship. Parcel-A citizens have been robbed of their homeland and turned into refugees. Parcel-B inhabitants have been swamped with refugees without a say in the matter, quite probably setting the stage for intense resource and cultural conflicts there. In the human case we immediately recognize what is going on here—brazen theft of land and resources and violations of sovereignty. It doesn't matter how carefully the relocation is handled to 'minimize harm'—we simply don't have the right to take control over lands already occupied by others.

Yet neither international law nor political theory condemns these brazen injustices in the case of wild animals. (Indeed, ironically, the very international laws adopted to uphold sovereignty in the human case seem to condone the denial of animal sovereignty.)[15]

Our proposal is that, as in the human case, these inter-community injustices are best addressed by extending rights of sovereignty to wild animals, and by defining fair terms of interaction amongst sovereign communities. We spell out the details below, but to begin with, it may help to contrast our model with a 'stewardship' model, found in some environmentalist literature (and in some public policy). In this model, habitat is set aside for wild animals in the form of wildlife sanctuaries, refuges, or a national park system. These wild areas are under the management or stewardship of humans, for the shared benefit of both humans and animals. Human access and use might be strictly limited, not as a recognition of animal sovereignty, but rather as an exercise of human management. This stewardship may be relatively interventionist or relatively hands off, but either way the relationship is conceptualized as one in which a human sovereign community has set aside a territory for a specific use, and to which the human community retains the right to unilaterally redefine boundaries and use.

On a sovereignty model, by contrast, recognizing another community's sovereign territory involves recognizing that we have no right to govern that territory, let alone to make unilateral decisions by stewards on behalf of wards. As citizens of one state, we may be free to visit and even inhabit the territory of a different sovereign state, but we are not free to control, settle, or unilaterally reshape it according to our needs and desires, or our conception of its needs and desires. A Canadian visitor to Sweden is free to move around the country and to enjoy its many pleasures, but she does not possess the rights of citizenship. She cannot set up shop, change the laws, vote, demand services in French and English, or access state benefits. Swedish citizens determine the shape of their own society, and set the terms upon which others may visit.

Similarly, when we talk of recognizing wild animals' sovereign rights to habitat, we are not talking about creating parks where humans retain sovereign authority, exercising stewardship over animals and nature. We are talking about relations between sovereign entities resting on similar claims to authority. This means that if and when we humans visit their territory, we do so not in the role of stewards and managers, but as visitors to foreign lands.[16]

In this respect, the problems with the stewardship model towards wild animals are similar to the wardship model we discussed in Chapter 5 with respect to domesticated animals. In each case, the fundamental problem is the treatment of animals as incompetent, and as passive recipients of our (benign or harmful) actions. A sovereignty model for wild animals, like a citizenship model for domesticated animals, focuses instead on the capacity of animals to pursue their own good, and to shape their own communities.

Recognizing the sovereignty of a territorial-based community means recognizing that the people inhabiting the territory have a right to be there and to determine the shape of their communal life; and that they have the ability to do so. This recognition means that a sovereign community has the right to be free both from colonization, invasion, and exploitation on the one hand, and also from external paternalistic management on the other. Sovereign peoples have the right to make their own decisions about the nature of their communal life, providing these do not infringe on the rights of other sovereign nations. This includes the right to make mistakes, and to follow paths that outsiders might see as misguided.

The autonomy of sovereign nations is not absolute, in either the human or animal case. There are many conditions under which outside assistance or intervention might be appropriate. We will discuss many such cases in relation to wild animals. However, as a general principle, a theory of sovereignty recognizes the importance for peoples, as for individuals, of leading self-determined lives, which, in turn, influences and constrains how we respond to their suffering.

The idea of animal sovereignty will undoubtedly strike many readers as unfamiliar, and perhaps as deeply counter-intuitive. And, indeed, the idea of animal sovereignty is a non sequitur according to some definitions. Sovereignty is sometimes defined as a supreme or absolute authority to make law, where law is understood as something separate from mere custom, habit, or social convention. Understood in this way, sovereignty requires the existence of an authority structure that 'stands apart from and over the community', since 'it is only with the emergence of this type of command structure that we find an institution in which the concept of sovereignty can be lodged' (Pemberton 2009: 17). Much of social life is regulated in tacit and informal ways, through socialization, tradition, the influence of peers, bargaining and fighting amongst individual group members, and so on, but sovereignty is said to be categorically different: it only arises 'through the establishment of a governing authority that can be differentiated from society and which is able to exercise an absolute political power' (Loughlin 2003: 56). In this sense, sovereignty 'stands in opposition to all that is merely mechanical or spontaneous in social development' (Bickerton, Cunliffe, and Gourevitch 2007: 11).

Defined this way, it is clear that animal communities lack the institutions needed for sovereignty. The self-regulation of wild animal communities may not be 'merely mechanical or spontaneous', but it is tacit and informal, not based on the promulgation of explicit legal commands by an authority separate from society. But we believe that this definition of sovereignty is unduly narrow, and not just in the animal case. It is too narrow to address the legitimate claims of human communities. So we will first discuss why we need a broader and more flexible account of sovereignty in the human case, and then discuss why this broader account can and should be generalized to wild animal communities.

If only societies with complex institutional differentiation are entitled to claim sovereignty, then some human communities will fail to pass the threshold. Indeed, most human communities throughout history have been stateless societies governed by custom. Does that mean they have no valid claim to sovereignty? This was the view adopted by European imperialists. When Europeans colonized the Americas, they denied this was a violation of the sovereignty of indigenous peoples on the grounds that indigenous peoples lacked any concept or practice of sovereignty—no individual or institution within indigenous communities was seen as having 'absolute political power' to issue legal commands binding on all members. Their self-regulation was seen to be 'merely mechanical or spontaneous'.[17]

This imperialist use of theories of sovereignty to dispossess indigenous peoples of their lands and autonomy was not an accident. Theories of sovereignty were developed precisely in order to justify the colonization of indigenous peoples (Keal 2003; Anaya 2004). A basic impetus for the elaboration of theories of sovereignty, and indeed of international law more generally, was to justify why European rulers should treat each other in one way (as civilized peoples to be treated with equality and consent) while treating non-Europeans in a very different way (as inferiors to be conquered and colonized). Theories of sovereignty were a move within this imperial game.

Some critics argue that such Eurocentric ideologies and hierarchies are inherent in any use of the term sovereignty, which should therefore be given up by anyone interested in justice for indigenous peoples (Alfred 2001, 2005). In this view, indigenous peoples shouldn't respond to their colonization by asserting indigenous sovereignty, but rather by repudiating the very idea of sovereignty.[18] Others argue that, even within its original European homeland, sovereignty is increasingly obsolete. The emergence of international human rights laws, and new forms of transnational governance such as the EU, make the idea of an 'absolute political power' meaningless. Indeed, various critics—including postmodernists, feminists, constructivists, and cosmopolitans—are 'convinced of the morally dangerous, conceptually vacuous or empirically irrelevant character of sovereignty' (Bickerton, Cunliffe, and Gourevitch 2007: 4; see also Smith 2009).

Our view, however, is that sovereignty can be rehabilitated, and can play a vital role in serving certain moral purposes, but we need to make these moral purposes more explicit. What then are the moral purposes of sovereignty? According to Pemberton, sovereignty is 'nothing more than a means of providing a secure space in which communities can grow and flourish. The crucial value at stake is thus autonomy' (Pemberton 2009: 7). This indeed is the view of most recent theorists of the moral purposes of sovereignty—sovereignty protects autonomy as a means of community flourishing.[19] Insofar as the flourishing of a community's members is tied up with their ability to maintain their own forms of social organization on their territory, then we commit a harm and an injustice when we impose alien rule on them, and sovereignty is the tool we use to protect against that injustice.

Viewed this way, the moral impulse of sovereignty is fundamentally anti-imperialist, and indeed Daniel Philpott argues that the two major historical 'revolutions in sovereignty'—the Treaty of Westphalia, which first created a recognizable principle of sovereignty, and the post-war decolonization movement, which diffused that principle around the world—were both inspired by struggles for local autonomy against imperial power (Philpott 2001: 254).[20]

Any normatively defensible concept of sovereignty, we believe, must be defined to serve this moral purpose. But if so, then the insistence that communities display a particular 'command structure' in order to qualify for sovereignty is clearly a moral distortion—it fetishizes legal form over moral substance. It should not matter whether indigenous peoples meet some threshold of complex institutional differentiation. What matters is their interest in autonomy. As Pemberton notes, 'the mere fact of [indigenous peoples'] independent existence as well as the value placed on it as evidenced by their resistance to state capture, should have been enough to establish their entitlement to be left alone'. Stateless societies may not have developed the High Modernist European concept of sovereignty, but 'nor could such peoples have been seen, in good faith, as mere numerical quantities, bereft of social organisation and recognisable interests' (Pemberton 2009: 130). Where peoples have an 'independent existence', 'place value upon it', and 'resist' alien rule, and where they have 'recognisable interests' in their 'social organisation', then we have the moral purposes that call for sovereignty.

In short, when evaluating whether and how to accord rights to sovereignty to particular communities, what matters is not the legal institutions they happen to possess, but rather whether they have interests in autonomy, which, in turn, depends on whether their flourishing is tied to their ability to maintain their modes of social organization and self-regulation on their territory. It is clear that, in the human case, such interests extend beyond those societies with specifically modern state forms. And so we see a clear trend towards developing new conceptions of sovereignty for indigenous peoples, nomadic peoples, and pastoralists that can operate within or across the boundaries of nation states.[21]

We can see a similar need to re-conceptualize sovereignty in relation to a range of protectorates or dependencies. Throughout history, smaller or vulnerable communities have sought protection by associating themselves with larger ones, for certain purposes, while insisting on their rights of internal self-government. A number of such cases remain around the world. While theorists of sovereignty puzzle about whether such communities have relinquished their sovereignty—and the UN's Commission on Non-Self-Governing Territories sometimes encourages such communities to (re)assert full-blown independence—there is no reason why such arrangements cannot be responsive to the underlying moral purposes of sovereignty.[22] We see similar innovations occurring within Europe, as people try to make sense of the way sovereignty is being unbundled and re-bundled at different levels of the European Union, with no single level being able to assert undisputed primacy.

In all these cases, we need to stop making a fetish of particular legal forms, and instead start by asking about the moral purposes that claims to sovereignty might serve, and then thinking about which forms or modes of sovereignty in fact serve those purposes. The result will inevitably be a rather disparate set of arrangements in which sovereignty will be nested, pooled, and shared in various forms of autonomies, dependencies, protectorates, confederations, and associations.[23]

In our view, all of this has definite implications for wild animals. Like stateless human communities, they may lack the concept of sovereignty, and may lack the sort of institutional differentiation that separates 'state' from 'society'. But, like human communities, they cannot be 'seen, in good faith, as mere numerical quantities, bereft of social organisation and recognisable interests' (Pemberton 2009: 130). They too have an 'independent existence' and have demonstrated the value they attach to it by resisting alien rule. Like human communities, their 'communal flourishing' depends on securing their lands and autonomy. (Indeed, the extent to which their well-being depends on maintaining specific traditional habitats is arguably greater for most wild animals than for humans.)[24] Hence they, too, should be seen as being 'entitled to be left alone'.

In short, once we make explicit the moral purpose of sovereignty, then we have no grounds for denying that wild animals qualify. Wild animals have legitimate interests in maintaining their social organization on their territory, they are vulnerable to the injustice of having alien rule imposed on them and their territory, and sovereignty is an appropriate tool for protecting that interest against vulnerability to injustice. Insisting on a particular 'command structure' as a requirement for sovereignty is morally arbitrary, in both the human and animal cases.

No doubt some readers will respond that there remains a fundamental difference between stateless human societies and wild animal communities. The former may not have an institutionally distinct legal order, but they are capable of rational reflection on their self-governance. Even if sovereignty does not require statehood, surely it at least requires some capacity for rational reflection and self-conscious decision-making. For sovereignty to be worth according or respecting, it must involve more than the 'merely mechanical or spontaneous' expression of instinctive behaviour. Even if imperialists were wrong to insist that indigenous peoples meet a Eurocentric 'standard of civilization', surely there are some standards of competence that claimants must meet?

We hope that our discussion of animal capacities for citizenship in Chapter 5 has already allayed some of these objections. As we discussed, it's a mistake to assume that animals are incapable of agency. But our discussion there was focused on the sort of agency that is possible for domesticated animals within mixed human–animal communities. Domesticated animals, we argued, are capable of expressing a subjective good that can and should be included in our political decisions about the common good. But this was tied to an idea of 'dependent agency' in which humans played an active role in interpreting this subjective good, and thereby enabling the exercise of animal co-citizenship—an idea which is itself dependent on the sort of relations of trust between animals and humans that domestication presupposes.

If we accord sovereignty to wild animals, by contrast, we are precisely rejecting this model of dependent agency: we are saying that individual wild animals do not want or need human assistance to interpret their good. Obviously the sort of competence required here is different from the competence involved in the exercise of co-citizenship by domesticated animals. If wild animals are to be accorded sovereignty, we need to show that they are competent to take care of themselves, and to manage their communities independently, separate from humans, which is very different from the competence for dependent agency within mixed communities.

What sort of competence is needed for sovereignty? We would argue that for wild animals—as indeed for humans—what matters for sovereignty is the ability to respond to the challenges that a community faces, and to provide a social context in which its individual members can grow and flourish. And in this sense, it seems clear that wild animals are competent. Sometimes this competence is 'mechanical and spontaneous', as when animals respond at an instinctual level to their bodily urges, and to the opportunities, challenges, and changes in their environment. And sometimes this competence is consciously learned (as when the bears in Yellowstone Park learn how to open the doors of minivans by bouncing on the roof, and pass on this learning to other bears).

Wild animals are competent both as individuals and as communities. As individuals, for example, they know what foods to eat, where to find them, and how to store them for winter use. They know how to find or construct shelter. They know how to care for their young. They know how to navigate vast distances. They know how to reduce the risk of predation (vigilance, hiding, diversion, counter-attack), and to guard against wastage of energy. For example, when deer flee a potentially dangerous human, they run just far enough to be out of the human's sightlines, but don't waste energy fleeing any further than necessary (Thomas 2009). And wild animals are competent as communities as well, at least amongst the social species. They know how to work together to hunt, or to evade predators, or to care for weak and injured

175

members of the group. New knowledge travels quickly amongst conspecifics. For example, ravens share information about food sources at the nightly roost (Heinrich 1999). A blue tit learns how to pierce the foil of milk bottles, and soon all the neighbourhood blue tits are using this new technique for raiding the cream layer from the top of milk bottles once delivered to front doorsteps in Britain.[25] Sometimes wild animals cooperate across the species divide—as in the case of the cooperative scavenging relationship between ravens and coyotes (described in Chapter 4, note 22), or cooperative hunting between grouper fish and moray eels (Braithwaite 2010).

In these and countless other ways, wild animals, both individually and collectively, confront the challenges of life in the wild, successfully tending to their needs and minimizing risks. In this sense, as Regan emphasizes, it is wrong to equate wild animals with defenceless children needing our protection.[26] Wild animal communities include animals of all ages and levels of competence. As parents and communities they socialize their young, and pass on the competence necessary for survival. There might be circumstances in which outside assistance from humans would be helpful and desirable (e.g., in the case of a large-scale natural disaster, or a ravaging and preventable disease, or in response to individual animals in distress)—we discuss such cases below. But in general, when it comes to the day-to-day management of the risks of living in the wild, it is reasonable to view wild animals as competent actors in a division of labour in which they take responsibility for mutual assistance in their own communities, and indeed are much more competent to do so than we would be on their behalf.

Someone might respond that wild animals are hardly competent to exercise sovereignty if they are unable to protect all of their own members from starvation or predation.[27] If a human community failed in this regard, we would likely view it as a 'failed state', or in any event one that requires some degree of external intervention. But in the context of ecosystems, food cycles and predator–prey relationships are not indicators of 'failure'. Rather, they are defining features of the context within which wild animal communities exist; they frame the challenges to which wild animals must respond both individually and collectively, and the evidence suggests that they respond competently.[28]

This competence argument is more compelling in relation to some animals than to others. Many mammalian species produce few offspring, and invest greatly in their care either as individual parents or larger social groups. Individual young have a real chance of surviving the challenges of their early years and making it to adulthood. Compare this with the many amphibian and reptile species who lay vast quantities of eggs and leave them to fend for themselves. Most eggs never hatch. Most hatchlings are quickly consumed by predators. Life for many a fish, turtle, or lizard amounts to a few brief moments after emerging from the shell until a larger fish or bird or reptile swoops in to devour them.

The scope for 'competent agency' varies across species, but should be recognized and supported where it does exist. For some species, it grounds a strong argument for respecting autonomy. For other species, the argument is weaker. On balance, however, we should still respect the sovereignty of wild animals, including those for whom there is minimal evidence of competent agency, because the argument is strongly buttressed by the earlier arguments about fallibility and flourishing. Given the complexity and interdependencies of natural processes, and our very fallible understanding of them, there is every reason to assume that any paternalistic intervention we undertake to protect wild animals will have unintended and perhaps perverse effects. And if this paternalistic intervention takes place on a broad scale, it is almost certainly going to undermine the ability of wild animals to exercise the capacities and dispositions that evolved precisely in response to their environment. If we are to respect wild animals as members of their own kinds of communities, autonomous and self-regulating, then interference in the defining features of their form of community would mean an end to their independence, to their ability to be the sorts of beings they are, and put them instead in a state of dependency on ongoing human intervention.[29]

Moreover, it's important to note that insofar as we can assess their preferences, wild animals do not accede to such interventions.[30] Wild animals, as we define them, are precisely those animals who avoid human contact. Unlike domesticated animals who have been bred for human environments, or the liminal animals we discuss in Chapter 7 who seek out human development and the opportunities afforded there, wild animals show a clear preference to be independent of humans. We could say that, on the sovereignty question, they 'vote with their feet'. And insofar as they exhibit no inclination to join into society with us, we must respect them as forming their own sovereign communities.

In our view, this presumption of competence amongst wild animals, and their demonstrated antipathy to human intervention, is sufficient to establish their claim to be recognized as having legitimate sovereign authority.[31]

This may seem like a roundabout way of getting back to where we started—namely, the long-standing ART view that in relation to wild animals we should simply 'let them be'. But as we have seen, the arguments ART has invoked for this view are rather ad hoc and underdeveloped, and the recognition of sovereignty provides a more secure normative and conceptual basis for it. Moreover, ART has not explained *how* to let them be. Respecting autonomy is a valid moral purpose, but we need legal and political tools to do so. As we noted earlier, some AR theorists have suggested that we can protect wild animals through the attribution of property rights (Dunayer 2004; Hadley

2005). But if we think again about the example of European imperialism, we can see the limits of this approach. European imperialists were often quite prepared to accept that indigenous peoples had property rights, even as they denied them sovereignty. The result was that indigenous individuals or families were able to maintain a plot of land, but lost their collective autonomy, as Europeans imposed their own laws, culture, and language on indigenous peoples.[32] Similarly, what wild animals need is not (or not only) a property right in an individual nest or den, say, but rather protection of their right to maintain their way of life on their territory—in short, they need sovereignty.

Moreover, respect for sovereignty is not just an injunction to let them be, in either the human or animal case. Respect for sovereignty does not require isolation or autarchy, but rather is consistent with various forms of interaction and assistance, and even with forms of intervention. This is clear enough in the human case, where self-governing communities exercise their sovereignty by entering into dense webs of mutual cooperation and mutual agreements (including agreements over the rules of humanitarian intervention). But even in the wild animal case, it is a mistake to think that respect for sovereignty requires a complete hands-off approach. Not all forms of human intervention threaten values of autonomy and self-determination. On the contrary, some forms of positive intervention may promote them. Imagine that human intervention could halt an aggressive and systemic new bacterium which is about to invade and devastate an ecosystem. Or imagine that human intervention could deflect a large meteor on a collision course for a wilderness zone populated by billions of wild animals. In these cases—and others we discuss below—human intervention can be seen as protecting the ability of wild animals to maintain their way of life on their territories.

More generally, sovereignty provides a framework within which we can address a range of issues that inevitably arise between communities, such as issues of boundaries and spillover effects, as well as the legitimate scope for intervention. As we noted at the start of this chapter, the traditional ART injunction to 'let them be' provides little or no guidance on these questions. Indeed, we believe that these questions simply cannot be addressed within any version of ART that focuses solely on the issue of individual capacities and interests. Any attempt to address questions of territory, boundaries, spillover effects, and intervention solely by reference to universal individual rights will inevitably fall prey to the 'too little–too much' dilemma we noted earlier. However, all of these questions become more tractable when they are situated within a larger framework of just relations between sovereign communities.

That, at any rate, is what we try to show in the rest of this chapter, by examining a series of concrete issues concerning the relations between humans and wild animals. As with our citizenship model in Chapter 5, invoking theories of sovereignty does not provide a magic formula for resolving some very thorny questions. But we try to show that sovereignty does provide a useful lens for addressing these issues, offering more coherent and compelling answers than those available in existing ART or ecological approaches. We start with the issue of intervention, to explore how ideas of sovereignty can both justify a general presumption against colonization or paternalistic management, while also providing criteria for acceptable forms of intervention that support sovereignty (section 3). We then turn to the issue of boundaries and territory (section 4), and spillover effects (section 5).

3. Positive Assistance and Intervention

As we noted earlier, one fundamental challenge facing ART concerns the question of positive obligations to wild animals. On the one hand, if we recognize animals as vulnerable selves, then surely their pain and suffering matters, even when caused by natural processes, and we should do what we can to mitigate or eliminate such suffering. This suggests, in Nussbaum's words, that ART should aim 'in a very general way, for the gradual supplanting of the natural by the just' (Nussbaum 2006: 400). On the other hand, the idea that we have a duty to intervene to provide food and safe shelter to wild animals seems a *reductio* of the very idea of animal rights. Confronted with this dilemma, AR theorists have offered a variety of arguments in favour of the 'laissez-faire intuition' that we should just let wild animals be, including arguments about autonomy, flourishing, fallibility, and discretion. However, these arguments often have a rather ad hoc appearance, and do not necessarily fit together in any clear or coherent fashion.

Moreover, as soon as we think about the full range of possible interventions, the idea that we could have a single simple rule—whether an interventionist commitment to 'supplant the natural by the just' or a non-interventionist commitment to 'let them be'—seems implausible. There are important variations between different types of interventions, some of which may be more permissible than others, and we need a version of ART that can capture the moral significance of these variations.

Not all human interventions in wild animal societies threaten their autonomy or habitat. Some human activity in wild animal territory might be benign—appreciation of the wilderness, or moderate resource extraction (e.g., sustainable collection of wild foods such as nuts, fruits, mushrooms, seaweeds, etc., leaving 'enough and as good' for others). Some interventions might actually be positively beneficial—as, for example, when selective logging increases light and air circulation in a closed forest environment in a way that enriches the ecosystem and benefits the animals living there. Although wild animals avoid human contact, they can sometimes benefit from the actions of humans, as, for example, when an individual animal is rescued after breaking through thin ice, or provided with emergency food or shelter.

Such small-scale interventions seem benign, and some large-scale interventions also seem desirable, such as the meteor deflection we mentioned earlier. We need to be very careful in justifying interventions into wild animal communities, but this does not mean that all interventions are illegitimate. Unfortunately, current versions of ART provide virtually no guidance in deciding which forms of intervention are appropriate. Can a theory of sovereignty for wild animals do better? Obviously sovereignty will not help if it is just a fancy word for 'letting them be'. But we have argued that sovereignty is more than this: it is rooted in a distinct set of moral purposes. Sovereignty is tied to a particular set of interests (communities have legitimate interests in maintaining their social organization on their territory) and to a particular set of threats (communities are vulnerable to the injustice of having alien rule imposed on them and their territories). Sovereignty is an appropriate tool for protecting this particular set of interests against that particular vulnerability to injustice.

Viewed this way, sovereignty is a far richer moral notion than simply 'letting them be'. Respect for sovereignty is not about isolation or autarchy, and does not forbid all forms of interaction or even intervention. What matters, rather, is upholding the value of self-determination, and while this rules out certain forms of intervention, it allows, and perhaps even requires, other forms of assistance.

The rules for distinguishing legitimate from illegitimate interventions in sovereign communities are highly contested, even in the human case. But we can identify some basic principles. On the one hand, sovereign communities have a right to protection from the aggression of foreign states (conquest, colonization, theft of resources), and from less violent forms of imperialism (paternalistic management or intervention in their internal affairs by outsiders, whether well-meaning or not). In other words, sovereignty is a form of protection against external threats of annihilation, exploitation, or assimilation. It provides the space for communities to develop along their own self-determining paths, under controlled conditions of interaction with outsiders, rather than being subjected to the unchecked force of powerful outsiders (regardless of the intentions of those outsiders).

However, it is not the goal of sovereignty to rule out all interactions between states. There are many potential benefits from mutual cooperation between states, in terms of trade, increased mobility, and, importantly, the possibilities of positive assistance. As a result, there are many instances in which states actively solicit the positive help of foreign states. Arrangements of mutual aid may be formalized in treaties, or merely cemented over years of interaction and mutual assistance. Such arrangements do not undermine sovereignty—on the contrary, they are ways in which states exercise sovereignty on behalf of their citizens.

A much thornier area is positive intervention that is not solicited or part of an agreed mutual agreement, as when a state is suddenly overwhelmed by an external threat, a natural calamity, or internal collapse. We usually consider that the international community has a duty to help in these situations, even if the afflicted state is not in a position to formally solicit assistance. But intervention to help others who have not requested our help (or in cases in which there is conflict about seeking outside assistance) can be problematic. Claims of providing positive assistance are frequently used to cloak acts of imperialistic power—consider the invasion of Iraq, for example, or the Nazi invasions of Czechoslovakia and Poland, which were defended on the basis of protecting internal minorities whose state had failed in its duty to protect them. On the other hand, it is generally agreed that the international community should have intervened in Rwanda to protect Tutsis from the sudden and catastrophic failure of that state to protect its citizens. External military interventions to protect basic rights of citizens are perhaps the most difficult issue, since these interventions occur almost inevitably against the wishes of the state government. But aid and assistance in response to natural disaster or failed development are also fraught. International response to the devastating 2004 tsunami in Asia is an example of international assistance which was welcomed by the people and communities in need, and was carried out in ways that were effective, and non-threatening to the sovereignty of those communities. However, there have been countless examples of so-called aid that are in fact thinly veiled efforts by the states offering assistance to access new markets, control resources, create dependencies, or extort obligations.

These issues are enormously complicated in human international relations, and there is no reason to think that they will be any less complicated in human–animal relations. However, we can identify some fundamental principles that are widely shared. First, if the people of a foreign state have suffered or are suffering a catastrophe (whether human-generated or an act of nature), and we are able to assist them, and our efforts to assist are not rejected, then we should indeed assist them to the best of our ability and resources. Second, we should offer assistance in a way that allows a community to get back on its own feet—that is, in a manner that supports its competence and viability as a sovereign state with a right to self-determination. We should not use the circumstances of vulnerability to undermine a state's independence, indebt it, weaken it, or impose on it our own conception of the good. These principles are not always easy to implement—there are complexities not just around the question of whether assistance should be provided, but also regarding how it should be provided, and by whom. At every stage, assistance can be undertaken in ways that respect the dignity of those being assisted (including their right to be citizens of self-determining communities) or ways that undermine their dignity.

However, it seems clear that there are instances of sovereign states being overwhelmed by catastrophe (e.g., natural tragedy) or suffering a total collapse of internal order and/or legitimacy ('failed state', genocide, etc.) where positive intervention is consistent with respecting the sovereignty of the people. Indeed, intervention can be viewed as protecting and helping to restore their sovereignty. In these instances, assuming intervention can be efficacious, we have a duty to assist.

We believe that these basic principles can also be applied to wild animal communities. Averting a meteor collision, for example, seems to fall clearly in the category of interventions that respect and help to restore sovereignty. By contrast, intervening to end predation, or to control natural food cycles, could only be achieved by subverting sovereignty, and by reducing wild animals to a state of permanent dependency and paternalism. As we discussed earlier, predation and food cycles are part of the stable structure of self-regulation of wild animal communities. Animals have evolved to survive under these conditions, and are competent to do so. Individual animals suffer from these natural processes, but the presence of predation and food cycles does not indicate that the sovereign community has suffered a disabling catastrophe, or a sudden failure of competence. Wild animals are not in the circumstances of justice with one another, and the survival of some individuals inevitably requires that other individuals die. This is a regrettable feature of nature, but any attempt to intervene to change these facts of nature en masse would require completely subjugating nature to our ongoing intervention and management. Not only is this impossible, but even if it were possible it would completely undermine the sovereignty of wild animal communities. Intervention in nature to end predation and food cycles is unjustifiable both in terms of motivation and effect. It does not meet the required trigger for intervention (overwhelming catastrophe, community disintegration, and/or request for external assistance), and it cannot meet the goal of intervention, which is to help a sovereign community get back on its feet as a viable and self-determining community.

Respect for sovereignty, therefore, rules out systematic intervention to end predation or natural food cycles (at least, insofar as we can currently envision such interventions). However, this leaves open the question of other kinds of positive assistance—ones that do not undermine the very stability of wild animal communities, or their ability to exist into the future as sovereign communities. We have already considered some interventions that meet this test—blasting the meteor out of space, or halting a runaway virus in its tracks before it invades a vulnerable ecosystem. These may sound like science fiction scenarios,[33] but we can imagine more prosaic small-scale interventions in which humans can benefit wild animal communities without undermining their sovereignty.[34] Scale matters here. As an individual human, I can save a starving deer without upsetting the balance of nature—that is, without compromising the sovereignty of wild animal communities. However, if the government undertakes a large-scale deer-feeding programme, this will have consequences—for deer populations, for their predators, for the plants that the deer would otherwise be eating, for their competitors for that food, and so on down the line. Systemic and ongoing human intervention would be required to manage all of these consequences.

This means that, as individuals or collectivities, we need to weigh our actions in a complex manner. On the one hand, my actions as an individual are unlikely to compromise the sovereignty of wild animal communities. On the other hand, my actions in concert with many others acting in the same way might do so. This doesn't prohibit me from feeding the deer. I may have fairly reliable knowledge, for example, that there aren't significant numbers of other individuals feeding deer and that my individual action is harmless in the larger scheme, not one that will snowball towards pervasive human interventions down the road.

However, concern about whether I am an individual actor, or one of many, is only one consideration. There is also the fallibility argument. Are my actions, even on an individual level, going to have the consequences I foresee, or am I potentially going to cause more harm where I seek to alleviate suffering? Elizabeth Marshall Thomas provides a detailed account of her reasoning process in considering whether or not to feed deer at her New Hampshire home.[35] Some of the potential unintended consequences she considers include: disrupting the social relations and power dynamics amongst the local deer community; contributing to diet imbalance; tempting the deer to risk exposure or predators in order to reach her food stations; and encouraging transmission of diseases between deer at the feeding station. On balance, she decides to take as many precautions as she can, and goes ahead and feeds the deer. She asks:

> Why did I feed these animals against all advice? Because we live in the same place, because they were individuals, because they had relatives, experience, a past, and desires, because they were cold and hungry, because they hadn't found enough to eat in the fall, because each had just one life. (Thomas 2009: 53)

In short, having weighed the consequences of her actions, in the end she is moved by a response of simple compassion. These are deer she has developed an individual relationship with. They are suffering, and she believes she is in a position to help them. So she helps them. Ultimately, in just about any situation of offering positive assistance, we have to trust our judgement as individuals to assess the specific circumstances and make the right choices.

Have I done my homework? Do I know enough about feeding deer to minimize the risk that I might actually harm them? Would my efforts to help others and alleviate suffering be better directed elsewhere? Have I thought about the larger ramifications of my actions, and the way they interact with the actions of others?

There is a nice description of this kind of dilemma in Hope Ryden's book about her experience with a colony of beavers at Lily Pond, in upstate New York (Ryden 1989). Ryden and the beavers gradually habituate to each other's presence, and she spends months observing them from a companionable distance, compiling some amazing documentation about their habits and social relationships. As a scientist, Ryden wants to observe beavers in their natural state as much as possible, without becoming a significant intervening force in their lives. She wants to observe their lives, not manipulate them. And yet, over the course of months of night-time observation (when beavers are most active), she naturally becomes greatly attached to the beavers. Then a crisis occurs. It is late in the winter, and a combination of events—delayed spring, unusually thick ice—has resulted in the beavers running out of food in their den. (Beavers can't escape the den until the ice cover breaks, so if they haven't stored sufficient food at the beginning of the winter they starve.) Ryden can tell from the absence of sounds emitted from the beaver house that they are on their last legs. Ryden agonizes, and finds she cannot stand by, so she chops open a section of ice next to the house, and brings enough branches to sustain the beavers for a few days until the weather breaks. Despite her adherence to a general principle of non-intervention, Ryden finds herself in an individual situation in which she feels she must intervene. Some would say this behaviour is contradictory, or a failure of duty on her part. But there is no contradiction, because Ryden is not legislating a universal duty of human intervention in beaver food cycles. Rather, she is in a very specific relationship to particular beavers: she knows them very well, and can understand that her actions are unlikely to have catastrophic spillover effects. Moreover, she has a duty of care that has been activated by her relationship with the beavers, including the many benefits she has drawn from this relationship.

Many scientists and naturalists have undertaken amazingly complex projects to assist wild animals—usually those who belong to species 'at risk'. Consider the efforts to help the waldrapp ibis relearn its traditional migration route by following behind humans in microlight aircraft. The ibis isn't a strong flier, and the birds are frequently blown off course. So far, several of them have been learning the migration route primarily from the back of a van![36] We may ask whether the fallibility and discretionary arguments are always sufficiently attended to in these undertakings—that is, are these interventions really causing more good than harm? Would efforts and resources be better directed elsewhere? We may also have concerns about whether the basic rights of the individual animals being assisted (as opposed to the species) are being respected. In other words, are the rights of individuals being compromised in order to benefit the species? These are all important questions. What we should learn from these efforts, though, is that humans are capable of incredibly creative and delicate interventions in the natural world, when we put our minds to it. And these interventions, under the right circumstances, can fully respect the rights of animals, both as individuals and as sovereign collectivities, while adding immensely to our understanding of them, and our ability to help them in future.

A wonderful account of such an intervention is naturalist Joe Hutto's decision to rescue abandoned wild turkey eggs from a farmer's field, incubate and hatch the eggs, and raise the turkeys to live in the wild (Hutto 1995). Hutto was fully committed to the implications of his decision. He knew that the turkeys would be dependent on him for a full year, not just to supply them with food and shelter, but to help them develop into fully independent creatures able to forage and fend for themselves, without becoming habituated to humans in the process. He set up an enclosure and roost for the turkeys where he could leave them safely at night. And during the day he took on the role of turkey parent, gradually introducing the young turkeys to their surroundings, accompanying them for countless hours of exploration and foraging in the woods and fields. For a year, Hutto lived the life of a wild turkey. He learned how to be in their company, how to move, where to forage, how to attend to changes in the environment, and how to signal snakes, berries, or other notable features. In this way he could keep a watchful eye on them during their vulnerable early months, while letting them develop a full range of natural wild turkey behaviours and experiences. And within a year, the turkeys were successfully weaned and integrated into the wild. Hutto's subsequent written account has added greatly to our understanding and appreciation of wild turkeys. Indeed, it looks like a clear case of a genuinely mutually beneficial relationship. The turkeys have a chance at life which would otherwise have been lost—and not a stunted life in captivity, but a full turkey life. And Hutto has a chance to learn, and develop a bond across the species barrier.

One could imagine a story starting with the same intervention (rescuing the eggs), but going in a very different direction—resulting in adult turkeys confined to a zoo for life, or so habituated to humans that even though released in the wild they wouldn't last long because, being drawn to human settlement, they would inevitably meet accidental or intentional harm there. Or one could imagine turkeys inadequately monitored during the vulnerable first months, or ill-prepared for life in the wild, thus becoming easy pickings for the first coyote or hawk to come along. These various grim scenarios remind us of why, in general, a hands-off principle towards wild animals is a sound one.

But Hutto's story reminds us that hands off isn't the only ethical choice for individuals in their relationships with wild animals.

Often, ecological theorists have taken a harder line than AR theorists regarding the inadmissibility of human interventions in processes of nature. This is strongly motivated by fallibility concerns (i.e., humans will inevitably do more harm than good),[37] but it is also motivated by a strain of anti-sentimentalism. According to this macho strain in ecological thought, nature's laws are harsh, and it is weakness and squeamishness to wish otherwise. Individual acts of compassion towards individual animals can't change the overall framework, so they are a futile form of sentimental sloppiness even if they don't lead to actual harm to animals or ecology. The desire to carry out such acts betrays a lack of understanding of nature, even a hatred of nature's processes (Hettinger 1994).

There are many problems with this view. For starters, it is wrong to suggest that deploring certain aspects of nature (e.g., that animals suffer) amounts to a hatred of nature per se (Everett 2001). Second, such a view rests on an implicit and indefensible assumption about humans and their actions being outside of nature: our empathetic response to the suffering of other species is itself a part of human nature, and is a response shared by other species as well (e.g., wild dolphins who help rescue humans). Third, it betrays callousness towards the fate of individuals. The fact that one cannot change natural processes of predation or food cycles, and hence cannot change the fate of animals on a large scale, doesn't mean that acts of caring towards individual animals are irrelevant or inconsistent. Such acts mean everything to the actual animal who has been fed, or rescued after falling thorough the ice. Some ecologists are led into this error because of the way they reify—even sanctify—nature's laws or (non-human) ecological processes. This is very different from the theory advanced here that animal communities must be respected as sovereign and self-determining.

Respect for wild animal sovereignty is not just letting them be. Sovereignty is critical for protecting the freedom, autonomy, and flourishing of wild animals, and in general this means that humans should be very cautious about intervening in nature. However, there are many kinds of assistance that do not compromise wild animal sovereignty. We have canvassed several— from efforts to avert natural disasters to small-scale acts of compassion and assistance—that do not undermine the sovereignty of wild animal communities. Far from being misguided or inconsistent acts of sentimentality, we would argue that these interventions are demanded by compassion (as a thoughtful response to another's suffering) and justice. (As we discuss below, such positive actions of intervention can also help temper the egregious risks and spillover costs we inevitably impose on wild animals.) The sovereignty of wild animals helps to explain why we have these two impulses:

(a) to leave nature in general to its own ways (preserving the space in which animals exercise agency to determine the course of their lives, and the future of their communities without humans 'calling the shots'); while (b) nevertheless responding in a time- and/or scale-limited fashion in order to reduce suffering or avert disaster, having carefully considered the consequences of doing so. These impulses are not inconsistent, but, rather, a reflection of a careful balancing of important values (autonomy and freedom on the one hand; the alleviation of suffering on the other) that frequently come into conflict in the wilderness where animals are not in the circumstances of justice with one another.

In short, we believe that sovereignty provides an appropriate framework for thinking through our positive obligations to wild animals—one that avoids the gaps and vacillations of existing ART. We ought not to intervene in the internal workings of wild animal communities (e.g., predation, food cycles) in ways that undermine their autonomy, effectively placing them under permanent and systemic human management. However, we have a duty to offer positive assistance when this is consistent with respect for sovereignty (and careful weighing of the fallibility and discretionary arguments). These requirements cannot be captured by some simple general formula such as 'always act to reduce suffering' or 'never interfere in nature'. We do not owe obeisance to some kind of sacred law of nature. We owe duties of justice to wild animals. In general, respecting their sovereignty means we should be very cautious about undertaking interventions in nature. But respect for sovereignty is consistent with undertaking many individual and time-limited or scale-limited acts of assistance which do not undermine the ability of wild animal communities to flourish as independent and self-regulating communities. When we can help animals without usurping their autonomy or causing greater harms, we should be moved by the plight of suffering individuals.

4. Boundaries and Territory

So far, we have tried to show how sovereignty for wild animals is a broader and richer notion than the traditional ART slogan of 'letting them be', rooted in a more complex set of moral purposes. However, a sovereignty framework is not without its own difficulties. Its moral purposes may be clear, we hope, but how it can be operationalized in practice is less clear. We have been talking so far in a rather loose way about the way norms of sovereignty can regulate interaction between distinct 'communities', each maintaining its own forms of social organization on 'its territory'. This suggests a picture in which we can neatly divide up the world into discrete communities exercising sovereignty over their discrete territories. Yet this is hardly a realistic picture. Nature did not assign discrete territory to different species. Different wild animal species occupy (and compete for) the same territory, and many species need to move large distances across territory occupied by other animals or by humans. Sovereignty, therefore, if it is to mean anything in practice, cannot be tied to a picture of neatly divided communities and territories.

In the rest of this chapter, therefore, we attempt to address some of the key challenges involved in implementing a sovereignty framework, including issues of boundaries, territory, and spillover effects.

The Nature of Boundaries: Shared and Overlapping Sovereignty

In everyday discourse, when we think of sovereign states, we think of traditional political maps with neat lines separating chunks of territory into defined states. Canada is to the north of the 49th parallel, the USA to the south. But of course it's more complicated than this. State boundaries do not neatly correspond with the boundaries separating nations or peoples with the inherent right to self-determination. Many states are actually multi-nation states, in which sovereignty is shared or overlapping between different nations or peoples, each of whom asserts rights to sovereignty and to self-determination. Within the boundaries of the USA or Canada, we find substate nations of various stripes—the Québécois, Inuit, and First Nations in Canada; American Indian tribes or Puerto Ricans in the USA. Typically, these instances of substate sovereignty are still territorially based—that is, we can point on the map to lands under the (partial and shared) sovereignty of different indigenous peoples or minority nations. In this sense, our ideas of sovereignty remain deeply connected to those of homeland or traditional territory. The existence of 'nations within' complicates the linking of sovereignty to territory, but does not replace that link.

When we turn to the animal case, the story is more complicated. In the case of some land-based animals, we can think about a form of substate territorial sovereignty. Like Quebec, Sami lands, or Puerto Rico, these would be examples in which the boundaries of a sovereign animal community are contained within, or overlap, the boundaries of a larger sovereign state encompassing other peoples. But when we think about birds and fish, the relevant boundaries can no longer be defined in simple two-dimensional geographic terms. Creatures of the water and air inhabit ecological dimensions that are often secondary in human conceptions of sovereign territory. Moreover, any conception of boundaries must account for the facts of migration. If the function of sovereignty is to protect a community's ability to maintain forms of social organization within which its members can flourish, then we need to recognize that these forms involve migrating across the territory of other species or peoples.

Consider some cases. Whitethroat (Sylvia) warblers winter in the Sahel region south of the Sahara desert, then migrate over Egypt and Western Europe to return to British woodlands each spring. What is their 'sovereign territory'? We might say that their two primary habitats in the Sahel and Britain constitute their primary sovereign territory, but their ability to enjoy that sovereign territory clearly depends on their right to use the land and air corridors in between. Some of this habitat is separate from human settlement, but much of it overlaps human sovereign territory, and so we need some account of how sovereignty is shared in those zones. The warblers don't harm us when they fly past, and so in addition to protecting their two primary habitats, we should be prohibited from erecting obstructions along their flight path, or degrading the waters and food sources at their vital resting spots.

Or consider the northern right whales, who roam between summer habitat off the coasts of New England and Nova Scotia, and winter calving grounds off the coast of Florida and Georgia. This is a perilous migration in light of the dangers of being struck by ships along the very busy eastern seaboard. Here again, we need some way of recognizing the sovereignty of ocean animals while sharing the use of territory. Humans, like warblers and right whales, have a right to migrate, to travel in the business of living. We might conceptualize this in terms of 'surface travel rights' to travel corridors through sovereign wild animal territory. But this 'right of way' for human travel is a limited right. Humans cannot exercise such a right without regard for those whose territory we are crossing. As it happens, in the case of right whales, humans are in fact taking important steps to protect them from deadly ship collisions, such as altering the route of Atlantic shipping lanes, and establishing whale monitoring systems to warn ships when they are in proximity to whale pods. In this way, we can say that humans are already recognizing an obligation to respect the sovereignty of whales as a side constraint on their activities as they traverse right whales' habitat.

Or consider the countless cases in which human highways cross wild lands in order to link separate human communities. This need not be inherently impermissible, but they should be seen as right of way corridors through sovereign wild animal territory. And, like ocean shipping lanes, we should be obliged to redesign them in order to limit harms to wild animals. We cannot exercise our right to mobility at the expense of their right to life and mobility. This might mean rethinking our highways in many ways: relocating them away from large wildlife populations; creating buffer zones, travel corridors, and tunnels; lowering speed limits and redesigning cars.

Respect for sovereignty is likely to involve some mix of designated territories and corridor/right of way rights. And this is true for both humans and animals. Just as humans need corridors through wild animal territory, wild animals need corridors through regions of intensive human settlement in order to be able to respond flexibly to population pressures, climate change, and so on.

Developing a framework of sovereignty that can accommodate these complexities is not easy. However, there are interesting analogies and precedents in the human case. We can find many cases where pastoralists, nomads, and ethnic or religious minorities have been accorded land corridors, rights of way, buffer zones, and shared sovereignty, so as to preserve access to their traditional destinations, sea ports, sacred sites, or co-ethnics.[38] For example, consider the situation of nomadic peoples such as the Roma, Bedouin, Sami, and countless others whose traditional migration patterns take them across modern state boundaries. In the case of nomadic peoples and other communities divided by international boundaries, the facts of membership cut across international boundaries, and efforts have been made to develop new forms of citizenship that recognize this.[39] Some of these peoples are stateless, some are citizens in one area and visitors elsewhere, yet others have forms of multiple citizenship. It's a work in progress, but human political theory is slowly developing new concepts for thinking about sovereignty and citizenship in ways that accommodate, rather than deny or suppress, the overlapping and mobile character of communities and territories.

This will obviously require abandoning the idea that sovereignty must be univocal and absolute. Human and animal sovereignty will necessarily involve some degree of 'parallel sovereignty'. Sovereignty is importantly tied to territory, since a community, especially most animal communities, cannot be ecologically viable, let alone autonomously self-regulating, without a land base to sustain it. But sovereignty need not be defined in terms of exclusive access or control over a particular territory, but rather in terms of the extent or nature of access and control necessary for a community to be autonomous and self-regulating.[40]

Consider the case of bonobos and humans sharing the forests to the south of the Congo River. One way of recognizing bonobo sovereignty would be to set aside a sizeable part of the forest and simply exclude humans, including those peoples who have traditionally inhabited the region for generations and whose way of life is tied to the land. This indeed has been the approach taken by some international conservation organizations. But dispossessing these humans in order to meet the claims of the bonobos is an injustice.[41] One solution to this problem has been compensation—that is, compensating dispossessed humans with land and opportunities elsewhere. But a better solution might be to recognize bonobos and local human communities as sharing overlapping sovereignty in this region. While bonobos have come under terrible pressure in recent history—due to war, resource development, and the bushmeat trade—there are examples of traditional societies who have lived sustainably and harmoniously side by side with bonobos for generations, and for whom harming them is taboo. There is no reason why their societies cannot coexist peacefully, sharing the land and its resources, each pursuing its independent course (providing the human footprint remains in balance). In relation to one another, sovereignty is shared or overlapping. But in relation to the outside world, their joint sovereignty can protect both parties from external interference and incursions (e.g., invasion, settlement, violence, development, or resource extraction by external human actors).[42]

Of course the Democratic Republic of the Congo (DRC) is home to countless other animal species as well, all connected in a complex ecological web. Thus we should think in terms of sovereign communities of multi-species animal ecologies, rather than single species. Here again we can find human equivalents. Various countries have endorsed the principle that indigenous peoples or national groups have inherent rights of self-determination, but in cases where such groups are either too small to govern themselves effectively, and/or are geographically interspersed with other such groups, the solution has been to create 'multi-ethnic autonomy regimes', in which a single geographic entity is seen as the vehicle for protecting and advancing the sovereignty of different peoples. We see these, for example, in Mexico (Stephen 2008), Nicaragua (Hooker 2009), and Ethiopia (Vaughan 2006).[43]

Whether we conceive of a particular territory as a single sovereign multi-species community, or a series of overlapping sovereign communities, the key point is that the territory is protected from external alien rule or depredations, and free internally to evolve along its own autonomous course.

In short, sovereignty need not be conceived in terms of strict geographical segregation. Sharing the world with animals would involve a variety of sovereign relationships. In some cases there would be strict territorial separation—that is, wilderness areas with very restricted access for humans. There might be other areas in which sovereignty is shared by particular communities of humans and animals, but is restricted with respect to outsiders. There may be other contexts in which sovereignty is conceived multidimensionally in order to accommodate migration patterns and travel corridors or other kinds of shared use.

To make room for such options, our conception of the boundaries of wild animal sovereignty must not be tied to an overly simplistic concept of territory—like the boundaries of a national park. It needs to be a more multilayered conception of sovereignty which can account for (a) ecological viability, (b) the multidimensionality of territory, (c) the facts of human and animal mobility, and (d) the possibilities for sustainable and cooperative parallel co-habitations.

Drawing Boundaries: The Fair Allocation of Territory

While not reducible simply to lines on a map, the recognition of sovereignty for humans and animals does require drawing boundaries. Even if the sovereignty of various wild animal and human communities can be overlapping in places, we still need some way of determining which animal and human communities have the right to be on which pieces of territory. But where should we draw the boundaries of sovereign human and animal communities?

This is a major challenge for a political theory of animal rights, in part because it is a major and unresolved challenge for political theory in the human case. In Avery Kolers' words, the issue of territorial rights is a 'shocking blind spot' in contemporary political philosophy, and indeed its 'most dangerous' omission (Kolers 2009: 1).

It is clear in the human case that we cannot resolve this question by developing some mathematical formula of a fair share of land per capita, or per country. The fact that Singapore has a population density of 18,000 people per square mile, whereas the United States has a density of only 81 people per square mile (and Australia has only 8 people per square mile), does not mean that Singapore should be granted sovereignty over part of the United States or Australia so as to equalize land per capita. We don't get very far by asking questions such as: Is Canada entitled to be as big as it is? Shouldn't Luxembourg be larger? Should there be fewer Chinese and Indian people, and more Swiss or Ugandans? In other words, we don't ask, in some abstract sense, how big sovereign territories should be, or how many people of each race/ethnicity/culture should exist.

Similarly, we won't get very far by asking: How many wild animals should there be, and how many humans? Or how much land are various groups of animals and humans entitled to? Rather, we need to start from the facts on the ground. All else being equal, existing humans and animals have the right to be where they are, and the fundamental task of a theory of sovereignty is to protect that right from threats of dispossession or conquest.

Of course, not all else is equal, and so these facts on the ground are just a starting point for the moral analysis, not the end of the story. Existing settlement and use patterns may need to be revisited in order to remedy certain injustices, or to meet ongoing and future needs. Recall the statistic we mentioned in the introduction about how the planet's human population has more than doubled since 1960, pushing human settlement into lands formerly occupied by wild animals, whose population has plummeted by a third. In effect, humans have been engaged in a dramatic conquest of animal-occupied lands, leading to the decimation of animal populations. Thus, when we think about the boundaries of sovereign animal territory we are immediately confronted with the question of whether we draw boundaries in line with current populations and where they live, or whether we address a history of unjust conquest.

This same problem plagues human political theory. The current boundaries of existing states were established unjustly, through conquest, colonization, and/or forced assimilation. Nevertheless, over time, what were initially unjust acts of settlement gave rise to legitimate claims. From the European conquest of the Americas to the Soviet colonization of the Baltic republics, the generations originally responsible for unjust colonization/settlement have given way to subsequent generations who know no other home, and have not themselves committed unjust acts of colonial occupation and conquest. Similarly, in the human–animal case, we must acknowledge that while it was (and is) wrong for humans to settle in animal-occupied land, nevertheless the human descendants of those settlers become new 'facts on the ground'. Justice requires us to take account of historical injustice, but it is impossible to turn back the clock without violating the rights of existing individuals.

A plausible political theory of territory has to start from the facts on the ground (where people currently live, and the boundaries of existing communities and states), while also attending to concerns of justice, both backward and forward looking. On the one hand, we must recognize the injustice of past actions, and perhaps, in some cases, offer compensation or restitution. On the other hand, we must start from the present—from individuals currently alive and inhabiting particular territories—and commit to justice for all going forward. We will return in a moment to the question of restitution for historic injustice. First, let us consider the question of forward-looking justice for wild animals.

Let us start with the 'facts on the ground'. Humans have drastically invaded and compromised wild animal habitat, but there are still large tracts of undeveloped territory inhabited by wild animals. This includes not just 'pristine wilderness', but large territories where humans have an extraction footprint (forestry, mining, domestic animal grazing, etc.) but minimal settlement. Wild animals are the de facto residents of these areas. So we begin with the proposition that all habitats not currently settled or developed by humans should be considered sovereign animal territory—the air; the seas, lakes, and rivers; and all remaining ecologically viable wild lands (whether 'pristine wilderness' or regreened lands, whether large tracts or small enclaves).[44] These lands are currently occupied by wild animals, and we do not have the right to colonize or displace the citizens of these spaces. This means, effectively, an end to expansion of human settlement. Our other incursions into sovereign animal zones—to log, mine, or graze domesticated animals, for example—carry our impact well beyond the boundaries of where we live, into areas that are inhabited by billions of wild animals. Many of these activities would be drastically curtailed or altered if we recognized the basic negative rights of animals. The numbers of grazing domesticated animals would be greatly reduced. Logging, mining, and wild food gathering would all be transformed to limit harms to animals. But recognizing these zones as sovereign animal territory would go further than cessation of direct harm in the process of resource extraction. While human activity would not necessarily cease within these zones, it would need to be renegotiated in light of the interests of wild animal communities who are sovereign or co-sovereign there. These interests extend beyond harm prevention to protection of the viability of ecosystems and the self-determination of wild animal communities. In other words, it would be renegotiated on the basis of reciprocal relations between sovereign equals.

Recognizing wild animal sovereignty thus places two enormous checks on human activity. First, it says 'this far and no further' with regard to human settlement sprawl. It means we build smarter, we build more efficiently, and we rebuild where we have already laid waste, but we no longer build outward, colonizing lands that are animal-occupied. Second, it means that our activity in sovereign animal territory (or shared territory) must be conducted on fair terms of cooperation amongst equals. This goes much further than ending our direct violence against wild animals. It means that human 'management' of wild animal territory must go through a process akin to decolonization, replacing unilateral extraction with fair trade, and replacing ecologically destructive cost-externalizing practices with sustainable and mutually beneficial ones.[45]

Although we can start from existing patterns of human and wild animal settlement, we will inevitably want to rethink some of these existing boundaries. Some of the earth's ecological zones support abundant life. Others are much more hostile environments. It could be that existing human settlement in rich or fragile ecosystems should be grandfathered, as it were, so that humans would retract their settlement footprint in these areas over time. Conversely, there may be areas in which human settlement can expand in a way that is consistent with increasing the vitality and diversity of wild animal populations. Consider, for example, the status of the enormous territories currently affected by livestock farming. These include vast tracts of land devoted to monocultural crop farming to produce animal feed, as well as many lands subject to cattle grazing. Both practices have decimated wild animal populations and diversity. With the end of livestock farming these areas could simply be returned to wild animals. Or, they could be shared with humans under sustainable models for agriculture, resource extraction, or wilderness/leisure activity. For example, hedgerows, managed forests, and a variety of no-till agricultural practices can support a wonderful diversity of species. Indeed, the end of livestock farming would free up enormous territorial zones in which we could negotiate a new relationship with wild animals (Sapontzis 1987: 103).

We should remember that in the human case, much grief has been caused by drawing arbitrary lines on maps which either fail to mirror the human geography of peoples and ethnic communities, or fail to provide a viable land base for the community in question. Luckily, we are learning a great deal about 'animal geography', and the nature of habitats, watersheds, ecosystems, and biospheres, which we can bring to the task of understanding critical boundaries for wild animal communities.[46] Our political boundaries for sovereign animal communities can be mapped onto ecologically-based boundaries to ensure the viability and stability of sovereign animal communities. Our decisions about which lands to 'rewild', which lands to share in stable symbiotic relationships, and which lands to maintain under more extensive human development or management can be informed by our growing understanding of ecosystems.[47]

Current settlement patterns may need to be adjusted, not only in light of future needs and ecological sustainability, but also to compensate for historic injustices. To be sure, not all past acts of violence against wild animals, or habitat destruction, were acts of injustice. At many times, and in many places, humans were not in the circumstances of justice vis-à-vis wild animals. Humans would not have survived without killing animals for food and clothing, or for self-protection. Having said that, humans have rarely, if ever, restricted themselves to killing out of necessity.[48] Humans have always killed animals for sport, for convenience, or for no reason at all. Indeed, our historic crimes against wild animals are staggering. Consider just one species, sperm whales. Rough estimates suggest that the sperm whale population in 1700 was around 1.5 million individuals. Yankee whaling in the eighteenth and nineteenth centuries is estimated to have reduced that population by about a quarter. Whaling activity dropped off in the latter part of the nineteenth century when spermaceti, used for lighting and lubrication, was replaced by petroleum and kerosene.[49] However, with the arrival of modern industrial whaling in the twentieth century, the industry was revived and approximately three-quarters of a million sperm whales were killed mid-century, before being protected under the International Whaling Commission treaty. Having been reduced to about a quarter of their original numbers, the population of sperm whales is very slowly starting to inch upwards again.

Spermaceti and whale-bone corsets were useful products for humans, but by no means necessities. The history of whaling is a clear case of wanton destruction of a wild animal population for human convenience. Close to a million and a half sperm whales used to roam the seas. Today, there are fewer than half a million. Forward-looking justice focuses on our treatment of existing whales— respecting their universal basic rights, and their communal sovereignty in ocean habitats. But what does justice require regarding humans' historical decimation of sperm whales? We cannot reanimate or compensate the original victims. In some cases of historic injustice, we can identify ways in which existing populations are worse off than they would have been due to the treatment of their ancestors.[50] Thus we may be able to offer compensation to currently living people as an appropriate remedy. In the case of sperm whales, however, it's not clear whether, and if so how, the descendants of the original victims have been harmed by the injustice to their ancestors.

Under these circumstances, it seems that the historical injustice has been 'superseded by circumstances' (Waldron 2004: 67), and the focus of our efforts should be forward-looking justice. Even so, we have strong reasons at least to acknowledge the facts of historic injustice, through education, memorials, collective apologies, and other forms of symbolic compensation. As Lukas Meyer notes, even where reparations are not possible,

> Acts of symbolic compensation make it possible for us to act in such a way as to express an understanding of ourselves as people who wish to, and would, carry out acts of real compensation if this were only possible. If successful we will have firmly expressed an understanding of ourselves as persons who would provide real compensation to the previously living person or people if this were only possible. We will also have expressed a firm commitment to prevent the repetition of such injustices. (Meyer 2008)

Perhaps there is nothing today we can do to repair the harm done from 250 years of whaling, but acknowledging that wrong should at least strengthen our commitment and obligation to ensure that we fully respect the sovereignty of existing whales.[51]

Time matters in thinking about justice. In the immediate aftermath of injustice, we may be able to effect restoration or offer compensation. In the longer term, the facts on the ground change, and forward-looking justice exerts a stronger pull. This makes it all the more urgent, of course, to interrupt injustice when and where it occurs. Aggressors and invaders know the significance of the passage of time and changing circumstances. There is a strong incentive to change the facts on the ground (e.g., by settling occupied territories, or engaging in ethnic cleansing), and then hold the ground until the balance of justice shifts towards the future. (On a more mundane level, we see this kind of behaviour in our everyday lives when, for example, someone violates a zoning regulation by building a prohibited structure, in hopes of creating new facts on the ground to pressure regulators to make an exception.) One of the obligations of forward-looking justice is to provide strong disincentives against efforts to establish such faits accomplis.

5. Fair Terms of Cooperation Between Sovereign Communities

So far, we have argued that a sovereignty framework provides an intellectually compelling way of articulating the presumption of non-interference, which is widespread but under-theorized in the ART literature. However, we believe that sovereignty also provides a normative framework for addressing another crucial issue that has been undertheorized—namely, spillover effects. As we noted earlier, wild animals are vulnerable to harm not just from direct violations of their basic rights, or from encroachment on their territory, but also from a range of inadvertent harms due to the impact of human activity. These include risks from climate change, pollution (e.g., oil spills, agricultural run-off), resource extraction, and infrastructure (e.g., dams, fences, roads, buildings, shipping lanes).

Some of these risks would be reduced if we stopped encroaching on the habitat of wild animals, but it's important to recall that there is no possibility of hermetically sealing human territory from wild animal territory. For one thing, many wild animals migrate over vast distances, including over or through areas of human settlement. Consider again the whitethroat warblers who migrate from the Sahel to Britain, or the northern right whales who migrate from the coasts off New England to Florida. Given that sovereign animal communities exist within, and in parallel with, human communities, all territory is, in a sense, border territory. We argued earlier that in regions of overlapping sovereignty (migration routes, mobility corridors, shared ecosystems, etc.), human communities are not free to pursue their interests in ways that ignore the interests of wild animal communities who are co-sovereign there. Indeed, there are few places in which human activity does not have a direct and immediate impact on sovereign wild animal communities, imposing significant risks of injury and death.

We should note that these risks are not all in one direction. Wild animals can pose a threat to human activity (e.g., road collisions with deer or moose; birds jamming airplane engines), or to public health (e.g., animal viruses), or indeed from direct attack (e.g., from grizzly bears or elephants).

Such risks are inevitable so long as both humans and wild animals continue to share the planet. And so a crucial task of a theory of animal rights is to determine the appropriate principles for regulating these risks. How should we take into account the interests of wild animals when designing our buildings, roads, shipping lanes, pollution codes, and so on? Is it our duty to 'minimize' risk? To impose only 'reasonable' risk? Or to eliminate entirely risks to wild animals? And conversely, what actions can we legitimately undertake to reduce the risks we face from wild animals? These are profoundly important questions which, yet again, are left unaddressed by the traditional ART injunction to 'let them be'.

At the moment, we treat these two issues in diametrically opposite ways. Where wild animals pose a risk to humans, no matter how small, we typically think we are entitled to take any measures to eliminate the risk, even the most lethal measures.[52] If coyotes or prairie dogs pose even a tiny risk to humans (or domesticated animals) we feel entitled to exterminate them en masse. But where our activities impose grave threats on wild animals, we often dismiss this as the price of progress.

A sovereignty framework, by contrast, insists that we treat the distribution of risks as an issue of justice between sovereign communities. And here we can learn from existing approaches to the imposition of risks and inadvertent harms in the human case.[53] Social life, in both the domestic and international context, invariably involves risks—accidental death and injury, transmission of disease, or destruction of property and livelihoods, to name some obvious examples. Allowing cars to go faster than 10 miles per hour, for example, increases risks for other drivers, pedestrians, and neighbouring property-owners, yet most of us think that such risks are worthwhile, given the costs to personal liberty and economic productivity if we banned quicker travel. Attempting to reduce risk to zero would paralyse social life. Yet not all forms of imposed risk are permissible or just. Imposing risks on others must meet a number of conditions, including:

(a) the imposed risks are genuinely necessary to achieve some legitimate interest, and are proportional to that benefit, and not just the result of negligence or callous disregard;

(b) both the risks and the attendant benefits are equitably shared overall—the people who suffer risk in one context benefit from risk in other contexts, rather than one group being continually the victims of imposed risk;

(c) society compensates, where possible, the victims of inadvertent harm.

We will say a few words about how these principles operate in the human case, and then show how they can also provide guidelines for thinking about fair terms of interaction between sovereign human and wild animal communities.

In evaluating risks, we first need to ask if they serve a genuine and legitimate interest. Consider again the case of highways. We could eliminate them, and the resulting traffic accidents and pollution, entirely. But this would have enormous economic and liberty costs. (It might also result in more direct deaths, not fewer, since it would drastically reduce the possibilities for emergency response.) And so, as a society, we make difficult choices about highways—whether to have them at all, whether to expand the system or gradually replace it with train networks, how much to invest in making high-ways as safe as possible (by widening them, adding lanes, lowering speed limits, cutting down roadside trees, or improving car safety), and how much to regulate drivers (in terms of age, impairment, and distractions).

These decisions may reduce risks, but cannot eliminate them entirely with-out unduly sacrificing a legitimate interest in mobility. This passes the first test—risks must be necessary and proportionate to some legitimate good. But this is not the end of the story. We also need to consider the distribution of these burdens and benefits. Many people benefit from highways, but others inevitably suffer, even die. Why is this not unjust?

One reason we do not consider this unjust is that no one is singled out in advance to pay the ultimate price for the benefit of others. It's not as if we literally select someone to sacrifice in order to appease an angry God or monster who demands a life in return for allowing passage along the road. Rather, (almost) all of us choose to drive (or be driven) on roads for the benefits we gain from mobility, albeit with the risk of harm. It is all of us who share in the benefits and risks of driving, as opposed to some humans being selected to die for the benefit of others.

It's true that the risks are not equally shared by all. Some people benefit economically from the highway without ever driving on it (say, a local store-owner who benefits from the increased traffic); others suffer from the highway without ever driving on it (say, a local recluse who wishes there was less traffic and pollution). But whether these variations violate our sense of fairness is likely to depend on the broader story about how risks are distributed in society. Fairness doesn't require that the risks and benefits of each individual collective decision be equally shared amongst all affected members of society. Rather, it depends on a general sense that since the elimination of all risk is impossible, and since everyone benefits from society in diverse ways and is at risk in diverse ways, risks and benefits should roughly even out over time and across domains (not that outcomes are equalized, but that general level of risk is roughly shared). Perhaps the person who is at greater-than-average risk of harm from automobiles is at less-than-average risk of harm from, say, work-place accidents, or food poisoning, or environmental pathogens, depending on where they live and work. These variations only tip over into injustice if they continually target the same group of people, perhaps because that group is already weak, stigmatized, or disadvantaged in society, such that risks imposed on it are discounted or ignored. If we start to think that a particular racial group, say, has been singled out to bear the risks of social policies or economic processes that primarily benefit others, then concerns of justice are raised. This may happen domestically or internationally. For example, an industry that primarily benefits middle-class people might deposit its unsafe waste in poor minority neighbourhoods, or a country may locate its polluting industries on its national borders, hoping that air or water will carry the pollutants into a powerless neighbouring country.

Even if social risk is in some sense fairly apportioned in general terms, and serves a legitimate public interest, there are further requirements of justice, including duties of care and compensation. The fact that risks are fairly distributed is not much consolation to the unfortunate person (or her family) who ends up in a car accident and is badly disabled as a result. This places a burden on society both to avoid unnecessary risk, and to compensate victims. Imagine that the risk potential of a highway derives not from ice and rock fall (which we might view as essentially uncontrollable risks), but rather from a single hairpin bend which has proven fatal time and again. The situation could be radically improved with some additional signage and a slight widening of the road. In this case, we are likely to say that the risk is no longer reasonable. If a serious risk can be eliminated at small cost, it is negligent not to do so, even if the risk is fairly distributed. As the costs of limiting risk rise, our sense of what is reasonable also shifts, as we consider whether those costs could be better spent elsewhere. Our judgement here will vary depending on the wealth of a particular society, and the relative costs of policy choices. Society A might have to weigh the costs of road repair against the costs of a few thousand anti-malaria nets. Society B might have to weigh the costs of road repair against the costs of seasonal decorations for its Main Street parade. They will come to different decisions about whether repairing the road is worth it.

Compensation is the other side of this equation. Collective life imposes inevitable risks on us all. But only some of us will pay a very high price and die or be injured in traffic accidents (for example). Society has a responsibility, not just to limit the chance of an accident occurring, but also to compensate victims when the inevitable accident does occur. By collectively assuming responsibility for a victim's medical and rehabilitation costs, or compensation to family, society can in some small way help to restore a fairer balance of benefit and risk. A society that fails to do this is failing in the original proviso to promote the equal sharing of the risks of social life.

These familiar principles from the human case provide helpful foundations for thinking about our duties of justice to wild animals. As we have emphasized, humans cause inadvertent harm to animals in countless ways. Pollution is an obvious example—water contamination, pesticide use, air pollution, and rapid climate change are all catastrophic for animal life. Most animals are far more vulnerable than humans to environmental degradation. Human settlement patterns and infrastructure also impose risks on animals. For example, nuclear power cooling plants decimate aquatic life, and glass siding and night lighting of skyscrapers kill countless migrating birds.

But since we have been relying on highway examples, let's stick with those. In fact, highways are a textbook example of a human infrastructure/activity that imposes enormous harms on wild animals in the form of 'road kill'. To give you a sense of the scale of the problem, there is a 3.5 kilometre causeway at Long Point, Ontario, which separates Lake Erie from an adjoining wetland (part of a World Biosphere Reserve). It is estimated that on a yearly basis 10,000 animals (of 100 different species, including leopard frogs, map turtles, fox snakes, and many small mammals) are run over on this short stretch of road. Granted, Long Point is a particularly egregious example, but it gives you some idea of the incomprehensible carnage that human roads inflict on wild animals.[54]

Is this incredible carnage a violation of our duties of justice to animals? In light of the principles discussed earlier, the answer must surely be yes. But let's consider the case more carefully to illuminate the nature of this injustice, and ways in which we might overcome it. The obvious problem is that the costs and benefits overall are not fairly shared. Humans benefit from roads, either directly or as part of a broader sharing of the risks and benefits of social cooperation. Wild animals, however, do not benefit from human highways,[55] or from human society more generally. Nor is the risk we impose on them offset by risks they impose on us. In general, the risks imposed on us by wild animals pale in comparison with the risks we impose on them. This incredible disparity of risk should ring alarm bells for our sense of justice. It is akin to one state exporting its pollution downstream or downwind to a neighbouring state, without any reciprocity of benefits or risks.

In this situation, how can we achieve justice in the distribution and imposition of risk? The most obvious implication is that we have a duty to reduce the disproportionate risks we impose on wild animals, wherever possible. This would include a variety of modifications to human development practices, such as locating and designing structures in light of animal habits and migratory patterns, constructing animal underpasses under roads, creating wildlife corridors, and fitting vehicles with wildlife warning devices. Retrofits might be expensive, but if such modifications were taken into account in the initial design and development stages, the costs would be minimal. This would ensure both a fairer distribution of risks, but also that we are not guilty of negligently disregarding risk to others. In the case of most human development practices, the costs to animals have never entered the picture.[56] It's not as if humans have made a careful assessment of whether the risks imposed on animals can be justified by the benefits—these risks have simply been ignored.

But this is the bare minimum. Wealthy human societies could take many more steps to mitigate inadvertent harms to wild animals without imposing unreasonable costs on human development. It might cost quite a bit of money to stop polluting the environments we share with animals, to redesign vehicles and buildings to reduce impacts, to construct diversions or barriers to protect fish from power plants, to redesign agricultural tilling and harvesting techniques to better protect small rodents and animals, or nesting birds—but the costs would not be crippling. As with many kinds of change, the transition would be challenging, but once new ways of thinking are in place they become second nature.

Consider the example of switching from a standard North American diet to a vegan one. At first, one might be obsessed with food—focused on the Roquefort or pork chops left behind, on learning new recipes and cooking techniques, on changes to the body, and so on. But over time, the new diet is normalized, and longer-term vegans spend no more time on food and nutrition planning/preparation than anyone else. And if the switch to veganism were accomplished on a societal scale, with food rituals reconceived and human ingenuity redirected to developing delicious vegan cuisine, the sense of deprivation would disappear altogether. When considering the costs to humans of making certain changes, we need to distinguish a transition period from the longer term. In the transition period there can be a sense of deprivation of past freedoms and opportunities, and a powerful awareness of the burden of new practices. So there needs to be a transition strategy to deal with this (e.g., incremental changes, lots of experimentation, compensations, and so on). But in judging what are reasonable efforts to bring about the circumstances of justice, the fundamental issue is not the transition costs (which can be offset), but whether the transition leads to fair and sustainable practices in the long term.

So far we have focused on one side of the equation of reciprocity: how humans impose risks on wild animal communities, which are not offset by the sharing of benefits from cooperation. Because wild animals are not part of a shared community with humans in which overall risks are balanced, the risks we impose on them are unmitigated and must be reduced.

Let us turn now to the other side of the coin—the risks that wild animals impose on us. Humans used to be at considerable risk from several species of wild animal. We have eliminated many of our natural predators, but we still face risks—from venomous snakes to tigers, grizzly bears, elephants, and crocodiles. We tend to look at any risk posed by wild animals to humans as unacceptable. However, considering the enormous risks we pose to animals, it is unreasonable to expect zero risk in the opposite direction. Instead, we should accept a certain level of risk from the presence of wild animals in areas of overlapping sovereignty. This does not mean we do not have the right to defend ourselves when under attack,[57] but human communities do not have the right to eliminate the general risks posed by the presence of wild animals in overlapping zones. So, for example, if we choose to live somewhere abutting wild lands in which coyotes, mountain lions, or elephants live, then we must accept a certain level of risk for ourselves, our children, and our animal companions. We cannot demand that the coyotes be killed so we can live risk-free. If we choose to drive on country roads at dusk, we must accept the risk of harm from an accidental collision with a deer or moose. We cannot demand that these animals be culled in order to reduce our risk. In other words, we cannot demand zero risk for ourselves, at the same time that human societies impose extraordinary risks on wild animal communities.[58]

There is never going to be total equity in the level of imposed risk, but we can certainly reduce the asymmetry by minimizing the risks we impose on wild animals, while learning to live with the risks they impose on us.[59] We can also reduce this asymmetry by thinking about the ways we can benefit wild animals. As we have noted, the injustice of the risks imposed by human development depends in part on the fact that wild animals do not benefit from this development. But as we discussed earlier, there may be ways that humans can benefit wild animals. While ART has been rightly cautious about human interventions in wild animal societies, we have argued that not all positive interventions are illegitimate. Some interventions can protect the interests and autonomy of wild animal communities, such as intervention to block the spread of a devastating virus. Another example would be rewilding projects that humans can undertake to enrich or revitalize degraded habitats. Insofar as humans can assist wild animals in these cases, the gross asymmetry of risk imposition can be mitigated to some extent. Our ability to help wild animals (under strict parameters) provides some opportunity for reciprocity in our relations with them. It doesn't obviate our responsibility to reduce the risks we impose on animals, but in many cases risk imposition will remain unavoidable. Justifiable positive interventions provide us an opportunity to partially right the balance.

Finally, consider the issue of compensation. Even if we reduce the risks we impose on wild animals, there will inevitably be inadvertent harm. What then do we owe the wild animal victims of our activity? Consider again the causeway at Long Point. The discussion so far makes it clear that humans have many duties to the local wildlife, at different stages of decision-making. In fact, the causeway is in the process of being rebuilt using wildlife barriers and tunnels. This will allow humans to continue to access Long Point without decimating other animals in the process.[60] Even the best designed causeway, however, is still going to result in some animal injuries and deaths, and so we have a duty of compensation to individuals as a way of mitigating the unequal burdens of risk. Compensation in this context would mean healing and rehabilitating injured animals where possible, and caring for orphaned offspring if they can be identified. This is hardly a novel idea: there are already many wildlife refuges that carry out this kind of work. However, at present, animal rescue reaches few victims, in part because it depends on a handful of unusually compassionate individuals responding to injured animals rather than a general social strategy for discharging our duty to care for animals suffering the consequences of risks that we impose on them.

Affirming a duty of compensation opens up a host of new questions. We must consider the specifics of *how* to compensate them. Some wild animals, injured by human roads or other activity, can be rehabilitated and safely released back into the wild. Those are straightforward cases. But in many other cases individuals are disabled in ways that make return to the wild impossible. While, in general, it is always a violation of the basic rights of wild animals to remove them from the wild and forcibly confine them—as pets or zoo exhibits—the case of disabled animals is a special case. For these animals life in the wild is no longer possible, and so we have a duty to provide them with appropriate care in some sort of refuge. Obviously such refuges should be designed to meet the interests of the disabled animals as far as possible—providing food, shelter, care, freedom of movement, privacy, and companionship.

Identifying the interests of wild animals in a refuge environment is not an easy matter. For example, it may not be in their interests for us to reconstruct for them a life that approximates as closely as possible life in the wild. There is a danger here of looking backwards—focusing too much on what has been lost, rather than on what is in an animal's interests looking forward. If they cannot be returned to the wild, and are under human care, then these animals become, in a sense, refugees from a former life which is no longer available to them. And at this point, we have a duty to welcome them as citizens of our community. It would obviously be preferable had they never become refugees in the first place, but once that die is cast we need to look forwards, not backwards. We need to shift from seeing them as members of a separate and autonomous community (or nation) pursuing its own destiny, to being co-members or citizens of our community, cooperating in our new shared destiny.[61]

Overemphasis on attempting to reconstruct a lost way of life can blind us to the new opportunities open to animals in changed circumstances. We shouldn't fetishize them as (damaged) exemplars of their wild counterparts, but respond to them as individuals with special needs and interests in a new environment. For example, many of these animals might eschew human contact, as is their choice. But others may become not only habituated to human contact (often unavoidable during the rescue and rehabilitation process), but may even thrive on human interaction. Some might form friendships with humans or animals of other species. A coyote disabled in a car collision who can no longer roam, hunt, or defend a territory has in some sense morphed into a new kind of being. In the context of a wildlife refuge she might bond with humans, or rabbits and squirrels, for that matter. She might develop a taste for obstacle courses, or for riding in vehicles, or watching rock videos. A disabled parrot might enjoy the challenges of learning Spanish or solving puzzles. The point is that once an unfortunate accident forces us to bring these animals under human care in shared human–animal society, we need to respond to them fully as individuals, not sacrifice them to fantasies of reconstructed wildness. Our duties to the animal should be based on an assessment of their current interests living in shared society, not on a commitment to ideas like 'naturalness' or 'species norm'—ideas which ignore the fact that the animals' community has changed.[62] Animal refuges should be designed not as pale copies of nature, but as stimulating, diverse environments in which unique animals can find new ways of being, if they so choose.[63]

In short, a sovereignty approach to imposed risks and inadvertent harms helps to identify a number of principles for governing fair terms of interaction between sovereign human and wild animal communities—principles of equity, reciprocity, and compensation. This would mean, for example, that we should relocate and redesign cars, roads, buildings, and other infrastructure to reduce animal impacts and create effective animal corridors and buffer zones. It also means that, when animals are inadvertently injured through contact with human activity, despite our best efforts to minimize these risks, we should set up wildlife rescue centres for their rehabilitation and, hopefully, release back to the wild. And we need to learn to live with reasonable risks from the presence of wild animals.

6. Conclusion

We began this chapter by outlining the myriad ways in which wild animals are vulnerable to human activity—direct violence, habitat destruction, inadvertent harms, and positive interventions. ART has focused primarily on direct violence towards wild animals. We agree that these violations must end, but this is only the beginning of sorting out the complexities of human relations with wild animals. We have argued that a sovereignty approach provides guidance on how to understand our diverse obligations to wild animals. Respect for wild animal sovereignty (the right of wild animal communities to lead autonomous, self-directed lives) places a strong check on human activity and on interventions in the wild. First of all, sovereignty anchors the right of individuals to belong to a specific territory and autonomous community—a community which cannot be invaded, colonized, or robbed by others. Thus, recognition of wild animal sovereignty would bring a halt to human destruction of wild animal habitat. It would force the recognition that these are inhabited lands, and that existing inhabitants have the right to maintain their forms of community life on that territory. Second, sovereignty provides a framework for cooperation between communities on a basis of equality and non-exploitation. As such, it would place significant constraints on human activity in areas of overlapping sovereignty, or in contexts of 'cross-border' effects, to minimize inadvertent harms to wild animals, and to compensate animals whom we injure.

Sovereignty also provides an appropriate framework for thinking through our obligations of positive intervention to wild animals. We must not intervene in the internal workings of wild animal communities in ways that undermine their autonomy, effectively placing them under permanent human management. However, some forms of positive assistance are consistent with respect for sovereignty. A duty of assistance can be triggered by natural disasters which undermine the viability of sovereign animal communities (and which we are in a position to relieve), or it can be triggered by external threats to wild animal communities from a destructive invader (e.g., a rogue bacterium, or giant meteor, not to mention human invaders). We do not have a duty to 'police the animal world' (Nussbaum 2006: 379), but we do have a duty to protect wild animals against threats to their sovereignty. We can see duties to protect and assist wild animals as part of the reciprocity of states in a system of sovereign communities. We benefit from the presence of wild animals; and from the resources we share with them. Sometimes we are harmed by wild animals, although these harms pale in comparison with the harms that we inflict in return. It is our duty to be aware of, and to minimize, the harms we cause to wild animals, and to try to balance these harms, when possible, through appropriate acts of positive assistance.

Finally, sovereignty helps make sense of our intuitions about why individual acts of assistance cannot be captured by any general formula about 'never interfering in nature'. We do not owe obeisance to some kind of law of nature. We owe duties of justice to wild animals. In general, respecting their sovereignty means we should be very cautious about undertaking interventions in nature. But respect for sovereignty is consistent with undertaking many individual and limited-scale acts of assistance which do not undermine the ability of wild animal communities to flourish as independent and self-determining communities.

In all of these ways, we believe the sovereignty approach provides more compelling answers than are currently available within the ART literature. In much of that literature, issues of intervention and inadvertent harm are either ignored entirely, or are reduced to the slogan of 'let them be'. As we have seen, that slogan simply cannot do the work that is needed in sorting out our ethical responsibilities to the wild animal communities around us.

As we noted in Chapter 1, other writers have also recognized the limits of an AR approach that focuses only on individual capacities and interests, and have argued for a more relational approach. Perhaps the most detailed example is the recent book by Clare Palmer (2010), who generates certain relational duties towards different groups of animals, depending on the role humans have played in generating particular vulnerabilities amongst those animals. Having made farm animals and companion animals dependent on us through domestication, we are now responsible for fulfilling their needs. Having made wild animals vulnerable through loss of habitat, we may be responsible for remedying that harm. But if we are not causally implicated in their vulnerability, then we have no positive duties towards them. In this sense, Palmer's 'relational' theory is in fact essentially remedial: we acquire relational duties only because we need to remedy harms we are responsible for, and which ideally should not have occurred in the first place. Relational duties are a second-best response when the first-best option of non-relationship is no longer possible, and these relational duties are remedial in nature.[64]

Our account, by contrast, is relational in a deeper way. Palmer defends the 'laissez-faire intuition' on the grounds that (in the absence of human-caused injustice) we lack positive moral obligations towards wild animals. Our approach defends the sovereignty of wild animals on the grounds that there is a great moral value at stake in the autonomy of wild animal communities, and that establishing relationships of sovereignty is the best way of respecting those moral values. Respect for the sovereignty of wild animals, like respect for the co-citizenship of domesticated animals, instantiates a morally valuable relationship, and fulfils our (positive) duty to relate to animals in ways that respect their interests, preferences, and agency. None of these positive values come through in Palmer's remedial account of relational duties: there is no account of the moral goods or purposes that underpin relations of sovereignty for wild animals (or co-citizenship for domesticated animals). And as a result, her account of what we in fact owe wild animals and domesticated animals is, we believe, seriously deficient. In the end, her account of justice towards wild animals, like traditional ART, says little beyond the need to avoid the direct harming of the basic negative rights of individual animals, or remedying these harms once we have committed them.

Palmer's view is one version of the 'concentric circles' model of relational duties. In this model, found in Callicott (1992) and Wenz (1988) as well as Palmer, our moral duties are determined by our (emotional, spatial, or causal) proximity to different groups of animals. We have positive duties to animals close to us (such as domesticated animals), but only negative duties to wild animals far from us. But, as Jac Swart (2005) notes, this is seriously misleading. It would be more accurate to say that we have duties of care and justice in both cases, but that the sort of actions that are called for differ. Swart himself explains this difference in terms of the nature of animals' dependency. Domesticated animals are dependent on their relationship to us for their food and shelter, and so we have duties of 'specific' care towards them, whereas wild animals are dependent on their relationship to their natural environment, and so our duties of care in this context are 'non-specific', and are focused on 'making efforts to maintain their living conditions and their dependent relationship with the environment' (Swart 2005: 258). In each case, we have a positive duty to ensure that animals have what they are dependent on. Part of what it means to meet a duty of care towards others is to care for the relationships on which others depend—that is equally true of wild and domesticated animals. They simply depend on different types of relationships. Contra Palmer, the fact that our duty of care towards wild animals is non-specific is a response to their needs, not evidence that we lack positive duties to respond to their needs.

Our relational view is obviously closer in this respect to Swart than to Palmer. Indeed, our account of the duty to respect and uphold the sovereignty of wild animal communities over their territory can be seen as simply a more 'political' way of restating Swart's idea that we have a duty to respect the dependency of wild animals on their environment. (Similarly, our account in Chapter 5 of the duty to accord co-citizenship to domesticated animals can be seen as a more political restatement of his idea that we have a duty of specific care to animals dependent on us.) But just as the political language of co-citizenship helps specify the duty of specific care to domesticated animals, so the political language of sovereignty helps specify the duty of non-specific care to wild animals, enabling us to address some fundamentally political issues about rights, property, territory, risk, and mobility. In this respect, both Palmer and Swart—and other relational theories within ART—remain locked within the field of applied ethics, disconnected from the political theories that govern our legal and political life.

Needless to say, adopting a sovereignty approach is not a magic formula, and our discussion so far leaves many questions unanswered, not least the political question of how to *enforce* wild animal sovereignty. In traditional human political theory, the right to be recognized as a sovereign authority has always been closely tied to the ability to assert one's sovereignty, both internally and externally. A state is recognized as sovereign because it has effective control over its territory. To be sure, there are different ways of enforcing sovereignty in the human case. In terms of external challenges, a state can assert its sovereignty through the possession of sufficient military power, but it can also do so through treaties of mutual protection and regional security (e.g., membership in NATO), or through upward delegation in multi-nation states (e.g., Canada's First Nations have delegated upwards to the Canadian state the responsibility for their defence), or through participation in international bodies which overlap or 'pool' the sovereignty of individual states.

What would be the comparable political processes in the case of wild animal sovereignty? Wild animals are usually not in a position to physically defend themselves from human interference. They cannot represent themselves in diplomatic negotiations or on international bodies. They cannot make collective decisions about delegating responsibility for the protection of their sovereign interests. So what then would be the political mechanism to assert or enforce animal sovereignty?

The answer lies in some form of proxy representation by human beings who are committed to the principle of animal sovereignty. At present, we have little idea what such a system of proxy representation would look like. As we noted in Chapter 5, a related question arises concerning the political representation of domestic animals within a scheme of co-citizenship. Various proposals have been made in that context for something like an animal ombudsperson or advocate. In their article envisaging 'Simian Sovereignty', Goodin, Pateman, and Pateman (1997) argue than a sovereign great ape nation would inevitably take the form of a protectorate, for which humans act as trustees. Such a trustee (or ombudsperson or advocate) would presumably have the mandate to protect wild animals from colonization, conquest, and the unfair imposition of risks, and also to evaluate the impact of proposed positive interventions.[65]

We do not have a detailed blueprint for such institutional mechanisms. As we argued in Chapter 5, our concern at this stage is not to advocate the creation of this or that institutional mechanism, but rather to clarify the underlying picture of human–animal relations that drives institutional reform. We need first to identify the goals of any new scheme of representation, which, we have argued, should be built around the idea of sovereignty for wild animals. Effective representation within this scheme will require institutional reforms at any number of levels, both domestic and international, covering issues of the environment, development, transportation, public health, and so on. In all of these institutions, the rights of wild animals as sovereign communities need to be represented.

7

Liminal Animal Denizens

In the previous two chapters, we have described a co-citizenship framework for domesticated animals, and a sovereignty framework for animals in the wild. In the popular imagination, these two groups of animals more or less exhaust the field: animals are either domesticated animals selected to live amongst us, or wild animals living out in the wilderness of forest, sky, and ocean—independent of human activities and designs, and avoiding human contact.

This domestic/wild dichotomy ignores the vast numbers of wild animals who live amongst us, even in the heart of the city: squirrels, raccoons, rats, starlings, sparrows, gulls, peregrine falcons, and mice, just to name a few. If we add in suburban animals, such as deer, coyotes, foxes, skunks, and countless others, it becomes clear that we are not dealing with a few anomalous species here, but rather a large variety of non-domesticated species who have adapted to life amongst humans. Wild animals live, and always have lived, amongst us.

We will call this group liminal animals, to indicate their in-between status, neither wilderness animals nor domesticated animals. Sometimes they live amongst us because humans have encroached on or encircled their traditional habitat, leaving them no choice but to adapt as best they can to human settlement. But in other cases, wild animals actively seek out areas of human settlement, which may offer greater food sources, shelter, and protection from predators as compared with traditional wilderness habitat. As we will see, there are in fact many different routes by which liminal animals come to live amongst us.

In one sense, the situation of liminal animals can be seen as a success story. Whereas wilderness animals have been declining in numbers, many liminal animals have been growing in numbers, and have proven remarkably success-ful in adapting to human settlement. However, this doesn't mean that all is well in the relationship between humans and liminal animals, at least from an animal rights (AR) perspective. On the contrary, liminal animals are subject to a wide range of abuses and injustices, and a persistent failure to recognize our distinctive relational obligations to them.

One problem, already noted, is that these animals are invisible in our everyday worldview. Given the way we draw a dichotomy between nature and human civilization, urban space is defined precisely in opposition to what is wild and natural. We therefore do not see liminal animals, at least when thinking and talking about how to design and govern our societies. For example, urban design rarely, if ever, gives any consideration to the impact of human decisions on liminal animals, and urban planners are rarely trained to consider these issues.[1] As a result, liminal animals are often the victims of inadvertent harms from our buildings, roads, wires, fences, pollution, rogue pets, and so on. Qua species, liminal animals may have adapted to these dangers of life with humans, but many individuals die gruesome and unnecessary deaths.

The invisibility of liminal animals does not just lead to indifference or neglect. Much worse, it often leads to a de-legitimization of their very presence. Since we assume that wild animals should live out in the wilderness, liminal animals are often stigmatized as aliens or invaders who wrongly trespass on human territory, and who have no right to be there. And as a result, whenever conflicts arise with humans, we feel entitled to get rid of them, either by mass trapping/relocation or even through mass extermination campaigns (shooting, poisoning). Since they do not belong in our space, we feel entitled to eliminate these so-called pests in the animal equivalent of ethnic cleansing.[2]

The situation of liminal animals is, therefore, a highly paradoxical one. From a broad evolutionary perspective, they have been amongst the most successful of animal species, finding new ways to survive and thrive in a human-dominated world. But from a legal and moral perspective, they are amongst the least recognized or protected animals. Whatever our mistreatment of domesticated animals and of wilderness animals, there is at least a grudging recognition that they have a right to be where they are. But the very idea of liminal animals—of wild animals living amongst us—is seen by many people as illegitimate, and as an affront to our conception of human space.[3] As a result, few voices are raised to protect them from our periodic bursts of ethnic cleansing, and few laws provide them with any protection.[4] For an extreme, but sadly typical, expression of the incompatibility of animals and urbanity, consider the statement by uber-urbanite Fran Liebowitz:

> I do not like animals. Of any sort. I don't even like the idea of animals. Animals are no friends of mine. They are not welcome in my house. They occupy no space in my heart. Animals are off my list ... I might more accurately state that I do not like animals, with two exceptions. The first being in the past tense, at which point I

like them just fine, in the form of nice crispy spareribs and Bass Weejun penny
loafers. And the second being outside, as in outside in the woods, or preferably
outside in the South American jungle. This is, after all, only fair. I don't go there;
why should they come here? (cited in Philo and Wilbert 2000: 6)

In our view, the idea that liminal animals do not belong in areas of human
settlement is fundamentally flawed. For one thing, it is entirely unrealistic. As
we will see, campaigns of mass relocation or extermination are futile; they
don't work, and often makes things worse. But, more importantly, they are
morally untenable. Liminal animals are not aliens or trespassers who belong
elsewhere. In most cases, liminal animals have no place else to live; urban
areas are their home and their habitat.

We therefore need to find ways of acknowledging their legitimate presence,
and of coexisting with them. Indeed, a central task of any plausible animal
rights theory (ART) is to develop guidelines for this coexistence. Yet ART, to
date, has said virtually nothing about liminal animals. Reflecting the preva-
lent domestic/wild dichotomy, animal rights (AR) theorists have talked about
domesticated animals who need to be liberated from humans and about wild
animals who need to be left alone to get on with their lives, but have not
talked about liminal animals.

Indeed, the very category of liminal animals is difficult to fit into the
imaginary of many AR theorists, which presupposes a natural geographical
separation between the human world and the world of wild animals. According to Francione, for example, one of the problems with domestication is that
it violates this natural geographical separation, and leads to animals being
'stuck in our world' where they 'do not belong' (Francione 2007: 4).[5] The
implicit assumption is that the appropriate or natural place for animals is out
there in the wild, and that the presence of animals within human communities can only be the result of illegitimate human activities of capture,
domestication, and breeding. This picture of a natural separation of animals
and humans renders liminal animals invisible.

AR theorists have not ignored the case of liminal animals entirely. When AR
theorists say that all animals have an inviolable right to life, and hence that
humans cannot kill animals except in self-defence, they often emphasize that
this is indeed a universal right that applies to all sentient animals, domesticated, wild, or liminal.[6] But this just reiterates the basic ART commitment to
inviolable basic rights, and does not tell us anything about the distinctive
nature of our duties to liminal animals, and how they differ from those to wild
or domesticated animals. Discussions of this latter question are either non-
existent or relegated to a footnote or parenthetical reference. For example,
Dunayer acknowledges liminal animals in passing, and implies that they are
an exception to the desired human–animal separation. However, she seems

unsure what to say about them, beyond the traditional AR injunction against direct interference or violations of inviolable rights:

> Eventually after emancipation, virtually all nonhumans would be free-living and non 'domesticated.' *Free-living nonhumans can't be completely isolated from humans*. Geese visit 'our' ponds: squirrels enter our backyards; pigeons roost on our buildings. We encounter bears in the forest and crabs on the seashore. Wherever they may be, nonhumans need protection against humans. They need *legal rights that prevent human interference*. (Dunayer 2004: 141, emphasis added)

This is a revealing passage that highlights the limitations of traditional ART. To say that liminal animals 'can't be completely isolated from humans' is a gross understatement, and reveals the theoretical problems for ART posed by animals who not only choose to live near humans, but seemingly thrive (qua species) in human-built environments. And to say that they need 'legal rights that prevent human interference' begs the question: what counts as 'human interference' with pigeons, squirrels, and house sparrows? Is it interference to put up netting to prevent pigeons from roosting in a building, or to seal up a hole through which mice enter a basement? Is it interference to put up hawk silhouettes to prevent song birds from flying into plate-glass windows? Is it interference to let dogs or children chase squirrels in a park? Whatever our obligations towards liminal animals, they cannot be captured by a principle of non-interference. Every time we erect a fence, build a house, or establish a park, we are interfering with the activities of liminal animals, sometimes in ways that benefit them, sometimes in ways that harm them.

AR theorists have traditionally said that the appro-

clearly hopes that the same principle of non-interference can apply to liminal animals. But the idea makes little sense in the liminal case. In the wilderness case, 'let them be' is a shorthand for saying that we should respect the sovereignty of wild animals over their habitat, and resist encroaching upon or colonizing their territory. But in the case of liminal animals, their habitat is our cities, and indeed our backyards and homes—in short, the same physical space in which sovereign human communities inevitably and legitimately exercise their self-government. The governance of human societies will unavoidably create all sorts of interference in the activities of the liminal animals who take up residence amongst us, and the task of ART is to figure out how to take those impacts into account.

One way to try to include the interests of liminal animals would be to extend citizenship to them. If liminal animals continue to live amongst us, perhaps we should think of them as our co-citizens, sharing in the exercise of our sovereignty. After all, this is what we recommend in relation to domesticated animals. But, as we noted in Chapter 5, the possibility of extending citizenship to domesticated animals is predicated precisely on the fact of their domestication. Domestication presupposes and further develops the possibilities for cooperation, communication, and trust between humans and animals, which are preconditions for relations of citizenship. Citizenship presupposes a level of sociability that makes possible reciprocal engagement, rule-learning behaviour, and socialization. It requires the ability to have physically proximate and socially meaningful interactions. Humans and domesticated animals need to be socialized into their relations of co-citizenship, and this requires trust and cooperation.

Liminal animals, by contrast, are not domesticated, and so do not trust humans, and typically avoid direct contact. We could try to change liminal animals to make them more sociable and cooperative. We could, in effect, attempt to domesticate them over time. But this could only be achieved through confinement, separation of families, controlled breeding, radical changes to diet and other habitual behaviours, and other violations of basic liberties like those that were imposed on domesticated animals as part of the historic domestication process. We could not protect house sparrows from hawks without caging one or both. We could not protect squirrels from food shortages without undertaking systematic management of their food supply and reproduction rates, and we could not protect them from cars or raccoons or weasels without confining them.

So we cannot view liminal animals as either sovereigns of their own territories or co-citizens of our territory. We cannot 'liberate' these animals from our communities. Nor can we simply 'let them be'. We need an entirely new way of thinking about our relationship with them.

We argue that the best way to conceptualize this relationship is in terms of *denizenship*. Liminal animals are co-residents of human communities but not co-citizens. They belong here amongst us, but are not one of us. Denizenship captures this distinctive status, which is fundamentally different from either co-citizenship or external sovereignty. Like citizenship, denizenship is a relationship that should be governed by norms of justice, but it is a looser sort of relationship, less intimate or cooperative, and therefore characterized by a reduced set of rights and responsibilities.[7] What determines the fairness of any scheme of denizenship is, in large part, the basis on which these rights and responsibilities are reduced. Denizenship can quickly become a source of exploitation and oppression if the rights and responsibilities are defined in such a way as to consign denizens to the status of a permanently subordinated caste group. But where the rights and responsibilities are reduced in a more reciprocal way, and done in order better to accommodate the distinctive interests of denizens themselves, then denizenship can serve as a vehicle for just relationships.

Our aim in this chapter is to outline what a model of denizenship might look like, and what sorts of rights and responsibilities it entails (and which rights and responsibilities would be waived). In doing so, we draw on various cases of human denizenship. There are many examples of humans who are residents in a particular society, and want to remain there, without becoming full participants in the prevailing scheme of citizenship. Just as liminal animals wish to live amongst us without being press-ganged into our social project of cooperative citizenship, with its distinctive forms of socialization, reciprocity, and rule-following, so, too, some human groups wish to live amongst us while resisting incorporation into the practices of modern citizenship. There are many historical examples of this, and Western societies continue to permit a broad range of people to, in effect, 'opt out' of citizenship, often in order to maintain a cultural or religious way of life that is inconsistent with the demands of citizenship.

We have already alluded in Chapter 3 to some examples of humans who inhabit a liminal zone in relation to the surrounding society, residing within a community without being eligible for (or interested in) full citizenship—including some types of refugees, seasonal migrant workers, illegal immigrants, as well as isolationist communities such as the Amish. As in the case of liminal animals, some of these groups of human denizens are stigmatized as aliens and trespassers who don't belong, and who are therefore at best neglected and at worst exploited or denied the right to reside amongst us. But in other cases, societies have developed models of denizenship that better _____ _____tions of such groups.

appropriate terms of denizenship for _____ characteristic set of interests and injustices that can accompany this status. Regrettably, these examples of human denizenship are understudied in the political theory literature. We do not have well-developed theories of what constitutes fair terms of denizenship in the human case, and so our discussion in this chapter is more provisional and speculative than in relation to domesticated animal citizenship and wild animal sovereignty. Yet there is no doubt that we need a theory of denizenship even in the human case: not all of our co-residents are able or willing to become our co-citizens. And once we recognize the need to make sense of the status of human denizenship, we can more readily see the relevance of denizenship for animals as well.

In one sense, this analogy is already a familiar one. Liminal animal species have frequently been derided as 'alien invaders' who threaten us with their imported diseases, dirty habits, or unruly behaviour.[8] In a fascinating article, 'How Pigeons Became Rats', Colin Jerolmack (2008) charts fluctuating attitudes towards sparrows and pigeons in the USA, and shows how the language and attitudes expressed towards bird 'pests' mirror those towards stigmatized human groups such as immigrants, the homeless, and homosexuals.[9] Unwanted animals are stigmatized by being equated with unwanted humans (and vice versa).

Our project works in the opposite direction. We do not seek to distance liminal animals by comparing them to feared and despised human groups. Rather, we wish to take some of the strategies for extending justice to human outliers—strategies of inclusion and coexistence—and use them to think about justice for liminal animals. We are not interested in human liminality as metaphor, but in the actual ways models of denizenship can be used to accommodate a fuller range of diversity in society, and to bring those perceived as deviant, foreign, second class, undesirable, or dangerous into just relations with the body politic.

1. The Diversity of Liminal Animals

Before we develop our conception of denizenship, we need to say a bit more about liminal animals, who constitute a rather broad and complex group. In everyday discussion, we tend to think of the non-domesticated animals who live amongst us as either opportunistic trespassers who really belong elsewhere and/or as pests whose very presence causes conflict and inconvenience to us. In reality, however, there are many different avenues by which wild animals come to live amongst us, as a result of various forms of both human and animal agency, leading to many different forms of interdependence and interaction, both conflictual and beneficial. The category of liminal animals includes so-called pests like rats whom we try to keep out, but equally it includes songbirds whom we actively welcome. And it includes many species that generate conflicting and contradictory impulses amongst humans: some residents feed pigeons while their neighbours poison them. Human attitudes to liminal animals are often intense, but rarely simple or consistent. For many people, liminal animals add great beauty and interest to the urban environment, while for others liminal animals contradict their image of cities as oases of human civilization in which nature is transcended or at least tightly policed.

So who are these liminal animals? As noted earlier, we are distinguishing liminal animals from both animals that are truly wild (those who avoid and/or are unable to adapt to human settlement) and animals who are domesticated. It is important to emphasize that these are not rigid biological classifications. Members of the same or related species can be found in all three categories: there are truly wild rabbits in the wilderness, for example, as well as liminal rabbits living in urban parks, and domesticated rabbits. Moreover, it is possible for animals to move along this continuum. So we have a matrix of human–animal relationships here, in which different animals show different and evolving degrees of interdependence, agency, and relationship.

Nonetheless, the situation of liminal animals does reflect a distinctive—and growing—type of human–animal relationship, characterized by a particular type of adaptation by wild (non-domesticated) animals to human environments. Liminal animals are those who have adapted to life amongst humans, without being under the direct care of humans.

We should note that not all wild animals in the urban/suburban contact zone are liminal animals, at least as we are using that term. As we discussed in Chapter 6, many truly wild animals spend time in urban and suburban areas. Consider a moose, temporarily disoriented, who wanders out of a wilderness area and has to be rescued from a backyard swimming pool, or an antipodal albatross, thrown drastically off course by a storm, who washes up on the shores of a Lake Ontario community.[10] Countless wild animals follow migratory routes that take them near human-developed areas for periods of time. And many others have had their lands colonized by human development, turning them into internally displaced refugees attempting to survive in small pockets of habitat.

These animals do not seek to live in areas of human settlement for opportunistic reasons, and typically do not benefit from this coexistence. Rather, they have been forced into contact by chance, or by the relentless pace of human expansion. Typically they struggle, unsuccessfully, to survive contact.[11] We argued in Chapter 6 that they should be viewed as citizens of sovereign wild ... humans have nation-to-nation duties such as:

deaths); (3) shared sovereignty of key international corridors (e.g., ... routes); (4) respect for the basic rights of visitors; and (5) extension of assistance to refugees. In other words, our duty is to enable them to exist as wild animal communities, while limiting the negative costs of their inevitable contacts with us.

Our focus in this chapter, however, is not with truly wild animals who temporarily enter into contact with humans, but rather with liminal animals who reside amongst us. A distinguishing feature of liminal animals is that in evolutionary terms, they have been able to survive, and in many cases flourish, by exploiting the opportunities of living near humans—for shelter and food, safety from predators, or simply because we've colonized the best water sources and microclimates.[12] Liminal animals are those who are drawn to, or adapt to, human settlement, rather than avoiding or fleeing it (or being destroyed by it), and this results in forms of dependency and vulnerability that distinguish them from both domesticated animals and truly wild animals. Recall that wild animals are highly vulnerable to human activity in terms of direct harms, inadvertent harms, and habitat loss. If humans were to disappear from the face of the earth tomorrow, this would be overwhelmingly good news for most wild animals, greatly reducing the threats to their existence.[13] For example, a study of British mammals (including both wild and liminal species) found that predation, competition, and other non-human factors have little impact on wild animal populations compared with human-generated risks such as climate change, habitat destruction, deliberate killing, pollution and pesticides, or road deaths. This study looked at overall population trends, not individual mortality, but many of the human-generated risks obviously involve direct harm to individuals. And the number of individuals harmed must be very high indeed if the mortality rate poses a significant risk to the overall species population (Harris et al. 1995). For most wild animals, life in the wild is safer than life in proximity to humans.

For most domesticated animals, the options for a life independent of humans are severely limited. Over time, under hospitable conditions, many domesticated species qua species could readapt to independent life, but if humans were to disappear overnight, the consequences for most domesticated animal individuals would be catastrophic. They are pervasively and specifically dependent on humans to feed, protect, and shelter them, and to address medical conditions arising from the process of domestication. Without humans, many would quickly succumb to starvation, exposure, predation, or disease.

Liminal animals occupy a different niche with respect to human communities. By definition, they have adapted to changes in the environment due to human activity, and in this sense they need, or at least benefit from, humans. But while liminal animals are dependent on human settlement and the resources it offers them, this dependency tends to be non-specific. Unlike domesticated animals, they don't rely on specific human individuals to care for them. Rather, their dependency is more generalized—a reliance on human settlement writ large. Within that context they typically fend for themselves, living independently of individual humans (with some exceptions, to be discussed). On the other hand, their proximity to humans, and inevitable conflicts over space and resources, makes them frequent targets of killing and other violent control operations, as well as victims of inadvertent harms. Thus, if humans were to disappear overnight, the consequences for liminal animals would be highly variable. Some would move on to greener pastures. Some would live off the embers of human society, gradually adapting to new ecological realities. Some would be extinguished with us.

In order better to understand these patterns of residency, adaptation, and dependence, and why denizenship is an appropriate response to them, it is useful to distinguish amongst different types of liminal animals. Liminal animals include opportunists (highly adaptive and mobile animals attracted to the opportunities of city life, like coyotes or Canada geese); niche specialists who are much less flexible in their dependency on particular forms of human activity; feral domesticated animals and their descendants; and escaped and introduced exotic species. In each case, we argue, these groups of animals must be seen as belonging *here*, rather than as aliens who somehow belong *out there*, and so programmes of deportation are typically unjust and indeed futile. But nor is co-citizenship a meaningful option, since it presupposes capacities for trust and cooperation that only emerged through processes of domestication, and to impose these processes on liminal animals would be unjust (and likely futile). What we need, therefore, are new ways of conceptualizing our relationship to liminal animals based on denizenship.

Opportunists

Opportunistic animals are highly adaptive species who have learned to survive, and indeed thrive, in human-built environments, greatly expanding their range and numbers in the process. They exist as wild animal populations but also as urban populations. For example, we have the wild coyote and the urban coyote; the wild migrating Canada goose and the resident suburban Canada goose. Opportunistic animals include grey squirrels, raccoons, mallard ducks, gulls, crows, bats, deer, foxes, hawks, and many others. By their nature these animals tend to be adaptive generalists, able to move into new niches that arise, altering their diet, forms of shelter, or nesting practices as circumstances change. A mallard duck does not need to build her nest in a

the crevices of an expa..

properties than a typical cave. Peregrine falcons can substitute tall buildings for escarpment cliff faces. Raccoons can shelter in an old shed, rather than a decaying tree stump. Crows take up residence along highways where they can live more easily off road kill than by scavenging in the wilds.

This flexibility allows opportunists to flourish in human-developed areas, while retaining their capacity, qua species, to thrive in wild circumstances. Most animal species, given time, can adapt to changing ecological circumstances. But some species have proven more adept. There is a continuum here, and opportunists are those species which have demonstrated particular flexibility to a range of circumstances, and rapid pace of change, especially when it comes to adaptations to human settlement.

Because opportunistic species are seen as having 'chosen' to live amongst us, and because some of their conspecifics continue to live in the wild, it is sometimes assumed that we have no positive obligations or responsibility arising from their presence. They live amongst us, presumably, because the mix of benefits and risks of urban life compares favourably with life in the wild, and if they no longer find that mix advantageous, they can return to the wild. Clare Palmer, for example, invokes this kind of reasoning to argue that we do not have relational obligations to opportunistic liminal animals in the city—they came because 'human-dominated spaces are as they are' (Palmer 2003a: 72).[14]

However, this argument moves too quickly from the species level to the individual level. As a species, opportunists are mobile and adaptable, but it is important to emphasize that *as individuals*, animals may not have the option of moving back and forth between wild or liminal situations. Sometimes wild animals are pushed by competition to explore opportunities in the suburbs or cities. But in many cases, urban opportunists are the descendants of former migrants, or refugees from human expansion into their habitat. The facts on the ground change over time. Imagine a fox who migrates into the city along an available habitat corridor. Soon afterwards, the corridor is lost due to development. Now the fox has lost the option of return to the wilderness. Many liminal animals end up inhabiting urban or suburban islands of this sort, their options cut off by physical barriers, or by conspecific population pressures from adjoining territories. And the descendants of the fox migrant face the same limitations on movement. Thus, we must keep in mind the difference between options at the species level, and options for individuals. At the individual level, it often makes sense to view opportunists as permanent members of our communities without a viable option for return to the wild. We cannot assume that just because there are viable groups of geese or coyotes in the wild, therefore the particular individual geese or coyotes living amongst us could survive relocation.

Opportunists tend to be dependent on humans in the non-specific sense. They live off of human settlement, but do not typically rely on a relationship with any specific human(s), and can often adapt to changes in human activity.[15] When one householder decides to store her garbage properly (or to stop leaving pet food bowls out on the porch, or to fit the chimney with a wire mesh) there's always another householder up the street who is a little sloppier in habit. Or there's the local dumpster, open air market, restaurant back alley, street litter, hot-air vent, abandoned building, garden shed, and countless other opportunities for those who have an omnivorous diet and are not fussy about their shelter requirements.

Many opportunists are viewed as nuisance species (e.g., resident geese) or potential threats (e.g., coyotes), and are the targets of lethal campaigns to limit their numbers. And as we discuss below, there can be legitimate (non-lethal) efforts undertaken to discourage or prevent new members of these species from taking up residence amongst us. But many, if not most, opportunist liminal animals belong here: they are the descendants of the original opportunist who moved from the wild to the city, and/or have lost the option of a return to the wild due to changes in habitat or demography. This is now the only home they have.

Within the larger category of opportunists, it is worth mentioning a sub-group of synanthropic species (DeStefano 2010: 75). Unlike other opportunists, synanthropic animals are almost exclusively identified with human settlement. Examples include European starlings, house sparrows, house mice, and Norway rats, amongst others. Unlike other opportunists, it's not obvious that synanthropics can thrive outside the context of human settlement. Whereas we can readily identify both wild and liminal populations of foxes or white-tailed deer, this is not the case with house sparrows or Norway rats. What the two groups share, however, is a high degree of flexibility. Sparrows can thrive on a varied diet. Rodents can nest in decaying leaf matter, but can do just as well with building insulation or old wool blankets.

As with other opportunists, synanthropics live amongst us regardless of whether we invite them, actively support them, or want them as part of the community. Many humans see very few benefits to the presence of these animals and have subjected them to rigorous campaigns of suppression and control. Yet, even more than for other opportunists, we must accept that they belong here amongst us: they have no wilderness option. And deportation almost certainly results in death.

Niche Specialists

specialists are much less flexible, and ... their environment. They have adapted to long-standing forms of human activity, and are inflexibly dependent on humans to maintain this role. For example, in regions where traditional agricultural practices have been stable for many generations, some species have adapted to the specific ecological niches created by these practices. The English hedgerow is a classic example, offering habitat to an amazing diversity of animals who feed on agricultural crops, weeds, insects, small rodents, and so on. Some species, like the (flexible opportunist) fox are not inflexibly dependent on the hedgerow. They can also thrive in wild settings, and in urban ones as well. Other species, however, like the hazel dormouse, have become dependent on the specific ecological niche created by the hedgerow, and if the hedgerow dies out, they will too.[16] In other words, a niche specialist cannot readily relocate to a new territory, or adapt to rapid change.

The corncrake is another striking example of a niche specialist. These birds thrived with the expansion of traditional agricultural practices in the UK. Then, as Kathleen Jamie describes:

> The grim reaper came for the corncrake in the form of the mechanized mower. In the days of the scythe, when hay was long and cut later in the year, then heaped on slow-moving wains, the corncrake had long grasses to hide and breed in. The chicks would be fledged before the meadow was mown, and had plenty of time to escape the swinging blade. With mechanization, however, and a shift toward earlier cutting for silage, corncrakes, eggs, fledglings and all have been slaughtered wholesale. (Jamie 2005: 90)

The corncrake is near extinction, surviving only in a few fields in the Hebrides that are too small for mechanized mowing. In general, the rapid transition from traditional farming practices to mechanized monocropping has been devastating for a wide variety of niche specialists. Their habitat isn't wilderness habitat unaltered by human activity, but it is vital habitat nonetheless. And human alterations to this habitat are as devastating for animals as incursions into pristine wilderness.

The devastating effects of rapid change on niche specialists raise concerns at both the species and individual level. Rapid change in their environment leads not only to suppressed population growth (and resulting possibility of extinction and loss of diversity), but also to the suffering of individuals. If a hedgerow is ripped out, the hazel dormouse living there has nowhere to go and will probably perish. If mechanized mowers are introduced to fields where corncrakes are nesting, the birds will be killed.

Niche specialists are vulnerable to change, and especially to a rapid pace of change, in their human-constructed environments. Unlike highly adaptive and invasive species, they are rarely the deliberate targets of human campaigns for eradication. However, they are particularly vulnerable to inadvertent harms and human negligence regarding their vulnerability in liminal ecosystems. Most of the time, we are completely unaware of the impact on these animals, for better or worse, of changes in human activity.

Introduced Exotics[17]

Classic examples of introduced exotics include captive animals from zoos or exotic pets that are released or escape, as well as deliberately released species such as rabbits and cane toads in Australia, pythons in the Florida everglades, carp in the Mississippi, or brown snakes in Guam. Some of these released species function as wild animals; but others gravitate to human-altered environments—crop land, suburbs—where they thrive as naturalized liminal species. Some of these species have been introduced deliberately (e.g., by a hunter stocking his acreage with a favourite species, or a farmer trying to control a pest by introducing a foreign predator), others through carelessness (during transportation, or when an exotic pet owner tires of her charge), or as a by-product of human mobility and mass transportation.

They are often seen as environmental nightmares, but the effects of released exotics are in fact quite diverse. For example, the red-masked parakeets of San Francisco (descended from wild birds captured in Ecuador and Peru) have adapted to life in their new location without any apparent negative impact on the local ecosystem.[18] Another South American parrot—the monk parrot—has established liminal colonies in Connecticut and elsewhere along the eastern US coast. Again, the local ecosystem and native birds seem none the worse for the addition of these new immigrants.[19] Yet, in both cases, there are voices calling for the extermination of the 'alien' and 'foreign' invaders, as though their mere presence contaminates the natural order of things.[20] Fear of so-called invasive species can be highly overblown. After all, ecological change (including change from in-migration of new species) is part of ecological vitality, and it's important to be able to distinguish change that is beneficial or neutral from change that has a genuinely destructive (and irreversible) impact on species diversity or ecosystem vitality.

In some cases, an introduced species might outcompete and suppress the population of a closely related native species, but without undermining the ecosystem more generally.[21] This seems to be the case with the American grey squirrel, which tends to displace the red squirrel after introduction, but doesn't have a drastic impact on general ecosystem vitality or biodiversity. The greys are more adaptable, and more disease-resistant than the red

grey squirrel, especially in the UK where there is a se[...] the disappearing red squirrel, due in part to 'Squirrel Nutkin' of Beatrix Potter fame (BBC 2006). As many critics have noted, these extermination campaigns often rely on myths about the interlopers attacking native red squirrels or infecting them with disease, or being destructive to native flora and fauna.[22]

Biologists have begun to question some of the hysteria regarding invasive species, arguing that many introductions have a benign effect, or even a positive impact, on diversity of the gene pool when they interbreed with closely related species (Vellend et al. 2007). Indeed, as scientists learn more about how to predict the behaviour of species introduced to new environments, some biologists advocate deliberate introductions as a way to save species that will be marooned by climate change (Goldenberg 2010).

The history of catastrophic introductions, especially of predators, should make us cautious about the deliberate introduction of species, especially given the scope and pace of such introductions in the modern world. When an animal is introduced to a new environment in which it has no predators, and native animals are not adapted to it, there is grave potential for the introduced exotic to flourish to an extent that threatens ecological vitality. For example, the cane toad has adapted to Australian environments ranging from mangrove swamps to coastal sand dunes to agricultural regions, and is blamed for reducing biodiversity in all of these regions. The toads also thrive in urban areas where they can reproduce in puddles, and dine on a variety of plants and animals, garbage, dog food, and carrion.[23] (Even in the case of cane toads, however, it should be noted that, over time, ecosystems tend to re-stabilize as native species learn how to prey on the toads without being poisoned.)

So we certainly do not advocate the deliberate introduction of exotics. On the contrary, humans violate the basic rights of these animals when they first capture and transport them to a new environment, and either keep them captive or release them into a radically new environment. Moreover, we violate the rights of sovereign animals in the release zone if an introduced species is a predator against whom they have no protection. And so we should, wherever possible, seek to prohibit the transportation and introduction of exotics. But here again, we cannot hope to eliminate this problem entirely. For one thing, it's important to note that not all introductions are deliberate. Some occur because of inadvertent human activity, or through the agency of animal stowaways. And once an introduction occurs, extermination campaigns are not an acceptable response. We need to find alternative ways of addressing the challenges that arise, to both humans and to native species, from these adaptive exotics.

Feral Animals

We use the term feral to refer to domesticated animals and their descendants who have escaped direct human control. Escaped or abandoned cats and dogs come readily to mind. But there are also large populations of feral farm animals, especially in Australia, where feral populations (including pigs, horses, cattle, goats, buffalo, and camels) number in the millions.[24]

First-generation ferals are almost invariably direct victims of human injustice. Either their humans have abandoned them, or treated them so badly that the animals have run away. Many feral animals, especially in less temperate zones, are unable to survive on their own, and one can imagine many horrible ends (exposure, starvation, disease, predation, accident, capture and vivisection by scientists, or capture and euthanization by animal control officers). At first glance, one might look at this grim situation and think that justice requires returning feral animals to their original state of domestication (and hence, in our view, domestic co-citizenship). This is likely the right answer for many feral animals—certainly for recent escapees or abandonees, and those individuals who are physiologically or psychologically unfit for survival. However, we should not assume that this is the case for all feral animals. If a feral population has become established, and the animals have started to adapt to their new circumstances, then they have effectively become a liminal species. It may not be in their interest to return to a closer relationship with humans, or to accept the trade-offs of citizenship in mixed human–animal society.

Some of these animals have truly become 'rewilded', such as the descendants of farm animals living in Australia's Northern Territories remote from human settlement. Other feral domestics, like pigeons, function very much like non-domesticated synanthropics, thriving exclusively in symbiosis with human settlement. Pigeons are adaptive generalists, able to thrive on a range of seeds, insects, and scavengings, and able to roost on building ledges instead of the rock faces favoured by their non-domesticated rock dove cousins. In general, pigeons are dependent on humans in a relatively flexible and non-specific sense. However, this may not always be the case. The flock of pigeons living at Trafalgar Square in London is an interesting example (Palmer 2003a). The pigeon population has increased in response to systematic human feeding. If direct human feeding were cut off, the pigeons would starve since neighbouring areas are already saturated in terms of pigeon population. In other words, the situation of this particular flock of pigeons (and similar flocks in St Mark's Square and elsewhere) is actually quite precarious—their dependency on humans is fairly inflexible and specific.

Most feral pets, like cats and dogs, tend to stick close to human settlement where they function like other highly adaptive animals—scavenging, preying on sm̶ ⸻⸻ ⸻ As adaptive ⸻ ⸻, like the Trafalgar ⸻ ⸻

more specific and inflexible dependency relationships.[25] For example, feral dogs and cats often develop specific relationships with humans (householders, groundskeepers, grocery shop or restaurant owners) who can be relied on to feed them scraps or set out water bowls.

A study of feral cats in the city of Hull (England) found an interesting diversity of human–feral cat relationships, in terms of the level of dependency on human feeding, shelter, and contact (Griffiths, Poulter, and Sibley 2000). Some cat colonies lived in abandoned areas of the city and avoided human contact. Others lived in closer proximity to humans—near homes, businesses, or on the grounds of large institutions, for example. These colonies were well known to humans, who provided the cats with food, water, and shelter, and there was a high degree of interaction between cats and humans. The population of some of the cat colonies was managed by catch-neuter-release programmes. Many of the cats seemed to live quite healthy and independent lives, counter to the stereotype that all feral pets must be suffering and in need of rescue by humans.

A more formalized arrangement exists in the city of Rome, where a cat sanctuary has been established in a large city block consisting of ruins of ancient temples. The area lies several feet below street level and is fenced off, but the fencing is sufficiently porous that cats can come and go as they please. Sanctuary volunteers provide the cats with food, shelter, and medical care, and they carry out a vaccination and sterilization programme. Visitors are welcome to hang out with the cats, and adoptions are sometimes arranged.[26]

The feral chickens of Key West, Florida, offer another interesting case. These are the descendants of escaped and abandoned chickens once kept by Key West residents for eggs, meat, and cock fighting. They seem to thrive as a feral population, with occasional assistance from humans, who keep an eye out for sick and injured animals. They are credited with keeping down the scorpion population, and other pesky bugs, and add a unique and colourful dimension to Key West life. Of course not everyone is a fan, and the chickens are also derided for their cacophonous and messy ways. Over the years attempts have been made to eradicate the chickens, but for now they have a protected status in the city, and residents continue to negotiate strategies for peaceful coexistence.

Feral domestics are often targeted for control when their numbers are perceived to be too large. Killing campaigns are carried out in cities around the world, but these are becoming more controversial. From Palermo to Bucharest to Moscow there is growing debate regarding how to respond to feral dogs, as increasing numbers of people seek ways to coexist with liminal animals rather than resorting to traditional violent (and ineffective) strategies.[27] In addition to being targeted as pests, feral animals are often derided for the same reason exotic species are, that is, they are perceived as ecological aliens whose mere presence contaminates natural ecosystems, especially when they disperse beyond urban boundaries and into the countryside beyond. And, as in the case of exotics, this perception is often highly exaggerated—the impact of feral animals on the ecosystem varies enormously from case to case (King 2009).

Finally, as former (or descendants of) domestic animal citizens, feral animals may provide a unique window for understanding domesticated animals, and a possible future relationship between humans and domesticated animals in which animals exercise greater agency and independence in establishing the terms of their relationships with us.

2. The Need for a Denizenship Model

In sum, liminal animals come to live amongst us for a variety of different reasons, and display a wide range of interactions with the larger human society. Although these various groups of liminal animals differ in important ways, they typically share two key characteristics: (1) there is no other place where they (qua individuals) belong, and so we cannot legitimately exclude them, and yet (2) they are not eligible or appropriate for a co-citizenship model. Under these conditions, we need a new model of human–animal relations, one that provides security of residence to liminal animals while exempting them from the requirements of co-citizenship. We believe that the idea of denizenship captures this goal.

To be sure, there are some potential exceptions to both of these generalizations. Not all liminal animals need to be accepted as belonging here. In the case of highly mobile opportunists, we have a prima facie right to regulate in-migration. After all, as we discuss below, we do this in the human case as well. Under conditions of reasonable justice between states, countries have a prima facie right to regulate human in-migration. A citizen of Canada might have a strong desire to emigrate and become a citizen of Sweden. But Sweden has the right to regulate this process in accordance with international law and agreements, and, ultimately, to say yes or no. The Canadian is neither stateless, nor the victim of international injustice, nor is she a refugee. She does not have an unrestricted right to mobility which allows her to choose her country of citizenship.

Where liminal animals in the wild have the option of staying there, then they, like the Canadian citizen, may be neither stateless, refugee, nor victim of international injustice. If so, then human communities do not have an obligation to create incentives to attract such liminal animals, to remove barriers to their free entry, or to welcome them as permanent denizens. On the contrary, human communities may erect barriers and create disincentives in order to limit the population of incoming liminal animals. For example, we can dramatically increase monitoring of international travel and shipping to prevent stowaways. We can use physical barriers to discourage in-migration from wild areas that brush up against highly populated human centres. We can reduce incentives that attract migrating animals to human communities. (For example, we can stop creating expansive lawns of Kentucky blue grass next to ponds—a microenvironment which is irresistible to the Canada goose.) Or we can use active disincentives (e.g., noise blasters, off-leash dog parks) to discourage liminal migrants from landing or settling.

However, as in the human case, this general presumption in favour of the right of human communities to use barriers and disincentives to discourage in-migration is subject to various provisos. First of all, control measures must respect the basic inviolable rights of all individuals: we cannot shoot the human or animal migrants attempting to enter our territory. Moreover, once liminal animals take up residence in human communities (i.e., if they have succeeded in evading border controls), the calculus starts to change. There may be cases in which an animal recently migrating from the wilds can safely be deported back to the wild. For most animals, though, once they have made the move into a new environment there is no turning back. As we noted earlier, the fact that opportunist species (or introduced exotics) thrive as wild populations does not mean that individuals have the option of return to the wild. Over time, opportunistic animals become embedded in the community, and the cost of uprooting them (e.g., by trapping and relocating to the wild) is likely to be severe—for example, separation of families, and release in an unknown and hostile environment. Many trapped and released animals die because they are unequipped to deal with predators or conspecific competitors; because they are separated from their kin support networks; or because they are unable to find food and shelter in an unfamiliar setting.

For the most part, then, we should recognize that, even in the case of mobile and adaptive opportunists, liminal animals are not aliens, but, rather, belong here. Once they are here, and established, we must accept the legitimacy of their presence, and adopt an approach of coexistence rather than exclusion.

But if we recognize liminals as permanent residents of our communities, then should we not offer them co-citizenship, like domesticated animals? If we were able to ask them their preference, would they not clamour to sign up for the benefits of full citizenship? (Free medical care! Central heating!) What is the justification for offering them only the status of denizens?

As we have seen, co-citizenship may indeed be feasible for some feral animals, who belong to species that have been bred for domestication. But for most liminal animals, co-citizenship is neither feasible nor desirable. We tend to think of citizenship as an unqualified good or benefit, but it is important to remember that citizenship also involves responsibilities, including the responsibility to be socialized into norms of civility and reciprocity regarding one's co-citizens. For some groups, the cost of being forced to participate in the cooperative project of citizenship can be very high. As we will see, this is true in the human case, but is even clearer in the case of liminal animals.

It's important to note that most liminal animals, like their wild animal cousins, tend to avoid contact with humans. (This is less true of feral domestics, although over time, as feral colonies become established, they too tend to practise human avoidance—no doubt a painfully learned response to the dangers of human contact.) Individual liminals can be tamed, but, in general, squirrels, coyotes, crows, and other liminal animals display caution or avoidance behaviour. They tolerate us, because we are one of the costs of living in a human environment with its attendant opportunities, but they do not seek our company or our cooperation. Put another way, liminal animals benefit from human environments, but not from human contact per se (although there are certainly individual exceptions to this general rule). They do not have the sociability with humans that characterizes domesticated animals. Therefore we cannot (typically) engage them in the same sort of process of reciprocal engagement, rule-learning behaviour, and socialization that is possible with pigs or cats.

We could try to change these liminal animals to become more sociable and cooperative. That is, we could attempt to domesticate them. But as we noted earlier, this could only be achieved through significant confinement, separation of families, controlled breeding, and other violations of basic liberties like those that were imposed on domesticated animals as part of their historic domestication process. Liminal animals live amongst us, but because they are not domesticated, they retain their own self-regulating mechanisms of social organization, reproduction, and raising of their young. Bringing them into conformity with the rights and responsibilities of standard citizenship would require replacing these self-regulating mechanisms with human management, leading to a drastic curtailment of their liberties and autonomy (confinement, and control over diet, mating, association, and other habitual behaviours).

This is not to say that we have no positive obligations to protect and promote the well-being of liminal animals. On the contrary, as we discuss below, any defensible model of denizenship will include such obligations. But we cannot extend the full protections of citizenship without intervening systematically and coercively in all areas of their lives, jeopardizing other important interests.

On balance, then, we would argue that liminal animals are better off with a form of denizenship status which releases them from some of the obligations of citizenship, while at the same time releasing humans from some of the obligations of comprehensive positive duties towards these liminal animals. This is obviously a judgement call: we cannot ask liminal animals whether they would prefer co-citizenship to a form of denizenship involving reduced benefits as well as reduced responsibilities. In this respect, denizenship for liminal animals differs from the human cases we discuss in the next section, where the package of reduced rights and responsibilities of denizenship emerges from a process of negotiation. In the animal case, the best we can do is (a) respond to behavioural cues, such as the tendency of liminal animals to avoid humans; (b) imagine what the trade-offs of regular citizenship would mean for these animals, and whether they would be in their interests (e.g., getting safety and food at the cost of severe restrictions on movement, food choices, and reproductive freedom);[28] and (c) respect the basic competence of liminal opportunists to negotiate many of the risks of their environment, a competence which would be undermined by human management of these risks on their behalf.[29] In our view, these considerations all tip clearly in favour of a denizenship model.

For the vast bulk of liminal animals, therefore, neither exclusion nor co-citizenship is a viable option. Some ferals may be eligible for (and benefit from) domestic co-citizenship, and we can try to keep out newly arriving opportunists or exotics. But the vast bulk of liminal animals are here to stay, and must be accorded a legal and political status that provides security of residence, without the forms of intimate trust and cooperation that define domestic co-citizenship. They need, in short, denizenship.

But what would be the fair terms of such a denizenship status? Denizenship combines secure residence with exemption from, or reduction of, some of the rights and responsibilities of citizenship. But which rights and responsibilities can be waived, and which should remain? Denizenship may not involve the intimate relations of trust and cooperation of co-citizenship, but it is still very much a relationship, involving the sharing of physical space, and dense webs of mutual impact. To put it bluntly, humans can make life miserable for liminal animals, and vice versa. What then do we owe each other? What would constitute fair terms for this unique relationship?

As we noted earlier, this question has barely been raised, let alone addressed, in the ART literature. We may be able to learn something, however, by considering some relevant examples of human denizenship.

3. Denizenship in Human Political Communities

As we have seen, the invisibility of liminal animals in both public discourse and ART arises from our tendency to put animals into two boxes: domesticated animals who have been bred to be part of human society; and wild animals who belong elsewhere. Liminal animals stubbornly refuse to fit into these categories, being neither part of our society nor external to it; neither fully in nor fully out. Denizenship is a response to this complexity.

We can see a similar dynamic at work in the human case. Here, too, we have a tendency to put humans into two boxes: they are either co-citizens who are one of us; or foreigners who belong elsewhere. Both the international world order and traditional political theory operate with a familiar picture in which human beings are neatly assigned to discrete political communities: everyone in the world would, ideally, be a member of one and only one political community. This is reflected in international conventions that, on the one hand, insist that no one should be stateless, and on the other hand, insist that dual citizenship should be discouraged.[30] As James Scott has shown, modern states like their populations to be 'legible': everyone in their place, and a place for everyone (Scott 1998). In this imagined world, people within the boundaries of a state would all be full citizens of the state, and all others would be firmly excluded, kept safely within the boundaries of whatever state they 'really' belonged to.

Yet, like liminal animals, human beings have stubbornly refused to fit into these standardized state-designed categories. There have always been, and will always be, some individuals residing within the territory of a state who wish to stay there, but who are ill-adapted to, or uninterested in, full citizenship. They wish to live amongst us without becoming one of us, and without taking part fully in our schemes of cooperative citizenship. In response to such cases, various forms of denizenship have been designed. Denizens enjoy rights of residence but with a looser connection to the surrounding society; they are ineligible for some of the standard rights of citizenship and reciprocally absolved from some of its standard responsibilities.

We consider two kinds of denizenship that have emerged within contemporary states: (1) opt-out denizenship, and (2) migrant denizenship.

Opt-Out Denizenship

One category of denizenship derives from the inclination of some individuals or groups to disengage from aspects of full citizenship. Modern democratic states are based on a certain social ethos of participation, cooperation, and affiliation. Government is by and for the people, who are conceived as engaging in a cooperative social project. Inevitably, some individuals and groups cannot or will not assent to this project, and wish to opt out of it. They may, for example, resist assuming some of the standard responsibilities of citizenship, perhaps because they view these responsibilities as conflicting with the demands of their conscience or their religion. If so, they may seek to negotiate their own form of opt-out status, in which they seek exemptions from both the rights and responsibilities of citizenship.

One well-known example is the Amish in the United States—a very traditionalist and isolationist ethnoreligious sect that seeks to minimize contact with the larger society and with state institutions, which they view as worldly and corrupt. As a result, the Amish resist calls to fulfil the responsibilities of citizenship: they do not wish to serve on juries or in the military, do not want to contribute to public pension schemes, and do not want their children educated into the practices and ethos of modern citizenship. But in return, they also waive many of the rights of citizenship: they do not vote, or run for public office, or use public courts to resolve their own internal disputes, or take advantage of public welfare or pension schemes.

Jeff Spinner refers to the Amish as exercising a form of 'partial citizenship' (Spinner 1994), but, as he himself notes, it is precisely the idea of 'citizenship' that the Amish are trying to opt out of. The status of citizen, with its attendant virtues, practices, and forms of socialization, is not part of their way of life. In this respect, it might be more accurate to describe them as seeking a form of denizenship: they want to live amongst us, but not as our co-citizens.

We will call this *opt-out* denizenship. Opting out can take a range of forms, from single-issue to comprehensive disengagement, from temporary to permanent, from legally sanctioned to illegal or dissenting. For example, in the case of a pacifist conscientious objector, disengagement applies to only one specific aspect of citizenship—the duty to defend one's country by force if necessary—without rejecting the status of citizenship more generally. In this case, it might be more accurate to describe it as a form of dissenting citizenship. In the case of the Amish, by contrast, disengagement occurs across a range of issues—from mandatory pension contributions to school-leaving age for children—negotiated with the state in the name of maintaining a traditional religious way of life that requires isolation from the institutions and influences of the larger society. Here, it is citizenship itself that is being opted out of. Other cases fall somewhere in-between. Some Roma communities in Europe have attempted (without much success) to negotiate alternative forms of belonging to accommodate their traveller lifestyle which does not sit easily with standard modern citizenship.

Some individuals opt out of citizenship by flouting certain laws or rejecting citizenship responsibilities in the areas of political and economic participation (e.g., by refusing to vote, or by participating in an underground economy, or by becoming a hermit or living rough). This sort of dissent from citizenship can be individual or it can take a more communal and organized form—as when alternative communities structure themselves around home-schooling, a barter economy, political disengagement, and a refusal to accept state benefits.

In short, for a variety of ideological, religious, or cultural reasons, some people simply are unable or unwilling to participate in the social project of modern state citizenship—its complexities, demands, pace of change, or moral compromises—and would prefer to opt out, and negotiate instead some alternative form of denizenship.

Can a healthy democratic community accommodate this desire without risking injustice or instability? What would be the fair terms of such an opt-out denizenship? As we noted earlier, the fairness of any denizenship status depends on reciprocity in rights and responsibilities. The more individuals or groups seek exemption from the responsibilities of citizenship, the more they should be willing to forego some of its rights. If individuals or groups seek exemption from certain citizenship responsibilities, reciprocity can be maintained by a comparable reduction in benefits, or the provision of alternate community service. For example, conscientious objectors might be obliged to perform development work in lieu of military participation. Communities that negotiate tax exemptions might need to accept a corresponding reduction of benefits. Groups that do not want their members socialized into the ethos of public deliberation should not expect to be able to shape that deliberation.[31]

Such reciprocally weakened forms of affiliation do not seem inherently unfair or unreasonable to us, although not all claims for denizenship are equally compelling, and there is likely to be considerable discretion in how these terms of denizenship are negotiated. On the one hand, there may be a stronger case for accommodating opt-out denizenship in cases where the claimants can make a compelling case that disengagement is a matter of conscience (and not just preference or cultural practice), and hence required by freedom of conscience. On the other hand, all forms of opt-out denizenship involve elements of free-riding. Those who disengage from the social project of modern state citizenship nonetheless depend on the existence of that social project. The Amish would be unable to maintain their traditional way of life in Pennsylvania or Wisconsin if the United States did not protect their basic legal rights and property rights from violations by either local neighbours or foreign countries. Those who opt out are, in this sense, free-riding on a framework of law and political stability to which they do not fully contribute.

How we evaluate these competing considerations is likely to depend on a number of factors including: (a) numbers; (b) exit options; and (c) vulnerability of individual members. In respect to numbers, Spinner argues that while democratic societies can safely afford a few free-riders, they may need to be more restrictive if the number of such groups continually grows, threatening the ability of the larger society to provide the political framework within which opt-out alternatives are possible. Whether we feel obliged to accommodate opt-out denizenship may also depend on the availability of alternatives for the group. If the USA bordered a new Amish state which was welcoming co-religionists as immigrants, this might reduce the obligation of the USA to accommodate alternative Amish denizenship within its own borders. A third consideration is that individuals and groups who disengage from citizenship can be rendered highly vulnerable by this status. They can be stigmatized as shirkers or outcasts. They can end up isolated and vulnerable to exploitation. Most importantly, vulnerable members of disengaged communities (e.g., people with intellectual disabilities, children, animals) can fall through the cracks of state laws and agencies mandated to protect them. The state may allow competent adults voluntarily to run the risks associated with disengaged denizenship, but it retains a responsibility to ensure that the basic rights of vulnerable members of such groups are protected. Competent adults may be free to waive their own citizenship rights and responsibilities, but they cannot unilaterally waive the rights of children, people with intellectual disabilities, or domesticated animals.

It is not easy to determine how to weigh these various factors. States have proven surprisingly willing to negotiate various forms of opt-out denizenship, but in a very contingent and uneven fashion, and with unresolved challenges. Opt-out denizenship may be an attractive option for accommodating individuals and groups who are not a good fit for modern, market-oriented, individualist, liberal–democratic societies. The challenge of this form of denizenship is to figure out how to accommodate it without creating unfair burdens, violating individual rights, or generating intolerance.

Migrant Denizenship

A second form of denizenship is tied to migration across international borders. In this case, migrants may have no religious or cultural objection to the ethos of modern citizenship per se, but they may not want to enact their citizenship in their current country of residence. They may continue to see themselves as participants in the citizenship projects of their country of origin, even when they live abroad for extended periods, and so may seek only denizenship rather than citizenship elsewhere. Where this is the case, we can talk about migrant denizenship.

It is important to emphasize that we are talking about a very specific type of case here. Not all forms of international travel lead to denizenship. To be a denizen, in our use of that term, migrants must be more than merely temporary foreign visitors. Citizens of other countries who are temporarily resident while they travel, conduct business, or study are visitors not denizens. But denizens are also different from traditional immigrants who have been recruited with the expectation and promise of full citizenship. Denizens fall in-between these two groups: they are long-term residents but not citizens.

The contemporary world is full of such migrant denizens. Some are illegal migrants who have crossed unauthorized into foreign territory in search of work. Others are state-sanctioned migrant workers, invited by the state on a seasonal or semi-permanent basis to take up certain kinds of employment without the expectation that this will lead to citizenship.[32] These migrant workers are expected to return to the foreign country where they hold citizenship, either at the end of each season or upon retirement. In some countries, like the United Arab Emirates, Kuwait, and Saudi Arabia, migrant workers form the backbone of the economy. In other regions, like Europe and North America, migrant workers tend to fill smaller niches in the labour market considered undesirable by native citizens (e.g., picking fruits and vegetables, working in slaughterhouses, doing cleaning and other domestic work). For example, workers from Mexico travel to Canada to pick fruit or harvest vegetables, returning in the late autumn to their families and communities in Mexico, where they hold full citizenship. Women from the Caribbean and the Philippines often spend years in Canada working as semi-skilled child or elder caregivers before returning home.

In some of these cases, the fact that long-term migrants remain denizens rather than citizens is an injustice. For all intents and purposes, the country of residence is where the migrants now belong, it is where they have built a home and a family, and where their lives have taken root. In such cases, migrants are likely to seek full citizenship, and justice requires that it be offered to them. Denying citizenship in such cases is not just unfair in and of itself, but often serves to perpetuate other injustices. Migrant denizens around the world face a high potential for exploitation: desperate individuals from poor countries are often willing to accept very harsh living and working conditions, and the lack of citizenship means they may be unable to exercise whatever legal rights they nominally possess.

For this reason, many commentators have argued that the goal should be to turn migrant workers into citizens as quickly and easily as possible, or that we should eliminate migrant worker programmes entirely (Lenard and Straehle forthcoming). Countries seeking to fill labour market gaps should admit permanent immigrants, not migrant workers, and thus all workers would be protected under the umbrella of full citizenship.

However, we shouldn't assume that migrant denizenship is always or inherently exploitative, or that citizenship is always the solution. Some migrants do not wish to build a home and family in their current country of residence, and may not wish to put down deep social roots in it, or to take part in its scheme of cooperative citizenship. The focus of their life projects may remain their country of origin. As Ottonelli and Torresi (forthcoming) note, seasonal and temporary workers may have perfectly rational and legitimate 'temporary migration projects'. The focal point of their lives may lie in their country of origin, and they simply wish to earn money or gain expertise in order to achieve those aims back home, such as building a house, supporting an extended family, or opening a business. They do not wish to settle permanently, uproot their families, and abandon their old lives. On the contrary, they want to engage in migrant work in order to achieve goals tied up with their lives and families back home. (Or, in the case of travelling youth, they may simply want the experience of extended travel and life abroad before settling down, and may seek to work abroad to fund their travel.)

In these cases, migrant workers are not likely to be interested in policies designed to integrate them more quickly into state projects of citizenship.

Where migrants have temporary migration projects, they may have little interest or inclination in mastering the norms of citizenship in their host country, and may resent efforts to force them to do so. It may not be rational for them to spend time or resources learning about the host country's political system or learning the national language. (Mexican seasonal workers in Canada may not wish to spend the time needed to learn English or French.) In short, they may want to live amongst us on an extended or seasonal basis, but not become one of us. In their own way, although for different reasons, migrant workers, too, may wish to opt out of citizenship.

Such cases pose a challenge to traditional liberal theories of justice, which rely on citizenship as the pre-eminent means of ensuring fairness. Migrants are highly vulnerable to injustice, but imposing citizenship on them is likely to be either ineffective (given that migrants would not invest the time and resources needed to exercise effectively their citizenship rights) and/or unfair (if the state forced migrants to invest the time and resources to learn the local language and become informed about the country's political system). Any attempt to press-gang migrants into mastering citizenship 'comes at a cost that has to be shared in part by immigrants, who will be unfairly forced to divert the relevant resources from their life plans and the projects they originally established' (Ottonelli and Torresi forthcoming). As a result, such migrants are 'hard to locate on the map of democracy' (Carens 2008a).

How, then, are we to protect migrants from injustice? How do we ensure that efforts to accommodate migrants do not degenerate into relations of subordination and caste hierarchy, as happens all too often around the world? In this context, justice arguably requires a form of denizenship that protects migrants from exploitation, while leaving them free to pursue life goals tied to their country of origin.[33] Denizenship offers a distinctive relationship to the host society that is weaker than citizenship, but not unfair or oppressive, since it is adapted to the legitimate interests of both parties.

Of course, much depends on the precise terms of this denizenship status. As we have seen, the fairness of denizenship requires that both the rights and responsibilities of citizenship be reduced in a balanced or reciprocal manner, and that this be done to respond to the legitimate interests of both parties, rather than as a unilateral imposition by one side on the other. It does not involve reducing rights while still imposing the full burdens of citizenship: that would be second-class citizenship.[34] Rather, it involves negotiating a different and weaker, but nonetheless reciprocal, relationship with the broader political community: both sides of the relationship exert weaker claims on the other.

For example, we might extend to migrant workers the full protections of the host country's law in the sphere of social rights (e.g., health care benefits; workplace safety, training, and compensation; access to visitor visas for family members), while denying access to full citizenship benefits (e.g., the right to settle permanently and sponsor family immigration, the right to vote or hold office) or responsibilities (e.g., taxation, military service or jury duty, language competence).

In this context, migrant denizenship typically involves a division of labour between states. In relation to seasonal workers, for example, the destination country extends equal protection and standing within the realm of seasonal work life (e.g., the same wages, protections, training, and health and safety provisions as for workers with citizenship in that country), while the sending country remains the primary vehicle of citizenship in other realms of life (home country work life, family life supports and benefits, political participation, retirement benefits, etc.). On this model, migrants are not 'perceived as helpless second-class citizens', but rather as people 'whose equality of status is secured not by their full inclusion within the host society but by the recognition of their special position and the public awareness of their contingent and temporary relation to that society' (Ottonelli and Torresi forthcoming).

We do not wish to underestimate the risks involved in such denizenship models. Lower-skilled migrant workers are always vulnerable to exploitation, given their lack of connections in the communities where they engage in seasonal work, their lack of power in the political process, language barriers, lack of education or knowledge of rights, and so on. To some extent this vulnerability is shared by all travellers, including business people, tourists, or visiting students. But migrant workers are especially vulnerable because they typically have less money, fewer options, and are more likely to be engaged in physically demanding and dangerous work in isolated locations. (Highly skilled foreign workers are much less vulnerable, given their greater options, bargaining power, and levels of education.) Perhaps this vulnerability could be assuaged through the establishment of effective domestic or international oversight to ensure that the rights of migrant workers are fully communicated and respected.[35]

So far we have been focusing on denizenship for authorized migrant workers. The case of unauthorized or illegal migrants is more complicated, since it raises the issue of initial entry. Insofar as illegal migrants have temporary migration projects, then we believe that, under certain conditions, something like migrant denizenship is an appropriate status. But specifying these conditions is not simple.

If we consider the best practices of liberal democracies in relation to illegal immigration, we can identify two principles at work. First, states have a legitimate right to try to prevent unauthorized entry. The state cannot of course shoot illegal immigrants, or otherwise violate their basic rights, but it can erect visa requirements, border controls, and barriers to prevent entry, and undertake policing efforts to identify and remove illegal migrants who do enter. It can also change the social conditions that act as an inducement for illegal entry in the first place. For example, it can punish companies that employ illegal migrants, or deny illegal immigrants access to certain benefits (e.g., driver's licence) in order to make life as an illegal immigrant less attractive.

However, if illegal immigrants have been able to escape detection and deportation for a certain period of time, then a second principle kicks in. Sooner or later they acquire a moral 'right to stay', akin to squatter's rights, reflected in the periodic amnesties that states often offer to long-term illegal immigrants (Carens 2008b, 2010). Migrants may have entered a community illegally, but over time, as they become enmeshed in that community, the moral costs of uprooting them become too high.

In some cases, this enmeshing is such that their country of residence becomes de facto their only home. They may have built a home and family, and may feel like strangers if they returned to their country of origin. If so, then amnesties should lead to full citizenship. But in other cases, illegal migrants have maintained close ties to their country of origin, and indeed engaged in illegal migration in the first place in order to pursue life goals tied to their homeland. In such cases, as with authorized migrant workers, denizenship can be a just solution.

In short, states can use barriers and disincentives to keep illegal migrants out, but once they are in, the calculus starts to change over time, requiring accommodation of the new facts on the ground.[36] In some cases, this accommodation should take the form of full citizenship, but in other cases, denizenship is more appropriate.

For both authorized migrant workers and illegal immigrants, then, the status of migrant denizenship is a potential outcome, one that provides firm protection for rights of residence (and other appropriate social rights) without demanding a commitment to full citizenship—a commitment that may not be desired by either side in the relationship.

As we noted, these forms of migrant denizenship carry the risk that the fair accommodation of difference will turn into relations of subordination and stigmatization. Migrant denizens may be perceived and treated as unworthy aliens or illegitimate invaders, rather than as moral equals with distinctive life projects and ties to other societies, eroding the potential reciprocity of the denizenship relationship. This risk is particularly relevant to illegal immigrants, but applies to authorized migrants as well. Whether this erosion takes place depends in large part on whether the host country is acting in good faith regarding its immigration policies. In reality, many states practise deceptive and hypocritical migrant worker policies. They turn a blind eye to illegal migration because legal immigration is a tough sell, but migrant workers are crucial for the economy. By allowing migrants to enter but refusing them legal status, states side-step the responsibility to provide any rights or benefits of denizenship, and industry benefits from the downward pressure on wages.

More generally, states often take a public position against migration, and present it as an undue burden on the economy, democratic self-determination, and/or cultural stability, while secretly allowing illegal migration, in order to reap its benefits and pay none of the costs. In addition to the obvious injustices, this sort of duplicitous state policy poisons citizens' attitudes towards migrants. Official silence on the need for, and benefits of, immigration results in a limited perspective of migrants as those who break the law, burden society, and/or threaten the social contract, rather than being contributing members of the community. Under these conditions, migrant denizenship is indeed a fragile and vulnerable status. But where states address issues of migration honestly and in good faith, denizenship can provide a stable framework for just relationships.

We have considered two basic forms of denizenship in modern liberal–democratic societies. Denizenship can arise both from migration across borders, and from various forms of disengagement with dominant practices of citizenship. In our view, the existence of such forms of denizenship is inevitable, given what Rawls calls 'the facts of pluralism'—the diversity of human cultures, behaviours, and practices that inevitably arises under conditions of freedom. As we said earlier, humans are stubbornly resistant to the effort of states and political philosophers to put them into rigid and exclusive categories. Not everyone is able or willing to accept the choice between full citizenship or full exclusion. Faced with the choice of 'in or out', some people, for good reasons, may prefer to negotiate a third option of denizenship.

However, while the status of denizenship may be inevitable given the facts of pluralism, and may comply with fundamental standards of fairness and reciprocity, it is also inherently prone to exploitation. The historical record suggests that full citizenship remains the most reliable protector of moral equality, and any acceptance of denizenship needs to be strongly hedged to prevent its deterioration into relations of subordination. What precisely these hedges are is undertheorized in the literature, but we would identify three clusters of issues:

1. *security of residency* In the case of migrant denizenship, regardless of how individuals come to take up residence in a community (legally or illegally), their right to stay and to be incorporated into the political community increases over time, and as opportunities to reside elsewhere diminish. Permanent residents cannot be expelled, but must be accorded secure residency, either as citizens or denizens.

2. *reciprocity of denizenship* Limitations on access to full citizenship rights of denizens can only be justified assuming that (a) they are part-time or temporary residents only who benefit from full citizenship in a foreign state; and/or (b) denizenship status is a mutually beneficial accommodation of interests and capacities, reflecting a mutual desire for a weakened form of affiliation or cooperation. In other words, there is a reciprocal reduction of citizenship benefits and burdens, and these represent a fair accommodation of interests, not a hierarchical relation of exploitation;

3. *anti-stigma safeguards* States have a special responsibility to ensure that denizens are not made vulnerable by their alternative status. Safeguards must be put in place to prevent denizenship becoming a source of stigma or caste hierarchy: denizens are differentially related to the political community, but are not for that reason inferior or unworthy, and must still be respected for their intrinsic moral status and for their contributions. These safeguards include such measures as robust anti-discrimination legislation, and full and equal protection of the law, and the avoidance of hypocrisy or bad faith in public debates about the role denizens play in the community.

Where these and other safeguards are in place, denizenship can arguably play a valid role in accommodating the diversity of human groups and communities, while still upholding fundamental values of moral equality and fairness.

4. Defining the Terms of Animal Denizenship

Can this discussion of human denizenship shed light on the case of liminal animals? We believe that it does, in part because liminal animals face many of the same dynamics of exclusion or invisibility as human denizens face. Just as modern states like to put every human being into rigid and exclusive citizenship categories—expecting individuals to be either fully a citizen or fully alien—so, too, societies like to put all animals into their place, either fully wild or fully domestic. Liminal animals are rendered invisible in this everyday picture, and continually perceived as somehow 'out of place'. They are seen, in effect, as aliens or foreigners who really belong somewhere else, even if we are not quite sure where else they belong. And so, like human aliens, they are subject to exclusion, although in this case the exclusion not only takes the form of disincentives, barriers, and deportation, but also more extreme forms of violence and killing.

The underlying logic, in both the human and animal cases, seems to be that anyone who wants to reside here must choose 'in or out': either full citizenship or exclusion. And just as this forced choice is insufficient to address the diversity of human relationships, so, too, it is inadequate in the animal case. Indeed, in many respects, it is even more inadequate in the animal case. In the case of human denizens, a forced choice between deportation and full citizenship is harsh, but both options are potentially viable. Human denizens may be able to adapt to either a return to their country of origin or to full citizenship, albeit with significant (and unfair) burdens and costs. In the animal case, by contrast, neither option is typically viable. The in or out choice means in effect a choice between deportation or domestication: being forced to leave areas of human settlement, or being forced to undergo the sort of confinement and breeding necessary to turn animals into domesticated companions of humans. As we have seen, neither option is adequate as a response to the realities of liminal animals. Rather, we need to accept that liminal animals belong here, but not under our governance, and with a different status from that of domesticated animals. They need, in effect, a form of denizenship.

But what would be the fair terms of such animal denizenship? Can the three principles of fair denizenship we discussed in the human case shed light on the animal case? We believe that they can. We cannot develop a systematic account of what these principles would entail in relation to all of the different types of liminal animals. As we discussed earlier, liminal animals differ in their vulnerabilities and adaptabilities. Denizenship for the hazel dormouse living in a hedgerow will obviously take a different form to denizenship for urban pigeons. However, we would like to say a few words about each of these principles.

(1) *Secure residency*: In both the human and animal cases, a core feature of denizenship is the right of residency—the right not to be treated as aliens or foreigners who really belong somewhere else, but as residents belonging here with us. While efforts can legitimately be undertaken to discourage or prevent the initial entry and reproduction of opportunist or exotic liminal animals, over time they come to acquire the right to stay. Regardless of how individuals come to take up residence in a community (legally or illegally, wanted or unwanted), their right to stay increases over time, and as opportunities to reside elsewhere diminish.

(2) *Fair terms of reciprocity*: In both the human and animal cases, denizenship involves a reciprocal reduction in rights and responsibilities, to accommodate the desire of groups to have a weaker relationship than that of full citizenship. Animal denizenship, however, will typically involve an even weaker form of mutual interaction and mutual obligation than human denizenship. If denizenship involves opting out of some aspects of full citizenship, the degree of opting out is much greater in the case of liminal animals compared with human denizens.

241

This is perhaps most obvious in relation to predation. In the case of human denizenship, we do not accept predation of some denizens by others, or the death of denizens by starvation or exposure. States have an obligation to protect all human residents, including denizens, from these basic threats to existence—the status of denizenship does not involve waiving such protections. By contrast, liminal animal denizens will still be subject to predator–prey relations: some animal denizens are predators (hawks), others are prey (house sparrows), and others are both (feral cats eat birds, and are sometimes eaten by coyotes).

What explains this difference? The answer, again, lies in the sort of threats to liberty and autonomy that are involved. Generally speaking, we can protect human denizens from threats of killing or starvation while still respecting robust rights of free choice and free movement. But it's worth noting that in cases where protection of human life can only be achieved with drastic limitations on liberty and autonomy, we tend to accept the risks to life and safety. For example, we don't compel people to report for regular medical check-ups, even though this is the only way to ensure we catch diseases in time. Similarly, we don't install cameras in every home, even though this might ensure that every infant receives sufficient love and nourishment. Human societies are constantly balancing liberty and autonomy against safety (and different societies legitimately make different trade-offs here). The lives of liminal animals involve levels of risk which we would consider unacceptable in the human case. However, reducing these risks would involve levels of coercion and confinement which we would also find unacceptable. Because the liberty/risk calculations work so differently for liminal animals, the resulting package of rights and responsibilities will also be different.

This weaker form of denizenship is appropriate for liminal animals as a mutually beneficial arrangement between liminal animals and humans in mixed communities. This reciprocal arrangement of reduced benefits and duties would release liminal animals from the drastic reductions of liberty necessary to bring them into conformity with full citizenship, and at the same time reduce the responsibility of the human community in terms of the provision of full citizenship benefits and protections. We have defended this position on the assumption that liminal animals (a) tend to avoid humans; (b) would prefer the risk of predation to confinement and other severe restrictions on liberty; and (c) have considerable competence for negotiating the risks of their environment, a competence that requires liberty (and risk) to develop.

However, for any *particular* liminal animal, circumstances might change to alter this equation drastically. After all, some liminal animals *do* seek out human company, developing relations of trust and a degree of mutual understanding. We could, in such cases, see the animal's actions as a vote for citizenship over denizenship. Or consider the case of an orphaned raccoon, or an injured squirrel, who could not survive on their own, and whom we could safely assist. For these animals, the trade-offs of citizenship would look quite attractive since in their situation denizenship involves not just greater risk, but, rather, a swift and certain death. In some cases, we might be able to rehabilitate the animal and return it to liminal denizenship, but in others it might be more appropriate to pursue their integration into the mixed human–animal community as regular citizens (with the accompanying trade-offs in terms of restricted liberty). This is analogous to the argument we made in Chapter 6 about our obligations to injured wild animals.[37]

Although we must be attentive to the circumstances of atypical liminal individuals who may need or desire closer relations to humans, this does not mean that we should encourage an increase in such individuals. Humans should be very cautious about encouraging closer relations with liminal animals—for example, by feeding or other attempts to befriend them. Many human–animal conflicts stem from these interventions. Population increase and habituation to humans leads to animals being viewed as nuisances or threats, and the result is invariably bad for animals. For example, 'problem' coyotes who attack humans and pets almost always have a history of having been fed by humans (Adams and Lindsey 2010). Feeding bears, deer, or geese may seem like a positive intervention that benefits animals (and sometimes this may be the case), but it should not be undertaken without a thorough understanding of the spillover effects.

Liminal denizenship, then, typically involves a far looser relationship than that of human denizenship, with a significantly weaker form of cooperation and obligation. Liminal animals reside amongst us, and their presence must be accepted as legitimate, but we have no right to socialize them into the practices of citizenship, and they have no claim to the full benefits of cooperative citizenship.

However, it's also worth emphasizing that denizenship, like citizenship, is an evolving relationship, and its future evolution is unpredictable. If humans were to recognize the liminal animals living in our midst, and begin the process of establishing relations of justice rather than abuse and negligence, then inevitably these animals would change their behaviour towards us. On the one hand, they might become less wary of humans, for example, and over time this could lead to opportunities for a more mutual form of citizenship than we are capable of imagining at this point. On the other hand, reduced wariness might also lead to greater conflict. For example, given the level of risk that coyotes may pose for infants or small domesticated animals, it would be foolhardy to interact with coyotes in ways that reduce their wariness of humans.[38] Similarly, there might be various kinds of liminal animals who pose genuine disease threats to humans or domesticated animals. And there are many cases in which reduced wariness of humans or domesticated animals might put liminal animals at increased risk. (For example, a chipmunk who grows accustomed to harmless domestic dogs may get a rude awakening when she encounters a feral hunting dog.) In the many cases where closer relations seem ill-advised, we can still treat liminal animals justly (i.e., we can respect their basic negative rights and reduce the risks which we inadvertently impose on them) without facilitating closer relations.

We need to keep an open mind about the possibilities and limits regarding relationships with liminal animals. Individually, and at the species level, liminals differ significantly in terms of how they interact with humans and the possibilities for mutuality. In general, we have argued for limits on the integration of liminals into the community of citizens, given the likelihood of creating conflict. Treating these animals justly does not entail befriending them, or increasing the range or depth of mutual relationship. However, we cannot predict how these relationships will evolve over time, and whether some liminal animals might be on a trajectory from denizenship to something closer to co-citizenship.

For the foreseeable future, models of denizenship should operate on the assumption of wary and minimal interaction, rather than trusting and intimate cooperation. However, this weaker form of relationship still carries with it important positive obligations. Liminal animal denizenship is weaker than human denizenship, but it is still much more than the traditional ART injunction to 'let them be'. Humans must not only respect the basic rights of liminal animals, but must take into account their interests in our decisions about how to design our cities and buildings, and how to regulate our activities.

One aspect of this, already discussed in Chapter 6, concerns a fair sharing of risk. At the moment, we are hypersensitive to any risk that liminal animals might pose to us—getting sucked into airplane engines, causing car accidents, chewing insulated electrical wires. Or we wildly exaggerate threats, especially in the case of disease.[39] Meanwhile, we ignore the countless risks we impose on liminals—cars, electrical transformers, tall structures and wires, window glass, backyard pools, pesticides, and many others. As we argued in Chapter 6, it is unfair to have a zero-tolerance policy as regards animal risks to humans, while completely disregarding the risks we impose on them. Fairness requires a balancing of risks and benefits between citizens and denizens. Fair sharing of risks would have significant implications for urban and suburban development, including changes to building codes regarding location, height, and window placement (to limit bird impacts), the creation of urban animal corridors (so liminal animals can avoid roads), use of warning devices and barriers, and revised codes for use of pesticides and other poisons for which animals often have a much lower tolerance than humans.

A related accommodation concerns the pace of change in human environments. Liminal animals, particularly niche specialists, are extremely vulnerable to changes in their environment, such as changes in land use and agricultural practices. This means we need to take these animals into account when deciding whether change is necessary, and how best to undertake it. Sometimes it might be enough to make changes gradually, ensuring that vulnerable animals have a chance to adjust or relocate. Čapek (2005) describes a striking incident involving cattle egrets, a liminal species associated with pasture and grazing animals. A tree grove in Conway, Arkansas was a nesting site for 8,000 pairs of cattle egrets. During the brief nesting season, the grove was bulldozed for development, resulting in a massive slaughter of birds. Had the project been delayed by two weeks, the egrets would have finished nesting and the slaughter could easily have been avoided. The developer claimed ignorance that the birds were there. In this situation there was no inherent conflict between human and egret interests. Rather, the birds were simply invisible (physically and ethically).

The positive obligations of humans towards liminal animals have their counterpart in various responsibilities that we can impose on liminal animals. Any viable scheme of coexistence in shared territory requires mutual restraints and mutual accommodations. For example, as in the case of domestic animals, liminal animals are unable to regulate their reproduction in light of their obligations to others in a shared political community. Humans do not need to intervene in the 'who, what, where, when' of liminal sexual activity, but we may need to regulate the total numbers of liminal animals if coexistence is to be possible (through methods such as birth control vaccines, or by fostering habitat conditions allowing for population dispersal, and the re-emergence of predators or competitors). Similarly, most liminal animals are unable to regulate their mobility in light of the rights of others to private property. This is another area in which humans can exercise control to protect the rights of all members of the community, including the (non-lethal) use of fences and nets and other barriers. In other words, the robust responsibilities of the human community towards liminal denizens are hedged by a robust right to exercise control over their total numbers and use of shared space.

In the human case, the rights of individuals carry corresponding duties to respect the rights of others. Invading someone's home without permission and posing a risk or nuisance to them would clearly be a violation of the obligation to respect their basic rights. Typically, such problems are avoided because humans can internalize reasonable behaviour, and an understanding of the need to regulate one's actions out of respect for the rights of others. In the case of mice, however, and other adaptive animal home invaders, we are dealing with parties who don't understand that they pose a risk or nuisance, and are incapable of understanding reasonable accommodation. In this, they are similar to children or others with limited intellectual capacities who sometimes need to be monitored and controlled for their safety as well as our own. Given that liminal animals cannot be held responsible for regulating their behaviour in relation to humans, it is up to humans to impose a framework of reasonable accommodation, one which recognizes the legitimacy of human concerns about safety (as well as aesthetic and other concerns), and balances this against risks imposed on animals. The ideal solution will be one in which the animal is not made worse off by an accommodation, although this might not always be achievable.

We have already discussed many strategies for restricting access of liminal animals, and for reducing total populations. Fences, physical barriers, and house-proofing measures are obvious steps. Disincentives such as annoying sound systems, unpleasant (but harmless) substances, or unleashed dogs can be effective. For example, some golf courses now encourage golfers to bring their dog companions along for the day. The presence of unleashed dogs discourages geese from landing on the greens. Off-leash dog parks could be deliberately located in areas where humans wish to discourage liminal animals—for example, next to garden allotments or public parks that are vulnerable to deer grazing. Similarly, a city park might encourage a colony of mute swans to take up residence. Swans are highly territorial, although there is debate about how effective they actually are in keeping geese at bay.[40]

Inevitably, conflicts will still emerge. Barriers and careful food/garbage storage practices may keep mice and rats out of the house and cupboards, but what if you buy an old house with rodent colonies already well established? There may be no option except to trap and relocate the animals. This will be stressful for them, but it could be managed in ways to minimize harm. For example, they could be relocated to a safe outbuilding, and provided with food and water on a gradually diminishing basis until they are able to fend for themselves.

The most effective measures for controlling liminal animal populations are those that limit food sources and nesting sites, and provide habitat networks and corridors that are sufficiently large to allow natural systems of population control to emerge (e.g., population dispersal, competition, predation). Populations increase in response to resources, and humans seem to go out of their way to provide food and nesting sites for liminal animals. Careless storage of food and litter is a major source of problems. Poorly considered choices for park and garden plantings act as magnets. And deliberate feeding also plays a major role. Public education campaigns highlighting the role of human actions in creating liminal animal 'pest' situations can be very effective. We have already discussed the 'Coexistence with Coyotes' campaign in Vancouver, which discourages feeding or friendly contact with coyotes. And the Animal Alliance of Canada has produced a superb guide for reducing conflicts between humans and Canada geese by redesigning urban, suburban, and agricultural landscapes in ways that reduce food, nesting, and security opportunities for geese (Doncaster and Keller 2000).[41]

Another highly effective campaign has significantly reduced urban pigeon populations in Nottingham, Basel, and other European cities (Blechman 2006: ch. 8). Developed by a Swiss biologist, the campaign is essentially a three-pronged strategy. First, safe, clean lofts for pigeons are set up at locations around the city. Volunteers regularly clean the lofts, and provide fresh food and water. In effect, the pigeons are provided with a safe location much like the dovecotes of old. The second strategy is to educate the public to stop feeding pigeons in other locations. (Pigeon lovers who want to feed the birds can do so at designated lofts.) Public education is the most challenging part of the strategy, and often requires serious penalties for a small minority of humans who insist on deliberately feeding birds outside the designated feeding locations. The final prong of the strategy is to control reproduction. Loft volunteers replace a certain percentage of pigeon eggs with fakes, thereby slowing the reproduction rate. The programme effectively limits pigeon numbers and locales, and has created détente between humans and pigeons where it has been adopted. This is in marked contrast to the brutality and ineffectiveness of traditional campaigns (shooting, poisoning, trapping, impaling) which have resulted in an increase in pigeon populations in other cities (Blechman 2006: 142–3).

The deliberate location and designation of pigeon lofts points to a general strategy for coexistence with liminal animals. Rather than negative campaigns of elimination or deportation, we should adopt positive campaigns for locating and managing populations in a spirit of coexistence. For example, feral cats in suburban areas pose a mortal threat to songbirds. One estimate is that 100 million birds die annually in the USA due to cat predation (Adams and Lindsey 2010: 141). However, regions with a liminal coyote population have a much higher population of songbirds than regions without coyotes (Fraser 2009: 2). Where coyotes patrol the suburban woods and wild patches, domestic and feral cats are afraid to roam, and as a result birds are spared from predation. In effect, the coyotes act as a barrier, establishing no-go zones for cats which become de facto sanctuaries for birds. Given these various facts, how can we best respect the interests of songbirds, coyotes, and feral cats? One solution is to create cat sanctuaries and feeding stations in areas of urban density (like the Rome sanctuary). Cats will be attracted by a variety of benefits (e.g., food, safety from coyotes), and the net effect will be far fewer birds at risk from the cats, and fewer cats, in turn, at risk from coyotes.

In general, the kinds of strategies we are advocating for controlling the population and movement of liminal animals—barriers, disincentives, reduced food supply, habitat corridors, safe zones—happen to be precisely the strategies which countless studies have demonstrated to be far more effective than traditional methods. Killing or relocating animals simply opens up a gap which will be filled—often by increased numbers. In general, animal populations are self-regulating in relation to food, shelter, and nesting opportunities, and the presence of hazards causing death. If humans increase food and shelter opportunities, then animal populations will increase accordingly. If humans reduce opportunities, then populations will reduce. If opportunities remain the same, but humans increase hazards (e.g., by culling, or inadvertent killing), natural rates of reproduction will increase to fill the void. For example, liminal black bears produce larger litters than wild black bears, probably because liminal bears have much higher rates of cub mortality (due largely to road deaths).[42] If humans reduce hazards, then fewer animals will be killed and, in turn, rates of reproduction will slow down.[43] In short, it's a 'build it and they will come' situation. If we provide opportunities, liminal animals will make use of them. If we limit overall opportunities, we will limit their total numbers. We can also deliberately locate opportunities, thus managing their presence in ways conducive to peaceful coexistence.

In these examples, we can begin to see the outlines of a fair scheme of denizenship, built around principles of secure residency and a weak but mutual scheme of responsibility and obligation, including norms of reasonable accommodation and minimizing risk.

(3) *Anti-stigma*: As we noted in the human case, one of the risks of denizenship is that denizens can become stigmatized, isolated, and vulnerable. While denizenship should not be seen as a mark of inferiority or deviance, denizens are less able than full citizens to protect themselves against this sort of stigma, leading to hostility and xenophobia. This is a threat that affects migrant denizens, opt-out denizens, and liminal animal denizens, all of whom have historically been treated as pariahs rather than as simply different.

Societies must be constantly vigilant that denizenship does not deteriorate into hierarchy and prejudice. There are several safeguards one can imagine here. It would be important that legal protections for denizens do not just exist on paper, but are backed up by full and equal protection of the law. For example, regulations to reduce harms to liminal animals when designing roads or buildings should be rigorously enforced, as should laws about negligence causing death (from road accidents, or construction and agricultural machinery, for example). We have already discussed the symbolic as well as material importance of such legal enforcement in Chapter 5.

But an equally important safeguard involves a commitment to transparency and consistency and a good-faith acknowledgement of our own role in creating human–animal conflicts. As in the case of human migrants, our response to liminal animals is highly inconsistent, and frequently based on misconceptions about the role they play in our communities, and the role we play in attracting them. We set up feeders for songbirds, but end up attracting squirrels, raccoons, bears, and deer who steal the food, not to mention raptors who prey on the songbirds. And then we complain about these invaders. We are careless with garbage or outdoor pet food bowls, and thereby attract a host of animals, from rodents to raccoons to coyotes. We plant vast lawns of clipped Kentucky blue grass next to ponds and water features, creating perfect habitat for Canada geese. It's not unusual for one neighbour to set up a deer feeder, while next door they're putting up electric fences and human scarecrows in an effort to save the tulips and ornamental shrubs. Sometimes the same family that sets up a feeder to enjoy some bird-watching also has a free-roaming domestic cat that preys on the birds, or a bank of tree-reflecting windows that serves as a death magnet. And, of course, human action is overwhelmingly responsible for the existence of exotic and feral animal populations.

Currently, there is an utter lack of transparency and consistency in human responses to liminal animals. As in the case of human migration, this is in part due to divergent opinions about the desirability of these denizens, extensive ignorance about the nature and habits of these individuals who share our communities and living spaces, misplaced fears about the dangers they pose, and utter blindness to the risks we impose in turn. We tend to see liminal animals in terms of their problem attributes (e.g., sparrows making too much noise, squirrels stealing the bird seed, pigeons fouling the park benches), while ignoring the ways we benefit from the same animals (scavenging human garbage, seeding new trees, eating insects, pollinating plants, controlling other liminal animal populations through predation).

Moreover, as in the human context, unethical politicians and business people often prefer to exploit ignorance and fear for their own gain, rather than educating the public about the benefits and possibilities of coexistence.[44] No matter what, there will always be differences amongst humans regarding attitudes towards liminal animals. Some people welcome these animals, and seek opportunities to live alongside them, enjoying the diversity, beauty, and other benefits they bring to community life. Others will never get beyond basic toleration. Transparency, careful planning, and public education can help to accommodate this range of attitudes.

Consider a similar kind of problem in human affairs. Ontarians flock to cottage country in the summer. For some, the ideal is a quiet lake where you can hear the loons call and the cicadas hum. For others, the ideal is an action-filled lake of jet skis, power boats, and water sports. The two ideals are incompatible, and lead to some measure of conflict in lake country. However, a partial solution can be achieved by covenants and power boat-free ordinances which channel quiet nature lovers to certain lakes, and water sports lovers to others. We could approach urban planning in a similar spirit, with some communities employing barriers and no-feeding ordinances to limit the liminal animal population, while other areas are more welcoming to liminal animals and the humans who are happy to coexist with them. We shouldn't underestimate human ingenuity for creating urban ecosystems that accommodate citizens and denizens, both human and animal. For example, the city of Leeds (UK) has embarked on an annual competition to design wildlife-friendly urban spaces. A recent winning entry was for an animal 'high-rise' intended to accommodate bats, birds, and butterflies in the heart of the metropolis, while simultaneously appealing to human inhabitants.[45]

5. Conclusion

Recognition of the rights of liminal animal denizens does not mean that humans must sit back and let them take over their cities and homes.[46] It means that we must recognize the legitimacy of those already present as residents of the community, and devise strategies for coexistence which recognize animals' rights as well as our own. If we operate on the idea that adaptive animals are illegal aliens in our cities who need to be apprehended and deported, we are going to fail. The animals will return, or be replaced by others. They are a fact of life of human settlement, and successful strategies will be premised on coexistence not banishment. Happily, the requirements of justice for denizens are quite compatible with strategies for successful coexistence.

Consider the scenario of the dog companions at a golf course, happily running the rounds to discourage geese from landing and fouling the greens. We can look at this scenario and see it as a sign of failure to find a permanent solution. Or we can see it as a successful coexistence strategy, one that recognizes the inevitability of geese and achieves a tolerable *modus vivendi*. Eradication isn't an option, either ethically or practically. We have argued that it is perfectly reasonable for humans to make cities a little less attractive to adaptive species (e.g., by reducing resources, and by using barriers, competitors, and predators), while making the wilds more attractive (by not colonizing them). In effect, this is a strategy for altering the risk calculus for liminal animals, making city life a less obvious improvement over life in the wild. But this will never be enough to discourage liminal animals from making a life in the city. City life is simply too messy, complex, and permeable to ever effectively barricade it from liminal animals. Besides, who would want to? Some liminal animals become pests, but they also provide welcome diversity and interest to city life. It would be terrible (and futile) if, in the name of solving a few serious animal–human conflicts, we cut ourselves off from the natural world. The more we can move towards accepting and accommodating animals' presence (even if there are some people who will never fully welcome them), and recognizing that cities are their own kind of animal kingdom, the more equipped we will be for discovering creative coexistence strategies.

The extent of our differences from liminal animals, and the resulting limitations on mutuality, mean that, for the foreseeable future, most of these animals will continue to be denizens not co-citizens. They live amongst us. We must respect their basic rights, and extend to them various positive obligations. These include reasonable accommodation of their interests in the way we develop the human-built environment, and positive forms of assistance when these can be undertaken without undermining their basic liberty and autonomy. At the same time, it is legitimate for humans to limit increases in liminal populations, and to manage their mobility and access.

So, on the one hand, liminal animals are residents of the political community and their interests need to be taken into account. On the other hand, there is an important sense in which liminals inhabit a parallel plane—a different city spatially and temporally, and one which operates by mechanisms (e.g., laws of nature) much closer to those that operate in sovereign animal communities than in the mixed community of humans and domesticated animals.

The resulting status is a complex one, and not without its moral ambiguities. It does not offer the seeming clarity of either citizenship for domesticated animals or sovereignty for animals in the wild. Denizenship is, by comparison, a hybrid status, with fewer clear fixed points of reference. And, as a result, it is indeed more vulnerable to being misused as a cover for subordination or neglect. But in our view, there is no alternative. The values of liminal denizenship are in fact the same as for domestic co-citizenship and wild animal sovereignty—values of moral equality, autonomy, individual and communal flourishing. But how to achieve these goals depends on the nature of animals' relationships with human political communities. And for the vast bulk of liminal animals, these values can only be achieved through recognizing their status as permanent residents of human environments, but as residents who retain the desire and capacity to remain independent of us. Trying to relocate liminals into a zone of wild animal sovereignty would threaten those values, as would trying to integrate them into cooperative schemes of co-citizenship with humans. What they need, and deserve, is denizenship.

8

Conclusion

We began this book by noting that the animal advocacy movement has reached both a political and an intellectual impasse, and that we hope to contribute to overcoming both. In the previous chapters, we have focused on the intellectual impasse, showing how a wide range of pressing issues regarding human–animal interactions cannot be resolved from within a traditional animal rights theory (ART) perspective that focuses solely on the intrinsic moral standing of animals. To address these issues, we have argued, requires attending to the variable ways that animals are related to political institutions and practices of state sovereignty, territory, colonization, migration, and membership. This more relational and political approach helps illuminate blind spots within ART, and clarifies some of its well-known paradoxes and ambiguities.

In this Conclusion, we'd like to return to the political impasse, which is considerably more daunting. We noted in the Introduction that while the animal advocacy movement has won some battles over the past century, it has essentially lost the war. The sheer scale of animal exploitation continues to expand around the globe, and the occasional 'victory' in reforming the cruelest forms of animal use simply nibbles at the edges of the systemic human mistreatment of animals.

For anyone concerned with the fate of animals, finding a way to overcome this political impasse is a priority. Developing new and expanded theories of animal rights may be intellectually stimulating and challenging, but can it make any difference to real-world campaigns and debates?

We are not optimistic about the prospects for dramatic change in the short term, and we certainly have no delusions that one can somehow change the world simply by articulating better moral arguments. Humans have built our societies—our cultures and economies—on animal exploitation, and many people have vested interests in perpetuating those practices in some form or another. Moral arguments are notoriously ineffective when they run so fully against the grain of self-interest and inherited expectations. Most of us are not moral saints: we're willing to act on our moral convictions when it costs us relatively little, but not when it requires us to give up our standard of living or way of life. People may be willing to ban fox hunting, but are notably less keen about giving up meat or leather, let alone ceasing colonization of wild animal habitat, extending co-citizenship to cats and cows, or embracing coexistence with pigeons and coyotes. Any theory that asks people to become moral saints is doomed to be politically ineffective, and it would be naïve to expect otherwise.

However, we do not believe that this is the whole story. In fact, one could argue that our addiction to animal exploitation is harming us, even killing us. Meat-centred diets are less healthy than vegetarian diets; moreover, the agricultural processes needed to produce that meat rival transportation as a leading cause of global warming.[1] Human colonization of wild animal territory is destroying the lungs of the planet, the vitality of our soils, the stability of weather systems, and the supply of fresh water. The simple fact is that the human species cannot survive on this planet if we do not become less dependent on the exploitation of animals, and destruction of their habitat.

Indeed, some commentators have argued that the system of animal exploitation will inevitably collapse of its own accord, even without any change in moral sensibilities. As Jim Motavelli puts it, 'we won't stop eating meat simply because it's "the right thing to do;"'—he thinks arguing people to give up meat 'is a losing proposition'—but nonetheless 'we'll be forced to stop'. UN studies have shown that, by 2025, there simply won't be enough water or land needed to sustain a meat diet for 8 billion people, and so 'meat will disappear except as a luxury available to few'.[2] Motavelli predicts that there will eventually be a shift to an ethic that rejects eating animal flesh, but this will follow, not precede, the environmental collapse of the meat industry. In this view, engaging in animal rights (AR) moral theory is pointless, not because it is powerless against the forces upholding animal exploitation, but because it is unnecessary given the long-term forces undermining animal exploitation.

There are interesting echoes here with scholarly debates about the abolition of slavery. Some argue that slavery ended as a result of the campaigns of abolitionists, who successfully managed to change people's moral sensibilities about the rights of blacks. Others argue that slavery collapsed of its own accord, as it proved increasingly economically inefficient. In the case of human slavery, most observers agree that both moral agitation and economic factors were important, and indeed that they were interconnected. Changing moral sensibilities encouraged people to identify potential self-interested reasons for abolishing slavery; changing economic self-interest encouraged people to rethink their previous moral commitments.

This complex and unpredictable interplay between moral conviction and perceptions of self-interest is a familiar refrain in the recent social science literature. It is widely accepted now that ideals and interests are not discrete and watertight categories, since people identify their self-interest in part based on their sense of who they are, and what sorts of relationships they value in the world. To take an extreme example, few people would argue that prohibitions on cannibalism are a 'burden' or 'sacrifice' of their self-interest. People do not think of themselves as having a self-interest in eating human flesh, because they do not think of themselves as the sort of people who would even want to engage in that behaviour. Similarly, we may hope that one day, humans will not view prohibitions on eating animal flesh as a burden or sacrifice, because people will not think of themselves as the sort of people who want to engage in that behaviour. In this way, changing moral sensibilities redefine our sense of self, and hence our sense of self-interest.

Indeed, our sense of who we are, and what we value, is shaped by more than either narrow selfish interests or explicit moral commitments. Our moral imagination can be enlarged by careful thought and reflection, and through compassionate relationship, but it can also be enlarged via scientific and creative impulses—our desire to explore, to learn, to create beauty, connection, and meaning. We need to engage this larger human spirit in the animal justice project.

Today, much of what ART demands will undoubtedly be seen by many people as an enormous sacrifice. The gap between the moral theory we are advancing and people's perceived interests or self-conceptions is vast. But that can change, in unpredictable ways, and perhaps more quickly than one might think. As the environmental and economic costs of our system of animal exploitation and colonization become increasingly apparent, it will become increasingly urgent to develop new conceptual frameworks to help identify alternative visions of human–animal relations.

We hope that this book contributes to that task, both in terms of the long-term vision it offers, and in terms of the short-term strategies it recommends. In terms of long-term vision, our approach offers a more positive picture of the future of human–animal relations than is offered by traditional ART. To date, ART has focused primarily on a set of negative prohibitions—thou shall not kill, use, or keep animals. In the process, ART has embraced a stark and simplistic conception of human–animal relations—domesticated animals should be extinguished, and wild animals should be left alone. In short, there should be no human–animal relations. We have argued that this vision is not only an empirical non-starter—humans and animals cannot be severed into hermetically distinct environments—but also a political liability.

Most humans come to understand and care for animals by having a relationship with them—observing them, hanging out with them, caring for them, loving and being loved by them. The humans who care the most for the fate of animals are typically those involved in relationships with them, as companions and workmates, or as wildlife observers, conservationists, and ecological restorationists. Overcoming the political impasse will require drawing on this energy and these motivations. And yet the underlying message of ART is that humans cannot be trusted to have relationships with animals. We will inevitably exploit and harm them, and therefore we must cut ourselves off. This is not a message likely to galvanize animal lovers to fight for animal justice.[3]

Rather than cutting off relations between humans and animals, our long-term vision seeks to explore and embrace the full possibilities of such relations. This entails recognizing animals not just as individual subjects entitled to respect of their basic rights, but as members of communities—both ours and theirs—woven together in relations of interdependency, mutuality, and responsibility. This vision is far more demanding than the classic ART position that our obligation to animals is to let them be. But it is also a far more positive and creative vision—one that recognizes that human–animal relations can be compassionate, just, joyful, and mutually enriching. Any theory of AR will require humans to give up their ill-gotten gains from animal exploitation/colonization. But a politically effective ART will identify not just the sacrifices that justice demands of us, but also the rewarding new relationships that justice makes possible.

And this, in turn, has implications for more short-term strategy. If our long-term goal is not just to abolish exploitation, but to build new relationships of justice, then even the short-term outlook is not quite as bleak as it first appears. The sheer scale of animal exploitation/colonization is increasing globally, but there are also countless experiments around the world in which humans are trying to find new ways to relate to animals. We have discussed several of these in the course of the book, but just to mention a few of them:

- Designated pigeon lofts (with feeding and fertility control programmes) manage feral pigeon populations at sites from Jaipur to Nottingham, gradually persuading sceptics to abandon their murderous killing sprees. Some cities involve artists in the design of the lofts, turning them into sites of public art and participation, as well as peaceful interspecies coexistence.

- The city of Leeds, UK, is considering a proposal for erecting habitat high-rise dwellings—vertical green towers designed to accommodate and welcome birds, bats, and other wildlife in the heart of the city.

- A wildlife refuge in eastern Ontario rescues animals in distress, from starving owls and orphaned squirrels, to turtles with shells smashed by car impacts. All receive careful medical attention—while limiting exposure to humans—in hopes of full rehabilitation and successful return to the wild.

- A California sanctuary rescues chickens. It cares for their shelter, nutrition, and medical needs, including specially designed pens and runs to protect the chickens from nocturnal predators, and from exposure to avian influenza. The chickens have extensive freedom of movement, and opportunity to form attachments and engage in a range of activities and behaviours. No chickens are killed. They live out their natural lives—often for many years after they stop producing eggs. The sanctuary owners collect and sell some of the eggs.

- More and more people describe their dog and cat companions as full 'members of the family', and demand access for these family members to top-notch medical care, emergency services, and public space on the same basis that human citizens take as their due.

- Conservationists around the world use their growing knowledge of animal migration patterns to redirect human development in ways that protect and re-establish wildlife corridors and viable habitats. Shipping routes are being relocated. Wildlife overpasses are being constructed. Green spaces are being reclaimed and linked.

In these and countless other examples discussed throughout this book, we see humans attempting to establish new, and ethical, relations with animals. These relations go far beyond ideas of humane treatment. They also go far beyond ideas of non-intervention and respect for basic negative rights. Implicitly, at least, they embody a more comprehensive conception of human–animal relations, one which recognizes that we are inevitably involved in complex relationships with animals, and owe to them extensive positive duties.

In our view, these experiments can be seen as the building blocks of a future zoopolis, and our goal has been in part to provide a theoretical framework that can make sense of them. Each, in its own way, is showing that new relationships of justice are possible and sustainable. Humans are distressingly reluctant to give up the benefits from animal exploitation/colonization, and that is unlikely to change in the foreseeable future. But there is also a great deal of unease about these ill-gotten gains, a great deal of creative energy invested in exploring new possibilities, and a great deal of learning to be gleaned from these experiments. And yet much of this is invisible in the existing mainstream philosophy of animal rights, which lacks the theoretical tools to make sense of the moral value of such experiments, either perceiving them as tangential to the primary AR project of dismantling factory farms and other direct forms of animal exploitation, or indeed condemning them out of hand for failing to stop using animals and learning to 'let them be'.

It is asking too much of moral arguments to expect them to overcome by themselves deeply entrenched cultural assumptions and the powerful forces of self-interest, but moral arguments should at least identify the moral resources that do exist, tapped and untapped, within our society, and should work to strengthen them. These moral resources for AR include ordinary folk who bond with their companion animals, dedicated members of wildlife organizations, and ecologists working for habitat conservation and restoration. These individuals don't typically identify themselves as supporters of animal rights and few of them are vegans who consistently denounce practices of animal exploitation in their daily lives. Nevertheless, there are important ways in which they are indeed working for animal rights—rights to sovereign territory, rights to fair terms of coexistence, and rights to citizenship. The AR movement needs to embrace an expanded conception of animal rights which can include all of these natural allies in the fight for animals.

We need to get people excited about the project of justice for animals, tapping into the enormous well of human creative, scientific, and affiliative energies. It will by now be no secret to readers that we are big fans of *Star Trek*, and its ethic for interspecies contact, coexistence, and cooperation. This ethic can be summarized as follows: encounters with new 'life forms' should be governed by caution, curiosity, and respect. Species not yet ready, or willing, to benefit from contact with the Federation should be left unmolested to develop along their own trajectories. 'First contact' is made with species on the cusp of intergalactic travel to assess the desirability of membership in the Federation's political community. And this critical first contact is entrusted to the Federation's most able diplomats, armed with the best science available and sophisticated technological resources to facilitate communication to the extent possible, and guided by an overriding injunction to do no harm. The USS Enterprise encounters many species incapable of producing Shakespeare (or Spock or Data), human language, or human moral reflection, and yet all are approached with the same ethic of respect for their own uniquely adaptive intelligence and consciousness.

It would be hard to imagine a more stark contrast to the reality of interspecies contact here on earth. Just imagine, though, how thrilled we'd be to discover an elephant or whale or parrot-like animal in another galaxy; how we'd spare no resource to learn about this wonderful new creature, to appreciate its uniqueness, and to make friendly contact to any extent possible. Imagine how appalled we'd be at the thought of killing off this species, or enslaving it, or robbing it of the resources needed to live. And yet this is exactly how we treat the unique and wonderful animals who share planet Earth. We seem incapable of perceiving them with the respect and awe that would undoubtedly characterize a fresh encounter, with new eyes, on neutral territory—divorced from the context of our largely tragic history together.

We hope this book offers a fresh set of lenses for considering animals as more than 'just animals', or interchangeable members of endangered species, or passively suffering victims. We offer instead a picture of animals as complex individual actors embedded in webs of social (not just ecological) relationship, and as political animals: citizens, and sovereigns of self-determining communities. This perspective provides the basis for a fresh start—for first contact all over again. Fortunately, most animal communities do not retain detailed intergenerational records of abusive treatment by humans. This means we can turn a new page more easily than in the context of human injustice where memories are often long and bitter, hampering the prospects for forward-looking justice. We face no such impediments in the animal case. It's down to us.

Notes

Introduction

1. From the beginning, animal advocates have been closely involved in advocacy for other vulnerable members of society such as slaves, children, prison inmates, women, and people with disabilities, and it remains true today that support for animal advocacy is positively associated with broader social justice values such as civil rights and gender equality (Garner 2005a: 106, 129–30). Yet, as Crompton notes, the potential for 'common cause' has been neglected (Crompton 2010).
2. See the statistics compiled by the Humane Society of the United States at: http://www.humanesociety.org/assets/pdfs/legislation/ballot_initiatives_chart.pdf. (All websites cited in this book were valid as of 27 April 2011.)
3. Our own country, Canada, lags woefully behind regarding even the most minimal reforms. See Sorenson 2010; International Fund for Animal Welfare 2008.
4. There is enormous variation in population trends for different kinds of animals. Losses have been greatest for freshwater animals, compared with terrestrial and marine animals. And losses have been greater in the tropics, and in developing countries, compared with more temperate zones where much habitat had already been decimated by 1970 and populations were starting from a lower baseline. Some of these animal populations have started to recover under conservation and management strategies. See the World Wide Fund for Nature's (WWF) Living Planet Index at: http://wwf.panda.org/about_our_earth/all_publications/living_planet_report/health_of_our_planet/.
5. Charles Patterson's *Eternal Treblinka: Our Treatment of Animals and the Holocaust* (2002) describes the connections and parallels between animal slaughter and the Holocaust, and profiles the many survivors (and descendants of survivors) who have been key activists in the animal movement. He takes his title from a line in an Isaac Bashevis Singer story, in which a character says: 'for the animals it is an eternal Treblinka'. We are aware that some people will find this comparison objectionable, as they may object to other comparisons we will be making in this book—whether it is comparing animal treatment to genocide, slavery, or colonization; comparing animal minds, emotions, and behaviour to human capacities; or comparing struggles for animal rights to human struggles for citizenship and self-determination. In our view, the test of such comparisons should be whether they illuminate aspects of injustice towards animals. We are not invoking these comparisons for polemical purposes, but only if and when they actually help capture features of the moral landscape which are otherwise difficult to see.

6. For debates and competing predictions about the long-term effects of ameliorist campaigns, see the online transcription of a debate between Gary Francione and Erik Marcus (25 February 2007) at: (http://www.gary-francione.com/francione-marcus-debate.html). See also Garner (2005b), Dunayer (2004), Francione and Garner (2010), and Jones (2008). On the debate between pacifism and direct action as an animal advocacy strategy, see Hall (2006), and a critique of her position by Steven Best and Jason Miller from the direct action community (Best and Miller 2009). See also Hadley (2009a).

7. 'The poll, conducted May 5–7, finds 96% of Americans saying that animals deserve at least some protection from harm and exploitation, while just 3% say animals don't need protection "since they are just animals".' (http://www.gallup.com/poll/8461/public-lukewarm-animal-rights.aspx).

8. It is important to note that 'welfarism' in the sense we are using the term—i.e., as the 'humane use' of animals—is different from 'welfarism' in the more technical sense used in moral and political philosophy. Philosophers often use welfarism to denote a commitment to a particular form of consequentialism—i.e., the view that morality is about maximizing overall welfare. Welfarism in this philosophical sense is opposed to 'deontological' views which say that some actions are wrong even if they would maximize welfare (e.g., if they violate human rights). Welfarism as a position about the humane use of animals is largely unrelated to philosophical welfarism. On the one hand, as we will see, most defenders of welfarism in relation to animals believe in deontological constraints (such as respect for human rights) in how we treat humans. They are welfarists in relation to animals but deontologists in relation to humans. Conversely, some philosophical welfarists reject mainstream views of the humane use of animals. Peter Singer, for example, is a philosophical welfarist who insists that animal interests should count equally with human interests in determining what promotes overall welfare, and that if we do so, few if any human uses of animals will pass the test, no matter how 'humane' they are (Singer 1975, 1993). Philosophical welfarism can therefore lead to a radical critique of mainstream views of the humane use of animals. Welfarism, in the sense we are using the term, is best understood as the mainstream 'common-sense' view of how we should treat animals, and not as the product of a particular philosophical view of moral reasoning in general. Anyone who finds this confusing can simply replace 'welfarism' in our discussion with 'the view that animal welfare matters morally, and so animals should be treated humanely, but they can be used for human benefit'.

   To further complicate matters, within the animal rights literature there is debate about whether Singer should be viewed as a 'new welfarist'. While Singer's theory denies the moral significance of species difference per se, and requires that similar human and animal interests be weighed equally in the utilitarian calculus, he also denies that most animals have an interest in the continuation of life, and argues that most human lives have greater intrinsic value than most animal lives because they are more psychologically complex. Since he is a utilitarian, this reopens the possibility that the lives of less complex beings can be sacrificed for the benefit of more complex beings, if this maximizes overall welfare. Many rights-based critics of Singer describe this as a 'new welfarism'. While we too reject Singer's approach, and defend instead a stronger rights-based approach, we do not consider him a 'welfarist' in the sense we are discussing, given his profound critique of mainstream assumptions about the 'humane use' of animals.

9. According to Gary Varner, 'most environmental philosophers believe that animal rights views are incompatible with sound environmental policy' (Varner 1998: 98).

10. One example of an advocacy campaign that clearly invokes a rights-based rather than welfarist framework is the Great Ape project (GAP)—a recent initiative stating that the great apes have the right not to be imprisoned or experimented on, no matter what the potential human benefits. This project was launched with the publication of a book with that title in 1993 (Cavalieri and Singer 1993), and has since engaged in legal and political advocacy in various countries, including a notable victory in Spain when a Spanish parliamentary committee endorsed the idea that the great apes are entitled to rights to life and liberty. See the GAP International website (www.greatapeproject.com), and the related GRASP (Great Ape Standing and Personhood) website (http://www.personhood.org/). The apparent success of this rights-based rhetoric in the context of great apes may reflect the fact that great apes are both very close to humans in evolutionary terms, yet very far from most of us in geographic and economic terms, such that granting rights to great apes involves little disruption in our everyday lives. Where animals look less like humans, and/or where they are more central to our systems of farming, hunting, pet ownership, or industrial use, rights-based advocacy has proven ineffective, and advocacy groups tend to focus instead on welfarist campaigns.

11. It is sometimes said that Western cultures are unique in taking an instrumentalized view of animals and of nature, whereas Eastern or indigenous cultures are said to have a more respectful view. As Preece (1999) shows, this sort of contrast is oversimplified, and ignores the diversity of views and of moral sources within cultures. We return to this issue of cultural differences in attitudes to animals in Chapter 2.

12. Anti-terrorism laws in the UK and the USA, viewed by the general public as a response to events like 9/11, have been manipulated by animal use industries to target animal rights activists as so-called domestic terrorists. The US Animal Enterprise Terrorism Act (2006), for example, encompasses acts of non-violent civil disobedience (e.g., trespassing at a factory farm to photograph illegal animal abuses, or rescuing animals from a research lab) within the purview of domestic *terrorism* (Hall 2006).

13. This is true not just of strong rights-based views, but also, interestingly, of utilitarian approaches. In principle, utilitarianism should support positive obligations to animals whenever they would increase overall well-being, or diminish overall suffering. In practice, however, utilitarian theorists like Singer haven't developed any account of positive obligations towards animals. Like other AR theorists, Singer's focus is on why we ought to stop killing, confining, and experimenting on domesticated animals, and in relation to wild animals, he says that given the complexities of intervention in nature, we 'do enough if we eliminate our own unnecessary killing and cruelty towards other animals' (Singer 1990: 227). Despite their differing foundational premises, utilitarian and rights-based accounts of

animal rights have, to date, both focused almost exclusively on universal negative rights.

14. See, for example, Sapontzis's claim that the question of 'how these most unfortunate [farm and laboratory] animals are to be treated after they have been released from their current travail is a question for a much better world than ours' (Sapontzis 1987: 83; see also Zamir 2007: 55). Francione implies a similar view when he acknowledges that ART to date 'has very little to say' about positive rights, and that while attributing personhood to non-humans entails the immediate end of 'institutionalized exploitation', it 'does not in and of itself specify the scope of the rights that will be held by these nonhuman persons' (Francione 1999: 77). We believe that the decision to defer these questions 'for a much better world' has led to intellectual and political paralysis.

15. Not all AR theorists advocate the demise of domesticated animals, but none, so far, has offered a compelling theory of positive rights to frame our relationships with them. See Tom Regan's cautious statement that 'In the case of domestic animals the great challenge is to figure out how to live in a mutually respectful symbiotic relationship. It is very difficult to do that' (undated interview with Tom Regan at http://www.think-differently-about-sheep.com/Animal_Rights_A_History_Tom_Regan.htm). Burgess-Jackson (1998) offers an account of our obligations to companion animals, to which we return in Chapter 5.

16. Indeed, some critics suggest that the idea of positive duties towards animals is a *reductio ad absurdum* of the entire ART approach (Sagoff 1984).

17. Experts continue to push back the date at which humans and dogs first became companions, a relationship which pre-dates domestication of other species by several millennia. For many years the accepted estimate was around 15,000 years (compared with the domestication of pigs, cows, and other animals which occurred in the last 8,000 years). More recent research, however, suggests that the partnership between humans and dogs may go back anywhere from 40,000 to over 150,000 years. If true, this would suggest that humans and dogs have literally co-evolved, engaging in a process of mutual domestication. Indeed, Masson claims that 'for at least the last 15,000 years and continuing down until today there have been hardly any human habitations without dogs', even in societies that did not domesticate any other animals (Masson 2010: 51). See also Serpell 1996.

18. For some examples, see: http://www.naiaonline.org/body/articles/archives/animalrightsquote.htm;www.spanieljournal.com/32lbaughan.html; http://purebredcatbreedrescue.org/animal_rights.htm; http://people.ucalgary.ca/~powlesla/personal/hunting/rights/pets.txt.

19. See also Benton's comment that 'Consideration of the diversity of social relations and practices through which both humans and animals may be brought into interest-affecting relations with one another reveals a complex and differentiated moral scene' (Benton 1993: 166). See also Midgley 1983, Donovan and Adams 2007.

20. Critics of ART differ as to whether their call for a more situated, relational, or communal conception of animal ethics is intended to *complement* ART's emphasis

on universal basic rights (Burgess-Jackson 1998; Lekan 2004; Donovan 2007), or to *replace* it (Slicer 1991; Palmer 1995, 2003a; Luke 2007).

21. In more recent work, Palmer suggests that her relational approach is in fact compatible with ART, and can be viewed as an expansion of ART (Palmer 2010). We discuss her revised view in Chapter 6.

22. For a related call to shift the animal question from applied ethics to political theory, see Cline 2005.

23. On the resurgence of citizenship as a core idea in political philosophy, and its role in mediating and transcending the liberal–communitarian debate, see Kymlicka and Norman 1994.

Chapter 2

1. Peter Singer is widely seen as one of the founders of the 'animal rights' field, but in fact he is a utilitarian, and so does not believe in inviolable rights for either humans or animals. His arguments for improved treatment of animals are, therefore, based on empirical claims that most of the harms we inflict on animals do not in fact serve the overall good, rather than on the rights-based claim that it would be wrong to harm animals even when it does serve the greater good. For critiques of Singer's utilitarianism from a rights-based AR perspective, see Regan 1983; Francione 2000; Nussbaum 2006.

2. For a more extended account of this shift from utilitarian to rights-based theories in political philosophy, see Kymlicka 2002: ch. 2.

3. It is important to note that inviolability is not absolute: there are circumstances, in both the human and the animal cases, where inviolable rights can be overridden. The most obvious example of this concerns self-defence, where we recognize the right of individuals to protect themselves from grievous assault by injuring, and even killing, their attacker. Another example is the temporary forcible confinement of an individual with a deadly contagion who poses an immediate threat to others and refuses to undertake voluntary quarantine. In other words, the inviolable rights of individuals can be overridden *in extremis*, when they pose an immediate threat to the basic inviolable rights of others (or, in some cases, when they pose such a threat to themselves). Inviolable rights are 'trumps' against being used for the greater good of others, but are not a licence to harm others. This is familiar enough in the human case, and we return to the permissible overriding of the inviolable rights of animals in section 5 below.

4. See, for example, Cavalieri 2001; Francione 2008; Steiner 2008. Tom Regan's *The Case for Animal Rights* (1983) is widely cited as the first systematic statement of a distinctly rights-based approach to animals (in contrast to Singer's utilitarian approach), and indeed many of his arguments arguably entail support for inviolability. But in that book, Regan himself pulled back from that conclusion, stating that while animals have rights, they are perhaps more violable than human rights. His more recent work is arguably more consistent in its commitment to a strong rights position (e.g., Regan 2003).

5. From now on, we use the terms universal rights, basic rights, and inviolable rights interchangeably to refer to those basic inviolable rights that are owed to all sentient beings.

6. Not all AR theorists accept sentience or selfhood as the basis for inviolable rights. Some authors—such as Regan (in his early work, 1983), DeGrazia (1996), Wise (2000), and others—have argued that inviolable rights require some further threshold of cognitive complexity, such as memory, autonomy, or self-consciousness (and hence limit inviolable rights to certain 'higher' animals). We reject such 'mental complexity threshold' views, for reasons explained below. Indeed, it's worth noting that these authors themselves express ambivalence about tying inviolable rights to cognitive complexity. For example, in his later work, Regan shifts to selfhood as the basis for inviolable rights (Regan 2003). And Wise (2004) acknowledges that mental complexity arguments are problematically tied to human-centric standards of mental life.

7. Note the similarity with Eva Feder Kittay's account of the personhood of humans with severe intellectual disabilities. As against philosophical accounts of personhood that require complex cognitive capacities, she insists that 'we know there is a person before us when we see . . . that there is "someone home" . . . In one who can scarcely move a muscle, a glint in the eye at a strain of familiar music establishes personhood. A slight upturn of the lip in a profoundly and multiply disabled individual when a favorite caregiver comes along, or a look of joy in response to the scent of a perfume—all these establish personhood' (Kittay 2001: 568).

8. Such religious arguments have sometimes been invoked by people charged with animal cruelty—see Sorenson 2010: 116.

9. The most recent addition to the literature is the striking new research supporting the likelihood that fish feel pain—see Braithwaite 2010, which also contains a very helpful discussion of the difference between nociception (the unconscious reflexive reaction triggered when pain receptors send information about an injury to the spinal cord) and the subjective sentient experience of pain in the brain. It used to be thought that fish lacked the latter, but as Braithwaite notes, this is simply because no one had actually researched the question—it was only in 2003 that the first studies were conducted on fish pain! As scientific research replaces uninformed prejudice, the evidence for animal sentience continues to expand.

10. A variation on this objection argues that to qualify as a rights-holder, one must have the capacity for rational choice, since to have a right to X is just to have the right to choose whether or not to X. This is often described as the 'choice theory' or 'will theory' of rights. This was once an influential theory of rights, but it is now widely rejected, since it would not only preclude any idea of animal rights, but also any idea that children, the temporarily incapacitated, or future generations might have rights. It would also render unintelligible the idea that we have a right to vote in jurisdictions where voting is mandatory. Most theorists today, therefore, endorse the alternative 'interest theory' of rights, according to which (in Joseph Raz's influential formulation) to say that X is a rights holder is to say that his or her interests are sufficient reason for imposing duties on others either not to interfere with X in the performance of some action, or to secure him or her in something

(Raz 1984). Whether animals, children, or the incapacitated have inviolable rights is, therefore, a question that can only be answered by examining the interests at stake.

11. As Stephen Horigan notes, there is a long history in Western culture of people 'responding to the discovery of boundary-threatening abilities in non-human animals by contentious re-conceptualization of human-definitive powers (such as language) so as to keep the boundary in place' (Horigan 1988, quoted in Benton 1993: 17).

12. For the most sustained discussion, see Dombrowski 1997.

13. Similarly, we reject the idea that humans and animals can be clearly categorized as being either moral agents or moral patients. Moral agency involves a cluster of capacities which vary across species, amongst individuals within species, and over time within individuals. See Bekoff and Pierce 2009, Hribal 2007, 2010, Reid 2010, and Denison 2010. We return to this question in Chapter 5.

14. *Star Trek: The Next Generation* fans will be reminded of episode 2 from season 2 ('Where Silence Has Lease') in which the Enterprise is ensnared by a species, represented by Nagilum, who are vastly superior to the Federation, at least in technological terms. The Enterprise crew are turned into rats in a maze, and are deeply affronted by this failure to recognize their basic rights and dignity.

15. Telepaths are just science fiction, but they have given even some erstwhile defenders of animal experimentation pause for thought. Michael A. Fox's 1988 book *The Case for Animal Experimentation: An Evolutionary and Ethical Perspective* is often cited as a sophisticated defence of the right of human beings to use animals for their benefit (Fox 1988a). But when Fox realized that his arguments could be used by superior alien species to enslave humans, he repudiated those arguments (Fox 1988b), and now defends a robust AR position (Fox 1999).

16. *Superintendent of Belchertown v Saikewicz* 370 Eastern Reporter 2d Series, 417–35 (Mass. Supreme Court 1977). For discussions of the relevance of this and similar cases for the rights of animals, see Dunayer 2004: 107; Hall and Waters 2000.

17. Sometimes, the moral hierarchy doesn't just have two tiers, but looks more like the great chain of being. Consider this recent statement by utilitarian philosopher Wayne Sumner: 'The hierarchy of sentience (capacity to feel pain) and intelligence determines a species' moral weight. Primates outrank other mammals; vertebrates outrank invertebrates. Seals rank with dogs, wolves, sea otters and bears—and ahead of cows' (quoted in Valpy 2010: A6).

18. As Angus Taylor points out, advocates of human exceptionalism, such as Somerville, 'cannot countenance just any ethical view that protects humans, for it is not enough to include all humans within the moral community—one must simultaneously exclude all non-humans. And this is crucial: *human exceptionalism is at least as much about whom we are determined to exclude from the moral community as about whom we wish to include within it.*' (Taylor 2010: 228, emphasis in original). This sort of human exceptionalism is not just philosophically suspect, it is also empirically pernicious. The evidence shows that the more people sharply distinguish between humans and animals, the more likely they are to dehumanize human outgroups, such as immigrants. Belief in human superiority over animals is empirically

correlated with, and causally connected to, belief in the superiority of some human groups over others. When participants in psychological studies are given arguments about human superiority over animals, the outcome is greater prejudice against human outgroups. By contrast, those who recognize that animals possess valued traits and emotions are also more likely to accord equality to human outgroups. Reducing the status divide between humans and animals helps to reduce prejudice and to strengthen belief in equality amongst human groups (Costello and Hodson 2010).

19. According to Silvers and Francis, 'Gaining an inclusive conception of personhood thus is posterior, not prior, to building out an adequately inclusive conception of justice. In other words, learning how to think more inclusively about personhood is an incremental benefit of building toward justice' (Silvers and Francis 2009: 495–6). See also Kittay 2005a, Vorhaus 2005, and Sanders 1993.

20. The idea that our capacity for moral agency is the foundation of human beings' inviolability (and animals' violability) is particularly perverse. As Stephen Clark notes, this argument says that the characteristic to be valued is our capacity to recognize other points of view than our own, yet the conclusion is that we don't need to consider the interests of others—in other words, 'we are absolutely better than animals because we are able to give their interests some consideration; so we won't' (Clark 1984: 107–8; see discussion in Benton 1993: 6; Cavalieri 2009b).

21. Indeed, these often seem like attempts to find a secular basis for older religious ideas about the special place of human beings within God's providential plan. According to the Bible, only humans possess an immortal soul, only humans were made in God's image, and God gave humans dominion over animals. The idea that only humans are entitled to inviolable rights may make sense for anyone who believes in this biblical creation story. But if we seek a secular account of the moral basis of rights, one consistent with evolution, we should not expect or assume that only human beings require the protection of inviolable rights.

22. Some readers may think that in equating selfhood and personhood we are simply losing a word, and that there are good reasons to reserve the term 'person' for that subset of 'selves' who have complex cognitive capacities. We disagree—as we have seen, there is no sharp line that would allow us to stably divide the world into persons and selves—but this is not essential to our argument. Anyone who objects to our references to animal 'personhood' can simply replace the word with 'selfhood', without any change in meaning or argumentation. Even if there are contexts where it is useful to distinguish personhood from selfhood, our claim is simply that this distinction cannot play a role in determining who is a bearer of inviolable rights. See Garner 2005b who says that while inviolable rights should be based on selfhood, we may nonetheless want an account of personhood for other conceptual purposes.

23. Martin Bell has a helpful discussion of these issues on the Vegan Outreach website: http://www.veganoutreach.org/insectcog.html. See also Dunayer 2004: 103–4, 127–32.

24. By scientific understanding we do not refer primarily to controlled lab experiments on animals, most of which are unethical. We refer to the understanding of animals learned through careful observation and ethical interaction. Many researchers

believe that understanding animals' minds is best achieved through ethical inter-action which assumes the existence of mindedness, and indeed helps bring it into existence. Sociological 'interactionist' theory begins from the premise that mind-edness and selfhood are established in relationship with other selves. Irvine (2004), Myers (2003), Sanders (1993), and Sanders and Arluke (1993) have explored animal minds on this interactionist model.

25. We are reminded here of another episode of *Star Trek: The Next Generation (STNG)* which nicely illustrates aspects of this dilemma. In season 1, episode 18, the crew encounters a 'chrystalline entity' on a distant planet. The species chasm is so wide that merely recognizing that there is 'someone home' is a fraught challenge, and coexistence is not possible. The *STNG* crew quarantines the entity's planet, to await a possible future when interaction might be possible.

26. Justice is about more than protecting the vulnerable, and we discuss other aspects of justice in later chapters (e.g., reciprocity), but protecting the vulnerable is one of the core goals of justice (see Goodin 1985), and is particularly central to justifica-tions for basic rights (see Shue 1980).

27. For similar moves, see Baxter 2005 and Schlossberg 2007.

28. There are a few extreme ecologists who seem to bite the ecofascist bullet. Finnish ecologist Pentti Linkola advocates authoritarian government to impose green liv-ing, and opposes the concept of human rights (e.g., he advocates eugenics and other coercive methods to reduce human population). For a brief discussion of his ideas see: http://plausiblefutures.wordpress.com/2007/04/10/extinguish-humans-save-the-world/.

29. As we have stated, recognizing the inviolability of selves (human and animal) is compatible with recognizing direct (non-instrumental) duties to non-sentient nature. We will not be exploring the nature of our direct duties to non-sentient nature in this book. However, it is important to note that the theory we elaborate provides extensive indirect protections to natural ecosystems via direct duties to animals. As we argue in Chapters 6 and 7, recognizing the sovereign and denizen rights of wild and liminal animals places an immediate check on expan-sion of human settlement and habitat degradation, while providing a compelling basis for re-wilding large territories currently devoted to animal agriculture, and for re-establishing key animal corridors and migration routes.

30. See also Sanders 1993; Sanders and Arluke 1993; and Horowitz 2009 regarding other efforts by animal researchers to learn the language of their research subjects, and how establishing interspecies communication (rather than detached observa-tion) is the basis for learning.

31. For a critique of this tendency to ignore the 'difference between animate and inanimate nature', see Wolch 1998, who notes that 'animals as well as people socially construct their worlds and influence each other's worlds . . . Animals have their own realities, their own worldviews; in short, they are subjects, not objects.' Ecological theory ignores this fact, and instead has 'embedded animals within holistic and/or anthropocentric conceptions of the environment and therefore avoided the question of animal subjectivity. Thus, in most forms of progressive environmentalism, animals have been objectified and/or backgrounded' (Wolch

1998: 121). See also Palmer's comment that within environmental ethics, 'animals become swallowed up into "environment" or the "nonhuman world". But the place of animals in urban environmental ethics is not adequately considered by subsuming them into discussion of the environment in general' (Palmer 2003a: 65).

32. Some recent authors have disputed the common presumption that we can kill others in self-defence. According to these revisionist theorists, even if someone is posing an imminent threat to our lives, it is only permissible to kill them if they are *culpable* for threatening us. If the threat is non-culpable, we have a duty to accept martyrdom at their hands. For versions of this argument, see McMahan 1994, 2009; Otsuka 1994. For defences of our common-sense intuition that we do not have a duty of martyrdom in the face of innocent threats, see Frowe 2008; Kaufman 2010.

33. In these lifeboat cases, some favour deciding by soliciting voluntary sacrifice, or by lottery, others by various criteria such as age (e.g., saving those who have the most years to live), well-being (e.g., saving those with the highest quality of life), dependency (e.g., saving those who have family members depending on them), social contribution (e.g., saving those who are most likely to contribute to the common good), or desert (e.g., saving those who have led a meritorious life). We take no view on this matter, except to emphasize that we must not take these criteria as evidence of unequal moral status, or of inequality in basic rights. You might think that people on a lifeboat who are older or who have a terminal illness should give up their lives for younger people, but it would be morally indefensible for society to experiment on older people to gain medical knowledge that would benefit younger people, or to enslave older people for the benefit of younger people. Outside the lifeboat, in the circumstances of justice, we all have the same basic inviolable rights. See also Sapontzis 1987: 80–1 on the fallacy of generalizing from emergency lifeboat cases. Of course, the factors that are invoked in lifeboat cases may be relevant for certain issues of distributive justice—for example, access to scarce medical care. We address such questions of distributive justice in Part II, since they can only be resolved within the broader context of a theory of a mixed animal–human political community, which is precisely what ART (and its critics) currently lacks.

34. All the available evidence suggests that humans are omnivores who can thrive on a vegan diet. If this were not true—if humans biologically needed meat to get adequate nutrition—this would affect the circumstances of justice (see Fox 1999). As we will see in Chapter 5, the issue of dietary need also arises in relation to our companion animals. Whereas dogs are omnivores who do not need meat to survive or thrive, cats are true carnivores, and this raises difficult questions about the diet we feed them.

35. A related obligation, discussed in Chapters 6 and 7, is to avoid the inadvertent harms to animals that arise from our everyday activities—for example, developing new crop harvesting techniques that minimize harm to animals, or altering road and building design.

36. See for example An-Na'im 1990 and Bielefeldt 2000 for this model of how Islamic societies can embrace human rights; and Taylor 1999 for Buddhist societies.

37. Some cultures and societies may think of themselves as untainted by impulses towards human domination of animals and nature, but, as Fraser notes, 'there were no benign human societies that took only as much as needed' (Fraser 2009: 117).

38. And, as Erika Ritter points out, vestiges of the old strategies also live on in the images of happy farm animals and pigs in chef's hats, all willingly offering themselves up for human consumption (Ritter 2009). See also Luke 2007.

39. See the discussion in Sorenson 2010: 25–7.

40. Again, this is true in both the human and animal cases. For the debate on enforcing human rights standards within indigenous societies, see Kymlicka 2001a: ch. 6.

41. According to Elder, Wolch and Emel, dominant groups in the USA interpret the way minorities treat animals 'through their own lens', and thereby 'simultaneously construct immigrant others as uncivilized, irrational or beastly, and their own actions as civilized, rational and humane' (1998: 82).

Chapter 3

1. Some cosmopolitans acknowledge this fact, and so seek to make room within their theories for national solidarities and attachments within bounded and self-governing political communities. This is often called the idea of 'rooted cosmopolitanism' (Appiah 2006). In this view, duties of justice extend beyond our national borders, but part of what it means to treat others justly is to recognize the legitimacy of their desire for national autonomy, and hence does not preclude the existence of autonomous bounded communities that regulate their membership (Kymlicka 2001b; Tan 2004). The view we develop in this book is compatible with this sort of rooted cosmopolitanism—indeed, extending citizenship theory to animals can be seen as the next step in developing the project of reconciling global duties of justice with acknowledgement of legitimate rooted attachments.

2. One of the very few to even mention the possibility is Ted Benton, who immediately dismisses it on the grounds that citizenship is only relevant where issues of participation and social stigmatization are at stake, and hence 'animals cannot be citizens' (Benton 1993: 191). As we go on to discuss, citizenship is relevant for more than participation and stigmatization, but we argue that even on these criteria, animals can indeed be citizens.

3. 'The gospel of liberalism, at least in its democratic variants included the message that the state, including its territorial dimension, is not the property of a dynasty, an aristocracy, or any other political elite, but rather "belongs" to the people' (Buchanan 2003: 234).

4. For Rawls and Habermas, public deliberation is not about the mere expression of preferences, or the making of threats and bargains, but rather about the giving of reasons that can be accepted by others.

5. Such as 'drawing or pointing at pictures, making sounds, jumping up and down, laughing or hugging' (Francis and Silvers 2007: 325).

6. As Arneil says, we need to replace the dichotomy of autonomy/independence/ justice versus disability/dependence/charity 'with a gradient scale in which we are all in various ways and to different degrees both dependent on others and independent, depending on the particular stage we are at in the life cycle as well as the degree to which the world is structured to respond to some variations better than others' (Arneil 2009: 234).

7. Francis and Silvers themselves acknowledge the possibility that their model developed to address disability could be extended to animals. They note that their account 'may allow individualized, subjective conceptions of their good to be constructed for nonhuman animals. There is nothing disturbing or threatening about such a result. Some nonhuman animals express preferences and assume roles in social scripts, from which we do not hesitate to extrapolate ideas of the good that we attribute to them' (Francis and Silvers 2007: 325). However, they pull back from explicitly endorsing this extension, suggesting that the ability to construct such scripts for animals may not be a sufficient condition for them to be owed justice (326). We argue below that the circumstances created by domestication not only make possible relations of dependent agency and co-citizenship with domestic animals, but also obligate us to do so.

8. For example, it is entirely possible that some species of animals in the wild—such as great apes or dolphins—have cognitive capacities that many domesticated animals lack. But this does not make them citizens of our political community. Citizenship is not accorded based on comparative intelligence, but on membership in morally significant relationships. There will be many highly intelligent individuals— humans and animals—who are not citizens of our community; and many individuals with cognitive limitations—humans and animals—who are citizens of our community.

9. http://www.ciesin.columbia.edu/wild_areas/.

10. For critiques of the invisibility of animal agency in classic ART, see Jones 2008; Denison 2010; Reid 2010.

11. For a discussion of the efforts undertaken for the tigers in Nepal, see Fraser 2009: ch. 10. As Fraser's book shows, 're-wilding' is rarely, if ever, simply about 'leaving them alone'. It often involves captive breeding programmes, reintroducing species of animals and plants, changing long-standing land use patterns, careful monitoring of population levels, and so on. See Horta 2010 on the ethics of (re)introducing predators.

12. The *locus classicus* for this discussion of the place of animals within modernist conceptions of space is the work of Bruno Latour (1993, 2004). For various applications see the essays in Philo and Wilbert 2000. For a fascinating discussion of the case of pigeons, see Jerolmack 2008, who shows that our conceptions of space have evolved in such a way that there is literally nowhere where pigeons are seen as belonging legitimately.

Chapter 4

1. Britannica Online Encyclopedia, 'Domestication' (www.britannica.com/EBchecked/ topic/168592/domestication). Note that the category of domesticated animals does

not include tamed wild animals, such as dolphins at a marine park, or captured birds and reptiles kept as pets. Individual wild animals can be tamed and trained by humans, but this is different from a programme of selective breeding of a species to alter its nature to serve human purposes and render it dependent on humans to meet basic needs. We deal with captive wild animals in Chapter 6. As for feral domesticated animals—dogs, cats, horses, etc. who have escaped direct human control and returned to something closer to a wild state—we deal with this group of animals in Chapter 7 with other human-adaptive liminal species.

2. As Palmer notes, there is a particularly insidious dynamic here, in which factory farming subverts the very sociability that domestication is based on: 'Domestication is predicated on relationship. Animals became domesticated because they were social communicators and could enter into relationships with one another and with human beings. But on a factory farm, neither relationship is possible' (Palmer 1995: 21).

3. Consider horses, for example. Until the invention of the internal combustion engine, horses were a primary source of transport and labour power. (Cars have generated their own problems, of course, but we shouldn't forget their role in liberating some horses, donkeys, and oxen.) When Anna Sewell wrote *Black Beauty* in 1877 (a period considered 'hell for horses'), horses were used not only in traditional farm, military, and human transportation work, but also in many newer industrial contexts such as mines, canal operations, etc. The numbers are staggering. For example, there were more than 10,000 hansom cabs operating in London in this period (each pulled by two horses). The abuse of these animals, many of whom died in the harness from sheer exhaustion and maltreatment, was of particular concern to Sewell. And that's just London cabs! It is estimated that 3,000 horses died at the Battle of Gettysburg, and as many as 8 million in World War I. As late as World War II, the famously modern, technological German Wermacht was still dependent on horses for more than 75% of its transportation and other needs (making the requisitioning of horses from occupied territories a major preoccupation of German war planners). See Hribal 2007 for a fascinating perspective on the history of working horses.

4. For examples of the reciprocity/implied consent argument see Callicott 1992; Scruton 2004.

5. Tuan 1984. Tuan's book is now dated, and we don't know the current statistics concerning abandonment of pets, but a clear pattern persists in which cute puppies and kittens are purchased/adopted, but then they become large, unruly, and/or needy animals; the kids move on to new novelties; changes in routine or travel patterns make the animal's presence inconvenient; or ill-health makes the animal an economic burden – and the animal goes back to the shelter.

6. For an overview of statistics concerning killing of companion animals, see Palmer 2006.

7. The authors include themselves amongst the ignorant with good intentions. In the early years of our life with Codie, our beloved dog, we simply did not understand the full extent of his social and physical needs. He frequently spent several hours at home, alone, awaiting our return from work. And his multiple daily walks did not

really add up to the hours of physical exertion that he would truly have enjoyed. Our understanding of his needs improved over time, but we wish we could undo the neglect of his early years.

8. It is estimated that 40,000–90,000 companion animals died in Hurricane Katrina and its aftermath. (As for other domesticated animals, it is estimated that millions died in the disaster.) Approximately 15,000 pets were saved by rescue organizations, most of whom were adopted by new families. There are many tragic accounts of humans being forced by officials to leave behind their animal companions during the evacuations. And many people who ignored early warnings to leave New Orleans did so because they did not want to abandon their animal companions, but had no option for taking them with them. Indeed, the Katrina events provide a clear illustration of the inadequacy of thinking of domesticated animals as the sole responsibility of their individual guardians. Communities have a collective responsibility for domesticated animals, and require communal institutions and mechanisms for protecting them (Irvine 2009; Porter 2008).

9. Many AR theorists and activists share Francione's view. Lee Hall says that 'declining to create more dependent animals is the best decision an animal-rights activist can apply' (Hall 2006: 108). John Bryant considers pets to be slaves and prisoners who 'should be completely phased out of existence' (Bryant 1990: 9–10, cited in Garner 2005b: 138).

10. Callicott later repudiated this view, acknowledging that it 'is to condemn the very being of these creatures' (Callicott 1992). But his revised view retracts his condemnation of existing domesticated animals by retracting his earlier condemnation of historic processes of domestication. He now suggests that these historic processes were not so bad, and indeed can be seen as reflecting a kind of fair bargain in which domesticated animals give up their lives for food and shelter. In this respect, Callicott's revised view shares a common assumption with Francione's view. Both theorists link the rightness/wrongness of the original process of domestication with the intrinsic status of currently existing domesticated animals. For Francione, the original intent/process was immoral, so any relationship we have with existing creatures is unavoidably tainted. Under Callicott's revised view, the original intent/process was not immoral (because it involved 'a kind of evolved and unspoken contract between man and beast'), and therefore the ongoing existence of domesticated animals is not inherently problematic. What neither view seems to allow is the possibility that the historic wrongness of domestication does not predetermine the current and future status of domesticated animals, or the sorts of ethical relationships we can develop with them.

11. Pet extinction quotes are carefully collected and circulated by organizations from spaniel breeders to purebreed cat rescue organizations to hunting enthusiasts. The quotes are marshalled (often in misleading or selective ways) to reveal the alleged 'hidden agenda' of animal rights organizations such as PETA and the Humane Society of the United States, and prominent activists such as Francione, Regan, and Singer. We cite examples in Chapter 1, note 18.

12. Francione calls his position the 'abolitionist approach' in part to draw connections with human slavery, and to highlight that abolition rather than reform is the

appropriate response to slavery. But what distinguishes his position is not just the abolition of domesticated animal slavery, but the further claim that we should seek the extinction of domesticated animals—a position that was obviously not part of the abolitionist approach to human slavery. This is why we call his approach an 'abolitionist/extinctionist' approach.

13. We do not assume that animals have a deliberate or conscious desire to perpetuate their species as such. As far as we know, most animals don't reflect on the future of their species. However, given liberty to decide for themselves, they would continue to procreate, based not on reflection about the value of species continuation, but on a more direct response to sexual instinct and the pursuit of pleasure and connection. In light of the fact that left to their own devices they would continue to reproduce, and undergo the experience of parenting, we need a strong argument to interfere in this process on paternalistic grounds. See Boonin 2003; Palmer 2006.

14. Note that our position here does not depend on any general claim about the value of existence versus non-existence. A world with 10 billion humans is not in and of itself better than a world with only 6 billion humans, and the same is true about numbers of domesticated animals. For debates about this issue, which is a hornets' nest in philosophy, see Benatar 2006; Overall (forthcoming). Our position does not rest on the intrinsic goodness or value of bringing more beings into the world, but rather on the interests of individual animals in reproducing (or at least in having this capacity restricted only on justifiable paternalistic grounds) and in our duty to remedy the historic wrongs of domestication.

15. It is surely not her intention, but Hall's claim that we shouldn't allow domesticated animals to reproduce 'because it's disrespectful to afford them an autonomy that's incomplete' (2006: 108) sounds very much like older arguments for eugenics and the forced sterilization of people with disabilities.

16. See Dunayer 2004: 119 for the claim that domesticated animals are 'inevitably subservient'.

17. This is a familiar refrain in the disability literature: people with disabilities suffer not just from their dependence (and hence the potential that their needs will not be met), but also from the exaggeration of their dependence (and hence the likelihood that efforts will not be made to enable the sorts of agency and choice they are capable of). As Kittay puts it, 'Both bearing the burden of unmet dependency needs, and being falsely seen to be dependent in ways that one is not, serve to exclude disabled people from full social participation and the possibilities of flourishing' (Kittay, Jennings, and Wasunna 2005: 458).

18. This was clearly demonstrated by the forty-year silver fox experiment undertaken by Dr Belyaev and colleagues in Russia (Trut 1999). At a fur farm they selected foxes over several generations for tameability, i.e., they allowed only those animals displaying higher degrees of tameness within each generation to breed. Otherwise, they did not engage in any efforts to interact with, tame, train, or selectively breed the foxes. Over the course of the experiment, the foxes became completely tame in their relations with humans. Moreover, a cluster of other juvenile traits came along for the ride—floppy ears, changes to head shape and physical markings, and a variety of other domesticated traits.

19. Interview with Richard Wrangham on Edge, posted 11 August 2009, at: http://www.edge.org/3rd_culture/wrangham/wrangham_index.html.
20. There is plenty of debate about the relationship between absolute brain size, relative brain size, and intelligence. Whatever the truth of the matter, domesticated animals and self-domesticated humans are in the same boat.
21. Dunayer briefly notes the inevitability of animals in human society, but doesn't explore its implications for domesticated animals (Dunayer 2004: 41).
22. Symbiotic and cooperative relationships are found throughout nature, not just between humans and animals. Animals (and plants) continually adapt to the opportunities afforded by the environment, including the activities of other species. Some of these instances of symbiosis involve quite intriguing forms of cooperation. A fascinating example concerns the scavenging relationship between ravens and coyotes (and wolves), observed in Wyoming and Montana. In winter, coyotes benefit from ravens' eyesight. Both species feed on deer who have died of exhaustion, starvation, or exposure in winter's deep snows. Wading through deep drifts is also costly for coyotes, so they watch the ravens who can spot a deer corpse from the sky and alert coyotes to its location. In the summer, ravens benefit from coyotes' sense of smell. Ravens cannot spot carcasses hidden by undergrowth, so they watch the coyotes instead and follow them to the spoils. On first reflection, it seems like these two species should be in straightforward competition for scavenged remains. In fact, they tolerate, and even seek out, one another in a mutually beneficial arrangement (Ryden 1979; Heinrich 1999).
23. See Budiansky 1999 and Callicott 1992.
24. One is reminded of mythical stories in which human communities appease monsters by offering the occasional human sacrifice. The alleged benefit to humans in this relationship is that the monster stops at one rather than devouring the whole community. But we wouldn't call this an ethical relationship. The fact that humans tolerate it simply tells us that they have limited options, not that the relationship is a just one.
25. And once full domestication is involved—i.e., forced confinement and breeding—even the appearance of consent or assent disappears. Forced breeding often seeks not only to produce beings that are more useful to exploit (often in ways that are directly harmful to animals' health, longevity, etc.), but also beings that are more compliant in their own exploitation (through erosion of their inclination to avoid humans). In such contexts, self-serving appeals to animal compliance in their exploitation are wholly illegitimate. But in rejecting the injustices of forced domestication, we must not lose sight of the realities of unforced symbiotic relations.
26. See Tom Regan's remarks at http://www.think-differently-about-sheep.com/Animal_Rights_A_History_Tom_Regan.htm: 'In the case of domestic animals the great challenge is to figure out how to live in a mutually respectful symbiotic relationship. It is very difficult to do that.'
27. We discuss the basic needs criterion in the next section on Nussbaum's capability approach.
28. See Rolston 1988: 79 for a similar view that 'domestic animals ought to be treated . . . with no more suffering than would have been their lot in the wild'.

29. In the case of animal companions, it is unclear why the relevant comparison life is in the wild. With the exception of some feral populations, most domesticated animal species have not lived in the wild for centuries, and are not adapted to do so. DeGrazia's motivation here—that we shouldn't make an animal worse off by taking it into our family—seems reasonable. However, why limit the comparable life requirement to a wild existence? Why isn't the relevant comparison the opportunities that the animal would have had if instead of being adopted by me, it was adopted by the Paradise family down the road (with the large farm, and lots of dogs and dog-loving people home all day)? When I adopt a dog I can't know what opportunities I have foreclosed for her. Would she have continued to languish in the shelter, or been adopted by the Paradise family? We need to ask why a comparable life requirement should be assumed to set a very modest threshold (life in the wild for an animal unsuited to it), rather than a more robust one. See Burgess-Jackson 1998 for a more demanding conception of an alternative life requirement and individual ethical duties stemming from closing off options for others. See also Hanrahan 2007.

30. As Zamir acknowledges, this argument is often given by those who defend killing farm animals after they've lived a couple of years of qualitatively tolerable life. Zamir rejects this on the grounds that it projects a distorting goal onto the life of the animal. He calls this a teleological constraint against 'bringing a being into a life form that is objectionable, even if the life offered is qualitatively reasonable—for example, bringing some people with a rare blood type into the world with the sole purpose of using them as donors later (while providing them with a qualitatively reasonable existence)' (Zamir 2007: 122). In his view, no-kill use of farm animals respects this teleological constraint, whereas killing them fails it. It is not clear to us that Zamir's appeal to this teleological constraint can in fact distinguish killing from no-kill uses of animals, but even if so, it still fails to capture the moral demands of membership. For other discussions of the limitations of arguments that appeal to non-existence as a moral baseline, see Kavka 1982; McMahan 2008.

31. See Palmer 2003a for a discussion of how relational duties can stem from both individual and collective actions.

32. Indeed, at the most abstract level, our own citizenship model could be described in broadly capability terms. Our objection is with the underlying theory of community within which Nussbaum embeds her capability approach.

33. Nussbaum's focus on species norm rather than community membership generates problems for both domesticated and wild animals. On the one hand, it misses the distinctive nature of the well-being of domesticated animals: defining flourishing in terms of a species norm may sometimes be appropriate for wild animals, but the flourishing of domesticated animals is in fact defined by interspecies community. On the other hand, her account also misses the distinctive nature of our relations with wild animals, since she implies that we have the same right or duty to intervene in the lives of wild animals as in the lives of domesticated animals. We do indeed have a duty to provide medical care (including prostheses) to our companion dogs, and to protect them from predators, but this is not because of their 'species norm'. If it were due to their species norm, then we would presumably

have the same obligations to provide prostheses for wild dogs (say, dingos in Australia) who are normally mobile. But as we discuss in Chapter 6, we do not have such a duty to all wild animals. This again reflects the moral significance of community membership, which creates both distinctive sources of well-being and distinctive sources of obligation that are not reducible to 'species norms'. We return to Nussbaum's interventionist approach to wild animals in Chapter 6.

34. It's not that Nussbaum's conception of flourishing rules out the possibility of interspecies relationship—indeed, she mentions (in passing) that a dog's species norm includes the 'traditional relationship between the dog and the human' (Nussbaum 2006: 366). But she doesn't explore this possibility of interspecies relationships and interspecies community in any depth, and typically instead talks about each species living 'in their own community'. Moreover, even in the case of dogs, it is a mistake to think of human–dog relations solely in terms of achieving a 'species norm'. The way in which we promote the capabilities and flourishing of companion dogs is not solely, or primarily, determined by their genetic inheritance, which after all they share with wild and feral dogs. Rather, it is determined by the fact that they (unlike their genetically similar wild/feral cousins) are living in mixed communities. It is the fact of community membership, not just DNA, that determines the relevant capabilities to be fostered.

35. Indeed, as we noted in Chapter 2, the evidence shows that socializing people to make this sharp separation leads to prejudice, not just against animals, but also against human outgroups, such as immigrants (Costello and Hodson 2010).

Chapter 5

1. This seems to be the implicit assumption in Rollin 2006, who endorses a guardian-ship/wardship model for fulfilling our relational duties to domesticated animals. Burgess-Jackson (1998: 178 n61) suggests in passing that companion animals could be seen as 'urban and suburban denizens', without explaining what sorts of rela-tional rights and responsibilities are involved in 'denizenship'. In Chapter 7, we argue that the idea of denizenship is appropriate for the *non-domesticated* liminal animals (e.g., squirrels, crows) who live amongst us in urban and suburban contexts without being full members of our community. But justice for domesticated ani-mals, we argue in this chapter, requires citizenship rather than denizenship or wardship.

2. Insofar as the threshold views we discussed in Chapter 4 assume (a) that humans 'call all the shots' (Zamir 2007: 100); and (b) that the default or benchmark position is one of non-existence or non-relationship, they can at best defend some sort of wardship model. By contrast, a co-citizenship model is responsive to animals' own expressed subjective good, and takes the fact of membership in a shared and mixed community as a given.

3. Rawls identifies two moral powers: the first is the capacity to form, revise, and pursue a conception of the good; the second is the capacity for a sense of justice. Rawls does not explicitly mention the third capacity on our list, but it is implicit in his account of the second, and in his assumption that citizens are capable of 'public reason'.

Other contemporary theories, such as that of Habermas, focus on the capacity to participate in co-authoring the laws, while implicitly presupposing the first two.

4. And let's not forget that women, racial minorities, and lower-caste groups have historically been denied citizenship status, and condemned to the status of permanent wardship, on the alleged grounds that they were too feeble-minded to be citizens, lacking the right to express their subjective good, or to participate in shaping collective decisions. It was the so-called white man's burden to exercise guardianship over vast populations thought to lack the intellectual capacities of citizenship.

5. For helpful histories/overviews of these citizenship struggles, see Prince 2009 (on Canada); Beckett 2006 (on the UK); Carey 2009 (on the USA).

6. See also Benton (1993: 51), who emphasizes the extent to which 'either similarities to humans with respect to sociality, behavioural adaptability, and forms of communication, or interdependence with human populations with respect to ecological conditions of existence (or both) are preconditions of domestication—not simply consequences of it'.

7. In the bioethics literature, it is common to distinguish a rationalist conception of 'informed consent' to medical treatment from less cognitively demanding conceptions of 'assent', and to recognize that even if the former is not possible for some individuals, the latter is often relevant.

8. As Francis and Silvers acknowledge, any theory of dependent agency must address a number of challenges such as difficulties with planning, attachment, and judgements of trust that characterize people with SID. Some think that these difficulties undermine the possibility of developing truly individualized scripts about the good for people with SID, and hence 'that the good for people with lifelong intellectual disabilities is objective, namely, having basic levels of key capabilities enabled for them' (Francis and Silvers 2007: 318–19, attributing this view to Nussbaum). Their article is in large part an extended effort to respond to this objection.

9. See also Kittay 2005a on the way moral and political philosophy (and society generally) neglects the moral capacities and impact of people with SID. Clifford also describes ways in which the sheer bodily presence of a person with SID is a form of participation, acting as an unruly, discordant, or discombobulating presence which can 'confront false assumptions and raise new avenues of dialogue' (Clifford 2009).

10. The importance of viewing people with disabilities as individuals with their own distinctive subjective good and own distinctive capacities, rather than treating people on the basis of categories of disability, is a recurring theme in the disability literature, and is often seen as the distinctive advantage of a citizenship approach— it forces us to see the person, not just the disability. See, for example, Carey 2009: 140; Satz 2006; Prince 2009: 208; Vorhaus 2006.

11. Carey concludes her book on the rights of the intellectually disabled with the same message: we all need help in exercising our rights. 'Citizens are embedded in relational contexts that provide various levels of support for claiming and exercising rights. As such, we are all disadvantaged in our participation and exercise of rights when our relationships and the social institutions with which we interact

establish barriers, and we are all advantaged when they support our participation' (Carey 2009: 221). People with SID are a clear case of this, but it is a lesson worth bearing in mind for all citizens.

12. In studies of humans and their dog companions, Sanders describes the process of humans 'doing mind'—acting 'as agents who identify and give voice to the subjective experience of their animals' (Sanders 1993: 211). This process of construction accrues through the course of daily ritual and interaction. 'Caretakers and their dogs ongoingly share activities, moods, and routines. Coordination of these natural rituals requires human and animal participants to assume the perspective of the other and, certainly in the eyes of the owners and ostensibly on the part of the dogs, results in a mutual recognition of being "together"' (Sanders 1993: 211).

13. For the moment we are not addressing the question of when the use of dogs for service is a form of exploitation. We will return to this question later.

14. Please note that names and locations have been changed to protect innocent animal advocates!

15. See Bekoff and Pierce 2009; Bekoff 2007; de Waal 2009; Denison 2010; and Reid 2010. Sapontzis 1987 was an early voice for the view that moral agency is a continuum within and across species.

16. There are many cases of wild dolphins acting to save imperilled humans, pushing them to safety (White 2007). Indeed, their reputation for helping humans is such that novelist Martin Cruz Smith's metaphor for the 'morally upside-down' nature of contemporary Russian society is a pair of dolphins who push a Russian out of safety into danger (Smith 2010: 8).

17. This is just one aspect of how play functions, for both humans and animals. There are many others, such as the opportunity to learn useful physical survival skills, to maintain physical fitness, to promote social bonding—not to mention for the sheer fun of it.

18. Mark Twain famously said that 'Man is the only animal that blushes. Or needs to.' It appears that canids may share the capacity and the need.

19. See Masson 2010 for an exploration of the special relationship between dogs and humans, and growing evidence of how we may have co-evolved for mutual understanding and cooperation. See also Horowitz 2009.

20. Bernard Rollin says that we don't always know what is in the best interests of companion animals (e.g., what kinds of training are enjoyable rather than oppressive), and that 'Until we can answer these and similar questions, we are blocked from moving towards a guardianship model for companion animals' (Rollin 2006: 310). We would put it the other way around: until we adopt a citizenship model for companion animals, we will lack the preconditions and dispositions that would enable us to answer these questions about what is in their best interests.

21. Some readers may be nervous about the way we have mingled scientific studies with more anecdotal accounts of animal behaviour in the foregoing discussion. We are all familiar with the tendency of some animal lovers to interpret their companion animals' behaviour in outrageously anthropomorphic ways, and we need to be wary of such projections. However, sociological studies confirm that human companions are often optimally placed to engage in the kind of long-term observation

that leads to genuine insight into other minds, and that our interpretations of the mental states of our animal companions are subject to the same ongoing processes of correction and refinement as our interpretations of the mental states of our human companions. As Sanders and Arluke say, 'the evidence employed by those involved in routine interactions with nonhuman animals in everyday situations to define the intentions of the animal-other and make judgements about his or her internal state is certainly as persuasive as that employed to establish the intersubjective groundings of human-to-human interaction in everyday situations . . . [and it is] at least as powerful as causal accounts solely premised on behaviourist or instinctivist presumptions' (Sanders and Arluke 1993: 382). Our projections regarding our companion animals need to be refined in light of evidence, but it is precisely our willingness to engage in such projections in the first place that opens up the possibility for learning: 'It is only through acknowledging that our animal companions are eminently conscious partners in social interaction that we will come to examine and understand their perspectives and behaviours' (Sanders and Arluke 1993: 384). 'Intimate familiarity with others—animal or human—is an effective teacher' (Sanders 1993: 211). See also Horowitz 2009.

22. Recall our discussion in Chapter 4, section 3 of the way that people with disabilities suffer not just from their dependence (and hence the potential that their needs will not be met), but also from the exaggeration of their dependence (and hence the likelihood that efforts will not be made to enable the sorts of agency and choice they are capable of). One frequently hears claims that dogs or cats have the intelligence of a human child. Animal advocates often object, and rightly so, to these sorts of comparisons of domesticated animals with children. Such comparisons frequently underestimate or obscure animals' capacity for independent agency, and for adult competency and experience. But this is only part of the story. Animals don't spring into the world fully grown. They, like us, start out as highly vulnerable infants in need of extensive care, including gradual socialization into the community. So, while it is inappropriate to compare all animals to children, it is not inappropriate to compare infants across species in relation to the question of basic socialization.

23. In the words of Joyce Poole, who has spent decades observing African elephants: 'I have never seen calves "disciplined". Protected, comforted, cooed over, reassured, and rescued, yes; but punished, no. Elephants are raised in an incredibly positive and loving environment. If a younger elephant, or in fact anyone in the family has wronged another in some way much comment and discussion follows. Sounds of the wronged individual being comforted are mixed with voices of reconciliation' (Poole 2001).

24. One manifestation of human ignorance is the view that dogs must be dominated by humans who establish themselves as alpha members of 'the pack'. As Horowitz 2009, Peterson 2010 and others have pointed out, canid social structure is based on relatively stable *families* of related members, not *packs* with fluctuating membership of often unrelated individuals. In unstable pack structures there is often continuous testing and assertion of dominance through swagger, display, physical intimidation, and sometimes violence. This is quite unlike the nature of authority

in family structures, which inheres in relationships of parent–child, elder–youngster, and sibling order. This authority is largely unquestioned and does not continuously need to be asserted through domination.

25. We are deeply discombobulated when animals escape confinement, forcing us to notice their unruly presence, as when a livestock truck overturns on the highway discharging pigs or cows or chickens. Owain Jones argues that it is precisely these moments of animals being 'out of place' that bring them into ethical focus, allowing us to see specific individuals rather than mere instances of a kind (Jones 2000).

26. See Carey 2009 on the struggle within the disability movement for the 'least restrictive environment' principle. The possible need for paternalistic restrictions in one domain, at one point in time, does not provide a licence for wholesale or enduring restrictions across other domains.

27. For the almost total failure of urban planning as a discipline and profession to consider the impact of their decisions on animals, see Wolch 2002; Palmer 2003a.

28. Mobility issues also arise in relation to horses, who may require more space than is practical in many contexts. But in their case, as we noted earlier, the option of re-wilding is more feasible than for budgies or goldfish, and we would have a duty to pursue that option before embracing the extinctionist approach. Note that most 'pet' reptiles, amphibians, fish, and birds are captured wild animals, not domesticated animals. We discuss them in Chapters 6 and 7. In this chapter, we are referring to species that have been bred in captivity for several generations and have begun to display traits, such as loss of fear of humans and loss of fitness for life in the wild, displayed by most long-domesticated species.

29. It would be interesting to compare 'no pets' rules with 'no children' rules. Some resorts or inns stipulate no children, and there may be legitimate reasons for people on vacation to be able to choose an adult-only environment. One could imagine a similar argument for having some no-pet inns or resorts. But insofar as no-children rules are appropriate in such contexts, it surely depends on the presumption that such rules are exceptions to the norm that children are full members of society, and are generally welcome in public space. It is precisely this presumption that is missing in the case of animals. (An important difference, here, is that some people suffer allergic reactions to the presence of dogs and cats—though this can also be misused as an excuse to express dislike of animals. On a citizenship model, the organization of public space would be negotiated to uphold the full membership of domesticated animals, while accommodating sufficient options for people with allergies.)

30. We agree with Francione 2000: 184 that there might be reasons for prosecution and punishment in the human case that do not apply in the animal case. However, he minimizes too quickly the possibility of prosecuting humans for the negligent or deliberate killing of animals.

31. The fact that states have special responsibilities to their own citizens may affect how certain laws are interpreted, particularly in cases such as negligence leading to harm or death. The duty to take reasonable precautions against causing harm is likely to be more demanding in relation to domesticated animals who are a

permanent part of our community than in relation to the often unpredictable interactions humans have with wild or liminal animals.

32. For a discussion of animal rescue in cases of disaster, see Irvine 2009. Interestingly, fire and rescue services seem to take account of animals in a way that many other professions, such as urban planners or social workers, do not (Ryan 2006).

33. This raises a question about future breeding, and the possibility of reversing the process. Due to breeding practices, not only can sheep not shed their own wool, but the increased volume of skin and wool makes them vulnerable to parasites and diseases. It is incumbent on us to allow different breeds of sheep to intermix and gradually reverse this process. However, this could take a long time. Moreover, while we should reverse breeding practices that make them uncomfortable, unhealthy, or disease-prone, it is not obvious that the mere fact of dependency on humans for wool shearing is problematic. In any case, the results of future breeding are not just in our hands, assuming we allow sheep to select their own partners and breeding opportunities. Humans can set general parameters (e.g., mixing flocks to increase the diversity of partners), but the future direction of sheep evolution will unfold through the choices of both sheep and humans, not rigid human control.

34. For a discussion of the Farm Sanctuary's philosophy of non-use, see http://farm-sanctuary.typepad.com/sanctuary_tails/2009/04/shearing-rescued-sheep.html. See also Dunayer's claim that humans 'have no right to treat what, in fairness, belongs to nonhumans as human property. Nonhumans should be regarded as owning what they produce (eggs, milk, honey, pearls...), what they build (nests, bowers, hives...), and the natural habitats in which they live (marshlands, forests, lakes, oceans...)' (2004: 142). We agree that what animals produce belongs to them, but that doesn't foreclose the question of the just use of those products. Citizens pay taxes on what belongs to them, and enter into exchanges to gain access to what belongs to others, or to help sustain what belongs in common to all. Recognizing that animal products belong to the animals that produce them does not necessarily lead to a 'no-use' policy; rather, it requires that use be justified as part of a fair scheme of citizenship, and of the give and take of social life.

35. Or creative ways—consider the animals (domestic and wild) who spontaneously participate in composer R. Murray Schafer's works performed in wilderness settings. The music stimulates participation from wolves, elk, birds, and the dog companions of human participants. For an example of Schafer's Wolf Music go to: http://beta.farolatino.com/Views/Album.aspx?id=1000393.

36. For interesting reflections on these issues, see the website of Black Hen Farm in California, explaining why they think it is ethical to sell the eggs of the chickens in their care: http://www.blackhenfarm.com/index.html.

37. As in the case of sheep, this raises the question of what efforts humans should make to reverse the health-distorting effects of selective breeding.

38. There are some contexts in which cow herds might be more practical than others. For example, the Hungarian grey cattle who pasture in the Neusiedler See region of eastern Austria graze for most of their food needs, and this grazing, rather than

destroying the grasslands, is key to maintaining the shortgrass meadow ecosystem and the wild plants and animals who thrive there (Fraser 2009: 91).

39. There is a further 'use' issue pertaining to cows and pigs, concerning the use of their skins after they have died a natural death. We deal with the treatment of animal corpses below, in the section on animal diets.

40. See the website of Fias Co Farm in Tennessee regarding their justification for selling goat's milk: http://fiascofarm.com/Humane-ifesto.htm. The farm never kills goats, and finds adoptive homes for male kids.

41. The situation for horses is far more doubtful. Horses typically reject bits, harnesses, and riders until they have been 'broken', i.e., subjected to extensive and coercive training, which is a violation of their basic rights. To the extent that human use of horses depends on harnessing or riding them (and most uses do, except for companionship and grazing), these uses would probably fail the test of citizenship.

42. This naturally raises the question of what justice requires in terms of the level of medical care for animal co-citizens. Here, as always, the answer will depend in part on what we take justice to require in the case of humans. Does justice in health care require enabling everyone to achieve certain key 'functionings', as capability theorists would tell us? (And if so, which functionings?) Or is the goal to achieve a certain basic level of well-being, as 'sufficientarian' theorists would tell us? Or is the goal to remedy undeserved inequalities in people's opportunity for welfare, as 'luck egalitarian' theorists would tell us? Or is the goal to enable everyone to fulfil their social roles as citizens, as 'democratic equality' theorists would tell us? Obviously these questions remain hotly contested in the human case, and, for the purposes of this book, we are not taking a stand on these debates. Our argument that domesticated animals are co-citizens of our political community does not depend on adopting any of these particular accounts of distributive justice, each of which will have different implications for animal health care. On Nussbaum's capability view, for example, the goal should be to enable domesticated animals to achieve the characteristic functionings that define flourishing for them, just as our health care aims to achieve the characteristic functionings that define flourishing for us. And in both cases, there would be limits to prevent health care funding becoming a bottomless pit that displaces all other social goods: we would not want to spend large sums for very minor gains in life expectancy or quality of life. Obviously the specification of these functionings, and of the relevant limits, will vary for different types of animals, depending on their physical and mental capacities, lifespan, health vulnerabilities, and so on.

43. See Boonin 2003 for an interesting discussion of animals' reproductive rights. As Boonin shows, a surprising number of AR theorists uncritically endorse the idea that humans have a right (and perhaps even a duty) to sterilize domesticated animals (e.g., Zamir 2007: 99), ignoring the fact that animals might have a legitimate interest in reproduction. We agree that such interests need to be taken into account, but they need to be taken into account within a broader theory of co-citizenship that governs the fuller set of rights and responsibilities amongst humans and animals, including the duty of humans to care for the offspring of domesticated animals. We believe that this broader theory provides grounds for

imposing some limits on reproduction. While in general AR theorists have failed to justify the violation of basic rights involved in sterilization, one exception is Fusfeld 2007, who defends mass sterilization on essentially utilitarian grounds, sacrificing the reproductive rights of existing animals to protect the interests of future animals not to be born into domesticated slavery.

44. Throughout much of the twentieth century, states engaged in the coercive sterilization of people with mental disabilities, on the grounds that they were unable to rationally self-regulate their sexual behaviour, and unable to look after their children. These coercive sterilization programmes have been abolished, partly on the grounds that they infringe basic rights to bodily integrity, and partly on the grounds that many people with intellectual disabilities are able to parent (with appropriate assistance). But it's worth noting that those who care for people with intellectual disabilities continue to engage in other, less invasive means of regulating their sex lives—for example, organizing group homes or group activities on a sex-segregated basis. The issue of how to deal with sex and reproduction amongst the mentally disabled remains controversial. See Carey 2009: 273–4 (on the USA); Rioux and Valentine 2006 (on Canada).

45. Readers may wonder about the implications of our argument in this section for animals in zoos. Capturing animals and putting them in zoos is a violation of their basic individual rights, and a violation of their rights as members of sovereign communities, as we argue in Chapter 6. However, what about animals who are already in zoos and who are no longer adapted for survival in the wild or for teaching their offspring how to survive in the wild? Should we prevent them from reproducing in captivity and cause captive zoo animals to gradually die out? Many species have low reproduction rates in captivity, and, left to their own devices, would gradually die out anyway. Others, however, do reproduce in captivity and will continue to do so unless humans prevent them. As in the case of domesticated animals, we would argue that restrictions on their sexual and reproductive choices must be justified in terms of the interests of the individual who is being restricted. Over time, these animals and their descendants may choose, under controlled conditions, to reintegrate into the wild, or into a semi-wild sanctuary. Others, however, may be trapped in a tragic dilemma—unable to re-wild, yet also unable to flourish in the sort of confined spaces that even the most 'progressive' sanctuaries provide. Their situation would then be similar to that of the budgies and goldfish discussed earlier for whom it is very difficult for humans to provide an environment of flourishing. Their condition in joint human–animal society may be intrinsically problematic in ways that abolitionists/extinctionists (wrongly) attribute to the condition of all domesticated animals.

46. For evidence on the health of vegan diets for dogs and cats, see http://www.vegepets.info/index.htm.

47. Some readers might wonder why eating eggs is not subject to the same worries as eating corpses. Can we eat eggs without this practice having spillover effects in terms of respect for chickens? This is one of several issues where it is difficult to disentangle the intrinsic wrongness of acts from their (variable and changing) cultural meaning. When it comes to eating frankenmeat grown from cells,

consuming corpses, using corpses for compost, or using bodily waste products for fertilizer, many people today would react with disgust if it were human cells, corpses, or waste products being used or consumed, but would happily accept using or consuming animal cells, corpses, or waste products. We think this differential treatment is morally suspect, but the remedy need not be to extend the same taboos from humans to animals. We might instead rethink our taboo against using human cells, corpses, or waste products, if we can do so in ways that respect human rights and human dignity. In the case of eggs, an obvious issue is the different practical characteristics of chicken versus human eggs. Chicken eggs are usable— they come enveloped in albumin with a handy hard shell coating to facilitate handling, storage, and cooking. If unfertilized human eggs were shed in this form, it's hard to know how we might react to using them. It's difficult to separate out disgust, taboo, and cultural tradition from the ethical considerations.

48. For a discussion of this position, and the failed attempt in a 2010 referendum to extend it across Switzerland, see http://www.guardian.co.uk/world/2010/mar/05/lawyer-who-defends-animals.

49. To take just one example, Ryan (2006) notes that although social workers often work within families and homes that contain domestic animals, and although their actions often have decisive impacts on those animals, they are given no professional training to consider animal well-being, and have no professional mandate to take their interests into account.

Chapter 6

1. For a critique of this tendency to ignore the 'difference between animate and inanimate nature', see Wolch 1998; Palmer 2003a.

2. For example, see Scully 2002 on the scope of the global hunting industry.

3. Within the AR advocacy community there is debate about whether the movement devotes too much attention to wild animal issues (such as hunting, fur trapping, zoos, and circuses) considering that farm animals constitute the overwhelming percentage of intentionally harmed animal victims. For example, the Vegan Outreach website notes that 'About 99% of the animals killed in the United States each year die to be eaten' (http://www.veganoutreach.org/advocacy/path.html). Note, however, that Vegan Outreach does not even mention unintentional killing of animals. Ten billion farm animals are killed in the USA annually. It is estimated that between 100 million and 1 billion birds are killed annually in the USA from building collisions alone (New York City Audubon Society 2007). This does not include deaths to birds from cars, electrical wires, domestic cats, pollution, habitat loss, and countless other hazards we impose on them. It is impossible to estimate all wild animal deaths from human causes, but the totals are staggering. Our point here is not to diminish Vegan Outreach's emphasis on the suffering of farmed animals, or their strategic decision about how to focus their efforts. Rather, it is to illustrate the lacunae in ART concerning inadvertent human killing of animals.

4. 'Wildlife managers should be principally concerned with letting animals be, keeping human predators out of their affairs, allowing these "other nations" to carve out their own destiny' (Regan 1983: 357).

5. 'Once we give up our right to claims to "dominion" over other species we have no right to interfere with them at all. We should leave them alone as much as we possibly can. Having given up the role of tyrant, we should not try to play Big Brother either' (Singer 1975: 251).

6. The fact that animals have a negative right not to be killed which humans must respect does not *logically* entail that animals also have a positive right to human aid or protection in the face of threats from other animals. But while there is no logical contradiction in affirming the former and rejecting the latter, the moral rationale for the former seems to push in the direction of the latter, and critics of ART are right to say that this moral tension has not been adequately addressed.

7. In the second edition of the book, Regan has revised this position, recognizing a duty of assistance:

    'The rights view can consistently recognize a general *prima facie* duty of benefi-cence that, in some circumstances, imposes actual duties of assistance. That such duties are not discussed in *The Case* is a symptom of the incompleteness of the theory developed there. In hindsight, I recognize that it would have been better had I said more about duties of assistance other than those owed to victims of injustice'. (Regan 2004: xxvii)

8. For another example, see Shelton 2004 regarding miscalculations by wildlife man-agers in the island ecosystem of Santa Cruz, California.

9. Fraser also discusses the case of 'ecological islands' in Venezuela which were created during flooding for a dam. Predators fled during the flooding, leaving behind howler monkeys and other smaller species. Far from being a predator-free paradise, however, the results were catastrophic. The monkeys increased in number, denuded the islands of vegetation, then suffered from starvation and collapse of their social structure (Fraser 2009: ch. 2). See also Ray et al. 2005 on the role of apex predators in ecosystems.

10. See Hadley 2006 for a critique of the flourishing argument. See also Nussbaum 2006, who denies that a species-norm conception of flourishing must uncritically accept what is natural (or species typical) as defining flourishing.

11. An early example is the article on 'simian sovereignty' (Goodin, Pateman, and Pateman 1997), although this was tied to the idea that the great apes, in virtue of their close proximity to humans and their high cognitive functionings, are partic-ularly entitled to sovereign political status.

12. See also Sapontzis:

    'Many animal liberation programs concerning wild animals express a deep respect for and desire to re-establish, safeguard, or expand the opportunities for these animals to lead independent, self-governing lives. While such programs may differ from those intended to make minorities and women "first-class citizens" and "full partners" in our social institutions, this difference is, once again, merely a consequence of the fact that animals have different interests than we do. Wild animals do not seem to want to be welcomed into our societies;

they seem to want, rather, basically to be left alone by us to pursue their own ways of life'. (Sapontzis 1987: 85)

13. It is unclear what weight Nussbaum accords sovereignty for wild animals. Sometimes she seems to advocate breathtaking interventions by humans in order to bring about 'the gradual formation of an interdependent world in which all species will enjoy cooperative and mutually supportive relations with one another'. As she acknowledges, 'Nature is not that way and never has been', and so she says that her approach 'calls, in a very general way, for the gradual supplanting of the natural by the just' (Nussbaum 2006: 399–400). It is difficult to see any respect for sovereignty in this picture. At other times, however, she backs away from such intervention, and notes that positive interventions must be balanced against 'appropriate respect for the autonomy of a species' (2006: 374). She provides no guidance on how to balance these conflicting agendas.

14. See also Palmer 2003b; Čapek 2005: 209 for other discussions of development as a process of colonizing animals and their territories, and the similarities with historic discourses of the colonization of indigenous peoples.

15. International norms of decolonization state that 'the right of peoples to use and exploit their natural wealth and resources is inherent in their sovereignty' (GA Resolution 626 (VIII) 21 December 1952), and that 'the rights of peoples and nations to permanent sovereignty over their natural wealth and resources must be exercised in the interest of their national development and of the wellbeing of the People of the State concerned' (1962 Resolution on Permanent Sovereignty over Natural Resources, Article 1, GA Resolution 1803 (XVII) 14 December 1962). As Eckersley notes, these wordings were adopted as part of the new 'sovereignty game' by which postcolonial states sought to restructure natural resource concessions made to foreign corporations during the colonial period, yet today they are seen as giving human communities unrestricted sovereignty over wild animals and nature, and the right (and indeed duty) to use them solely for human benefit (Eckersley 2004: 221–2). State laws in the USA have similar formulations. For example, legislation in the state of Ohio states that 'the ownership of and the title to all wild animals... is in the state, which holds such title in trust for the benefit of all the people' (Ohio Rev. Code Ann. § 1531.01, cited in Satz 2009: 14n79).

16. The issue of wildlife documentaries would be an interesting test case here. As Mills (2010) notes, we currently take it for granted that we have the right as stewards and managers to film wild animals, even in their most intimate settings (e.g., dens), and even in cases where animals themselves clearly avoid camera crews whenever they are aware of them. Wildlife documentaries often celebrate how cleverly they use hidden cameras to ensure wild animals are unaware of their presence. If we thought of ourselves as visitors to wild animal territory, rather than paternalistic managers, we would need to rethink this practice. Recall Smut's account of her interaction with baboons, and how responding to their indications to her to 'get lost' was key to establishing respectful relations (Smuts 2001: 295, and our discussion in Chapter 2).

17. This perception was manifestly false with regard to many indigenous societies such as the Incas, who clearly did have state-like structures. To circumvent this,

apologists for imperialism argued that pre-existing sovereignty (where it existed) was only worthy of respect if it met a certain 'standard of civilization', as defined by European norms and values (e.g., no polygamy). For overviews of the ways (the lack of) sovereignty was invoked to justify European imperialism, see Keal 2003; Anaya 2004; Pemberton 2009. Even as late as 1979, the Australian High Court ruled in *Coe v Commonwealth* that indigenous peoples lacked sovereignty based on an 'extremely Eurocentric test for the recognition of Aboriginal sovereignty, asserting that an Aboriginal nation had to have distinct legislative, executive and judicial organs before its sovereignty could be recognized' (Cassidy 1998: 115).

18. Alfred argues that indigenous peoples need to renounce patterns of thought that promote colonization 'beginning with the rejection of the term and notion of indigenous "sovereignty"', and should be guided instead by traditional modes of indigenous community life, in which there was 'no absolute authority, no coercive enforcement of decisions, no hierarchy, and no separate ruling entity', and which therefore exhibited 'sovereignty-free regimes of conscience and justice' (Alfred 2001: 27, 34). See also Keal 2003: 147, who notes that some indigenous peoples 'reject European notions of sovereignty in which the state exercises authority over civil society'.

19. See Reus-Smit 2001; Frost 1996; Philpott 2001, and Prokhovnik 2007, all of whom argue that we need to re-examine our theories of sovereignty by focusing on their underlying 'moral purposes' or 'moral dimensions', which they all link (in different ways) to autonomy.

20. According to Philpott, both revolutions 'claimed sovereignty in a similar moral fashion, on behalf of a similar value–freedom . . . Both revolutions sought sovereign authority as a protection for a people, for their local prerogatives, for their immunities, for their autonomy, all of this as a shield from the impositions of a more universal entity'. Sovereignty therefore advances a form of liberation in the sense of 'self-determination: the assertion of groups of people to freedom from the oppression of some larger, centralized authority' (Philpott 2001: 254).

21. For discussions of indigenous sovereignty, see Reynolds 1996 and Curry 2004 on Australia; Turner 2001 and Shadian 2010 on Canada; Bruyneel 2007 and Biolsi 2005 on the USA; and Lenzerini 2006 and Wiessner 2008 on the international debate.

22. In the famous American Supreme Court case of *Worcester v Georgia*, Judge Marshall said that 'the settled doctrine of the law of nations is that a weaker power does not surrender its independence—its rights to self-government—by associating with a stronger, and taking its protection' (31 US (6 Pet.) 515 1832). Note the parallel between the argument we are making here and the discussion in Chapter 5 regarding dependent agency for individual citizens. Dependency (or interdependency) of states is not the antonym of independence (in Arneil's terms), but rather its precursor.

23. In rehabilitating the idea of sovereignty in this way, we are aware of the risks involved. As Pemberton notes, while sovereignty is often justified on the grounds of serving community flourishing, too often its effective purpose becomes the maintenance of sovereignty itself at the expense of community members

(Pemberton 2009: 118). Given this, some people might think we are better off abandoning the term sovereignty, and instead using terms such as self-determination or autonomy. But all of these terms are vulnerable to abuse, and, at the end of the day, the only remedy is to insist that claims to sovereignty—human or animal—be explicitly linked to the underlying moral purposes. What matters for our argument is that there are such valid moral purposes behind claims to sovereignty, and that they arise for both human and wild animal communities. Whether or not we use the word 'sovereignty' as a label for such claims is not essential.

24. Recall our discussion in Chapter 3 about the way many wild animals are 'niche specialists' (rather than 'adaptive generalists'), highly dependent on specific ecosystems.

25. http://www.britishbirdlovers.co.uk/articles/blue-tits-and-milk-bottle-tops.html.

26. See Regan 2004: xxxvi–viii, and the discussion in Simmons 2009: 20.

27. Wild animals could turn the tables here, pointing to the sustainability of sovereign animal communities compared with the rapacious ecological footprint of human communities which is quite possibly leading us all towards ecological collapse. If living within one's means is a requirement of competent sovereignty, as Rawls says, it may well be humans not animals who are failing the test.

28. To adapt some of Dworkin's terminology, facts of food cycles and predation should be seen as 'parameters', rather than 'limitations', of wild animals' agency: they define the challenge to which animals either respond well or badly (Dworkin 1990). And, in general, the evidence suggests that wild animals respond competently to these challenges. (By contrast, domesticated animals have been bred in a way that diminishes their competence to deal with these challenges, while enhancing capacities relevant for domesticated life amongst humans.)

29. In any event, the idea that humans could somehow end predation is absurd. Nature is full of relations of predation, and all creatures—including us humans—are dependent on its ongoing existence. Even if all humans followed a vegan diet, we would still be completely dependent on the processes of nature that enable the seeding and pollination of plants, replenishment of soil, filtration of water and air, control of animal populations that feed on plants, and so on—processes that involve predation at various levels of the food chain.

30. In the human case, consent is often said to be a necessary condition for legitimate intervention (e.g., Luban 1980). Indeed, Ignatieff (2000) says that the consent of the local population is the 'first and primary' condition on a legitimate intervention— 'the people must be demanding our help'. Not all theorists say that consent is a necessary condition—see, for example, Caney 2005: 230 and Orend 2006: 95—although they too say that its presence strengthens the overall case for intervention, and that intervening in the absence of consent must pass especially stringent burdens of justification.

31. In their defence of sovereignty for the great apes, Goodin insist that they are 'perfectly capable of running [their] lives on day-to-day basics', and 'perfectly capable of crafting an autonomous existence for themselves' (Goodin, Pateman, and Pateman 1997: 836).

32. See Pemberton 2009: 140, who notes that imperialists often acknowledged the property rights of indigenous peoples even as they established European sovereignty over them.

33. Indeed, *Star Trek* fans will recognize that similar scenarios have been explored in *Star Trek: The Next Generation*. In 'Pen Pals' (season 2, episode 5) the people of Drema IV are going to die due to the planet's tectonic instability. The Enterprise crew debates their 'prime directive' not to intervene with the autonomous evolution of planets deemed not yet ready for contact with, and integration into, the federation of planets. They eventually decide on a one-time intervention to save the planet, using an easy technological fix. Then they erase the Dreman's memory of the intervention so the people can continue on their own self-determined course of development.

34. Fink (2005: 14) discusses the case of insect larvae that feed and grow in the nostrils of reindeer, and gradually suffocate the animals in a slow and agonizing death. It seems quite possible that humans could figure out a way of killing this insect, or inoculating reindeer against its effects. And it's quite possible that such an intervention, performed cautiously, might have negligible impact on the ecosystem. It would result in fewer deer dying, so reproduction rates might need to adjust downwards to compensate (either naturally, or by further human intervention), but this intervention would not seem to implicate humans in systematically regulating reindeer lives, or undermining their freedom and competence to continue as a self-directed community. This looks like an example of a possible intervention that supports, rather than undermines, wild animal sovereignty. Another case concerns the sea turtles living off the coast of Florida. Occasionally there are freak weather events that cause sea level temperatures to drop to levels too low for sea turtles to withstand. When this happens the turtles suffer cold shock, go into a torpid state, float to the water surface, and eventually die. A serious cold snap occurred in January 2010. Hundreds of turtles in cold shock were plucked from the water by humans, kept in warm water till the freak cold snap was over, and returned to the sea unharmed. Given the unusual nature of this weather event, it is hard to see how human assistance undermined the autonomy of sea turtles or their larger ecological community. This would be true even if human intervention were not independently justified by the fact that turtle populations have been drastically decimated by human impacts.

35. See also Haupt 2009: ch. 6 for a careful weighing of the choice to raise and release an orphaned crow, or rescue and release an injured one.

36. For a droll account of efforts to assist the migrating ibis, see Warner 2008 (entitled 'Survival of the Dumbest'). For the 2010 migration, see Morelle 2010. For an overview of articles about the waldrapp ibis programme see: http://www.waldrapp-team.at/waldrappteam/m_news.asp?YearNr=2010&lnr=2&pnr=1.

37. The fallibility argument can take weak or strong forms. The weak form is that given the complexity of nature and the limits of human knowledge, human interventions are bound to bungle things. A strong form is that nature 'by definition' gets things right, and so any human intervention is problematic. Under the influence of James Lovelock's 'gaia thesis' (Lovelock 1979), there is a tendency to see natural

ecosystems as intrinsically coherent, as part of an overall system that functions holistically and inevitably to support life. Generally, when humans interfere in this system it is a negative intervention—destructive of life and biodiversity. Peter Ward (2009) has recently challenged the gaia thesis, arguing that nature, without human interference, is neither effectively self-regulating, nor tending towards the support of life. Ward argues that nature goes terribly wrong sometimes, causing catastrophic destruction of ecosystems. (He claims that most of the great extinction events were caused by living systems of bacteria and plants that ran amuck.) Ward argues that there are times when humans should insert themselves into the equation, altering nature's course in order to prevent catastrophe and promote life.

38. See Henders 2010 for a discussion of some of these provisions in the Minority Treaties after World War I, intended to protect minorities who were cut off from their 'mother country' or from international markets.

39. See Fowler 2004 on 'fuzzy' citizenship for Hungarian minorities in Romania and Slovakia; Aukot 2009 on nomads in Africa.

40. In the human case, Iris Young has argued that self-determination should be understood not as absolute or exclusive, but as relational—the right not to be dominated by others, even in conditions where substantial interaction and interdependence exists (Young 2000). So too, we would argue, with animal sovereignty.

41. Indigenous rights advocates have long complained that Western conservation efforts ignore their rights, and indeed turn them into 'conservation refugees' (Dowie 2009; see also Fraser 2009: 110).

42. For bonobo conservation projects that work with indigenous peoples, see the website of the Bonobo Conservation Initiative (www.bonobo.org/projectsnew. htm). See Tashiro 1995 regarding the recent erosion of the traditional taboos against harming bonobos. See also Thompson et al. 2008 regarding how bonobo populations are actually higher in non-park areas where they live amongst indigenous people who maintain the traditional taboo against killing bonobos, as compared with established park areas that exclude indigenous peoples, where bonobos have been decimated by poachers. We can see here the outlines of what schemes of joint and parallel sovereignty might look like. In another case, Fraser discusses the efforts in Chitwan National Park, Nepal, to involve local people who want to benefit from the forest (to collect mulch, grass, leaves, herbs, fruit, and firewood) by hiring them to do anti-poaching security work as well (Fraser 2009: 245). Vaillant (2010) discusses traditional coexistence strategies between indigenous peoples and the Siberian tiger in the Primorye region of eastern Russia. See also the website for Elephant Voices, the animal advocacy organization directed by Joyce Poole. Elephant Voices works from the premise that helping elephants requires fostering relationships between humans and elephants, not attempting to isolate elephants from humans (http://www.elephantvoices.org/).

43. For a particularly complex example of multi-ethnic autonomy, see the discussion of the 'Southern Nations', Nationalities' and Peoples' Regional State' in Ethiopia in Vaughan 2006.

44. What about unexploited habitats shared by animals and humans in traditional sustainable relationships? (Consider indigenous cultures in the Amazon, or long-

term resource extraction zones in which stable symbiotic relations between wild animals and human activity have arisen.) We address some of these complexities later in this chapter. As for similar symbiotic relationships occurring in developed zones (e.g., sustainable agricultural lands), these will be dealt with in the chapter on liminal animals.

45. Some readers may think that we need a third check: namely, limits on human population growth. We are unlikely to comply with the first two checks if human population continues to grow. However, the relationship between human population and land/resource use is a complicated one. For one thing, we should not underestimate the human capacity for moving towards much smarter, more efficient, more sustainable, and more just use of resources. Also, societies are free to make their own trade-offs between total numbers of citizens and standard of living. We cannot ask or expect animals to give up their territories so that growing numbers of humans can sustain a particular standard of living. But a society may be able to grow in numbers without taking animal territory if it is willing to accept a lower standard of living. Rather than stipulating an 'ideal' human population target and then allocating territory accordingly, we should instead secure the fair territorial claims of existing humans and animals, and then allow human societies to regulate population within those constraints of justice.

46. See Hadley 2005 for a discussion of the predictability and stability of animal land use, which he invokes to explain why it is feasible to recognize wild animals' right to private property. In our view, such facts are better used to recognize rights to sovereignty.

47. Relevant factors here include the fact that certain ecological zones support a far greater abundance and diversity of animal life than others, and the fact that many animals are niche specialists without the ability to readily adapt to new environments (whereas humans, by virtue of their technological know-how, are quite versatile in terms of the zones that we can inhabit and flourish in).

48. As Fraser notes, 'There were no benign human societies that took only as much as needed' (Fraser 2009: 117). See also Redford 1999.

49. These days we are inclined to lament the impact of petroleum and the invention of the internal combustion engine on the environment: cars are the enemy. It is a useful corrective, however, to think about the numbers of animals who have escaped murderous exploitation—and not just whales. As discussed in Chapter 4, horses have been perhaps the greatest beneficiaries. This doesn't alter the negative impacts of cars on animals, from climate change to road deaths, but it does remind us to look forward in our search for solutions rather than romanticizing the pre-technological era.

50. For an attempt to calculate the ongoing losses suffered by contemporary African Americans due to slavery, see Robinson 2000.

51. For related discussions of compensatory justice for wild animals harmed by human injustice, see Regan 2004: xl; Palmer 2010: 55, 110.

52. This includes countless situations in which we are directly responsible for having made animals more dangerous to us. Bradshaw (2009) explores how human violence towards elephants has caused the breakdown of elephant societies, producing

psychologically damaged rogue elephants who pose a serious threat to humans. Vaillant (2010) discusses the extraordinary case of a Siberian tiger who was harassed one too many times by hunters and set out on a programme of systematic revenge.

53. For useful discussions, see Sunstein 2002; Wolff 2006.

54. Long Point Causeway Improvement Project (http://longpointcauseway.com/). Improvements to the causeway have significantly reduced road deaths in the last few years.

55. There are some interesting exceptions, such as crows and other scavengers who take up residence along highways because roadkill provides easier pickings than scavenging in traditional settings!

56. As we noted in Chapter 5, existing development practices rarely if ever consider their impact on animals. See Wolch 1998; Palmer 2003a. An interesting exception is the recent International Wildlife Crossing Infrastructure Design Competition for a wildlife overpass along a notorious section of the I-70 in Vail, Colorado. This stretch of highway takes a terrible toll on animal lives (and a much smaller but terrible human toll as well). The initiative was prompted more by concern for human life and rising insurance costs due to vehicle damage than concern for animals. Nevertheless, the initiative could be enormously important for reducing the road risks we impose on animals, since the designs are intended to be adaptable to a range of settings. Hundreds of designers and architects responded to the challenge to design an animal overpass which would be effective and ecologically sound while improving on the costs, flexibility, and labour-intensive construction characterizing existing wildlife overpass models (like the ones in Banff, Canada). The top five designs can be viewed online at: http://www.arc-competition.com/welcome.php. The New York City Audubon Society (2007) has produced a terrific guide for designing city buildings to reduce bird impacts. Also, the Jackson Hole (Wyoming) Wildlife Foundation provides information about the 'firefly flapper' designed to reduce bird collisions with electrical wires (http://www.jhwildlife.org/).

57. As we noted in Chapter 2, there is a revisionist camp within moral philosophy which denies that it is legitimate to kill an 'innocent aggressor' in self-defence, but we are assuming the mainstream view that there is a right to self-defence in such cases (see Ch. 2, note 32 above).

58. We should note a different kind of hypocrisy regarding wildlife risk. Animal lovers in developed countries—which have largely wiped out large dangerous animals—expect people in developing nations to live with the risks imposed by poster species such as tigers and elephants in the name of habitat and species conservation. Meanwhile, the people of Germany and Austria went crazy over the alleged risk posed by a single black bear, Bruno, when he wandered down from the Italian Alps. He was shot by a hunter with the blessing of the Bavarian Environment Ministry (Fraser 2009: 86–8). On the hypocrisy of Western attitudes in this respect, which are often reflected in Western-funded (or even Western-imposed) conservation programmes, see Wolch 1998: 125; Eckersley 2004: 222; Garner 2005a: 121.

59. We should note the position we are advocating here is importantly different from that of ecologists such as Val Plumwood, who also object to the human demand for

zero risk in relation to wild animals. Plumwood's view is that we should accept that we are part of natural processes, including predator–prey relations, and hence that we can eat others so long as we accept the risk of being eaten (Plumwood 2000, 2004). Our conception of reciprocity is not based on an idea of accepting what is 'natural', but rather on a conception of fair dealing between sovereign communities. What counts as fair risk management will therefore vary depending on who has sovereignty over the relevant territory. Humans don't have a right to enter sovereign animal territory and impose invasive measures to reduce risk to ourselves—e.g. by fencing territory or fitting animals with tracking devices. If we enter animal sovereign territory, we must accept the risks. But in sovereign human areas we do have the right to reduce our risk by using barriers, or relocation of dangerous wild animals, for example.

60. We might ask, given the density of animal life at that particular location, whether it's an appropriate place for a causeway in the first place. Perhaps this particular ecosystem should simply be a no-go (or low-impact) zone for humans, since the costs of human activity may pose too many risks for too many animals—risks that are not warranted in the name of an inessential human activity (tourism). But let's assume that in this case, it really is vital for humans to be able to drive along that 3.5 km stretch of road.

61. MacLeod 2011 contains several biographies of rescued wild animals from the Hope for Wildlife Society in Nova Scotia, Canada. As long as rehabilitation and release is an option for rescued animals, their contact with humans is limited as much as possible. However, if staff determine that an animal's injury means survival in the wild is not possible, the animal's treatment undergoes a dramatic shift to intensive contact with humans in a wide variety of circumstances in order to introduce the animal to the possibilities of its new society—a multi-species society including the staff of the rescue centre, other animals who live there on a permanent basis, and visiting members of the public.

62. The idea that we should treat animals according to their species norm lies at the heart of Nussbaum's approach to animal rights (Nussbaum 2006). We have already challenged that position in Chapter 4, section 5. One implication of disabled wild animals joining the mixed human–animal community is that we become responsible for their diet, which of course raises the puzzle of what to do regarding animals that are naturally carnivorous. We have already discussed this in Chapter 5, section 4 in relation to domestic cats, and the same principles would apply here.

63. Consider the multiple contrasts between refuges as described here, and traditional circuses and zoos. Zoos and circuses are designed for human ends. Animals are abducted from the wild or bred in captivity where they are trained to perform in various ways for human visitors. They are showcased in faux 'natural' environments in the case of many zoos. They are coerced/trained into performing stunts in circuses. Even in the most progressive zoos, the abduction, transportation, captive breeding, confinement, and management of able-bodied animals is a gross violation of their most basic rights. Nothing in the above discussion of disabled animal refuges should be taken to justify the existence of circuses or zoos. An animal refuge exists only to care for animals who are no longer fit to live in the wild, and to care

for them according to our best understanding of their interests as individuals. See Hribal 2010 for a fascinating account of resistance by circus, zoo, and aquarium animals to their captivity and abuse.

64. Paul Taylor (1986) offers a similar remedial theory regarding our obligations to wild animals. We should not harm them, or interfere with them. But if we do, then we should compensate them, and honour any dependencies we have created.

65. According to the Great Ape Project, we 'have considerable historical experience with the United Nations acting as a protector of non-autonomous human regions, known as United Nations Trust Territories. It is to an international body of this kind that the defense of the first nonhuman independent territories and a role in the regulation of mixed human and non-human animal territories could be entrusted' (Cavalieri and Singer 1993: 311; see also Singer and Cavalieri 2002: 290; Eckersley 2004: 289 n14).

Chapter 7

1. Urban geographers have started to question the invisibility of the vast numbers of non-domesticated animals who share human settlement. Jennifer Wolch has called for 'zoopolis'—a new kind of theorizing about human cities which acknowledges the full range of animal social groups, the ethical significance of our relations with them, and the need to challenge ideas of human culture or civilization which are defined in opposition to nature (Wolch 1998). See also Adams and Lindsey 2010; DeStefano 2010; Michelfelder 2003; Palmer 2003a, 2010; Philo and Wilbert 2000.

2. This feeling of entitlement to subordinate liminal animals to human interests in areas of human settlement is often thoroughly unreflective, but see Franklin 2005: 113 for an attempt to defend it.

3. Jerolmack traces this progressive delegitimization in the case of pigeons. As he notes, 'pigeons are now a "homeless" species: the past century has redefined an ever-increasing number of spaces as off limits to them (and other animals), until there seems nowhere humans live that is considered legitimate for pigeons' (Jerolmack 2008: 89).

4. Laws that protect migrating birds, for example, do not apply to liminal bird populations like pigeons or resident Canada geese. Nor do animal cruelty laws. It is striking that even environmental groups rarely object to extermination campaigns against liminal animals, since they are neither endangered species nor parts of wilderness ecosystems.

5. For a similar statement implying that the presence of animals amongst human society can only be the result of 'forced participation', and that the goal of ART is not to protect animals 'within society' but rather that 'nonhumans should be allowed to live free in natural environments, forming their own societies', see Dunayer 2004: 17.

6. When AR theorists say that animals have a basic right not to be killed, critics often ask whether this extends to 'pests' as well, or whether an exception should be made when humans and pests come into ineliminable conflict. The general AR view is that humans can kill animals only in situations of self-defence, and other circumstances

in extremis, as in the human case. These rights do not evaporate simply because an animal is viewed as a pest by humans. We can't kill pesky humans, and so with animals, too, we must seek less extreme methods to avoid and defuse conflicts. There are some kinds of liminal animals—e.g., house-loving venomous snakes— with whom arguably we are not in the circumstances of justice, since we cannot share living space with them without putting ourselves in peril. We may be justified in taking extreme measures to protect ourselves, including lethal ones, if barriers, relocation, quarantine, infection control, and other methods are inade- quate for our safety. However, as we discuss below, such measures are only justifi- able in a larger context in which we drastically circumscribe our own lethal impact on animals. In other words, we cannot hold animals to a standard of never endangering human life, while, for our part, heedlessly disregarding the violence and mayhem we impose on them. Otherwise, we must try to prevent conflicts from arising (e.g., by storing garbage and food carefully, or by adopting building codes that keep animals out of homes) or, when this fails, use non-lethal means to deal with unwanted animals. These might include relocation, repellants, birth control, attraction of competitors—or learning to live and let live. We return to this issue below.

7. We emphasize that the absence of trust between liminal animals and humans does not mean that principles of justice are inapplicable. In this respect, we differ from Silvers and Francis, who argue that justice presupposes trust, and hence there are no obligations of justice to animals prior to domestication (Silvers and Francis 2005: 72 n99). Trust is a precondition of relations of co-citizenship, but it is not a precondition of justice *tout court*.

8. As Michelfelder notes, liminal animals 'are often perceived as creatures out of place and as unwelcome visitors, somewhat akin to illegal aliens who do not speak the local language and never will. The operative words here are "nuisance" and "pest"—even when the population poses no direct and immediate threat to human safety or health…And, consistent with treatment of illegal aliens and criminals, members of urban wildlife populations perceived as nuisances are often subdued by government authorities and translocated back to the "great outdoors"' (Michelfelder 2003: 82; cf. Elder, Wolch, and Emel 1998: 82).

9. The tarring process works in several directions. Animals are tarred by association with denigrated human groups. Meanwhile humans and animals are tarred by association with animals widely considered to be less desirable, such as rats. See Costello and Hodson 2010 on the psychological mechanisms linking negative attitudes towards animals to the dehumanization of human outgroups.

10. For an account of the albatross, who was cared for at the Sandy Pines Wildlife Refuge in Napanee, Ontario, see: http://www.sandypineswildlife.org/. After several months of care and attempted rehabilitation with the aim of release back to the south seas, the albatross developed an incurable disease and was euthanized.

11. Some animal groups do survive contact, shifting over time from being wild animals to liminal ones. For example, the San Joaquin kit foxes in California started out as wild animals whose habitat was colonized by human development, but who

subsequently have been able to adapt and survive as a liminal species, though their situation is precarious.

12. For example, New York City is an ecological hot spot, teeming with a diversity of liminal animals much richer than in the surrounding counties. This makes sense, since animals are attracted to the region for the same reasons humans originally were—a resource-rich confluence of rivers, islands, and marshlands that persist amidst the modern metropolis (Sullivan 2010).

13. A possible exception would be endangered wild animal populations currently under management by humans to promote their survival and increase their populations. Even in these cases, though, the main threats to species tend to be humans and human activity.

14. Palmer distinguishes opportunists in this regard from other liminals, such as ferals or exotics, whose presence in the city is our responsibility (as we discuss below).

15. One can imagine exceptions, as when a human befriends a liminal animal and establishes a pattern of care which leads to expectation on the part of the animal, and a specific kind of dependency. In this case, the human has assumed an individual responsibility which goes beyond the general responsibility shared by all human members of the community towards liminal animals, as when humans take domestic animals into their care.

16. The dormouse is adapted to the raised corridors created by the densely interwoven branches that characterize managed hedgerows. See http://www.suffolk.gov.uk/NR/rdonlyres/CF03E9EF-F3B4-4D9D-95FF-C82A7CE62ABF/0/dormouse.pdf.

17. Note that the categories we are using are non-exclusive. For example, some opportunist, synanthropic, and feral species have been introduced to new environments where they function as introduced exotics.

18. These are the birds made famous by Mark Bittner's book *The Wild Parrots of Telegraph Hill* (Bittner 2005), subsequently made into a film.

19. See the write-up on the Connecticut Audubon Society's website: http://www.ctaudubon.org/conserv/nature/parowl.htm.

20. In the case of the monk parrots, this call is driven by the utilities companies who face considerable inconvenience from the fact that monk parrots build their giant communal nests on hydro poles and fixtures. Eradication efforts, which are defended in terms of the dangers of foreign interlopers, are actually motivated by cost and inconvenience.

21. Actual extinctions caused by new introductions are fairly rare. See Zimmer 2008.

22. See http://www.grey-squirrel.org.uk/ for defence of the grey squirrels, and http://www.europeansquirrelinitiative.org/index.html for the anti-grey squirrel campaign.

23. http://www.nt.gov.au/nreta/wildlife/animals/canetoads/index.html.

24. See the government of Australia senate report on feral animals at: http://www.aph.gov.au/SENATE/committee/history/animalwelfare_ctte/culling_feral_animals_nt/01ch1.pdf.

25. It should be noted that other liminal animal groups can also develop more specific relationships of dependency on individual humans. This might be particularly true for weak, injured, or orphaned animals who only survive because humans provide temporary or long-term shelter and food.

26. See the Torre Argentina Roman Cat Sanctuary website (http://www.romancats. com/index_eng.php).

27. See Eva Hornung's novel *Dog Boy* for a fascinating perspective on the feral dogs of Moscow (Hornung 2009).

28. Domesticated animals face the same kinds of restrictions. However, they are already highly adapted to associating with humans, and to communicating their needs and wants to us. As we argued in Chapter 5, this means that coexistence can be negotiated to some extent, not simply imposed on domesticated animals. They can be socialized into citizenship in ways that foster freedom and opportunity, as opposed to simply being subjected to human control. Most liminal animals avoid humans, and distrust humans, and this limits the possibilities for communication and relationship necessary for mutual citizenship. Thus, what initially appear to be similar restrictions on liberty would in fact be very different in terms of their impact on the autonomy and well-being of liminal and domesticated animals.

29. Note that these are roughly the same considerations that tip in favour of recognizing limitations on human interference in sovereign wild animal communities.

30. The 1930 Hague Convention explicitly sought to discourage dual citizenship—a position that has only recently been amended in European law.

31. Spinner argues that whereas the Amish are consistent in rejecting both the rights and responsibilities of public participation, some Hasidic Jewish communities seek to retain their full rights to shape public decisions (e.g., by voting), while still resisting the obligation to learn the virtues and practices of civic cooperation with the members of other groups. This latter approach, he argues, fails the test of reciprocity (Spinner 1994).

32. Some migrant worker programmes can function as stages on the route to full citizenship. Canada's live-in caregiver programme is one such example. Our focus here is on those migrant worker programmes that lead to denizenship, not citizenship.

33. This is not to say that states have an obligation of justice to create migrant worker programmes. States can choose an immigration policy that admits only permanent residents with rights to citizenship, not temporary migrants. Our point, rather, is that migrant worker programmes are not necessarily unjust, even if they do not lead to citizenship, so long as they uphold a fair scheme of denizenship that is responsive to the distinctive interests of those with temporary migration projects.

34. Where rights and responsibilities are asymmetric, then we have what Cairns (2000) calls 'citizenship minus' (a term he uses to describe the second-class status of Aboriginal peoples in Canada until the 1970s), or what Cohen (2009) calls 'semicitizenship' (a term she uses to describe the historic status of groups such as people with disabilities, felons, and children). Denizenship, as we are using the term, could involve such unfair forms of status, but it need not—it could instead represent a mutual decision to develop a weaker sort of relationship than that implied by full citizenship.

35. Indeed, the United Nations adopted a Convention on the Protection of the Rights of All Migrant Workers and Members of Their Families in 1990, which is monitored by a UN Committee. However, the Convention is very weak in its substantive

requirements, and even weaker in its enforcement mechanisms, not least because none of the major destination countries has signed or ratified the Convention.

36. These two principles sometimes operate at cross-purposes: granting amnesties to long-settled illegal migrants can be seen as giving an incentive for new illegal migrants to come, and to put up with the temporary hardships, reducing the effectiveness of the barriers and disincentives. But there is no alternative: both principles are morally compelling.

37. Recall that while we should respect the sovereignty of wild animal communities, when we encounter injured individual wild animals we should respond to the radical change in their circumstances. If healing and rehabilitation to the wild are possible that is preferable, but if not, the animal may benefit from becoming a citizen of the human–animal community, even with the drastic curtailment of liberty involved, rather than being left to die. See Chapter 6 for more discussion of this point.

38. See Adams and Lindsey 2010: 228–35 for a discussion of the successful urban coyote management programme in Vancouver, Canada. The 'Coexisting with Coyotes' programme focuses on public education to reduce incentives for coyote habituation (e.g., feeding, leaving pet food outside) and promote active disincentives. For example, adults who see coyotes are encouraged to chase them, yell at them, or use noise makers to disturb them in order to encourage coyotes to maintain a wary distance. The programme's website is at: http://www.stanleyparkecology.ca/programs/conservation/urbanWildlife/coyotes/.

The Cook Country Coyote Project is another excellent resource for successful human–coyote coexistence strategies. Their website is at: http://urbancoyoteresearch.com/ Coexistence for humans and coyotes requires both parties to keep a respectful distance. We should note, here, that supporters of coyote culls and bounties frequently argue that killing coyotes is necessary to teach them to keep a respectful distance from humans. This is a perverse idea. A dead coyote cannot employ her newly learned avoidance behaviour, nor will she have the opportunity to pass on this knowledge to her offspring. Moreover, coyote culls don't result in net decreases in the coyote population, so the strategy is self-defeating (Wolch et al. 2002).

39. For example, myths persist about the dangers of 'dirty' pigeons, even though there are no recorded cases of pigeon-to-human transmission of disease. While pigeon faeces pose some risk to immune-compromised humans if handled (or breathed in unventilated spaces), the danger is no greater than from any other animal, such as cats, dogs, etc. (Blechman 2006: ch. 8).

40. Mute swans are a native species in the UK and elsewhere in Europe and Asia, and an introduced species in North America, where debate rages about whether they are a dangerous invader or a benign immigrant whose role in the ecosystem is similar to native North American swans. For different perspectives, see: http://www.savemuteswans.org/ and http://www.allaboutbirds.org/guide/Mute_Swan/lifehistory.

41. Animal Alliance also has helpful guidance on conflicts with other liminal animals, such as deer and coyotes. Available at: http://www.animalalliance.ca.

42. Adams and Lindsey 2010: 161. On the other hand, wild squirrel populations reach sexual maturity earlier than their urban cousins, presumably because urban squirrels have higher rates of offspring survival.

43. We still have much to learn about how animal populations regulate their numbers. At first glance, it seems that regulation for some species is completely external. For example, liminal white-tailed deer populations, if not controlled by predators, will exceed local carrying capacity, i.e., they will outgrow their food supply and die of starvation. Fraser discusses a similar phenomenon of monkey overpopulation on islands where predators have been removed (2009: 26), and the case of elephants confined to wildlife parks out-eating their environment. However, the herbivore carrying-capacity problem seems to be an effect of confinement to ecological 'islands'—whether literal islands, fenced parks, or suburban enclaves. If corridors exist to connect herbivore populations to larger territories, then they seem to regulate their population through migration (Fraser 2009).

44. Blechman discusses how pigeon pest control companies happily reaped a bonanza of fear-based commissions during the West Nile Virus and avian influenza outbreaks, even though pigeons don't carry either disease (Blechman 2006: ch. 8).

45. See http://www.metrofieldguide.com/?p=74.

46. In this respect, we would differentiate our model from the more enthusiastic descriptions some authors give of the place of liminal animals. Wolch, for example, says that 'To allow for the emergence of an ethic, practice, and politics of caring for animals and nature, we need to renaturalize cities and invite the animals back in, and in the process re-enchant the city. I call this renaturalized, re-enchanted city *zoopolis*' (Wolch 1998: 124). As the title of our book indicates, we are inspired by her ideas, but we would not say that humans have a duty to 'invite animals back in': we can take reasonable steps to keep would-be opportunistic animals out. Similarly, Michelfelder says that liminal animals who 'inhabit and have found a home in urban settings are our nonhuman neighbors. As a result we have a moral obligation to respond to them accordingly and treat them as the neighbors that they are ... As a basic principle, it could be said that actions that serve to make such a community more cohesive are morally preferable to those actions that would divide it' (Michelfelder 2003: 86). We agree that liminal animals need to be seen as our neighbours or co-residents, but we've insisted that the goal is not to create a more 'cohesive' community with them. This should be our goal with respect to domesticated animals, with whom we should aim to strengthen relations of trust and cooperation and to build ideas of shared membership in a mixed community. But in relation to liminal animals, the goal is a much looser and less cohesive relationship, one that is consistent with (and in some cases requires) preserving relations of wariness and distrust. Ideas of denizenship, we believe, capture this dialectic of co-residence without co-membership.

Chapter 8

1. UN 2006. For a critique of some of the calculations in the UN report, see Fairlie 2010.

2. Jim Motevalli, 'Meat: The Slavery of our Time: How the Coming Vegetarian Revolution will arrive by Force', *Foreign Policy*, http://experts.foreignpolicy.com/posts/2009/06/03/meat_the_slavery_of_our_time.

3. Recall Singer's claim that 'Once we give up our right to claims to "dominion" over other species we have no right to interfere with them at all. We should leave them alone as much as we possibly can. Having given up the role of tyrant, we should not try to play Big Brother either' (Singer 1975: 251). Is this the limit of our moral imagination—that our only possible ways of relating to animals are as tyrants or Big Brothers?

Bibliography

Adams, Clark and Kieran Lindsey (2010) *Urban Wildlife Management*, 2nd edn (Boca Raton, FL: CRC Press).

Alfred, Taiake (2001) 'From Sovereignty to Freedom: Toward an Indigenous Political Discourse', *Indigenous Affairs* 3: 22–34.

——(2005) 'Sovereignty', in Joanne Barker (ed.) *Sovereignty Matters: Locations of Contestation and Possibility in Indigenous Strategies for Self-Determination* (Lincoln: University of Nebraska Press), 33–50.

Alger, Janet and Steven Alger (2005) 'The Dynamics of Friendship Between Dogs and Cats In the Same Household'. Paper presented for the Annual Meeting of the American Sociological Association, Philadelphia, PA, 13–16 August 2005.

Anaya, S. J. (2004) *Indigenous Peoples in International Law*, 2nd edn (Oxford: Oxford University Press).

An-Na'im, Abdullahi (1990) 'Islam, Islamic Law and the Dilemma of Cultural Legitimacy for Universal Human Rights', in Claude Welch and Virginia Leary (eds) *Asian Perspectives on Human Rights* (Boulder, CO: Westview), 31–54.

Appiah, Anthony Kwame (2006) *Cosmopolitanism: Ethics in a World of Strangers* (New York: W.W. Norton).

Armstrong, Susan and Richard Botzler (eds) (2008) *The Animal Ethics Reader*, 2nd edn (London: Routledge).

Arneil, Barbara (2009) 'Disability, Self Image, and Modern Political Theory', *Political Theory* 37/2: 218–42.

Aukot, Ekuru (2009) 'Am I Stateless Because I am a Nomad?', *Forced Migration Review* 32: 18.

Barry, John (1999) *Rethinking Green Politics* (London: Sage).

Baubock, Rainer (1994) *Transnational Citizenship: Membership and Rights in Transnational Migration* (Aldershot: Elgar).

——(2009) 'Global Justice, Freedom of Movement, and Democratic Citizenship', *European Journal of Sociology* 50/1: 1–31.

Baxter, Brian (2005) *A Theory of Ecological Justice* (London: Routledge).

BBC News (2006) 'Jamie "must back squirrel-eating"' BBC News online, 23 March. Available at http://news.bbc.co.uk/2/hi/4835690.stm

Beckett, Angharad (2006) *Citizenship and Vulnerability: Disability and Issues of Social and Political Engagement* (Basingstoke: Palgrave Macmillan).

Bekoff, Marc (2007) *The Emotional Lives of Animals: A Leading Scientist Explores Animal Joy, Sorrow, and Empathy – and Why They Matter* (Novato, CA: New World Library).

Bekoff, Marc and Jessica Pierce (2009) *Wild Justice: The Moral Lives of Animals* (Chicago: University of Chicago Press).

Benatar, David (2006) *Better Never to Have Been: The Harm of Coming into Existence* (Oxford: Oxford University Press).

Bentham, Jeremy (2002) 'Anarchical Fallacies, Being an Examination of the Declarations of Rights Issued During the French Revolution', in Philip Schofield, Catherine Pease-Watkin, and Cyprian Blamires (eds) *The Collected Works of Jeremy Bentham: Rights, Representation, and Reform: Nonsense upon Stilts and Other Writings on the French Revolution* (Oxford: Oxford University Press; first published 1843).

Benton, Ted (1993) *Natural Relations: Ecology, Animal Rights, and Social Justice* (London: Verso).

Best, Steven and Jason Miller (2009) 'Pacifism or Animals: Which Do You Love More?', *North American Animal Liberation Press Office Newsletter* April 2009, 7–14. Available at www.animalliberationpressoffice.org/pdf/2009-04_newsletter_vol1.pdf.

Bickerton, Christopher, Philip Cunliffe, and Alexander Gourevitch (2007) 'Introduction: The Unholy Alliance against Sovereignty', in their *Politics without Sovereignty: A Critique of Contemporary International Relations* (London: University College London Press), 1–19.

Biolsi, Thomas (2005) 'Imagined Geographies: Sovereignty, Indigenous Space, and American Indian Struggle', *American Ethnologist* 32/2: 239–59.

Bielefeldt, Heiner (2000) '"Western' versus 'Islamic' Human Rights Conceptions?', *Political Theory* 28/1: 90–121.

Bittner, Mark (2005) *The Wild Parrots of Telegraph Hill: A Love Story...with Wings* (New York: Three Rivers Press).

Blechman, Andrew D. (2006) *Pigeons: The Fascinating Saga of the World's Most Revered and Reviled Bird* (New York: Grove Press).

Bonnett, Laura (2003) 'Citizenship and People with Disabilities: The Invisible Frontier', in Janine Brodie and Linda Trimble (eds) *Reinventing Canada: Politics of the 21st Century* (Toronto: Pearson), 151–63.

Boonin, David (2003) 'Robbing PETA to Spay Paul: Do Animal Rights Include Reproductive Rights?' *Between the Species* 13/3: 1–8.

Bradshaw, G. A. (2009) *Elephants on the Edge: What Animals Teach Us about Humanity* (New Haven: Yale University Press).

Braithwaite, Victoria (2010) *Do Fish Feel Pain?* (Oxford: Oxford University Press).

Brown, Rita Mae (2009) *Animal Magnetism: My Life with Creatures Great and Small* (New York: Ballantine Books).

Bruyneel, Kevin (2007) *The Third Space of Sovereignty: The Postcolonial Politics of U.S. Indigenous Relations* (Minneapolis: University of Minnesota Press).

Bryant, John (1990) *Fettered Kingdoms* (Winchester: Fox Press).

Buchanan, Allen (2003) 'The Making and Unmaking of Boundaries: What Liberalism has to Say', in Allen Buchanan and Margaret Moore (eds) *States, Nations and Borders: The Ethics of Making and Unmaking Boundaries* (Cambridge: Cambridge University Press), 231–61.

Budiansky, Stephen (1999) *The Covenant of the Wild: Why Animals Chose Domestication* (New Haven: Yale University Press; first published by William Morrow 1992).

Bunton, Molly (2010) 'My Humane-ifesto'. Available at http://fiascofarm.com/ Humane-ifesto.htm.

Burgess-Jackson, Keith (1998) 'Doing Right by our Animal Companions', *Journal of Ethics* 2: 159–85.

Cairns, Alan (2000) *Citizens Plus: Aboriginal Peoples and the Canadian State* (Vancouver: University of British Columbia).

Callicott, J. Baird (1980) 'Animal Liberation: A Triangular Affair', *Environmental Ethics* 2: 311–28.

——(1992) 'Animal Liberation and Environmental Ethics: Back Together Again', in Eugene C. Hargrove (ed.) *The Animal Rights/Environmental Ethics Debate* (Albany, NY: State University of New York Press), 249–62.

——(1999) 'Holistic Environmental Ethics and the Problem of Ecofascism', in *Beyond the Land Ethic: More Essays in Environmental Philosophy* (Albany, NY: State University of New York Press), 59–76.

Calore, Gary (1999) 'Evolutionary Covenants: Domestication, Wildlife and Animal Rights', in P. N. Cohn (ed.) *Ethics and Wildlife* (Lewiston, NY: Mellen Press), 219–63.

Caney, Simon (2005) *Justice Beyond Borders: A Global Political Theory* (Oxford: Oxford University Press).

Čapek, Stella (2005) 'Of Time, Space, and Birds: Cattle Egrets and the Place of the Wild', in Ann Herda-Rapp and Theresa L. Goedeke (eds) *Mad about Wildlife: Looking at Social Conflict over Wildlife* (Leiden: Brill), 195–222.

Carens, Joseph (2008a) 'Live-in Domestics, Seasonal Workers, and Others Hard to Locate on the Map of Democracy', *Journal of Political Philosophy* 16/4: 419–45.

——(2008b) 'The Rights of Irregular Migrants', *Ethics and International Affairs* 22: 163–86.

——(2010) *Immigrants and the Right to Stay* (Boston: MIT Press).

Carey, Allison (2009) *On the Margins of Citizenship: Intellectual Disability and Civil Rights in Twentieth-Century America* (Philadelphia: Temple University Press).

Carlson, Licia (2009) 'Philosophers of Intellectual Disability: A Taxonomy', *Metaphilosophy* 40/3–4: 552–67.

Casal, Paula (2003) 'Is Multiculturalism Bad for Animals?', *Journal of Political Philosophy* 11/1: 1–22.

Cassidy, Julie (1998) 'Sovereignty of Aboriginal Peoples', *Indiana International and Comparative Law Review* 9: 65–119.

Cavalieri, Paola (2001) *The Animal Question: Why Nonhuman Animals Deserve Human Rights* (Oxford: Oxford University Press).

——(2006) 'Whales as persons', in M. Kaiser and M. Lien (eds) *Ethics and the politics of food* (Wageningen: Wageningen Academic Publishers).

——(2007) 'The Murder of Johnny', *The Guardian*, 5 October 2007. Available at http://www.guardian.co.uk/commentisfree/2007/oct/05/comment.animalwelfare.

——(2009a) *The Death of the Animal: A Dialogue* (New York: Columbia University Press).

——(2009b) 'The Ruses of Reason: Strategies of Exclusion', *Logos Journal* (www.logosjournal.com).

——and Peter Singer (eds) (1993) *The Great Ape Project: Equality Beyond Humanity* (London: Fourth Estate).

Clark, Stephen R. L. (1984) *The Moral Status of Animals* (Oxford: Oxford University Press).

Clement, Grace (2003) 'The Ethic of Care and the Problem of Wild Animals', *Between the Species*, 13/3: 9–21.

Clifford, Stacy (2009) 'Disabling Democracy: How Disability Reconfigures Deliberative Democratic Norms', American Political Science Association 2009 Toronto Meeting Paper. Available at http://ssrn.com/abstract=1451092

Cline, Cheryl (2005) 'Beyond Ethics: Animals, Law and Politics' (PhD Thesis, University of Toronto).

Clutton-Brock, Janet (1987) *A Natural History of Domesticated Animals* (Cambridge: Cambridge University Press).

Cohen, Carl and Tom Regan (2001) *The Animal Rights Debate* (Lanham, MD: Rowman & Littlefield).

Cohen, Elizabeth F. (2009) *Semi-Citizenship in Democratic Politics* (Cambridge: Cambridge University Press).

Costello, Kimberly and Gordon Hodson (2010) 'Exploring the roots of dehumanization: The role of animal-human similarity in promoting immigrant humanization', *Group Processes and Intergroup Relations* 13/1: 3–22.

Crompton, Tom (2010) *Common Cause: The Case for Working with Our Cultural Values* (World Wildlife Fund-United Kingdom). Available at http://assets.wwf.org.uk/downloads/common_cause_report.pdf.

Curry, Steven (2004) *Indigenous Sovereignty and the Democratic Project* (Aldershot: Ashgate).

DeGrazia, David (1996) *Taking Animals Seriously: Mental Life and Moral Status* (Cambridge: Cambridge University Press).

——(2002) *Animal Rights: A Very Short Introduction* (Oxford: Oxford University Press).

Denison, Jaime (2010) 'Between the Moment and Eternity: How Schillerian Play Can Establish Animals as Moral Agents', *Between the Species* 13/10: 60–72.

DeStefano, Stephen (2010) *Coyote at the Kitchen Door: Living with Wildlife in Suburbia* (Cambridge, MA: Harvard University Press).

de Waal, Frans (2009) *The Age of Empathy: Nature's Lessons for a Kinder Society* (Toronto: McClelland & Stewart).

Diamond, Cora (2004) 'Eating Meat and Eating People', in Cass Sunstein and Martha Nussbaum (eds) *Animal Rights: Current Debates and New Directions* (Oxford: Oxford University Press), 93–107.

Dobson, Andrew (1996) 'Representative Democracy and the Environment', in W. Lafferty and J. Meadowcroft (eds) *Democracy and the Environment: Problems and Prospects* (Cheltenham: Elgar), 124–39.

Dombrowski, Daniel (1997) *Babies and Beasts: The Argument from Marginal Cases* (Champaign: University of Illinois Press).

Doncaster, Deborah and Jeff Keller (2000) *Habitat Modification & Canada Geese: Techniques for Mitigating Human/Goose Conflicts in Urban & Suburban Environments*. Animal Alliance of Canada, Toronto. Available at http://www.animalalliance.ca.

Donovan, Josephine (2006) 'Feminism and the Treatment of Animals: From Care to Dialogue', *Signs* 2: 305–29.

——(2007) 'Animal Rights and Feminist Theory', in Josephine Donovan and Carol J. Adams (eds) *The Feminist Care Tradition in Animal Ethics* (New York: Columbia University Press), 58–86.

——and Carol J. Adams (eds) (2007) *The Feminist Care Tradition in Animal Ethics* (New York: Colombia University Press).

Dowie, Mark (2009) *Conservation Refugees: The Hundred-Year Conflict between Global Conservation and Native Peoples* (Cambridge, MA: MIT Press).

Dunayer, Joan (2004) *Speciesism* (Derwood, MD; Ryce Publishing).

Dworkin, Ronald (1984) 'Rights as Trumps', in Jeremy Waldron (ed.) *Theories of Rights* (Oxford: Oxford University Press), 153–67.

——(1990) 'Foundations of Liberal Equality', in Grethe B. Peterson (ed.) *The Tanner Lectures on Human Values*, vol. 11 (Salt Lake City, UT: University of Utah Press), 1–119.

Eckersley, Robyn (1999) 'The Discourse Ethic and the Problem of Representing Nature', *Environmental Politics* 8/2: 24–49.

——(2004) *The Green State: Rethinking Democracy and Sovereignty* (Cambridge, MA: MIT Press).

Elder, Glenn, Jennifer Wolch, and Jody Emel (1998) 'La Practique Sauvage: Race, Place and the Human-Animal Divide', in Jennifer Wolch and Jody Emel (eds) *Animal Geographies: Place, Politics and Identity in the Nature-Culture Borderlands* (London: Verso), 72–90.

Everett, Jennifer (2001) 'Environmental Ethics, Animal Welfarism, and the Problem of Predation: A Bambi Lover's Respect for Nature', *Ethics and the Environment* 6/1: 42–67.

Fairlie, Simon (2010) *Meat: A Benign Extravagance* (East Meon, UK; Permanent Publications).

Feuerstein, N. and J. Terkel (2008) 'Interrelationship of Dogs (*canis familiaris*) and Cats (*felis catus L.*) Living under the Same Roof', *Applied Animal Behaviour Science* 113/1: 150–65.

Fink, Charles K. (2005) 'The Predation Argument', *Between the Species* 5: 1–16.

Fowler, Brigid (2004) 'Fuzzing Citizenship, Nationalising Political Space: A Framework for Interpreting the Hungarian "Status Law" as a New Form of Kin-State Policy in Central and Eastern Europe', in Z. Kántor, B. Majtényi, O. Ieda, B. Vizi, and I. Halász (eds) *The Hungarian Status Law: Nation Building and/or Minority Protection* (Sapporo: Slavic Research Council), 177–238.

Fox, Michael A. (1988a) *The Case for Animal Experimentation: An Evolutionary and Ethical Perspective* (Berkeley: University of California Press).

——(1988b) 'Animal Research Reconsidered', *New Age Journal* (January/February): 14–21.

——(1999) *Deep Vegetarianism* (Philadelphia: Temple University Press).

Francione, Gary L. (1999) 'Wildlife and Animal Rights', in P. N. Cohn (ed.) *Ethics and Wildlife* (Lewiston, NY: Mellen Press), 65–81.

——(2000) *Introduction to Animal Rights: Your Child or the Dog?* (Philadelphia: Temple University Press).

——(2007) 'Animal Rights and Domesticated Nonhumans' (blog). Available at http://www.abolitionistapproach.com/animal-rights-and-domesticated-nonhumans/.

Francione, Gary L. (2008) *Animals as Persons: Essays on the Abolition of Animal Exploitation* (New York: Columbia University Press).

——and Robert Garner (2010) *The Animal Rights Debate: Abolition or Regulation?* (New York: Columbia University Press).

Francis, L. P. and Anita Silvers (2007) 'Liberalism and Individually Scripted ideas of the Good: Meeting the Challenge of Dependent Agency', *Social Theory and Practice* 33/2: 311–34.

Franklin, Julian H. (2005) *Animal Rights and Moral Philosophy* (New York: Columbia University Press).

Fraser, Caroline (2009) *Rewilding the World: Dispatches form the Conservation Revolution* (New York: Metropolitan Books).

Frey, Raymond (1983) *Rights, Killing and Suffering* (Oxford: Oxford University Press).

Frost, Mervyn (1996) *Ethics in International Relations: A Constitutive Theory* (Cambridge: Cambridge University Press).

Frowe, Helen (2008) 'Equating Innocent Threats and Bystanders', *Journal of Applied Philosophy* 25/4: 277–90.

Fusfeld, Leila (2007) 'Sterilization in an Animal Rights Paradigm', *Journal of Animal Law and Ethics* 2: 255–62.

Garner, Robert (1998) *Political Animals: Animal Protection Politics in Britain and the United States* (Basingstoke: Macmillan).

——(2005a) *The Political Theory of Animal Rights* (Manchester: Manchester University Press).

——(2005b) *Animal Ethics* (Cambridge: Polity Press).

Goldenberg, Suzanne (2010) 'In Search of a Home away from Home', *The Guardian Weekly*, 12 March 2010: 28–9.

Goodin, Robert (1985) *Protecting the Vulnerable: A Reanalysis of Our Social Responsibilities* (Chicago: University of Chicago Press).

——(1996) 'Enfranchising the Earth, and its Alternatives', *Political Studies* 44: 835–49.

Goodin, R., C. Pateman, and R. Pateman (1997) 'Simian Sovereignty', *Political Theory* 25/6: 821–49.

Griffiths, Huw, Ingrid Poulter, and David Sibley (2000) 'Feral Cats in the City', in Chris Philo and Chris Wilbert (eds) *Animal Spaces, Beastly Places: New Geographies of Human-Animal Relations* (London: Routledge), 56–70.

Hadley, John (2005) 'Nonhuman Animal Property: Reconciling Environmentalism and Animal Rights', *Journal of Social Philosophy* 36/3: 305–15.

——(2006) 'The Duty to Aid Nonhuman Animals in Dire Need', *Journal of Applied Philosophy* 23/4: 445–51.

——(2009a) 'Animal Rights and Self-Defense Theory', *Journal of Value Inquiry* 43: 165–77.

——(2009b) '"We Cannot Experience Abstractions": Moral Responsibility for "Eternal Treblinka"', *Southerly* 69/1: 213–23.

——and Siobhan O'Sullivan (2009) 'World Poverty, Animal Minds and the Ethics of Veterinary Expenditure', *Environmental Values* 18: 361–78.

Hailwood, Simon (2004) *How to be a Green Liberal: Nature, Value and Liberal Philosophy* (Montreal: McGill-Queen's University Press).

Hall, Lee (2006) *Capers in the Churchyard: Animal rights advocacy in the age of terror* (Darien, CT: Nectar Bat Press).

——and Anthony Jon Waters (2000) 'From Property to Persons: The Case of Evelyn Hart', *Seton Hall Constitutional Law Journal* 11/1: 1–68.

Hanrahan, Rebecca (2007) 'Dog Duty', *Society and Animals* 15: 379–99.

Hargrove, Eugene (ed.) (1992) *The Animal Rights/Environmental Ethics Debate: The Environmental Perspective* (Albany, NY: State University of New York Press).

Harris S., P. Morris, S. Wray, and D. Yalden (1995) *A review of British mammals: population estimates and conservation status of British mammals other than cetaceans* (Peterborough, UK: Joint Nature Conservation Committee).

Hartley, Christie (2009) 'Justice for the Disabled: A Contractualist Approach', *Journal of Social Philosophy* 40/1: 17–36.

Haupt, Lyanda Lynn (2009) *Crow Planet: Essential Wisdom from the Urban Wilderness* (New York: Little, Brown and Company).

Heinrich, Bernd (1999) *Mind of the Raven: Investigations and Adventures with Wolf-birds*. (New York: HarperCollins).

Henders, Susan (2010) 'Internationalized Minority Territorial Autonomy and World Order: The Early Post-World War I Era Arrangements' (paper presented at EDG workshop on International Approaches to the Governance of Ethnic Diversity, Queen's University, September).

Hettinger, Ned (1994) 'Valuing Predation in Rolston's Environmental Ethics: Bambi Lovers versus Tree Huggers', *Environmental Ethics* 16/1: 3–20.

Hooker, Juliet (2009) *Race and the Politics of Solidarity* (Oxford: Oxford University Press).

Horigan, Steven (1988) *Nature and Culture in Western Discourses* (London: Routledge).

Hornung, Eva (2009) *Dog Boy* (Toronto: Harper Collins).

Horowitz, Alexandra (2009) *Inside of a Dog: What Dogs See, Smell and Know* (New York: Scribner).

Horta, Oscar (2010) 'The Ethics of the Ecology of Fear against the Nonspecieist Paradigm: A Shift in the Aims of Intervention in Nature', *Between the Species* 13/10: 163–87.

Hribal, Jason (2006) 'Jessie, a Working Dog', *Counterpunch*, 11 November 2006. Available at www.counterpunch.org/hribal11112006.html.

——(2007) 'Animals, Agency, and Class: Writing the History of Animals from Below', *Human Ecology Review* 14/1: 101–12.

——(2010) *Fear of the Animal Planet: The Hidden History of Animal Resistance* (Oakland, CA: Counter Punch Press and AK Press).

Hutto, Joe (1995) *Illumination in the Flatwoods: A season with the wild turkey* (Guilford, CT: Lyons Press).

Ignatieff, Michael (2000) *The Rights Revolution* (Toronto: Anansi).

International Fund for Animal Welfare (2008) *Falling Behind: An International Comparison of Canada's Animal Cruelty Legislation*. Available at http://www.ifaw.org/Publications/Program_Publications/Regional_National_Efforts/North_America/Canada/asset_upload_file751_15788.pdf.

Irvine, Leslie (2004) 'A Model of Animal Selfhood: Expanding Interactionist Possibilities', *Symbolic Interaction* 27/1: 3–21.

Irvine, Leslie (2009) *Filling the Ark: Animal Welfare in Disasters* (Philadelphia: Temple University Press).

Isin, Engin and Bryan Turner (eds) (2003) *Handbook of Citizenship Studies* (Thousand Oaks, CA: Sage).

Jackson, Peter (2009) 'Can animals live in high-rise blocks?', BBC news online, 7 June. Available at http://news.bbc.co.uk/2/hi/uk_news/magazine/8079079.stm.

Jamie, Kathleen (2005) *Findings* (London: Sort of Books).

Jamieson, Dale (1998) 'Animal Liberation is an Environmental Ethic', *Environmental Values* 7: 41–57.

Jerolmack, Colin (2008) 'How Pigeons Became Rats: The Cultural-Spatial Logic of Problem Animals', *Social Problems* 55/1: 72–94.

Jones, Owain (2000) '(Un)ethical geographies of human-non-human relations: encounters, collectives and spaces', in Chris Philo and Chris Wilbert (eds) *Animal Spaces, Beastly Places: New Geographies of Human-Animal Relations* (London: Routledge), 268–91.

Jones, Pattrice (2008) 'Strategic Analysis of Animal Welfare Legislation: A Guide for the Perplexed' (Eastern Shore Sanctuary & Education Center, Strategic Analysis Report, August 2008, Springfield Vermont). Available at http://pattricejones.info/blog/wp-content/uploads/perplexed.pdf.

Kaufman, Whitley (2010) 'Self-defense, Innocent Aggressors, and the Duty of Martyrdom', *Pacific Philosophical Quarterly* 91: 78–96.

Kavka, Gregory (1982) 'The Paradox of Future Individuals', *Philosophy and Public Affairs* 11/2: 93–112.

Keal, Paul (2003) *European Conquest and the Rights of Indigenous Peoples* (Cambridge: Cambridge University Press).

King, Roger J. H. (2009) 'Feral Animals and the Restoration of Nature', *Between the Species* 9: 1–27.

Kittay, Eva Feder (1998) *Love's Labor: Essays on Women, Equality and Dependency* (New York: Routledge).

——(2001) 'When Caring is Just and Justice is Caring: Justice and Mental Retardation', *Public Culture* 13/3: 557–79.

——(2005a) 'At the Margins of Moral Personhood', *Ethics* 116/1: 100–31.

——(2005b) 'Equality, Dignity and Disability', in Mary Ann Lyons and Fionnuala Waldron (eds) *Perspectives on Equality: The Second Seamus Heaney Lectures* (Dublin: Liffey Press), 95–122.

Kittay, Eva Feder, Bruce Jennings, and Angela Wasunna (2005) 'Dependency, Difference and the Global Ethic of Longterm Care', *Journal of Political Philosophy* 13/4: 443–69.

Kolers, Avery (2009) *Land, Conflict, and Justice: A Political Theory of Territory* (Cambridge: Cambridge University Press).

Kymlicka, Will (1995) *Multicultural Citizenship* (Oxford: Oxford University Press).

——(2001a) 'Territorial Boundaries: A Liberal Egalitarian Perspective', in David Miller and Sohail Hashmi (eds) *Boundaries and Justice: Diverse Ethical Perspectives* (Princeton: Princeton University Press), 249–75.

——(2001b) *Politics in the Vernacular: Nationalism, Multiculturalism and Citizenship* (Oxford: Oxford University Press).

——(2002) *Contemporary Political Philosophy*, 2nd edn (Oxford University Press, Oxford).

——and Wayne Norman (1994) 'Return of the Citizen: A Survey of Recent Work on Citizenship Theory', *Ethics* 104/2: 352–81.

Latour, Bruno (1993) *We Have Never Been Modern* (Cambridge, MA: Harvard University Press).

——(2004) *Politics of Nature* (Cambridge, MA: Harvard University Press).

Lee, Teresa Man Ling (2006) 'Multicultural Citizenship: The Case of the Disabled', in Dianne Pothier and Richard Devlin (eds) *Critical Disability Theory* (Vancouver: University of British Columbia Press), 87–105.

Lekan, Todd (2004) 'Integrating Justice and Care in Animal Ethics', *Journal of Applied Philosophy* 21/2: 183–95.

Lenard, Patti and Christine Straehle (forthcoming) 'Temporary Labour Migration, Global Redistribution and Democratic Justice', *Politics, Philosophy and Economics*.

Lenzerini, Frederico (2006) 'Sovereignty Revisited: International Law and Parallel Sovereignty of Indigenous Peoples', *Texas International Law Journal* 42: 155–89

Loughlin, Martin (2003) 'Ten Tenets of Sovereignty', in Neil Walker (ed.) *Sovereignty in Transition* (London: Hart), 55–86.

Lovelock, James (1979) *Gaia: A New Look at Life on Earth* (Oxford: Oxford University Press).

Luban, David (1980) 'Just War and Human Rights', *Philosophy and Public Affairs* 9/2: 160–81.

Luke, Brian (2007) 'Justice, Caring and Animal Liberation', in Josephine Donovan and Carol Adams (eds) *The Feminist Care Tradition in Ethics* (New York: Columbia University Press), 125–52.

Lund, Vonne and Anna S. Olsson (2006) 'Animal Agriculture: Symbiosis, Culture, or Ethical Conflict?', *Journal of Agricultural and Environmental Ethics* 19: 47–56.

Mackenzie, Catriona and Natalie Stoljar (eds) (2000) *Relational Autonomy: Feminist Perspectives on Autonomy, Agency and the Social Self* (Oxford: Oxford University Press).

MacKinnon, Catherine (1987) *Feminism Unmodified* (Cambridge, MA: Harvard University Press).

MacLeod, Ray (2011) *Hope for Wildlife: True Stories of Animal Rescue* (Halifax, NS: Nimbus Publishing).

McMahan, Jeff (1994) 'Self-Defense and the Problem of the Innocent Attacker', *Ethics* 104/2: 252–90.

——(2002) *The Ethics of Killing: Problems at the Margins of Life* (Oxford: Oxford University Press).

——(2008) 'Eating Animals the Nice Way', *Daedalus* 137/1: 66–76.

——(2009) 'Self-Defense Against Morally Innocent Threats', and 'Reply to Commentators', in Paul H. Robinson, Kimberly Ferzan, and Stephen Garvey (eds) *Criminal Law Conversations* (New York: Oxford University Press), 385–94.

——(2010) 'The Meat Eaters', *The New York Times* 'Opinionator', 19 September 2010. Available at http://opinionator.blogs.nytimes.com/2010/09/19/the-meat-eaters/.

Masson, Jeffrey Moussaieff (2003) *The Pig Who Sang to the Moon: The Emotional World of Farm Animals* (New York: Ballantine).

Masson, Jeffrey Moussaieff (2010) *The Dog Who Couldn't Stop Loving: How Dogs Have Captured Our Hearts for Thousands of Years* (New York: HarperCollins).

Meyer, Lukas (2008) 'Intergenerational Justice', *Stanford Encyclopedia of Philosophy* online. First published April 3/02. Revised 26 February 2008.

Michelfelder, Diane (2003) 'Valuing Wildlife Populations in Urban Environments', *Journal of Social Philosophy* 34/1: 79–90.

Midgley, Mary (1983) *Animals and Why They Matter* (Athens: University of Georgia Press).

Miller, David (2005) 'Immigration' in Andrew Cohen and Christopher Wellman (eds) *Contemporary Debates in Applied Ethics* (Oxford: Blackwell).

——(2007) *National Responsibility and Global Justice* (Oxford: Oxford University Press).

——(2010) 'Why Immigration Controls are Not Coercive: A Reply to Arash Abizadeh', *Political Theory* 38/1: 111–20.

——(2010) 'Territorial Rights: Concept and Justification' (unpublished).

Mills, Brett (2010) 'Television Wildlife Documentaries and Animals' Right to Privacy', *Continuum: Journal of Media and Cultural Studies* 24/2: 193–202.

Morelle, Rebecca (2010) 'Follow that microlight: Birds learn to migrate', BBC online 27 October 2010. Available at http://www.bbc.co.uk/news/science-environment-11574073.

Murdoch, Iris (1970) 'The Sovereignty of Good Over Other Concepts', in *The Sovereignty of Good* (London: Routledge & Kegan Paul), 77–104.

Myers, Olin E. Jr. (2003) 'No Longer the Lonely Species: A Post-Mead Perspective on Animals and Sociology', *International Journal of Sociology and Social Policy* 23/3: 46–68.

New York City Audubon Society (2007) *Bird-Safe Building Guidelines*. Available at: http://www.nycaudubon.org/home/BirdSafeBuildingGuidelines.pdf.

Nobis, Nathan (2004) 'Carl Cohen's 'Kind' Arguments *For* Animal Rights and *Against* Human Rights', *Journal of Applied Philosophy* 21/1: 43–59.

Norton, Bryan (1991) *Toward Unity among Environmentalists* (Oxford: Oxford University Press).

Nozick, Robert (1974) *Anarchy, State and Utopia* (New York: Basic Books).

Nussbaum, Martha (2006) *Frontiers of Justice: Disability, Nationality, Species Membership* (Cambridge, MA: Harvard University Press).

Oh, Minjoo and Jeffrey Jackson (2011) 'Animal Rights vs Cultural Rights: Exploring the Dog Meat Debate in South Korea from a World Polity Perspective', *Journal of Intercultural Studies* 32/1: 31–56.

Okin, Susan Moller (1979) *Women in Western Political Thought* (Princeton: Princeton University Press).

——(1999) *Is Multiculturalism Bad for Women?* (Princeton: Princeton University Press).

Orend, Brian (2006) *The Morality of War* (Peterborough, ON: Broadview).

Orford, H. J. L. (1999) 'Why the Cullers Got it Wrong', in Priscilla Cohn (ed.) *Ethics and Wildlife* (Lewiston, NY: Mellen Press), 159–68.

Otsuka, Michael (1994) 'Killing the Innocent in Self-Defense', *Philosophy and Public Affairs* 23/1: 74–94.

Otto, Diane (1995) 'A Question of Law or Politics? Indigenous Claims to Sovereignty in Australia', *Syracuse Journal of International Law* 21: 65–103.

Ottonelli, Valeria and Tiziana Torresi (forthcoming) 'Inclusivist Egalitarian Liberalism and Temporary Migration: A Dilemma', *Journal of Political Philosophy*.

Overall, Christine (forthcoming) *Why Have Children? The Ethical Debate* (Cambridge, MA: MIT Press).

Pallotta, Nicole R. (2008) 'Origin of Adult Animal Rights Lifestyle in Childhood Responsiveness to Animal Suffering', *Society and Animals* 16: 149–70.

Palmer, Clare (1995) 'Animal Liberation, Environmental Ethics and Domestication', OCEES Research Papers, Oxford Centre for the Environment, Ethics & Society, Mansfield College, Oxford.

——(2003a) 'Placing Animals in Urban Environmental Ethics', *Journal of Social Philosophy* 34/1: 64–78.

——(2003b) 'Colonization, urbanization, and animals', *Philosophy & Geography* 6/1: 47–58.

——(2006) 'Killing Animals in Animal Shelters', in The Animal Studies Group (ed.) *Killing Animals* (Champaign: University of Illinois Press), 170–87.

——(2010) *Animal Ethics in Context* (New York: Columbia University Press).

——(ed.) (2008) *Animal Rights* (Farnham: Ashgate).

Patterson, Charles (2002) *Eternal Treblinka: Our Treatment of Animals and the Holocaust* (New York: Lantern Books).

Pemberton, Jo-Anne (2009) *Sovereignty: Interpretations* (Basingstoke: Palgrave Macmillan).

Pepperberg, Irene M. (2008) *Alex & Me* (New York: HarperCollins).

Peterson, Dale (2010) *The Moral Lives of Animals* (New York: Bloomsbury Press).

Philo, Chris and Chris Wilbert (eds) (2000) *Animal Spaces, Beastly Places: New Geographies of Human-Animal Relations* (London: Routledge).

Philpott, Daniel (2001) *Revolutions in Sovereignty: How Ideas Shaped Modern International Relations* (Princeton: Princeton University Press).

Pitcher, George (1996) *The Dogs Who Came To Stay* (London: HarperCollins).

Plumwood, Val (2000) 'Surviving a Crocodile Attack' *Utne Reader* online, July-August 2000. Available at http://www.utne.com/2000-07-01/being-prey.aspx?page=1.

——(2004) 'Animals and Ecology: Toward a Better Integration', in Steve Sapontzis (ed.) *Food For Thought: The Debate over Eating Meat* (Amherst, NY: Prometheus), 344–58.

Poole, Joyce (1998) 'An Exploration of a Commonality between Ourselves and Elephants', *Etica & Animali* 9: 85–110.

——(2001) 'Keynote address at Elephant Managers Association 22nd Annual Conference', Orlando, Florida (November. 9–12, 2001). Available at http://www.elephants.com/j_poole.php.

Porter, Pete (2008) 'Mourning the Decline of Human Responsibility', *Society and Animals* 16: 98–101.

Potter, Cheryl (n.d.) 'Providing Humanely Produced Eggs'. Available at http://www.blackhenfarm.com/index.html.

Preece, Rod (1999) *Animals and Nature: Cultural Myths, Cultural Realities* (Vancouver: University of British Columbia Press).

Prince, Michael (2009) *Absent Citizens: Disability Politics and Policy in Canada* (Toronto: University of Toronto Press).

Prokhovnik, Raia (2007) *Sovereignties: Contemporary Theory and Practice* (Basingstoke: Palgrave Macmillan).

Rawls, John (1971) *A Theory of Justice* (Oxford: Oxford University Press).

Ray, Justina C., Kent Redford, Robert Steneck, and Joel Berger (eds) (2005) *Large Carnivores and the Conservation of Biodiversity* (Washington DC: Island Press).

Raz, Joseph (1984) 'The Nature of Rights', *Mind* 93: 194–214.

Redford, Kent (1999) 'The Ecologically Noble Savage', *Cultural Survival Quarterly* 15: 46–8.

Regan, Tom (1983) *The Case for Animal Rights* (Berkeley: University of California Press).

——(2001) *Defending Animal Rights* (Champaign: University of Illinois Press).

——(2003) *Animal Rights, Human Wrongs: An Introduction to Moral Philosophy* (Lanham, MD: Rowman & Littlefield).

——(2004) *The Case for Animal Rights*, 2nd edn (Berkeley: University of California Press).

Reid, Mark D. (2010) 'Moral Agency in *Mammalia*', *Between the Species* 13/10: 1–24.

Reinders, J. S. (2002) 'The good life for citizens with intellectual disability', *Journal of Intellectual Disability* 46/1: 1–5.

Reus-Smit, Christian (2001) 'Human Rights and the Social Construction of Sovereignty', *Review of International Studies* 27: 519–38.

Reynolds, Henry (1996) *Aboriginal Sovereignty: Reflections on Race, State and Nation* (St Leonards, New South Wales: Allen and Unwin).

Rioux, Marcia and Fraser Valentine (2006) 'Does Theory Matter? Exploring the Nexus between Disability, Human Rights and Public Policy', in Dianne Pothier and Richard Devlin (eds) *Critical Disability Theory* (Vancouver: University of British Columbia Press), 47–69.

Ritter, Erika (2009) *The Dog by the Cradle, The Serpent Beneath: Some Paradoxes of Human-Animal Relationships* (Toronto: Key Porter).

Robinson, Randall (2000) *The Debt: What America Owes to Blacks* (New York: Dutton).

Rollin, Bernard (2006) *Animal Rights and Human Morality*, 3rd edn (Amherst, NY: Prometheus Books).

Rolston, Holmes (1988) *Environmental Ethics: Duties to and Values in the Natural World* (Philadelphia: Temple University Press).

——(1999) 'Respect for Life: Counting what Singer Finds of No Account', in Dale Jamieson (ed.) *Singer and His Critics* (Oxford: Blackwell), 247–68.

Rowlands, Mark (1997) 'Contractarianism and Animal Rights' *Journal of Applied Philosophy* 14/3: 235–47.

——(1998) *Animal Rights: A Philosophical Defence* (New York: St. Martin's Press).

——(2008) *The Philosopher and the Wolf: Lessons from the Wild on Love, Death and Happiness* (London: Granta Books).

Ryan, Thomas (2006) 'Social Work, Independent Realities and the Circle of Moral Considerability: Respect for Humans, Animals and the Natural World' (PhD, Department of Human Services, Edith Cowan University, Australia). Available at http://ro.ecu.edu.au/cgi/viewcontent.cgi?article=1097&context=theses.

Ryden, Hope (1979) *God's Dog: A Celebration of the North American Coyote* (New York: Viking Press).

——(1989) *Lily Pond: Four years with a Family of Beavers* (New York: Lyons & Burford).

Sagoff, Mark (1984) 'Animal Liberation and Environmental Ethics: Bad Marriage, Quick Divorce', *Osgoode Hall Law Journal* 22/2: 297–307.

Sanders, Clinton R. (1993) 'Understanding Dogs: Caretakers' Attributions of Mindedness in Canine-Human Relationships', *Journal of Contemporary Ethnography* 22/2: 205–26.

——and Arnold Arluke (1993) 'If Lions Could Speak: Investigating the Animal-Human Relationship and the Perspectives of Non-Human Others', *Sociological Quarterly* 34/3: 377–90.

Sapontzis, Steve (1987) *Morals, Reason, and Animals* (Philadelphia: Temple University Press).

——(ed.) (2004) *Food for Thought: The Debate over Eating Meat* (Amherst, NY: Prometheus Books).

Satz, Ani (2006) 'Would Rosa Parks Wear Fur? Toward a nondiscrimination approach to animal welfare', *Journal of Animal Law and Ethics* 1: 139–59.

——(2009) 'Animals as Vulnerable Subjects: Beyond Interest-Convergence, Hierarchy, and Property', *Animal Law* 16/2: 1–50.

Schlossberg, David (2007) *Defining Environmental Justice: Theories, Movements, and Nature* (Oxford: Oxford University Press).

Scott, James (1998) *Seeing Like a State: How Certain Schemes to Improve the Human Condition Have Failed* (New Haven: Yale University Press).

Scruton, Roger (2004) 'The Conscientious Carnivore', in Steven Sapontzis (ed.) *Food For Thought: The Debate over Eating Meat* (Amherst, NY: Prometheus), 81–91.

Scully, Matthew (2002) *Dominion: The Power of Man, the Suffering of Animals, and the Call to Mercy* (New York: St Martin's Press).

Serpell, James (1996) *In the Company of Animals: A Study of Human-Animal Relationships* (Cambridge: Cambridge University Press).

Shadian, Jessica (2010) 'From States to Polities: Reconceptualising Sovereignty through Inuit Governance', *European Journal of International Relations,* 16/3: 485–510.

Shelton, Jo-Ann (2004) 'Killing Animals That Don't Fit In: Moral Dimensions of Habitat Restoration', *Between the Species* 13/4: 1–19.

Shepard, Paul (1997) *The Others: How Animals Made us Human* (Washington DC: Island Press).

Shue, Henry (1980) *Basic Rights: Subsistance, Affluence, and U.S. Foreign Policy* (Princeton: Princeton University Press).

Silvers, Anita and L.P. Francis (2005) 'Justice through Trust: Disability and the 'Outlier Problem' in Social Contract Theory', *Ethics* 116: 40–76.

——and Leslie Pickering Francis (2009) 'Thinking about the Good: Reconfiguring Liberal Metaphysics (or not) for People with Cognitive Disabilities', *Metaphilosophy* 40/3: 475–98.

Simmons, Aaron (2009) 'Animals, Predators, the Right to Life, and the Duty to Save Lives', *Ethics And The Environment* 14/1: 15–27.

Singer, Peter (1975) *Animal liberation* (New York: Random House).

Singer, Peter (1990) *Animal Liberation*, 2nd edn (London: Cape).

——(1993) *Practical Ethics*, 2nd edn (Cambridge: Cambridge University Press).

——(1999) 'A Response', in Dale Jamieson (ed.) *Singer and His Critics* (Oxford: Blackwell), 325–33.

——(2003) 'Animal Liberation at 30', *New York Review of Books* 50/8.

——and Paola Cavalieri (2002) 'Apes, Persons and Bioethics', in Biruté Galdikas et al. (eds) *All Apes Great and Small*, vol. 1: *African Apes* (New York: Springer), 283–91.

Slicer, Deborah (1991) 'Your Daughter or Your Dog? A Feminist Assessment of the Animal Research Issue', *Hypatia* 6/1: 108–24.

Smith, Graham (2003) *Deliberative Democracy and the Environment* (London: Routledge).

Smith, Martin Cruz (2010) *Three Stations* (New York: Simon and Schuster).

Smith, Mick (2009) 'Against Ecological Sovereignty: Agamben, politics and globalization', *Environmental Politics* 18/1: 99–116.

Smuts, Barbara (1999) 'Reflections', in J. M. Coetzee, *The Lives of Animals*, ed. Amy Gutmann (Princeton: Princeton University Press), 107–20.

——(2001) 'Encounters with Animal Minds', *Journal of Consciousness Studies* 8/5–7: 293–309.

——(2006) 'Between Species: Science and Subjectivity' *Configurations* 14/1: 115–26.

Somerville, Margaret (2010) 'Are Animals People?', *The Mark*, 25 January 2010. Available at http://www.themarknews.com/articles/868-are-animals-people.

Sorenson, John (2010) *About Canada: Animal Rights* (Black Point, Nova Scotia: Fernwood Publishing).

Spinner, Jeff (1994) *The Boundaries of Citizenship: Race, Ethnicity, and Nationality in the Liberal State* (Baltimore, MD: Johns Hopkins University Press).

Steiner, Gary (2008) *Animals and the Moral Community: Mental Life, Moral Status, and Kinship* (New York: Columbia University Press).

Stephen, Lynn (2008) 'Redefined Nationalism in Building a Movement for Indigenous Autonomy in Southern Mexico', *Journal of Latin American Anthropology* 3/1: 72–101.

Sullivan, Robert (2010) 'The Concrete Jungle', *New York Magazine* (online), 12 September 2010. Available at http://nymag.com/news/features/68087.

Sunstein, Cass (2002) *Risk and Reason* (Cambridge: Cambridge University Press).

——and Martha Nussbaum (eds) (2004) *Animal Rights: Current Debates and New Directions* (Oxford: Oxford University Press).

Swart, J. (2005) 'Care for the Wild: An Integrative View on Wild and Domesticated Animals', *Environmental Values* 14: 251–63.

Tan, Kok-Chor (2004) *Justice Without Borders: Cosmopolitanism, Nationalism, and Patriotism* (Cambridge: Cambridge University Press).

Tashiro, Yasuko (1995) 'Economic Difficulties in Zaire and the Disappearing Taboo against Hunting Bonobos in the Wamba Area' *Pan Africa News* 2/2 (October 1995). Available at http://mahale.web.infoseek.co.jp/PAN/2_2/tashiro.html.

Taylor, Angus (1999) *Magpies, Monkeys, and Morals: What Philosophers Say about Animal Liberation* (Peterborough, ON: Broadview Press).

——(2010) 'Review of Wesley J. Smith's *A Rat is a Pig is a Dog is a Boy: The Human Cost of the Animal Rights Movement*', *Between the Species* 10: 223–36.

Taylor, Charles (1999) 'Conditions of an Unforced Consensus on Human Rights', in Joanne Bauer and Daniel A. Bell (eds) *The East Asian Challenge for Human Rights* (Cambridge: Cambridge University Press), 124–45.

Taylor, Paul (1986) *Respect for Nature: A Theory of Environmental Ethics* (Princeton: Princeton University Press).

Thomas, Elizabeth Marshall (1993) *The Hidden Life of Dogs* (Boston: Houghton Mifflin).

——(2009) *The Hidden Life of Deer: Lessons from the Natural World* (New York: HarperCollins).

Thompson, Dennis (1999) 'Democratic Theory and Global Society', *Journal of Political Philosophy* 7: 111–25.

Thompson, Jo Myers, M. N. Lubaba, and Richard Bovundja Kabanda (2008) 'Traditional Land-use Practices for Bonobo Conservation', in Takeshi Furuichi and Jo Myers Thompson (eds) *The Bonobos: Behavior, Ecology, and Conservation* (New York: Springer), 227–45.

Titchkovsky, Tania (2003) 'Governing Embodiment: Technologies of Constituting Citizens with Disabilities', *Canadian Journal of Sociology* 28/4: 517–42.

Tobias, Michael and Jane Morrison (2006) *Donkey: The Mystique of* Equus Asinus (San Francisco: Council Oak Books).

Trut, Lyudmila (1999) 'Early Canid Domestication: The Farm-Fox Experiment', *American Scientist* 87: 160–9.

Tuan, Yi-Fu (1984) *Dominance and Affection: The Making of Pets* (New Haven: Yale University Press).

Turner, Dale (2001) 'Vision: Towards an Understanding of Aboriginal Sovereignty', in Wayne Norman and Ronald Beiner (eds) *Canadian Political Philosophy: Contemporary Reflections* (Oxford: Oxford University Press).

United Nations (2006) *Livestock's Long Shadow: Environmental Issues and Options* (Rome: Food and Agriculture Organization).

Vaillant, John (2010) *The Tiger: A True Story of Vengeance and Survival* (New York: Alfred A. Knopf).

Valpy, Michael 'The Sea Hunt as a Matter of Morals', *Globe and Mail*, 8 February 2010, p. A6.

Varner, Gary (1998) *In Nature's Interests? Interests, Animal Rights, and Environmental Ethics* (Oxford: Oxford University Press).

Vaughan, Sarah (2006) 'Responses to Ethnic Federalism in Ethiopia's Southern Region', in David Turton (ed.) *Ethnic Federalism* (London: James Currey), 181–207.

Vellend, Mark, Luke Harmon, Julie Lockwood, et al. (2007) 'Effects of Exotic species on Evolutionary Diversification', *Trends in Ecology and Evolution* 22/9: 481–88.

Vorhaus, John (2005) 'Citizenship, Competence and Profound Disability', *Journal of Philosophy of Education* 39/3: 461–75.

——(2006) 'Respecting Profoundly Disabled Learners', *Journal of Philosophy of Education* 40/3: 331–28.

——(2007) 'Disability, Dependency and Indebtedness?', *Journal of Philosophy of Education* 41/1: 29–44.

Waldron, Jeremy (2004) 'Redressing Historic Injustice', in Lukas Meyer (ed.) *Justice in Time: Responding to Historical Injustice* (Baden-Baden: Nomos), 55–77.

Ward, Peter (2009) *The Medea Hypothesis: Is Life on Earth Ultimately Self-Destructive?* (Princeton: Princeton University Press).

Warner, Bernhard (2008) 'Survival of the Dumbest' *The Guardian* online, 14 April 2008. Available at http://www.guardian.co.uk/environment/2008/apr/14/endangeredspecies.

Wenz, Peter (1988) *Environmental Justice* (Albany: State University of New York Press).

White, Thomas (2007) *In Defense of Dolphins: The New Moral Frontier* (Oxford: Blackwell).

Wiessner, Siegfried (2008) 'Indigenous Sovereignty: A Reassessment in Light of the UN Declaration on the Rights of Indigenous People', *Vanderbilt Journal of Transnational Law* 41: 1141–76.

Wise, Steven (2000) *Rattling the Cage: Toward Legal Rights to Animals* (Cambridge, MA: Perseus Books).

——(2004) 'Animal Rights, One Step at a Time', in Martha Nussbaum and Cass Sunstein (eds) *Animal Rights: Current Debates and New Directions* (Oxford: Oxford University Press), 19–50.

Wolch, Jennifer (1998) 'Zoöpolis', in Jennifer Wolch and Jody Emel (eds) *Animal Geographies: Places, Politics, and Identity in the Nature-Culture Borderlands* (London: Verso), 119–38.

——(2002) 'Anima urbis', *Progress in Human Geography* 26/6: 721–42.

——, Stephanie Pincetl, and Laura Pulido (2002) 'Urban Nature and the Nature of Urbanism', in Michael J. Dear (ed.) *From Chicago to L.A.: Making Sense of Urban Theory* (Thousand Oaks, CA: Sage), 369–402.

Wolff, Jonathan (2006) 'Risk, Fear, Blame, Shame and the Regulation of Public Safety', *Economics and Philosophy*, 22: 409–27.

——(2009) 'Disadvantage, Risk and the Social Determinants of Health', *Public Health Ethics* 2/3: 214–23.

Wong, Sophia Isako (2009) 'Duties of Justice to Citizens with Cognitive Disabilities', *Metaphilosophy* 40/3–4: 382–401.

Wood, Lisa J. et al. (2007) 'More Than a Furry Companion: The Ripple Effect of Companion Animals on Neighborhood Interactions and Sense of Community', *Society and Animals* 15: 43–56.

Young, Iris Marion (2000) *Inclusion and Democracy* (Oxford: Oxford University Press).

Young, Rosamund (2003) *The Secret Life of Cows: Animal Sentience at Work* (Preston UK: Farming Books).

Young, Stephen M. (2006) 'On the Status of Vermin', *Between the Species* 13/6: 1–27.

Zamir, Tzachi (2007) *Ethics and the Beast: A Speciesist Argument for Animal Liberation* (Princeton: Princeton University Press).

Zimmer, Carl (2008) 'Friendly Invaders' *The New York Times*, 8 September 2008. Available at http://www.nytimes.com/2008/09/09/science/09inva.html?pagewanted=1&_r=4& ref= science.

Index

Lightning Source UK Ltd.
Milton Keynes UK
UKOW07f0354141114

241592UK00001B/3/P